The Classical Tradition in Modern American Fiction

BAAS Paperbacks

Published titles

African American Visual Arts
Celeste-Marie Bernier
The American Short Story since 1950
Kasia Boddy
American Imperialism: The Territorial Expansion of the United States, 1783–2013
Adam Burns
The Cultures of the American New West
Neil Campbell
The Open Door Era: United States Foreign Policy in the Twentieth Century
Michael Patrick Cullinane and Alex Goodall
Gender, Ethnicity and Sexuality in Contemporary American Film
Jude Davies and Carol R. Smith
The United States and World War II: The Awakening Giant
Martin Folly
The Sixties in America: History, Politics and Protest
M. J. Heale
Religion, Culture and Politics in the Twentieth-Century United States
Mark Hulsether
The Civil War in American Culture
Will Kaufman
The United States and European Reconstruction, 1945–1960
John Killick
American Exceptionalism
Deborah L. Madsen
American Autobiography
Rachael McLennan
The American Landscape
Stephen F. Mills
Slavery and Servitude in North America, 1607–1800
Kenneth Morgan
The Civil Rights Movement
Mark Newman
The Twenties in America: Politics and History
Niall Palmer
American Theatre
Theresa Saxon
The Vietnam War in History, Literature and Film
Mark Taylor
Contemporary Native American Literature
Rebecca Tillett
Jazz in American Culture
Peter Townsend
The New Deal
Fiona Venn
Animation and America
Paul Wells
Political Scandals in the USA
Robert Williams
Black Nationalism in American History: From the Nineteenth Century to the Million Man March
Mark Newman
The American Photo-Text, 1930–1960
Caroline Blinder
The Beats: Authorships, Legacies
A. Robert Lee
The Classical Tradition in Modern American Fiction
Tessa Roynon

Forthcoming titles
American Detective Fiction
Ruth Hawthorn
Staging Transatlantic Relations, 1776–1917
Theresa Saxon
American Poetry since 1900
Nick Selby
The US Graphic Novel
Paul Williams
The Canada US Border: Culture and Theory
Jeffrey Orr and David Stirrup

www.edinburghuniversitypress.com/series/BAAS

The Classical Tradition in Modern American Fiction

TESSA ROYNON

EDINBURGH
University Press

Edinburgh University Press is one of the leading university presses in the UK. We publish academic books and journals in our selected subject areas across the humanities and social sciences, combining cutting-edge scholarship with high editorial and production values to produce academic works of lasting importance. For more information visit our website: edinburghuniversitypress.com

Edinburgh University Press Ltd
The Tun – Holyrood Road
12(2f) Jackson's Entry
Edinburgh EH8 8PJ

Typeset in 10/12 Adobe Sabon by
IDSUK (DataConnection) Ltd, and
printed and bound in Great Britain.

A CIP record for this book is available from the British Library

ISBN 978 1 4744 3404 1 (hardback)
ISBN 978 1 4744 3405 8 (webready PDF)
ISBN 978 1 4744 3403 4 (paperback)
ISBN 978 1 4744 3406 5 (epub)

Contents

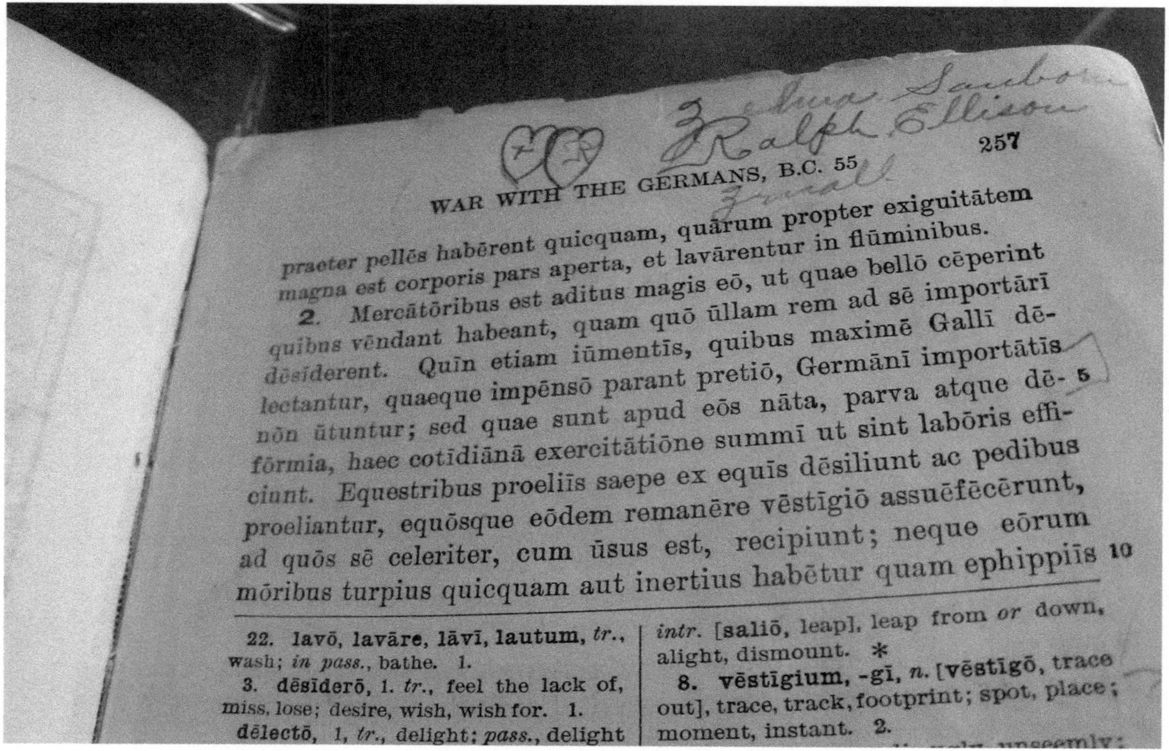

257

WAR WITH THE GERMANS, B.C. 55

praeter pellēs habērent quicquam, quārum propter exiguitātem magna est corporis pars aperta, et lavārentur in flūminibus.

2. Mercātōribus est aditus magis eō, ut quae bellō cēperint quibus vēndant habeant, quam quō ūllam rem ad sē importārī dēsīderent. Quīn etiam iūmentīs, quibus maximē Gallī dēlectantur, quaeque impēnsō parant pretiō, Germānī importātīs nōn ūtuntur; sed quae sunt apud eōs nāta, parva atque dēfōrmia, haec cotīdiānā exercitātiōne summī ut sint labōris efficiunt. Equestribus proeliīs saepe ex equīs dēsiliunt ac pedibus proeliantur, equōsque eōdem remanēre vēstīgiō assuēfēcērunt, ad quōs sē celeriter, cum ūsus est, recipiunt; neque eōrum mōribus turpius quicquam aut inertius habētur quam ephippiīs

22. **lavō, lavāre, lāvī, lautum,** *tr.*, wash; *in pass.*, bathe. 1.

3. **dēsīderō,** 1. *tr.*, feel the lack of, miss, lose; desire, wish, wish for. 1.

dēlectō, 1, *tr.*, delight; *pass.*, delight

intr. [**saliō**, leap], leap from *or* down, alight, dismount. *

8. **vēstīgium, -gī,** *n.* [**vēstīgō**, trace out], trace, track, footprint; spot, place; moment, instant. 2.

A page from Ralph Ellison's high school copy of Caesar's *Gallic Wars*

Preface and Acknowledgements

This is a book about the allusions to ancient Greece and Rome, and to their cultural legacies, in modern and contemporary American fiction. Both explicitly and implicitly, this is also a book about reading habits, education, and the nature of high school and university curricula. Each of my chapters begins with an overview of the role of Classics and classicism in a selected author's intellectual formation: Willa Cather studied both Latin and Greek to a high level, for example, while Philip Roth never studied either. At the same time, my study as a whole deliberately reaches out to the very many contemporary readers – students, teachers and scholars alike – who have little or no prior knowledge of the classical tradition. Each and every one of us, I contend, can participate in the analysis of ancient presences in modern texts.

Due to the ongoing changes in what is taught at secondary or high school, only a tiny minority of those who read American fiction today will have any knowledge of classical languages, literature or mythology. It is all too easy to feel shut out from what appears to be a vast and distant world of high culture, replete with unpronounceable names, to which great prior erudition (the preserve of a privileged and often privately educated few) is the only passport. But antiquity need not and should not be the preserve of an already-initiated elite. From the glossary and the list of resources at the end of this book to the online editions of classical texts and reference works held by many university libraries, as well as in the vast (and inevitably uneven) resources of the internet at large, there are numerous aids to decoding and contextualising a classical allusion. A few seconds of detective work can enable us to access numerous provocative cultural resonances and aesthetic-political implications, both deep and broad, of any initially opaque word or quotation. So, for all readers who are wary of classical references, and hence of this book in turn, one imperative stands out above all others: *if in doubt, look it up!* The rewards of so doing are great.

I am indebted to many people for their guidance and support in the completion of this book. Michelle Houston at EUP, the BAAS Paperbacks series editor Martin Halliwell and the anonymous reviewers of my original proposal have all provided invaluable advice and generous insights, and have been enthusiastic and encouraging about this project from the outset. I have been fortunate in the wonderful colleagues, endlessly patient librarians, ample office space and bottomless coffee at the Rothermere American Institute in Oxford. The APGRD (Archive for the Performance of Greek and Roman Drama) has also been an important source of companionship and food for thought, and the English Faculty Librarians have done all they can to support my work. Throughout the writing of this book and for the duration of my academic career I have been encouraged and supported by Marc Conner of Skidmore College, by Elleke Boehmer and Stephen Tuck at Oxford, and by Kasia Boddy and Sarah Meer at Cambridge.

In the summer term of 2019, Julia Adamo, a student on her Junior Year Abroad from Kenyon College, Ohio, bravely took a course of eight tutorials with me in which, each week, she read one chapter of my book manuscript along with the novels discussed in that chapter. I am hugely grateful to her for her enthusiasm and insights. Daniel Orrells of King's College London – my friend, former PhD co-supervisor and erstwhile co-editor – has patiently responded to frequent unsolicited texts and emails demanding on-the-spot answers to random questions about antiquity. Stephen Harrison, of Corpus Christi College, Oxford, has met with me several times throughout the research and writing process. He has fielded numerous queries and pointed me in the direction of crucial resources. In the final stages of completion he has read the whole manuscript from beginning to end, correcting countless errors and basic confusions on my part about the classical world. He has held erudition, rigour, tact, kindness and encouragement in perfect balance, and his perspective on this material is second to none. All remaining mistakes are, of course, my own.

I am grateful to my mother, Patsy Roynon, and to my husband, Patrick Watt; their many kinds of support have largely made this unsalaried endeavour possible. Patrick's unwavering belief in my work is equalled only by his much-needed humour and his skill and stamina both as cook and as bottle-washer. Although spending most of every day glued to my laptop has left me little time for siblings, friends and neighbours, I am indebted to all of those, both in Oxford and further afield, who have sustained and looked out for me nonetheless.

This book is dedicated to the memory of my beloved father, Gavin Roynon, who always taught me that work is a blessing. He died very suddenly, on a snowy Friday morning in March 2018. I had been reading about the books in Faulkner's library that very day. And as he above all people would have wished, this book is also dedicated to my daughters. It is for Hermione, Olivia and Frances Watt: brilliant and long-suffering graces all.

Tessa Roynon
Oxford, June 2019

Introduction: Greek and Roman Presences in the Modern American Novel

'If an increasingly pluralistic America ever decides to commission a new motto,' writes the narrator of Paul Beatty's satirical novel, *The Sellout* (2015), 'I'm open for business'. 'I've got a better one than *E pluribus unum*,' he continues. It's '*tu dormis tu perdis* . . . you snooze, you lose' (13). In the same darkly comic tone, the narrator comments wryly on the disjunction between aspiration and reality in the US capital city:

> Washington, D.C., with its wide streets, confounding roundabouts, marble statues, Doric columns, and domes, is supposed to feel like ancient Rome (that is, if the streets of ancient Rome were lined with homeless black people, bomb-sniffing dogs, tour buses, and cherry blossoms). Yesterday afternoon, like some sandal-shod Ethiop from the sticks of the darkest of the Los Angeles jungles, I ventured from the hotel and joined the hajj of blue-jeaned yokels that paraded slowly and patriotically past the empire's historic landmarks. (4)

Beatty's text not only constitutes a sharply ironic comment on the centuries-old identification between dominant American culture and classical antiquity. In so doing, it stakes out a position for itself in the ever-widening galaxy of modern American novels that engage, in numerous ways and to numerous ends, with the cultures, histories, literatures and mythologies of the ancient world.

This book examines how and why so much modern, postmodern and/or contemporary US fiction, occupying every position on the realist-to-experimentalist spectrum, makes such varied and extensive use of classical Greek and Roman tradition. It offers detailed studies of seven major authors of the twentieth and twenty-first centuries – Willa Cather, F. Scott Fitzgerald, William Faulkner, Ralph Ellison, Toni Morrison, Philip Roth and Marilynne Robinson – whose works are characterised by widespread and complex allusiveness to the classical past, as well as to later receptions and reworkings of that past. In close readings of texts dating from Cather's *My Ántonia*, published in 1918, to Robinson's *Home*, of 2008, it asks what's at stake in a specific reference to a hero from Greek tragedy or Roman epic; to pastoral poetry, or to a Roman emperor; to a neoclassical sculpture or architectural style? What's the significance of Pygmalion in Ellison's posthumous *Three Days Before the Shooting . . .* (2010), or of Prometheus in Roth's *I Married a Communist* (2008)? Classical allusions in these texts are never merely an aesthetic phenomenon. They are always ideological in effect, playing a central role in a novel's interactions with the historical, political and cultural contexts which it is shaped by and which it shapes. Each of the novelists discussed in this book deploys classical culture to construct specific versions of individual racial, socio-economic and/or gendered identities and experiences. Emerging from and during a range of significant moments in the history of the United States – the First World War, the Great Black Migration, the rapid modernisation and urbanisation of the 1920s, the Depression, the Second World War, the Cold War, the Vietnam War, the Civil Rights Movement, and so on – they each create and/or subvert specific narratives of national (and transnational) history and self-definition. In illuminating and critiquing these processes, my book both constitutes and advocates deep thinking about the active and transformative classical presences in the modern American canon.

In 2001, John Shields published a meticulous study of allusions to Greece and Rome in seventeenth- to nineteenth-century American literature: *The American Aeneas: Classical Origins of the American Self*. Meanwhile, in her 2008 monograph, *The Quest for Epic in Contemporary American Fiction*, Catherine Morley persuasively argues that the works of John Updike, Philip Roth and Don DeLillo are at once indebted to and revise the European epic. There also exist various one-volume studies of classical allusiveness in single authors, many of which have been invaluable in the chapters that follow.[1] Scholarly discussion of classical mythology in the canonical modernist poets such as T. S. Eliot and Ezra Pound, meanwhile, is too copious to enumerate here, while in recent years both Americanist and classical scholars have conducted extensive research in the reception of Greek drama by American playwrights and on the American stage.[2] This is the first book, however, both to survey and to read closely the persistence of classicism in the works of key American novelists that date from the last one hundred years.

The decades between 1918 and 2008 – when *My Ántonia* and *Home* respectively were published – witnessed a range of notable and often controversial cultural moments and contexts from (and sometimes against) which my chosen texts have emerged. These include the waxing and waning of the high modernism epitomised by James Joyce's *Ulysses* (published in 1922); the Great Books tradition that took hold during World War II and held great sway in the early 1950s; the postmodernisms (and reactions against them) of later decades; the 'culture wars' that began in the 1980s; and the identity politics that were so inextricable from those, while being taken to task themselves in recent years. Both separately and together, my readings shine new light on the multivalent classicism that is a striking feature of so much modern American fiction's always fraught, always political and always evolving articulations of our present-day lives, of our pasts, and of our futures. My analyses reveal the sometimes-surprising extent to which classicism shapes the dilemmas about authority, legitimacy or authenticity that animate modern American culture. These are dilemmas with continuing implications for our conceptions of ethnicity, race, nationhood and the globe; of feminism and masculinity; of wealth, poverty and inequality; of faith and spirituality, and of the nature of the academy itself.

My rationale for writing this book is my sense that as twenty-first-century readers we tend to be at once too terrified by and too deferential towards the classical allusions that we encounter in modern literature. Despite the burgeoning of classical reception studies in the last two decades – a field that draws attention to the ideologically motivated uses and abuses of the classical tradition in numerous spheres of modern life – within American literary studies (of the novel in particular, perhaps) we often assume that the classicism we run into is somehow at once neutral, 'universal', ennobling and unquestionably a 'good thing'. Classical references can appear to us as at once discrete and part of the 'natural order of things', leading either to blind assumptions about their perceived 'wholesomeness', or to the celebratory, reaffirming endorsement that characterises some scholars' and reviewers' responses to American novelists' allusiveness. In this book I encourage a sceptical scrutiny of the sophisticated dynamics at play in the many intertextual dialogues that American fiction's classicism involves. As do the novels and novelists discussed here, and as does the best in classical reception theory and practice, our readings should traverse with confidence the institutional and disciplinary boundaries that demarcate the 'ancient' and the 'modern', and that separate 'Classics' from 'literary studies'.

This kind of analysis, I contend, inevitably and usefully develops our understanding of authors such as Cather or Morrison in relation to modernism, transnationalism and other key cultural processes. It thereby complicates the way major works that survey American fiction – such as Leonard Cassuto's *Cambridge History of the American Novel* (2011) or Lawrence Buell's *Dream of the Great American Novel* (2014) – categorise and position their authors. My book is deliberately conceived and structured as a series of studies rather than as a monograph: it does not seek to advance one argument about modern American novelists' classicism, but rather, by drawing attention to an under-discussed dimension of the field, and by combining an overview of the existing critical discourse with new close readings, it aims to open doorways or illuminate pathways to numerous future studies. In particular it eschews the kind of unifying formula or paradigm on which Shields's reading of the nineteenth century in terms of the 'American Aeneas' depends. When Shields writes of the 'classical half of the American self' he harks back to the 'old' or 'myth and symbol' school of American studies which emerged in the 1950s (Shields x), and to R. W. B. Lewis's conception of the 'American Adam', which epitomises that approach in his 1955 work of that title. As we approach the third decade of the twenty-first century, there is no one classical hero or archetype that can symbolise or unify what Buell calls the 'pluriverse in motion' of the American novel (8), or, for that matter, of American identities themselves. It is of course my hope that the analyses in these pages reflect on and refract in new ways key works of intellectual history and cultural theory to which classicism is fundamental – from Erich Auerbach's *Mimesis* (1946) to John Guillory's *Cultural Capital* (1993) or Paul Gilroy's *The Black Atlantic* (1993) and beyond. I absolutely intend, however, to leave my readers with more questions than answers, and to provoke numerous new interpretations both of American fiction, and of the cultures and politics of which it is a symbiotic part.

The tracing of literary influences and intellectual antecedents is of course a notoriously ambiguous and contested process. There are, however, several traditions and/or cultural 'currents' – by definition American and European at once – that contribute, in different ways and to a greater or lesser extent, to modern American novelists' predilection for invoking antiquity. One is the idea of the 'American epic': reaching back to the conscious quest for a 'national' American literature that animated the early years of the new republic, it ranges from Joel Barlow's Pope-like *Columbiad* of 1807 to the resolutely non-classical Walt Whitman in *Song of Myself* (1855).[3] The impulse towards epic next found expression in the canonical novels which were to become the American 'classics' – beloved, not coincidentally, by nearly all the modern fiction writers discussed in this book – such as Hawthorne's *The Scarlet Letter* (1850), Melville's *Moby-Dick* (1851) and Twain's *Huckleberry Finn* (1884).[4] These texts were (paradoxically) at once self-consciously 'American' and in explicit dialogue with Egyptian, Greek and Roman (as well as biblical) traditions. The idea of the 'American epic', moreover, is of course closely linked to the equally metamorphic and equally tenacious concept of the 'Great American Novel' which, as Buell has documented, was first articulated by one John W. De Forest in 1868,[5] and which continues to compel and infuriate both writers and readers to this day.

A second cultural genealogy is the English literary tradition that the authors in this study encountered over the course of their own educations. For the most part, this tradition was privileged over the American one in the high school and undergraduate curricula during the years (from the late nineteenth century to the 1960s) during which these novelists undertook their studies. To pan across these novelists' literary enthusiasms, from the Renaissance through the Neoclassical satirists and the Romantics to the Decadents and beyond, is to see both the changing nature of the tradition and the persistence of antiquity therein. Marlowe, Shakespeare, Swift, Keats, Swinburne, Wilde and A. E. Housman, to name but a few, are all utterly dependent, but in contrasting ways and to contrasting effects, on the cultural legacies of Greece and Rome.[6] In addition, as antecedents in the blending of these English canonical traditions with the 'American epic' (that Cather et al. continue) are the vast fictional outputs of Henry James and Edith Wharton, whose writing in both its subject matter and its form epitomises both the interconnectedness of America and Europe, and the transition from the Victorian to the modern era. And the work of the late-nineteenth-century author Sarah Orne Jewett, the early-twentieth-century novelist Theodore Dreiser and the playwright Eugene O'Neill also merits mention here – for being at once replete with classical allusions and beloved by authors such as Cather, Fitzgerald and Faulkner respectively. At the same time, however, it is at once striking and regrettably unsurprising that the numerous African American literary ancestors who play a key role in the genealogy of American cultural classicism – ranging from Phillis Wheatley and David Walker to Alexander Crummell, Anna Julia Cooper, Charles Chesnutt, W. E. B. Du Bois and Pauline Hopkins – are almost never invoked in my chosen authors' reflections on the reading enthusiasms and the formal education of their youth. In a realm in which so much is at stake in terms of cultural value and the canon, this conspicuous and troubling absence speaks for itself.

Perhaps the most significant way in which Cather, Fitzgerald, Faulkner, Ellison, Morrison, Roth and Robinson encounter antiquity is directly – by which I mean through their own unmediated reading of works by Homer, Aeschylus, Plato, Aristotle, Virgil, Ovid, Petronius et al. As I document in the first section of each of the chapters that follow, for some of these novelists, some of this reading was in the original Greek or Latin texts. Predominantly, however, these writers' sensibilities were shaped by reading widely in English translations, and in scholarship, and also in 'middlebrow' writing, about the classical world. The canonical high modernists, T. S. Eliot, James Joyce and Ezra Pound (and the less canonical ones such as H.D.), were probably more fluent in both Latin and Greek (and French and Italian) than any of the fiction writers whom I analyse in detail here. But each of my chosen novelists herself or himself valorises the experience of the direct interaction with antiquity, the leaping over centuries of tradition back to a (perceived) original and deeply enriching source, that is a defining impulse in modernism. While this classically allusive strand of modernism was not only profoundly formative for each of these writers, several of them (namely Cather, Fitzgerald, Faulkner, Ellison and to some extent Morrison) are themselves part of this cultural moment and process.

And in the case of Roth and Robinson (and again, to some extent, Morrison) they indubitably stand in significant and conscious relation to it.

Of the nineteen novels and one series of manuscripts (Ellison's) that I read closely in this book, only two – Cather's *My Ántonia* (1918) and Fitzgerald's *This Side of Paradise* (1920) – pre-date the 'annus mirabilis' for classically allusive high modernism that was 1922, in which both T. S. Eliot's *The Waste Land* and Joyce's *Ulysses* were published.[7] Joyce's *Portrait of the Artist as a Young Man*, meanwhile, depicting the *Bildung* of a quasi-epic artist-hero and bookended by its references to Ovid's *Metamorphoses*, had of course appeared in 1916. It would be difficult to overstate the influence of both Joyce and Eliot – in particular of these three texts – on all of the classically allusive American fiction that post-dates them. Among the seven authors whom I discuss here, it is Fitzgerald, Faulkner, Ellison, Morrison and Roth for whom Eliot and Joyce are especially formative. Joyce's influence is particularly interesting in the case of the two African American authors, whose work constitutes a counter-epic and alternative-modernist perspective.

It is a contentious generalisation, but perhaps a useful one nonetheless, to state that it is from Eliot that these fiction writers inherit a means of articulating a modernist sense of self, in its alienation, conscious incoherence and fragmentedness. It is from Joyce, meanwhile, that they inherit this same embattled selfhood interwoven with a representation of national identity and history that is dependent on the epic forms that it transforms. In Eliot, in other words, many modern American novelists encounter a conception of modernity that is not exceptionally 'American' but to which American culture in the early twentieth century is key. In Joyce, meanwhile, they encounter a way of representing the past and the present, a way of using heroic tradition and contemporaneity to reflect on and refract each other in prose fiction, that can be readily transposed from an Irish to an American and/or African American context.

Of equal importance to any consideration of classicism in twentieth-century US fiction is Eliot's famous 1923 essay on Joyce, '*Ulysses*, Order, and Myth', in which he not only declares that novel to be one 'from which none of us can escape', but in which he also elucidates the 'mythical method' of the 'parallels to the *Odyssey*', which he asserts 'have the importance of a scientific discovery' (165–7). The essayist's perception of Joyce's synthesis of 'psychology, . . . ethnology, and The Golden Bough' alerts us to the formative influence of Freud, Jung and the anthropologists of the Cambridge Ritualist School in particular, who are as important in any consideration of the modern American novel's engagement with antiquity as they are to that of Joyce, or of Eliot himself. Yet, as numerous critics have observed before now, and as the discussions in the chapters that follow make clear, there is something misleadingly tidy or wishful about Eliot's major claim, that 'manipulating a continuous parallel between contemporaneity and antiquity' is 'simply a way of controlling, of ordering, of giving a shape and a significance to . . . contemporary history' (167).

It is noticeable but not surprising that America's 'Great Books' tradition, initiated by Robert Maynard Hutchins from the early 1930s onwards, includes in its first incarnation no texts from the 'high modernist' movement that was at this time barely itself yet on the wane.[8] This method of teaching the liberal arts through Socratic debate about a fixed canon of valorised translated 'classic' texts (such as those by Homer, the Greek tragedians, Aristotle, Herodotus, Virgil and a range of more recent European writers who pre-date the twentieth century) was still at its zenith at the University of Chicago when Philip Roth arrived there in 1954. Together with the closely related neo-Aristotelian school (which also emerged from Chicago), its influence is evident in the classes available to Morrison at Howard University between 1949 and 1953, and would indubitably have left its traces both on the curriculum at Tuskegee, where Ellison studied between 1933 and 1936, and on the way Robinson was taught at Brown's Pembroke College some fifteen years later. Its legacies persist at Chicago, at Columbia and various liberal arts institutions to this day.

While, as we shall see, the American fiction that emerged when the 'Great Books' were in vogue often challenges and complicates its constructions of culture, the canon, and concomitant ideologies of individualism, liberalism and Eurocentric nationalism, there are two aspects of the movement that are particularly relevant to the concerns of this book. The first is the fact that, from 1943 onwards, 'Great Books' became a commercial venture in addition to an intellectual or pedagogical one, in that Hutchins and his colleague Mortimer Adler launched (with Britannica) the publication of their 'Great Books of the Western World' series.[9] Following on from Charles Eliot's 'Harvard Classics' (which Ellison himself read, and which are also read or referenced by characters in certain texts by Cather, Fitzgerald and Faulkner), this came to involve door-to-door sales of the books, as well as a nationwide network of 'Great Books' discussion groups to which the public were encouraged to belong.

The middlebrow dimensions of this project are important because they reveal the way in which antiquity became repackaged as less the preserve of highly educated experimental writers and their erudite readers, and more a force for the 'common good'. Following the lead of *Bulfinch's Mythology* (first published in 1867 and frequently reprinted thereafter) were works such as Edith Hamilton's *Mythology*, first published in 1942.[10] Hamilton's book became a bestseller and a staple of the high school curriculum, and while it remained separate from the formal 'Great Books' tradition it is closely related to this phenomenon. While of course testifying to the inseparability of culture and capitalism in the United States, these processes also go some way to explaining the impressive autodidacticism of figures such as Faulkner and Ellison, who compensated for their lack of formal degrees with independent reading (including in Classics) of extraordinary breadth and depth. It is striking, as well, that the reissue and expansion of the published Great Books that took place in 1990 – one that aimed and ultimately failed to boost the series' sales – includes works by Cather and Joyce (anthologised in Volume 88) and those by T. S. Eliot, O'Neill, Fitzgerald and Faulkner (anthologised in Volume 99).[11] This demonstrates usefully how the once-avant-garde soon becomes itself a staple of the canon, and reminds us that Ellison, Morrison and Roth read and were shaped by Fitzgerald and Faulkner as much as by Eliot and Joyce, and by the Greek and Roman classics on whom all of them draw in turn.

The 1950s match the early 1920s in this account as a moment of highly significant convergences in the United States. The investment in liberal ideology and in liberal arts, fuelled by Cold War commitment to a strong sense of exceptional American identity, underpinned the valorisation of antiquity that both neo-Aristotelianism and the 'Great Books' phenomenon involved. Simultaneously and not at all coincidentally, this investment drove the emergence of an American studies that was itself deeply committed to the consolidation and perpetuation of a specific national mythology.[12] And yet, as the civic architecture of Washington DC makes immediately clear, the idea of modern (or post-independence) America as a kind of 'new' ancient world, an ideal democracy built on classical models, did not, of course, begin in the 1950s. As numerous works of cultural history have demonstrated, the legacies of Greece and Rome have for centuries been fundamental to dominant American culture's self-conceptions and self-presentations.[13] From the Founding Fathers' predilection for classical pseudonyms to the nineteenth-century predilection for Greek tragedy in performance; or from antebellum slave-holders' self-serving sense of their analogical relationship to the slave societies of ancient Greece and Rome (which extended to the fashion for giving slaves classical names) to the exuberantly postmodern construction of the iconic Caesar's Palace hotel in Las Vegas, American historiography, art and architecture, and popular culture have performed and even fetishised a variety of 'neo-classicisms'.[14] The fiction that I discuss in this book is inseparable from these contexts. It is never an uncomplicated articulation of them, of course, but instead constitutes cultural expressions that variously challenge, revise and re-voice the American classicisms that undergird that nation's dominant narratives about war, about empire, about slavery and freedom, about individualistic progress, and so on.

In his invaluable study *Joyce in America* (1993), Jeffrey Segall demonstrates that the complex and paradoxical reception of *Ulysses* in the United States is characterised by its differing appeal, on differing grounds, to Marxists, New Critical conservatives and liberals in the decades following its publication. '*Ulysses*', Segall writes, 'became a cultural nexus over which critics with opposed ideological perspectives did battle' (3). This insight is helpful not least because it applies equally to the classical tradition itself. Any overview of the history of the cultural and political deployments of antiquity in America must attend not only to hegemonic deployments of classicism, but also to its usefulness, in various guises and constructions, to Communism, and to the struggles for gender and racial equality. For example, as Edith Hall et al. (in *Ancient Slavery and Abolition* (2011)) and Margaret Malamud (in *African Americans and the Classics* (2016)) have separately shown, while nineteenth-century defenders of slavery relied heavily on classical precedents in arguing their case, abolitionists mined antiquity just as energetically and strategically to further their own cause. As key classical reception studies anthologies such as Stephens and Vasunia's *Classics and National Cultures* (2010) and Hardwick and Harrison's *Classics in the Modern World: A Democratic Turn?* (2013) have argued, the legacies of Greece and Rome are infinitely malleable, receptive to any number of interpretations, and ripe for pragmatic deployment in the 'authentication' of a huge range of conflicting ideological agendas.[15] When in 1954 W. B. Stanford published his pioneering and profoundly influential work of what was not yet called reception studies – *The Ulysses Theme: A Study in the Adaptability of a Traditional Hero* – his subtitular emphasis on 'adaptability' articulates precisely what is invaluable to modernity about the ancient past.

It is not coincidental that the field of 'Black Classicism' – which plays such a key role in the story of American uses of antiquity – has evolved in tandem with that of reception studies. In 2005, classicist Michele Ronnick (building on her work of the 1990s in the theory and practice of what she then termed 'Classica Africana') published a definition of 'Classicism, black' in the second edition of Gates and Appiah's mammoth *Encyclopedia Africana*. Subtitling this entry 'the history and study of the relationship between Greco-Roman civilization and people of African descent' (120), Ronnick here gave a name to, and hence increased the visibility and circulation of, a multifaceted concept and a complex genealogy of exchanges that had of course existed without such a name for centuries.[16] While Ronnick's *Encyclopedia* discussion includes modern literary writers such as Phillis Wheatley, W. E. B. Du Bois, Melvin Tolson, Ralph Ellison and Toni Morrison, scholars such as Patrice Rankine (in *Ulysses in Black* (2006)), Tracey Walters (in *African American Literature and the Classicist Tradition* (2007)), William Cook and James Tatum (in *African American Writers and Classical Tradition* (2010)) and myself (in *Toni Morrison and the Classical Tradition* (2013)) enact detailed readings of numerous African American authors' classical allusiveness that are both shaped by and expand the parameters of black classicist theory.[17] Considered alongside the recent illuminations of the role of antiquity in the long history of transatlantic slavery and the ongoing struggle for civil rights (for example by Hall et al. and by Malamud), this aspect of American classicism constitutes a crucial context to our readings not just of the black authors selected for close study in this book (Ellison and Morrison), but also of the white authors (in particular Faulkner, Roth and Robinson) who engage directly with issues of race and racism, and with African American experience.

Related works such as Barbara Goff and Michael Simpson's *Crossroads in the Black Aegean* (2007) and Justine McConnell's

Black Odysseys (2013) consider African, African American and Caribbean works in parallel. In this they are useful for illuminating the transnational dynamics not just of black diasporic cultural production but also of the classical tradition itself. They constitute an invaluable corrective to readings that conceptualise the American novel's allusions to antiquity in a purely nationalistic framework.[18] Continuing their refractions of United States classicism through a postcolonial lens is John Levi Barnard's *Empire of Ruin* (2017), which explores how black American writers and visual artists ranging from Wheatley and Charles Chesnutt to Kara Walker critique triumphalist dominant American deployments of the Greek and Roman past in order to protest slavery and the persistence of racial discrimination and injustice.

All of the black classicist scholarship mapped out here engages either explicitly or implicitly with the first volume of Martin Bernal's *Black Athena* trilogy, which was published in 1987, and subtitled 'the Afroasiatic roots of classical civilization'. Bernal's commitment to illuminating the previously obscured interconnections between Africa, the Middle East and Greece and Rome have inspired groundbreaking essays such as Toni Morrison's 'Unspeakable Things Unspoken' (1989), which drew attention to Bernal's emphasis on the '*process*' of the 'fabrication of Ancient Greece' as a whitened, pure and hence purifying force, deployed during the Enlightenment and its aftermath to bolster ideologies of empire, colonialism and slavery' (374, original italics). Yet, as Bernal would be the first to attest, what I have termed elsewhere 'the Africanness of classicism' is in no way a concept invented with his work.[19] Black American authors from Phillis Wheatley through Pauline Hopkins to Ishmael Reed pre-date Bernal in their insistence on the crucial interrelatedness of Africa, Greece and Rome, many arguing that, in Paul Gilroy's words, 'the roots of European civilization lay in African sources' (*Black Atlantic* 130). Both Ellison and Morrison, as my readings go on to demonstrate, are significant modern presences in this black classicist genealogy.

Gilroy's definition of tradition as 'the living memory of the changing same' usefully articulates the complex relationship between the texts discussed in this book, as well as between those texts and the classical antecedents on which they draw (*Black Atlantic* 18). While the concept of 'tradition' and the metaphor of 'genealogy' are useful and compelling, however, it is important to recognise that the story of American novelists' uses of antiquity is characterised as much by discontinuity and disjunction as it is by continuity and conjunction. With regard to the novels chosen for close study here, for example, Philip Roth's 'American trilogy' articulates the perspectives of both 1950s liberal humanism and postmodern self-reflexivity, while Robinson's texts implicitly locate a political radicalism in that very 1950s humanist education in which Roth's liberalism is grounded. Robinson insists on classical, humanist learning's connections with rather than separateness from the civil rights and feminist movements that were gathering momentum at that time, and in so doing implicitly critiques the less obviously politicised postmodernisms of recent decades. I determined on the specific seven authors selected here not because they are the only or even necessarily the most obvious classically allusive modern American fiction writers, but because while each individual novelist's specific engagements with antiquity reward close analysis, the texts and their authors when considered all together resonate within, refract and resist each other in numerous fascinating ways.[20]

Furthermore, no tidy scheme or universally applicable rationale has dictated either my choice of novels or the nature of each close reading. On the one hand I have elected to analyse the novels by each author most likely to be taught – such as Cather's *My Ántonia* (1918), Fitzgerald's *The Great Gatsby* (1925) or Morrison's *Song of Solomon* (1977). On the other hand I have consciously shone a spotlight on texts in which the significance of classical allusiveness is usually overlooked: Cather's *Sapphira and the Slave Girl* (1940), Faulkner's 'The Fire and the Hearth' from *Go Down, Moses* (1942) or Robinson's *Home* (2008). Often I conduct an overview of the engagements with antiquity as they pertain to a novel as a whole – so that in the case of Ellison's *Invisible Man* (1952) or *Housekeeping* (1980) my analyses constitute an exploration of these texts' numerous key themes. At other times, however – for example in my discussions of Faulkner's *Absalom, Absalom!* (1936), Roth's *The Human Stain* (2000) or selected sections of Ellison's posthumous manuscript *Three Days Before the Shooting . . .* (2010) – I home in on very specific motifs, authorial practices and/or passages in order to add new depth to pre-existing broad understandings.

As Lorna Hardwick charts in her foundational survey, *Reception Studies* (2003), scholars use a striking range of metaphors to describe both the ways in which modern writers and artists engage with antiquity, and the ways ancient texts re-present themselves in modern cultural practice. These include concepts of 'migration' (1), 'routes' (4), 'transplantation' (10) and 'transmission' (16). Ideas of 'excavation', 'accretion', the 'palimpsest' and even '*sparagmos*' also usefully articulate this complex relationship, and all of these terms illuminate the nature of the dialogues between modern American fiction and the classical past with which my book is concerned.[21] The allusions I discuss in the chapters that follow range from direct and exact quotation from canonical classical texts (in the case of Cather's transcriptions of lines from Virgil, for example) to the imprecise but nonetheless significant resonances of classical motifs or style (in Roth's depiction of Sylphid as a harpist in *I Married a Communist*, for example).[22] Following both Hardwick in *Reception Studies* and Stephen Hinds in his important analysis of literary relationships within Roman poetry, *Allusion and Intertext* (1998), my analyses of the selected fiction privilege the reader's 'response' over any 'original' authorial intention.[23] So, for example, my contention as a reader of Robinson's *Housekeeping* that certain scenes in that text recall Aeneas's visit to the underworld in the *Aeneid*, or that the first Eclogue is a significant presence in Morrison's *Jazz*, has value whether or not Robinson or Morrison consciously alludes to those poems. And their 'intentions' are something we can never know for certain, anyway. As the chapters that follow demonstrate, to read with an openness to the 'allusive inexactitude' that Hinds theorises is to enable innumerable rich and valuable interpretations of these complex and generative novels (25).

Notes

1. Besides works mentioned in the chapters that follow, see for example Ludot-Vlasak on Melville; St. Jean on Dreiser.
2. See for example Andreach; H. Foley; Bosher et al.
3. On Barlow and the Connecticut (Hartford) Wits see Shields 75–164.
4. See Shields chapters 8 and 9; on Twain see Solomon; Deneen.
5. See Buell 23.
6. Modern French literature was another classically allusive influence, particularly on Cather, Fitzgerald and Faulkner.
7. Both of these authors might, of course, have encountered the serialised chapters of *Ulysses* that appeared in *The Little Review* (published in New York) between 1918 and 1920. On this serialised version of *Ulysses* see Hutton.

8. Hutchins was president and then chancellor of the University of Chicago between 1938 and 1951. On the 'Great Books' see Beam; Boddy.
9. See Beam 79.
10. *Bulfinch's Mythology* by Massachusetts-born Thomas Bulfinch (1796–1867) begins with 'Stories of Gods and Heroes' in its first section, 'The Age of Fable' (see Bulfinch; also at <http://www.gutenberg.org/cache/epub/4928/pg4928-images.html> (last accessed 30 April 2020)).
11. Beam 220.
12. On the evolving nature of American studies see Maddox.
13. See for example Reinhold; Richard; Winterer (*Culture* and *Mirror*); Malamud (*Ancient Rome*); Wyke. The significant and longstanding cultural dialogue between US culture and that of ancient Egypt – also an important presence in modern American fiction – is regrettably beyond the scope of this study.
14. Shields also illuminates the significant classical allusiveness of Puritans such as Edward Taylor and Cotton Mather, who pre-date the Founding Fathers (38–74).
15. Centred on the USA are essays by Melton and by Connolly in each respective collection.
16. See also Ronnick's 2011 article, 'Black Classicism'.
17. See also Fertik and Hanses on Du Bois and antiquity.
18. For an invaluable overview of the key 'new directions' in black classicism during crucial years for the field, 2005 to 2007, see Greenwood.
19. See Roynon, 'The Africanness of Classicism'. The introduction to Orrells et al., *African Athena* (2011) surveys many of the key responses to Bernal's work, among which it is itself significant.
20. I reference many of the numerous other modern American novels that engage classical antiquity in my conclusion to this book.
21. On *sparagmos* as a metaphor for classical reception see McConnell, 'Postcolonial *Sparagmos*'.
22. Hardwick's theory of 'fuzzy connections' between modern and classical cultural forms is useful here; see Hardwick, 'Fuzzy Connections'.
23. See Hardwick, *Reception Studies* 8.

CHAPTER 1

Willa Cather (1873–1946)

Cather and the Classics

It is hard to find material written by Willa Cather that does *not* engage with the classical tradition. Each of her twelve novels – published between 1912 and 1940 – significantly and variously invokes the cultures and legacies of ancient Greece and Rome. The same is true of her earliest published work: of the copious journalism of the years 1893 to 1912 (when she was both student and paid professional); of the 1903 poetry collection, *April Twilights*, and of the 1905 story collection, *The Troll Garden*. Classical heroes (both historical and mythological), classical literature, classical sculpture and architecture, and ancient Mediterranean archaeological sites and landscapes make their presences felt throughout her oeuvre. In short, it would be hard to overstate the ubiquity and the importance of classical antiquity in Cather's intellectual formation, in her interpretations of her own life experiences and of the world around her, and in her literary output as a whole.[1]

This writer's extensive and varied non-fiction, including her letters, constitutes ample testimony to her early immersion in and passion for both Latin and Greek, as languages and as literature.[2] She was powerfully drawn to classical antiquity and to its extensive legacies in both European and American literature and art. As the numerous biographies and the memoirs by those who knew Cather attest, she was someone with huge intellectual curiosity and drive, one whose informal education through broad and deep reading from childhood onwards was as significant as her formal one, and who possessed a prodigious memory.[3] It is perhaps not surprising that accounts of Cather's intellectual formation occasionally exhibit a mythologising tendency themselves; there is undoubtedly something striking and unforgettable about the story of this writer's intellectual *Bildung* or apprenticeship. As with Ralph Ellison, this is due in part to her own self-fashioning in autobiographical reflections and statements, and in part to the extensive use she makes of her own reading, her own education, and her own artistic apprenticeship within her fiction.

As a woman, Cather indubitably and inevitably became something of a trailblazer, both as a student at the University of Nebraska and in the professional worlds of journalism and literary publishing in which she went on to excel. From the outset there was something exceptional about her passion for learning and her ambitiousness. As a young child she already identified personally and strongly with heroic figures of the classical past who captured her imagination: a childhood game, for example, was to sit in an upturned chair, playing the role of Cato in his chariot.[4] At the age of nine, when she first moved to Nebraska from Virginia with her family, she did not immediately attend school. Instead she encountered books with and through her maternal grandmother, Rachel Boak, who read to her from, among other things, a popular Victorian compendium for children known as *Peter Parley's Universal History*. This work claims to be 'a clear outline of the story of mankind' (Goodrich vi), and places key moments in the lives of ancient Greek and Roman historical figures (such as Alexander the Great or Julius Caesar) alongside similarly momentous events in different continents, including in America since European conquest.[5] Particularly striking is the way it holds the histories of multiple regions and eras in parallel, thereby implicitly encouraging eclectic comparisons and connections. The formative influence of this book on young Willa was considerable.

Cather's curriculum at her school in Red Cloud (which she attended from 1884 until 1890) included Latin and French. During these years she also made the most of her access to the personal book collection of a neighbouring family called the Wieners: her reading ranged from *Pilgrim's Progress* and Shakespeare's plays (including *Julius Caesar* and *Antony and Cleopatra*) to the highly allusive poetry of Milton, Keats and Housman, the prose of Carlyle and the novels of Flaubert and Tolstoy. Biographers agree that it was primarily from out-of-school 'tutorials' with the local and unconventionally learned storekeeper, William Ducker, that Cather gained real proficiency in both Latin and Greek. With Ducker she learned to read and translate the poetry of Homer, Virgil and Ovid, and his sudden death (he was purportedly reading the *Iliad* at the time) made a great impression on her. Passing on his torch of informal instruction, she went on to teach texts by Virgil and Caesar's *Gallic Wars* to her brother Roscoe during her vacations from university.[6]

Having graduated from high school with the top marks in Latin, Cather attended the Latin School in Lincoln for one year, thereby fulfilling the preparatory requirements for the University of Nebraska. She enrolled at the university (at that time 'a little Renaissance world') in September 1891 (Slote 42).[7] Initially intending to focus on science and to become a doctor, she switched to literary studies and Classics, and studied extensively in Greek, Latin, English and French literature. In February 1884, during her junior year, she played the part of Electra in a student dramatic performance which was a collage of scenes from Greek tragedy.[8] It must be said, however, that Cather did not unambivalently embrace academic approaches to either languages or literature. While she was passionate about the texts she encountered and the ancient civilisations of which they were part, she didn't like grammar (scholars have detected grammatical errors in the Latin that she incorporates into her fiction), and she found the linguistic preoccupations of several of her professors in both Classics and English to be uninspiring and frustrating.[9] After graduating from the university in June 1895, there came a turning point that was perhaps a blessing in disguise: her application for an academic post there was unsuccessful. She then continued to develop her classical enthusiasms through her job as a high school teacher in Pittsburgh between 1901–2 and 1904–5, through her journalism as a theatre and art critic, and through travels in Europe in 1902 and in 1908–9.[10]

Cather's lifelong preoccupation with conceptions of the heroic was inspired and nourished by many sources. Carlyle's lecture series of 1840, *Heroes and Hero Worship*, may well have influenced the young student, especially in its implicit analogy between 'the hero as poet' and 'the hero as king'.[11] While Carlyle's subjects are all 'Great Men' (Carlyle 1), Cather's conception of her heroic protagonists – pioneers, explorers, artists, intellectuals, and survivors of difficult circumstances, both male and female – has clear affinities with the Victorian writer's description of the hero's 'radiance' as 'the living light-fountain, which it is good and pleasant to be near' (2).[12] That her fictional heroes and heroines were informed not just by those of myth but also by the historical figures whom she personally revered is suggested by her response to a bust of Julius Caesar that she encountered in the Archaeological Museum in Naples in 1908. Rhapsodising in a letter about this 'wonderful head of Caesar', she recalls that there had been a photo of this sculpture in her high school textbook edition of Caesar's *Gallic Wars*. Going on to exclaim, 'Such a head!', she doubts 'whether the world has produced another such head in all the centuries since' (Jewell and Stout 110). A notably similar emphasis on the splendour of a heroic head recurs time and again in her fiction. Whether in early stories such as 'The Namesake' or in her last novel, *Sapphira and the Slave Girl*, Cather's remarking on a character's impressively wrought or strikingly held head always signifies that individual's greatness.

The novelist's recurring interest in the statuesque or in frieze-like images also expresses her impulse to create meaningful experience by arresting time, as Keats does in his 'Ode on a Grecian Urn'. Her depictions of individuals, natural landscapes and cities in the modern world certainly borrow from the classical traditions of pastoral and elegy in their laments over time's passing, and in recollecting a now-vanished Golden Age. Yet her references to classical sculpture usually express her concurrent faith in the power of the arts to memorialise and to distil an essence that is universal or permanent.[13] And as my close readings of the three novels demonstrate, classical epic animates a similar paradox or dialectic throughout her fiction. Cather repeatedly invokes the *Aeneid* and the *Odyssey* in particular to articulate both outward and returning journeys; both new experiences and the sanctuary of the familiar; both homesickness or dispossession and belonging or reconnection; and to suggest continuity amid seismic change.

Writing in 1961 of the importance of Classics to Cather, L. V. Jacks enlists the novelist's fascination with antiquity to advance the claim that she 'was more interested in the past than the present' (295). As my book as a whole demonstrates, however, it is too simplistic to understand classical allusiveness as solely constituting a preoccupation with the past. Cather's evident interest in elegy and remembrance, for example, is inseparable from her concomitant interest in the political and cultural dilemmas of her own times, both within and outside the United States. Her classicism should be seen not as peripheral but as central to ongoing critical debates about her stance and her position: as a regionalist and/or a cosmopolitan modernist; as a nostalgic reactionary and escapist and/or as an engaged progressive; as a conventional, tradition-bound novelist and/or as a radical, experimental one.

The Critical Field and Scholarly Debate

Cather's classicism has not always attracted critical attention. The fact that her contemporaneous reviewers scarcely mention her allusiveness reveals the extent to which dominant cultural 'literacy' in or expectations about the classical world have changed over the past one hundred years. While early readers occasionally deploy a classical allusion as part of their own analytical idiom, not one review of the three novels discussed in this chapter comments on the allusive elements that have impressed, unsettled and preoccupied later critics.[14] Scholarship in recent decades has made up for lost time, however; since Curtis Dahl's 1955 discussion of *My Ántonia* as 'An American Georgic', there have appeared a host of articles on classicism in single novels. For the most part focusing either on that text or on *The Professor's House*, these are as recent as Edith Hall's discussion (in her 2015 essay, 'The Migrant Muse') of Euripides in that later novel. The year 1990, meanwhile, proved to be an important moment in the study of Cather's classicism: two monographs on this subject – by Mary Ruth Ryder and by Erik Ingvar Thurin – appeared at this time.[15]

Matthew Hokom's 2015 essay, 'Pompeii and the House of the Tragic Poet in *A Lost Lady*', is a rare but welcome in-depth analysis of allusiveness in a relatively under-discussed text, and there is great scope for new analyses of this kind across Cather's oeuvre.[16] Hokom holds in parallel close reading of both the Cather and ancient texts with relevant details from the novelist's biography and from late-nineteenth-century American cultural trends. This is a process of positioning Cather within American intellectual history as a whole (by teasing out her relationship with Ralph Waldo Emerson, for example) that is absent from both of the full-length studies. Ryder's book, for example, is comprehensive in its coverage, and persuasive in the numerous mythical intertexts and resonances that it detects. In its restricted focus on 'myth as structuring principle' (Ryder 2), however, its exegesis of the psychology of and relationship dynamics between the characters conveys little sense of Cather's place in an American and/or modernist literary trajectory. Thurin's study is more wary of hagiography: it persuasively detects a 'mystique' in the Virgilianism of *My Ántonia*, for example (204). Yet it similarly eschews situating Cather's classicism within wider critical discourse. Thurin's study is also self-limiting as its arguments rest on a conception of 'classical humanism' as a stable body of fixed meaning. While he argues that 'there can be no doubt what this stands for' (12), in truth classicism can be made to mean all sorts of conflicting things. As the seven authors discussed in this book all make clear, and as reception studies has amply theorised, the classical tradition is anything but stable and fixed.

In contrast to Ryder and Thurin, Walter Benn Michaels reads Cather's classicism as part of her politics, and the much-feted study in which he does so, *Our America* (1995), remains a key critical contribution to Cather studies. While Catherine Morley (in *Modern American Literature* (2012)) is not alone in disputing Michaels's reading of Cather as a nativist (that is, someone invested in a pure American identity as a means to resist the cultural changes that immigration threatens), his argument that in Cather's story 'The Namesake' it is the *Aeneid* that signifies Lyon Hartwell's American identity is convincing.[17] One shortcoming of the Michaels argument, however, is that he uses this specific text and reading to imply that classicism throughout Cather's oeuvre means just one thing: an assertion of a distinct and distinctive American identity. Across her works, this novelist in fact deploys different aspects of the classical tradition to articulate a range of ethnic and racial identities, several of which are completely unlike the Americanness that Lyon Hartwell so proudly claims. The multivalence of this allusiveness adds weight to Stout's thesis that we should not compartmentalise Cather as a pure romanticist, or as always reactionary, or as always nativist, but instead regard her as a writer whose work is replete with 'conflict, evasion, and unresolved ambiguities' (*Willa* xi–xii).[18] Cather's classicism works to intensify these conflicts and ambiguities, not to resolve them.

To recognise the interdependence between this novelist's classicism and her conflictedness is to concur with those who position her work as typical of rather than antithetical to both the aesthetic and thematic tendencies of international modernism.[19] As Morley argues, to be 'regionalist' need not necessarily imply either a small canvas or an anti-modernist stance, and her own grouping of Cather with Faulkner (and others) under the title 'Regional American Modernism' is significant and useful.[20] By contrast, in his 2011 *History of the American*

Novel, editor Leonard Cassuto situates Tom Lutz's essay on Cather between studies of Dreiser and Wharton. Even though Lutz persuasively argues within the essay itself that 'regional literature . . . is cosmopolitan literature' and notes that Cather's classical allusiveness is part of her cosmopolitanism (441–3), the fact that Cather is placed two whole sections before the one named 'Modernism and Beyond', which covers Stein, Fitzgerald, Ellison, Faulkner et al., regrettably distances her from those writers and that movement (Cassuto viii).

'What would happen if Miss Cather's writing were given the same kind of textual attention that has been given to Eliot, Pound and Joyce?' asked Bernice Slote in 1966 (92–3). Close analysis of Cather's classicism, I contend, illuminates the major insight implied by Slote's question: her modernism – in particular, the manner and the effects of her classical allusiveness – has much more in common with the canonical male high modernists than critics are usually willing to concede. For the most part, Cather invokes the classical world in analogical rather than genealogical relationship to her own time. For example, in 'A Chance Meeting' the head of Flaubert's niece is like, or analogous to, a bust of a Roman noble woman; in *A Lost Lady* Mrs Forrester is like Helen of Troy. Rather than asserting a linear tradition or unbroken inheritance, in other words, which is how her indebtedness to the classics is commonly viewed, she enables a synchronic universalism, or a sense of commonalities across time. The effect is on the one hand simple, not dissimilar to that of the *Parley's Universal History* of her childhood. On the other hand it is complex, in the manner of Ezra Pound's high modernist sequence *Cantos*, or of his and Ernest Fenellosa's conception of the Chinese character in which each aspect or dimension of that calligraphic figure impresses at the same time.[21]

The fact that Cather's classically informed writing often disrupts historical chronology proves her analogical rather than genealogical stake in antiquity. For example, in her 1902 article on her travels in Provence, she observes – in a striking inversion of linear time – that the Roman builders of Arles must have possessed 'a Chicago like vehemence in adorning their city' (Curtin 950). This disruption is similar to the moment when Jim in *My Ántonia* rather incongruously moves from art to nature rather than vice versa, comparing the evening star over the prairie to 'the lamp engraved upon the title-page of old Latin texts' (255). The nature of Cather's classicism should make us think hard about what she means, in her preface to

Not Under Forty, when she asserts that 'the world broke in two in 1922 or thereabouts' (812). These much-quoted words are usually understood as indicative of an emphatically reactionary perspective. But is Cather really distancing herself here from that watershed moment in modernism, that year in which both Eliot's *The Waste Land* and Joyce's *Ulysses* arrived? Or is she fully aware that the ambiguities of her own texts make them broken at least in two, if not into the fragments that characterise the writing of the male modernists to whom she alludes without naming in this preface?

Cather's writing, particularly when most engaged with the classical world, often echoes and even anticipates *The Waste Land*. In 1924, for example, she wrote in a letter about her love of the Pincian Gardens in Rome, which she describes as 'all the many Romes of many ages heaped up together' (Jewell and Stout 361); Eliot's 'heap of broken images', as well as his juxtaposition of different cities across time, surely resonate here (*Waste Land* l. 22).[22] More striking still is Cather's profound insight about the surviving writings of Sappho, which she wrote in an article on women poets in 1895, a full twenty-seven years before *The Waste Land*'s appearance: 'Those broken fragments', she attests, 'have burned themselves into the consciousness of the world like fire' (Curtin 147).

My Ántonia (1918)

The role of classicism in the instability and ambiguity of *My Ántonia* is evident from its title page onwards. The original Houghton Mifflin edition of 1918 includes the novel's Latin epigraph, '*Optima dies . . . prima fugit*' ('the best days . . . flee first'), not on a page of its own, as is now the convention, but right there on the title page, immediately beneath Cather's name.[23] These words then reappear within the novel itself, some 250 pages later, when Jim Burden quotes them as he recounts his studying of their source, Virgil's *Georgics*. Readers usually resist the temptation to conflate the perspectives of Willa Cather, the author, with the recollected narration of Jim Burden, the fictional character; instead, critics rightly impute great significance to the slippage between the real author, the fictional author in the introduction, and the memoirist, Jim. Yet as it is both Cather and Jim who make much of Virgil, to whom should we attribute the predilection for classical allusions, and for the mythologising of the past, in this text? Does it belong only to Jim, who thereby incurs

Cather's implicit critique? Or is the unambivalent engagement with the classical tradition a tendency that the author shares with and therefore endorses in her narrator-protagonist?

It is inevitable that the boundaries between Cather as author and Jim as character-narrator are permeable and always shifting because the novelist drew so heavily on her own life experience and memories in creating this work.[24] Among many other things, of course, Cather and her created narrator share a love of classical literature. Modelling her own experience, Cather has Jim study the subject both informally, on his own initiative, at home, and formally at the University of Nebraska, Lincoln, where his decorating his rented bedroom with a map of ancient Rome mimics what the novelist (when a student) had actually done.[25] This aspect of Jim's biography – his own classical fluency – enables the apparently organic allusiveness of his narrative that numerous critics have discussed. For in its glorification of agricultural life and rural landscapes, as well as the mourning of their loss, this text is indebted not only to the *Georgics* but to Virgil's more overtly pastoral and elegiac poem, the *Eclogues*, as well. In its heroic conception of its protagonists and its investment in the idea of a newly founded settlement it is informed by the *Aeneid*. And in its conception of Jim's life story as a journey and its preoccupation with homesickness and homecoming it engages the *Odyssey* as well.

The novel's formal qualities, too, themselves bear witness to classical forms. The stories within stories – Jim's entire account, or Ántonia's retelling the tale of Peter, Pavel and the wolves, or the Widow Steavens's account of Ántonia's early motherhood – recall the way stories are told as memories by individual characters within both the *Odyssey* and the *Aeneid*. The sometimes-multiple framing devices also recall those of Ovid's *Metamorphoses*. Crucially, at each moment where Jim's allusiveness is at its most intense – in his childhood on the farm and in town; at university; and in middle age when re-encountering Ántonia – his classical sensibility works not to stabilise or to guarantee a specific meaning, but to reinforce the oscillation and indeterminacy of Cather's text.

Interestingly, it is when he is describing his childhood on the farm and his teenage years in Black Hawk that Jim appears most self-aware about his own tendency to mythologise experience, and/or, as Frances Harling suggests to him, to romanticise it. Perhaps not coincidentally, in the novel's first two books (which describe the time prior to his education in the classics) Jim does not make any *explicit* classical allusions – there are no direct quotations and no naming of classical authors or texts. In these pages his account of his memories repeatedly switches between an epic register and one that overtly pokes fun at or subverts that register. As an epicist, he describes the prairie grass as being 'the color of wine-stains' (14), recalling Homer's famous 'wine-dark sea' in the *Odyssey*.[26] His descriptions of the landscape often implicitly recall classical writers' depictions of the Golden Age: the unfarmed land, 'the material out of which countries are made', brings to mind the unboundaried and unapportioned land recalled in the first Georgic (7).[27] Enthusiastically depicting his Nebraskan childhood in the heroic mode, he undertakes some grand comparisons which are at once beautiful, sublime and somewhat incongruous; the moonlit sky one summer apparently reminds him of Homer's Troy or Virgil's Carthage: 'the quay of some splendid sea-coast city, doomed to destruction' (134). He also compares a sun-shot landscape both to the burning bush in the biblical Book of Exodus and to an epic past in which 'heroes died young and gloriously' (39). Within the same chapters, on the other hand, in anti-epic mode, Jim includes many myth-busting details about the all-too-real difficulties of agricultural life: the immense stamina required to do chores after a day in the freezing fields, or the near starvation of the inexpert Shimerda family.

In his depiction of his pre-university days, Jim draws implicit analogies between the stories and/or myths of different cultures – not solely classical ones – in his construction of a richly hybrid world. Fairy tales, Bohemian forests, the Mormons' trek and the three Marys' antics are all on a mythical par. The comparison between the formerly heroic Mr Shimerda and an 'old portrait' of a Virginian gentleman positions the immigrant within a tradition of classically enthusiastic Founding Fathers (23), and his grave becomes a sacred, mythical spot. Even in the account of the black American pianist, Samson (or 'Blind') d'Arnault, the mythologising impulse is evident, in this case working both to reinscribe and to undermine the racism inherent in that representation. At first, d'Arnault is a non-heroic stock character imported from the Southern pastoral tradition, but Cather's ensuing description of his talent in action allies him, albeit only for three or four brief sentences, with the heroic artists (such as Thea Kronborg in *The Song of the Lark* (1915)) who punctuate her work.[28] Yet repeatedly Jim explodes his own myths in these first two books: the savage winter light is like 'truth itself' (167), while that season goes on to become 'stale and shabby', making people 'shrunken and pinched' (175). The accounts of Mr Shimerda's suicide or of Wick Cutter's attempted rape of Ántonia, moreover, involve a specificity in their psychological and physical detail that places them squarely in the non-archetypal, anti-mythical realm of the all-too 'real'. Jim's awareness of the simultaneously heroic and mock- or anti-heroic aspects of his experience in these chapters is epitomised by his account of his killing the rattlesnake. At first he believes the snake he kills to be 'like the ancient, eldest Evil' (45), and he now feels 'equal' to any rattler on the prairie. Subsequently, however, he realises that the encounter had been 'in reality . . . a mock adventure' (48).

Once Jim's immersion in the poetry of Virgil begins, once he perceives his life as having a literary context, he ceases to countenance the non-mythological (or 'mock') dimensions of his own and his fellow Nebraskans' environment and experience. From the moment Jim begins 'scanning the *Aeneid* aloud' (224), thereby fashioning himself as a fusion of a heroic auto-didact and an epic hero, the reader questions the mythologising processes at work but the narrator no longer does so.[29] In the first chapter of 'Lena Lingard', Jim charts in painstaking detail and with great sincerity the two 'awakenings' to which his classical education is fundamental: his 'mental awakening' (24) and his sexual one, namely his love affair with Lena. He does observe that his learning about antiquity serves primarily not to make him a scholar but to shape his perception of his own history: analogous to the 'white figures against blue backgrounds' that Gaston Cleric's classical instruction conjures, Jim realises that the 'places and people of [his] own infinitesimal past' now 'stood out strengthened and simplified' (254). But although he recognises the ways in which classicism is shaping his self and his interpretation of the world, he nonetheless succumbs fully to that process, and never again challenges it.

Critics have expressed both admiration for and scepticism about Cather's and Jim's deployment of Virgil in these first two chapters of 'Lena Lingard'. While Sutherland points out the skill with which Cather recreates the resonance and plangent mood of Virgilian verse in her own original English prose, several scholars agree that the version of the Roman poet that appears in these pages is a strategic fabrication.[30] For example, in his reverential account of his interactions with Virgil, Jim ceases to distinguish between the primary concerns of the *Aeneid* (the life story of a hero who founds a new civilisation) and those of both the *Georgics* (in their detailed celebration of the minutiae of agricultural life) and the unnamed but thematically present *Eclogues* (a series of staged pastoral reminiscences). Furthermore, the key quotation, '*Optima dies . . . prima fugit*' ('the best days . . . flee first'), takes on a nostalgic implication in Cather's text which is barely there in the original Georgic it quotes. Virgil writes these words while giving practical advice on how to breed horses and cattle, observing that this is best done during the animals' 'lusty youth', because 'life's fairest days are ever the first to flee for hapless mortals'.[31] To learn of the not-very-elevated context of these words' original source is an amusing surprise that to some extent subverts Jim's heroic and highbrow stance at this point in his narrative. On the other hand, however, the narrator's quotation is apposite, in that Virgil here is writing about desire, fertility and creativity, and these are the key themes at this moment in the novel. And it is Virgil, not Cather or Jim, moreover, who extends the observation to apply to all 'hapless mortals'.

It is certainly in these first two sections of 'Lena Lingard' that the effects of the classical allusiveness in this novel are at their most complex, multi-voiced and multivalent. Of Jim's synthesising of Cleric's gloss on the lines '*Primus ego in patriam*' with his own reading of the third Georgic, many critics argue that Cather is thereby staking out her claim as the first literary voice of Nebraska, asserting herself as the first to 'bring the Muse' to that region and to articulate its history in both epic and pastoral terms (256).[32] This is to some extent true, but it is also an oversimplification. Significantly, Jim pays great attention to Cleric here: he is not directly identifying his own self and ambitions with those of Virgil, but instead (at least ostensibly) equating Cleric and Virgil, wondering whether the New England coast is Cleric's own quasi-Virgilian *patria* (or 'homeland'). There are of course thematic connections between the homesickness of Cleric, the regional loyalty of Virgil, the longing for or attachment to a *patria* or homeland expressed both by Aeneas in the *Aeneid* and by other Virgilian characters, and Jim's own multiple homesicknesses.[33] These all resonate in Jim's repetition, as the chapter's closing words, of the phrase '*Optima dies . . . prima fugit*' (262). Yet the overall effect of the narrator's allusiveness in these two chapters is not that of a linear tradition or of a solo protagonist clearly re-voicing a single literary ancestor. Instead it is one of simultaneity and not-always-harmonised multiple voices. This polyphony (not unlike that of Pound's *Canto* I) is at its most intense when Cather has Jim recall Cleric repeating the poet Statius, who in the *Divine Comedy* articulates Dante's veneration for Virgil.[34] Here literature and 'reality', classical, Renaissance and contemporary voices are all imposed on each other and weave through each other in no orderly chronology or genealogy.

Several scholars have pointed out the unwarranted audacity in Jim's claim that there is an intimate relationship between 'girls like [Lena] and the poetry of Virgil' (262). Jim would appear to be deceiving himself here in at least two ways. First, the relationship between romantic passion and poetic inspiration is far stronger in poets like Dante or Shakespeare than in Virgil.[35] And second, Jim's final assessments of Ántonia suggest less that young women are a pre-condition of great literature, and more that great literature is the pre-condition of Jim's relentlessly mythologising conception of women, in particular of this childhood friend. While Lena has long been subjected to Jim's classicising impulses (witness his dream in which she is an alluring shepherdess figure), his closing observations about Ántonia are at once uplifting and disturbing.[36] His constructions of Ántonia as a compound of Demeter, the Great Mother Earth, and a fertility goddess are on the one hand inspiring in their promise of 'universal and true' meaning that transcends the passing of time (342). On the other hand, they are disturbing in their fixity and totalising aspects, for the way they objectify the woman and harness her to Jim's own needs. Although he is at least honest with Ántonia – 'you really are a part of me', he tells her (312) – there is something unsettling in his comparison of her to a woodcut or (in imagining her with her hand on a crab apple tree) to a pre-Raphaelite image such as Edward Burne-Jones's *Pomona* (c. 1900).[37] This is a woman who has been sexually used and abandoned by one man; nearly raped by another; neglected for a long time by her erstwhile friend, Jim; whose identity is magnificently but exclusively that of mother to countless children, and who noticeably never gets to tell her own story.

Readers have long been divided about Jim's classically informed presentation and preservation of Ántonia. Does Cather share Jim's misogynistic mythologising impulse, does she critique it or is she conflicted about it, oscillating between endorsement and subversion of his narrative framing? When Jim likens Ántonia to 'the founders of early races', implicitly comparing her both to Aeneas and to the

Spanish conquistadors whose history he rehearses to her on their long-remembered summer day out (235–6), are he and Cather hereby granting full American status to Ántonia, and hence to all Eastern European immigrants?[38] Or is Jim's simile absurd in its incongruity, a sentimentalist's attempt to use the classical tradition not only to gloss over the violence of colonialism but also to obscure Ántonia's real life: one of economic hardship and sexual subordination and ethnic discrimination with which he himself never had to contend?

Not even the novel's (fictional) introduction will help us in resolving that perpetual dilemma. Though it does give us information about Jim, it tells us nothing about his predilection for classicism and classicising. Strikingly, the writing in these introductory pages is itself entirely without classical allusions, either explicit or implied; the fictional author writes of memory and of a shared sense of an exceptional past, but not in terms of mythical analogy. This conspicuous absence only adds to the complicating effects of the classicism in the novel as a whole.

The Professor's House (1925)

Texts by Euripides, Plato, Lucretius, Ovid and Plutarch all resonate, together with the *Odyssey* and the *Aeneid*, in Cather's seventh novel. In its focus on the eponymous middle-aged professor Godfrey St Peter – on his distaste for the materialist concerns of his own wife and daughters, and for the commercialisation of the intellectual legacies of his now-dead star student, Tom Outland – this work asks questions about what is valuable, about change and about what endures, and about how to live a worthwhile life. Classical allusions operate on two levels simultaneously: the two protagonists, Godfrey and Tom, both explicitly make use of classical writers and texts, while the author's omniscient, third-person narrative is punctuated by classical analogies and echoes. As in *My Ántonia*, Cather is profoundly concerned with heroism – with what constitutes heroic endeavour and with the nature of the individuals whose actions may or may not make them exceptional. As disagreements within existing criticism on the novel demonstrate, there are conflicting ways in which to understand the life stories both of Godfrey and of Tom.[39] Is each a true hero, a flawed hero, or a mere self-deluded parody of a hero? The ambiguous effects of their identities' dependence on classicism are key to the novel's indeterminacy on this point.

The novel's structure ensures that readers first encounter Tom as an absent but mythologised hero: he is already dead at its opening, and his history is revealed first through Godfrey's memory and then through a quasi-transcript of his spoken words. Louie Marsellus's account to Sir Edgar constructs Tom's legendary status through giving equal weight to two of his heroic feats: meeting 'death and glory' as a casualty in World War I, and 'revolutionizing aviation' as 'a brilliant . . . scientist and inventor' (42). Already, Tom is by implication both a mythological fallen warrior and a composite of the ill-fated Daedalus and Icarus of Ovid's *Metamorphoses*. Godfrey contributes to this sense of his late protégé's exceptionalism when he rejects Rosamund's offer to share in Tom's financial legacy: as Tom represented the single 'remarkable mind' he has encountered in his career, he 'will not have' his friendship with him 'translated into the vulgar tongue' (63). In this atmosphere of near-hagiography and constant eulogising, it is no surprise that Scott confesses Tom is no longer 'real' to him, and wonders whether he was just 'a glittering idea' (110). Although Godfrey is provoked by this remark into a concerted effort to remember the 'real' young man, his memories only reinscribe the heroic conception of Tom.

Cather introduces her young protagonist, through the professor's recollections, as someone who demonstrates his determination to succeed through his aptitude for Latin literature. Tom is at once more disadvantaged, less formally educated and less conflicted about his studies than is *My Ántonia*'s Jim, but like Jim he can recite long Latin passages from memory. Cather's choice of the texts in which Tom is proficient reflects her personal expertise and passion, but it is also strategic: both of Tom's favoured texts, Caesar's *Gallic Wars* and the *Aeneid*, anticipate his own future as a soldier and casualty in war, and also reflect on his past. The fifty lines from the *Aeneid* which Tom quotes to Godfrey to establish his credentials are from the epic's second book, in which Aeneas relates at length to Dido the full horrors of the Trojan War and of his subsequent voyage to Carthage.[40] In the opening line that Cather quotes in Latin in the novel, Aeneas paradoxically talks of his 'grief' that is 'unspeakable' at having to recall his traumatic past.[41] Tom's quotation is apposite because it expresses his own reluctance to speak about his own traumatic history. Moreover, through going on to insert within the third-person narrative the complete first-person narrative of the quasi-novella 'Tom Outland's Story', Cather mirrors the narrative technique of the

Aeneid that is evident in this very passage Outland quotes. Virgil in turn took this method of long, embedded first-person accounts from the *Odyssey*, and this formal replication in *The Professor's House* works to consolidate Tom's status as a long-suffering and resilient epic hero.

Tom relates to Godfrey that when he began his work with Roddy, as a cattle minder in New Mexico, he brought his 'Caesar' along with him and dutifully translated 'a hundred lines a day' (186). But he claims that after their argument, when he is all alone on the Blue Mesa for several months, it is the memorising and recitation of Virgil that kept him sane. His assertion that he now perceives in his copy of the *Aeneid* an image of the cliff dwellings superimposed on the image of Virgil's Carthage ('a dark grotto' and 'crystal spring' (252)) constitutes one of Cather's several constructions of an equivalence between the ancient Anasazi settlers and ancient classical civilisations.[42] Cather has Tom draw frequent implicit analogies between these 'fine people' (212), this example of a group who has 'lifted itself out of brutality' (220), and the once-great, now-ruined cities of the Greek, Roman and Egyptian past. Tom observes that the 'city of stone' is 'as still as sculpture' (199), and Father Duchêne compares the pottery found there to that of Minoan Crete.[43]

Critics have interpreted this classical equivalence in two ways. Catherine Morley along with Sean Lake and Theresa Levy separately suggest that, through Roddy's selling of the archaeological finds, Cather extends the equivalence to protest the commercial and colonialist exploitation of both cultural legacies in equal measure.[44] Helen Dennis, on the other hand, implicates Tom (and Cather) in that same, Enlightenment-derived colonialist impulse to appropriate and 'master a savage space', and to derive personal fulfilment and wellbeing from that process (Dennis, 'Tonight' 44–5). Although Alison Donnell in turn argues that Tom's valorisation of this culture is politically problematic because it depends on its being both 'othered' or exoticised, and dead and gone (Donnell 55), I contend that here Cather suggests a somewhat different relationship between Tom's present and the past. In a rather overdetermined sentence, Tom tells us he had 'read of filial piety in the Latin poets', and that he knew that 'that was what he felt for [this] place' (250). However speculative or unrealistic, Tom feels not his difference from but his affinity or identification with this lost group.[45] His mention of 'filial piety' recalls Virgil's '*pius Aeneas*' ('pious' or 'dutiful' Aeneas, as he is repeatedly described in the *Aeneid*), the epic hero renowned both for his filial duty and for founding the city of Lavinium, which was the forerunner to Rome.[46] Through Tom's words, Cather attempts to use the *Aeneid* to construct Cliff City as a kind of epic text in itself. She thereby seeks to guarantee an epic tradition or genealogy for American culture – one not derived from but analogous to the classical trajectory – in which Tom is the current heroic protagonist.

Ryder's critical analysis extends the significance of the relationship between Tom and the *Aeneid* by describing Roddy Blake as the equivalent to Aeneas's loyal comrade, 'faithful Achates' (227). Yet while Roddy goes on to betray Tom through selling the archaeological finds in his absence, Tom goes on to feel life-defining guilt for his rage towards and dismissal of his erstwhile companion. Without making any explicit classical allusion, it is clear that Tom now thinks of himself not as Aeneas but as an anti-Aeneas: 'Anyone who requites faith and friendship as I did, will have to pay for it,' he tells Godfrey (252). Critics have paid insufficient attention to the way Cather plays on this kind of opposition – the way she exploits the powerful disjunction between a classical ideal and a flawed reality – at several key moments in this text. For example, she emphasises the ironic disparity between the classical style of the civic architecture in Washington DC and the corruption of its institutions. On his arrival in the city, the Capitol building's 'white dome against a flashing blue sky' inspires a 'religious feeling' in a not-yet-disillusioned Tom (223). But his encounter with the greed of Smithsonian officials and the all-consuming material ambitiousness of the couple with whom he lodges makes him perceive dissonance all around him: between the slavish bureaucrats who work at the Treasury, for example, and the 'white columns' of that building (232–3).[47]

It is interesting that after Tom's death, Godfrey quotes Mark Antony's comments on corruption in Shakespeare's *Julius Caesar* in order to express his own despair at the plutomania that the young man's lucrative invention has unleashed. In addition, the professor frequently formulates his distaste for the corrupt and corrupting materialism in his own classical terms: his perception of the way Kathleen has turned 'green with envy' of her sister (85), and of the way both Lillian and Rosamund have 'changed and hardened' with their wealth (159), resonates with Ovid's depiction of Envy's venomous effect on the jealous sister Aglauros, and with his tale of Midas's catastrophic touch.[48] Critics have for the most part taken Cather's stated heroic conception of the non-materialistic Godfrey, and Godfrey's heroic conception of himself, at face value.[49] Perhaps influenced by Carlyle's inclusion of the 'man of letters' among his own heroic elite (Carlyle 143), Cather describes the professor's scholarly endeavours in epic terms: her description of his intellectual 'defeats and triumphs' allies him with the Spanish conquistadors that are his life's work (*Professor's House* 30).[50] The author bestows upon this protagonist her own trademark signifiers of greatness: his strikingly shapely head is compared to a classical bronze sculpture; like Aeneas or Odysseus he is often overcome by nostalgia or homesickness for his past life and its landscapes; and he is associated with Napoleon through his first name (which is itself a tradition in his family).[51]

Yet, arguably, Cather also deploys classical allusions to critique Godfrey's ways of interacting with the world. She imbues her account of his eccentric attachment to the 'forms' (Augusta's dressmaking mannequins) that populate his study with distorted echoes of Ovid's tale of Pygmalion – the frigid and purity-obsessed sculptor who creates a statue that comes to life and with which he then falls in love.[52] Moreover, as Anne Baker has persuasively argued, to interpret these 'forms' as Plato's unattainable 'forms' or 'ideas' is to understand Godfrey's troubled journey in this novel as a whole as a necessary abandonment of an impossible Greek idealism. Baker's suggestion that this Greek philosophical perspective might not in fact be the best one for the professor to live by brings into question the effects of his Greek-inflected identity and outlook elsewhere in the text. It is conventional to interpret Cather's comparison between his swimming-hatted head and the helmeted Parthenon warriors as sincere. But bearing in mind that heads in swimming caps often look more ridiculous than heroic, it is possible to argue either that Cather is overambitious in this simile, or that she is critiquing Scott McGregor here (who is watching Godfrey swim, and to whose consciousness we are closest at this moment) for idolising his father-in-law.[53]

This in turn permits a scepticism about the two occasions when Godfrey explicitly casts his own predicament in a grandiose, Greek context: when he compares himself to Medea, and when he envies the reputedly misanthropic and misogynistic Euripides.[54] As with certain incongruous classical allusions in Philip Roth's 2000 novel *The Human Stain* (see Chapter 6), it is worth thinking cool-headedly about these invocations. Even if Godfrey conceives of himself as a tragic hero, Medea is hardly an apt reference. And in his identification with Euripides, again is Cather overreaching in her classical register, taking Virgil's technique of 'comparing small things with great' to a regrettable extreme, or is she satirising her professor for a hopeless academicism that is ultimately absurd in its effect?[55] Of Augusta's rescue of Godfrey in the novel's closing pages, Baker writes that in pulling him out of the attic, the seamstress is saving him 'from his infatuation with the world of ideas and abstractions', and is the 'midwife for his journey out of Platonism' (Baker 266). But if we allow the 'attic' to pun as 'Attic', in the sense of the ancient Greek region of 'Attica' (which encompassed Athens), we can understand both Augusta and Cather to be rescuing the professor not just from Plato, but from an ultimately life-denying infatuation with Greek antiquity as a whole.

At the end of one of his lectures, Godfrey embarks on a long discourse on art and religion in answer to a student's question. 'What makes men happy,' the professor declares, is their 'believing in the mystery and importance of their own little individual lives' (68). Through her explorations of the nature of the heroic in this novel – whether heroism is attainable, desirable, maintainable – Cather subjects the idea of the significance of small individual lives to close scrutiny. Her widespread and various deployments of classical tradition are key to the ultimate undecidedness of the text on this point. The ambiguity extends beyond Tom Outland, keenly aware of his own fall from greatness, and beyond Godfrey, who is persuaded away from an indulgent Greek-inspired conception of himself: it also defines apparently peripheral characters such as his son-in-law Louie Marsellus. Godfrey does his best to demonise the financially adept younger man, and Cather's depiction of him at times falls prey to anti-Semitic stereotyping. Yet Godfrey is repeatedly surprised by Louie's magnanimity and goodness. It is surely significant that Cather gives this character a surname ('Marsellus') that sounds identical to that of an ancient Roman family ('Marcellus') who were famous for their public service. In the *Aeneid*, 'being a Marcellus' embodies the military greatness and promise of an ideal elite Roman.[56] Given that the novel's end looks forward to 'the advent of a young Marsellus' (273), it would seem that Cather's thinking about heroism, and about 'ordinary' people's capacity for epic greatness, remains unresolved.

Sapphira and the Slave Girl (1940)

Critical studies of Cather's engagement with the classical tradition have to date paid scant attention to her final novel. Ryder, for example, devotes only four pages to *Sapphira and the Slave Girl*, arguing that 'Cather virtually ignores the possibility of presenting the novel's central conflict in mythic terms' (273).[57] It is of course true that, unlike many of the earlier works, *Sapphira* does not invoke classical authors by name, nor quote directly from their writings. Yet this novel – set primarily in 1856, in the pre-Civil War Virginia of Cather's ancestors – both reflects and critiques the central place of classical pastoral, epic and tragic traditions in the dominant ideology of the slaveholding South and in the discourse of Confederacy's 'Lost Cause'. As Janice Stout has persuasively argued, this novel is profoundly ambiguous and ambivalent about the Civil War and its defining moral conflicts. Cather eulogises the landscapes and the comforts of the privileged white lifestyle of antebellum Virginia, but in her focus on the threat of rape to which the slave girl, Nancy, is repeatedly subjected before she escapes, the author challenges the whole system of slavery on which Southern society depended. Classical tradition is key to the novel's conflictedness: it informs the depiction of Sapphira, the mistress, as a deeply flawed yet partly heroic character, and at the same time it imparts mythical resonance to Nancy's plight through implicitly associating her with Persephone. The explicit epic-making work effected by the epilogue, 'Nancy's Return', then, makes it not the ill-fitting addition that many contemporaneous reviewers perceived it to be, but rather the logical grand finale to a subtly but consistently classically allusive text.[58]

The highly significant revisions that Cather made to the epilogue are evidence of the motivated nature of her engagement, throughout the novel as a whole, with a heroic tradition inherited from antiquity. Scholars have rightly pointed out that in its sudden divergence from the narrative that precedes it – being set in 1881 and narrated in the semi-autobiographical first person by Cather remembering her childhood self – this closing section of the novel has a destabilising effect. But scholarship has made surprisingly little of the fact that the entire first section of this epilogue (a five-page sweeping view of the Civil War and of the changes that have come to pass in Winchester, Virginia, during the intervening twenty-five years) was not part of Cather's first draft. The surviving manuscript of the original version reveals that only one single paragraph, now excised, in which Cather explains that 'at this point I, myself, came into the story', preceded what is now Part II of the epilogue.[59] That Cather chose at a later date to add the simultaneously rose-tinted and highly conflicted details about how the local community survived the war, how the fighting supposedly created 'few enmities' despite the population's divided loyalties, of the Confederates' dignity in defeat, and of the liveliness of current society suggests the huge significance of these perspectives to her personally (*Sapphira* 270). Significantly, this late addition includes the classically allusive and highly lyrical digression about the community's reverence for the historical local war hero, Turner Ashby, whom 'the old-time Virginians admired, *Like Paris handsome and like Hector brave*' (269). In this unattributed quotation from Elizabeth Barrett Browning's poem 'The Battle of Marathon' (written during the Victorian poet's youth and first published in 1820), Cather once again glorifies a young man's death in terms of Homeric and Virgilian heroic tradition. Her casting of the Rebel army's dead in classical, epic terms is typical of Confederate memorialising processes across the postbellum South.[60]

In his 2001 study, *Race and Reunion*, historian David Blight illuminates the contrasting 'reconciliationist', 'white supremacist' and 'emancipationist' responses to the Civil War in the nation's cultural memory. He demonstrates how the romantic, reconciliationist perspective on the war, which privileged reunion between white Southerners and Northerners, came to eclipse the emancipationist struggle for racial equality.[61] As Stout persuasively argues, Part I of *Sapphira*'s epilogue 'serves the reconciliationist impulse' ('Daughter' 140); indeed, it epitomises the 'sentimental remembrance' that Blight describes (Blight 2). Yet (as Stout continues), in the novel as a whole this impulse co-exists with rather than trumps the anti-slavery perspective, and the epilogue's Part II, which focuses on Nancy's successful post-escape life and her triumphant visit to her former home, clearly champions emancipation. Through the epic ambitions of the first section of her epilogue, Cather positions herself among the many reconciliationist commemorators of the war, documented by Blight, who drew Homeric analogies and who created a 'direct line from Thermopylae to Gettysburg' (Blight 73). Yet in attributing heroic characteristics to many black characters as well as white, and in particular through associating Nancy with Persephone,

Cather simultaneously continues the subversive classicism of black American writers such as W. E. B. Du Bois and Pauline Hopkins, who deploy antiquity to resist the reconciliationist whitewash of the issue of race. Just as both pro-slavery and abolitionist arguments harnessed the classical world in defence of their stances before the Civil War, in its aftermath those of all ideological perspectives harnessed antiquity to their vastly differing ends.[62] *Sapphira and the Slave Girl* – in its ubiquitous but always-vexed pastoralism, in its narrowly averted tragedy, and in its unstable relationship with epic – is defined and animated by this paradox.[63]

Although critics commonly assert that *Sapphira and the Slave Girl* is notable for nature writing in which idyllic landscapes are expressive of an idealised authorial nostalgia, in fact it is difficult to find a passage describing nature in this novel in which there are not undertones of danger, unease or conflict. There is no innocent pastoral here. For example, there is something sinister in the vines and creepers bedecking the slave cabins, while even the most lyrical of the landscape writing, describing 'the rich flowering and blushing and blooming of a Virginia spring' in the opening of Book IV, is framed by the 'Double S' in the road, with all its ominous Satanic and serpent-in-paradise connotations (117). Cather's focus on the neoclassical nature of several of the significant buildings in this novel is similar in effect to these depictions of the natural world as a corrupted or deeply vulnerable idyll. That the Mill House, for example, 'was built on very much the same pattern as Mount Vernon' is a double-edged observation (23).[64] Through associating her protagonists with the much-mythologised George Washington, Cather imbues them with his archetypal heroism. At the same time, however, lurking within these words is the irony that this famous defender of liberty was also the owner of slaves, and that the beautifully neoclassical Mount Vernon was a slave plantation. The novelist plays further on the murky relationship between the antiquity-loving Founding Fathers and slavery through selecting the names of 'Washington' and 'Jefferson' for two of the Colberts' slaves.

Cather misses no opportunity to point out the classical aspirations of Southern houses: Nancy's mother, Till, wistfully muses on the wealthy Winchester dwellings that have 'porticos' and 'tall columns' (76), while in her epilogue Cather mentions no fewer than three times in seven pages that both her own family home and many neighbouring houses have 'porticos' (267, 272, 273). Comparisons between the first and published versions reveal that Cather made notable changes to these sentences mentioning Graeco-Roman architectural features, and this suggests their significance in her mind.[65] Just as the classically informed ideal of Southern hospitality is polluted by Sapphira's machinations with her nephew, there is no unambivalent or ideal way of life within these 'ambitious' neoclassical homes (267). In addition, through the fact that the name of the ill-fated poor white boy whom Rachel helps has been corrupted to 'Lawndis' from the name of the Spartan military hero 'Leonidas', the novelist suggests the corruption of the entire region (125). 'The hill people could do queer things with unfamiliar names,' Rachel reflects (125); Cather suggests that 'queer things' are ubiquitous in this idealistic but flawed society as a whole.[66]

It is perhaps in her depiction of Sapphira herself that the author maintains the most complete and unresolved dialectic between the anti-heroic or evil and the heroic. Sapphira is a deeply conflicted figure whose instincts include both ingrained racism, calculated, vicious cruelty and moments of unsettlingly humane kindness towards the black people she owns. Without for a moment condoning her behaviour – and while depicting Nancy's near-defenceless fear and trauma in minute detail – Cather nonetheless does not depict her white protagonist as a monster. When Sapphira mentally unravels during the night following Jezebel's funeral, she is revealed as a deeply flawed hero *manqué*, resembling a kind of admixture of Iago and Othello. As she descends into a panic attack after witnessing the clear emotional connection between Henry and Nancy, her thoughts become reminiscent of Clytemnestra's or Medea's: she believes she is trapped in a 'shattered, treacherous house' (108). It is perhaps the author's depiction of Sapphira's pitiable interior anguish that enables this character's rehabilitation as a heroic figure in the novel's closing pages, in spite of her former heinousness. While Till's loyalty to her mistress remains troubling to the end, her account of her mistress dying in courageous and elective solitude, 'upright in her chair' (287), nonetheless leaves a lasting impression of Sapphira's archetypal fortitude.

In her well-known critique of this novel in *Playing in the Dark* (1992), Toni Morrison writes that 'Nancy has to hide her interior life' (23), and that she is 'rendered voiceless, a cipher, a perfect victim' (24). It is arguable, however, that the opposite is in fact the case. Undoubtedly it is an ideologically unresolved or uncommitted text, and therefore a troubling one. Yet as one written by a white novelist in the 1930s, about the 1850s, it is remarkable (as Faulkner's work is) for the attention it does pay to the interiority and the heroic resilience of several of its black characters, and of Nancy most of all. We are privy to Jezebel's memory through the backstory of her capture in Africa and her astonishing rebellion and fortitude during the Middle Passage; we learn about Till's traumatic childhood experience of watching her own mother burn to death.[67] Importantly, Cather's narrative also includes the courageous Sampson, who in a moment of brief but heroically Frederick Douglass-like resistance defies his slave status by looking the predatory Martin Colbert in the eye, and then goes on to speak to Henry about Nancy's endangered state.[68] The portrayal of Nancy's own interior life is particularly noteworthy for its level of detail: Cather explores Nancy's dislike of having to sleep outside Sapphira's room during the winter months, not just because of the threat she faces, but because it is cold compared to her mother's beloved 'snug' and 'homelike' cabin (64). After Nancy narrowly escapes Martin Colbert's intended assault in the night-time corridor, Cather deploys free indirect discourse to convey the girl's relief and her cherished affection for 'the home folks and the home place and the precious feeling of belonging' (196). And during her escape, though she doesn't express her feelings to her companions, Cather tells us 'her mind was frozen with homesickness and dread' (233). So, although the slave girl strategically hides her inner life from white people, the novelist does not hide it from her readers – rather she ensures that Nancy possesses a subjecthood to equal and implicitly to contend with that of Sapphira. Moreover, Nancy is no mere 'cipher' or agency-less victim: she repeatedly takes steps to save herself, for example in her ploy of rushing into Sapphira's bedroom, or in twice turning to Rachel for help. If there is an unambiguous hero in this novel, Nancy is surely she.

In claiming that the depiction of Nancy and Till constitutes 'a wholly unanalysed mother-daughter relationship' (*Playing* 21), Morrison makes no mention of the frequent resonances of the Demeter-Persephone myth with which Cather imbues her story. Cather constructs an extended dialogue with this myth of the flower-picking girl who is forcibly taken by Hades, as it is rendered in the *Homeric Hymn to Demeter* and in Ovid's *Metamorphoses*.[69] Nancy loves to pick flowers for Henry Colbert, and when she persuades Rachel to accompany her on her fraught trip to the woods, the pair pick laurels (resonant also of Daphne's escape from Apollo) among plants that include the 'maidenhair fern' (*Sapphira* 171).[70] Furthermore, Nancy escapes 'when the wheat harvest was nearly over' (213); a profoundly mythological 'ferryman' takes her across the Potomac (231); and the book that describes the aftermath of her escape is titled 'The Dark Autumn' (241).

Morrison chides Cather for depicting Nancy as 'voiceless' and for allowing Till to utter only one question on the topic of Nancy's fate: 'You ain't heard nothin', Miss Rachel?' (Morrison, *Playing* 21–2; Cather, *Sapphira* 245). Yet as the later novelist herself demonstrates in *The Bluest Eye*, silence is often a powerful and subversive mode of feminist protest and resistance. Indeed, in *Sapphira and the Slave Girl* Cather employs a strategy that Morrison herself uses to powerful effect: that of making myth speak volumes on behalf of characters whose spoken words carry negligible weight.[71] Through expressing Till and Nancy's story in terms of Demeter and Persephone, Cather achieves several things at once. She imbues Nancy's situation with the intense emotional charge of an archetypal story of female suffering; she invests a widespread significance to these individual circumstances (without diminishing the specific experience of those individuals); and in deploying the classical tradition to express an African American perspective she implicitly asserts black equality with white. She insists, in other words, that the classical tradition is not the preserve of any one group in society. The structuring presence of Demeter and Persephone, therefore, is key to the political dialectic and the impasse in this text.

Cather's strategic classicism continues to operate in several directions and to conflicting ends throughout the epilogue. There is great significance in its title, 'Nancy's Return'. The first implied 'return' both invokes and supersedes the Demeter-Persephone myth: it is spring time and Nancy has returned like Persephone, yet at the same time she has escaped a mythical fate, for when her visit to Back Creek is over she will go back not to Hades but to her free and emotionally fulfilled life in the North. But the most important dimension of the word 'return' in this title is its association with the Greek concept of *nostos*, itself meaning 'homecoming' or 'return'. As we have seen, the *Odyssey*'s unifying plot structure and emotional impulse (often expressed as nostalgia or homesickness) is a recurring theme in Cather's oeuvre. While this title therefore associates Nancy's escape, independent life and visit to her former home with the heroic wanderings of both Odysseus and Aeneas, it also speaks to a range of other 'homecomings'. For example, Part I of the epilogue imparts a Homeric resonance to the return of those who fought in the Civil War; Till relates the reunion or the return of good relations between Sapphira and Rachel (286); and she recounts Sapphira's death (somewhat problematically?) as a return to her former position among the 'fine folks' (287).

Last but not least, Cather enacts a personal homecoming in this epilogue, returning to the specific location and particular circumstances of her early childhood for her final novel, and positioning herself as the narrator of this closing section. Fittingly, she invokes her grandmother's readings from *Parley's Universal History* here: her childhood self notes how the word 'history' in its title, spoken in a Southern accent, sounds different from the Northern-inflected 'his-to-ry' that Nancy relates (277). This apparently minor detail reminds us of a hugely significant fact: that Cather's immersion in classics from her earliest childhood onwards is fundamental to the fragmented, conflicted, allusive and provocative versions of history that constitute not just *Sapphira and the Slave Girl*, but the entirety of this novelist's oeuvre.

Notes

1. For a useful chronology of Cather's life and publications see Lindemann xiv, 222–3.
2. Cather's non-fiction has been published in collections such as Curtin, *The World and the Parish* (1970); Cather, *On Writing* (1949); Slote, *The Kingdom of Art* (1966); and Bohlke, *Willa Cather in Person* (1986). The *Selected Letters* are edited by Jewell and Stout (2013). For her digitised correspondence (in progress) see the Willa Cather Archive: <https://cather.unl.edu/writings/letters> (last accessed 15 May 2020).
3. For discussion of Cather's classicism by her biographers see: Bennett 1–137; E. K. Brown 3–73; Lee 37–62; O'Brien 11–248; P. Robinson 35–75; Stout, *Writer* 12–45; and the memoir by Lewis 14–60. My account here is indebted to all of these works.
4. See O'Brien 26; E. K. Brown 19–20. Cather may have been an admirer of Addison's 1713 play, *Cato*; Winterer documents the popularity of this play in the USA from the late eighteenth century onwards (see Winterer, *Culture* 25).
5. Peter Parley is the pseudonym of Samuel Griswold Goodrich, who published numerous editions of this compendium from 1837 onwards.

6. See E. K. Brown 34–5; P. Robinson 63–4.
7. See E. Lewis 30; also Cather's letter of 31 May 1889 on her success and her love of 'Caesar' (Jewell and Stout 8).
8. For photographs of Cather as Electra see O'Brien 208; Ryder np. For Cather's own review of the whole performance see Curtin 74.
9. See Sutherland 157; E. K. Brown 53–5.
10. The first stint, in 1901 at Central High School, included teaching Latin; she found this stressful and challenging (Sutherland 156).
11. See Slote 36; Carlyle, 'Contents' (np).
12. See O'Brien 82 on American textbooks' construction of classical heroes as anticipating venerated heroes and/or embodiments of the American dream.
13. On Cather's dialogue with Keats see Bohlke 137; Ryder 29, 91, 125, 225; Thurin 115. On her interest in funerary sculpture in Paris see O'Brien 208.
14. For the contemporaneous reviews see O'Connor.
15. Scholarship on the three novels read closely in the following three sections is discussed in those sections. Further useful articles are by Arnold; Hughes; Swift.
16. There is also great scope for further discussion of the significance of Ovid's *Heroides*, perhaps functioning as a displaced version of Mrs Forrester's perspective, in *A Lost Lady*.
17. See Michaels 36–7; Morley, *Modern* 115.
18. Compare Lutz on Cather's 'basic technique of oscillation' (445); and Reynolds on Cather's 'ideological complexity' and tendency to shift between polarities (vi).
19. See Dennis iii–v; Morley, *Modern* 105, 113; also Morley, 'Willa' 118–20.
20. See Morley, *Modern* v–vi, 105.
21. Pound translated and published Fenellosa's essay 'The Chinese Written Character as a Medium for Poetry' in 1918; see Pound and Fenellosa, esp. 102–4 and 107.
22. Compare Freud in his later (1930) work, *Civilization and its Discontents* 7–10; see also my introduction here.
23. *Georgics* III.66–7, translated in the Loeb edition as 'the fairest days are ever the first to flee'. All page references to *My Ántonia* here are to the University of Nebraska Scholarly Edition (1994). Its text is the 1918 version, not the 1926 version (which has an abbreviated introduction). For a photograph of the original title page including the Latin epigraph see O'Connor 78. The Virago 1994 edition exemplifies the epigraph's more recent placement.
24. On the biographical/fictional overlaps see Woodress 369–402.
25. See E. Lewis 30.
26. See *Odyssey* I.178.

27. See *Georgics* I.125ff, for example. See also Ovid, *Met.* I.89ff. Compare also *My Ántonia* 132ff.
28. On Cather's problematic presentation of d'Arnault see Donnell; also Roynon, *Morrison* 80.
29. Jim hereby anticipates Tom in *The Professor's House.*
30. On Cather's subjective and/or creative interpretations of Virgil see Dahl 49; Sutherland 165–9; Swift 110.
31. See *Georgics* III.65–7. Jim has abbreviated the longer Latin lines to imbue them with a more nostalgic meaning.
32. See *Georgics* III.10–11: 'I first, if life but remain, will return to my country, bringing the Muses with me . . .'
33. For example, Tityrus and Meliboeus in the first Eclogue (also discussed in Chapter 5 here) anticipate being homesick for their beloved *patria* on the eve of their dispossession. Cather's Jim is homesick for the farm days when in Black Hawk, for Black Hawk days when in Lincoln, and for his Lincoln days when in New York.
34. For example on 253. Statius appears in Cantos 20 and 21 of Dante's *Purgatorio.*
35. See Sutherland 174.
36. As Stephen Harrison observed to me (discussion, 27 June 2019), 'lena' is the Latin word for 'procuress'. This is a stock-figure in love-elegy (for example by Tibullus, Ovid or Propertius).
37. For an image of Burne-Jones's Pomona tapestry see <http://collections.vam.ac.uk/item/O18150/pomona-tapestry-panel-burne-jones-edward/> (last accessed 4 May 2020). Cather visited Burne-Jones's studio in London in 1902 (see Curtin 913–16), though in a letter of 1934 she expressed ambivalence about that experience and that artist (see Jewell and Stout 501). Ovid's tale of the moneylender, Vertumnus, who rapes Pomona, resonates in Wick Cutter's attempted rape of Ántonia.
38. This reading refutes Walter Benn Michaels's interpretation of Cather as a nativist (see 1.2 here), for whom the conferral of classical genealogy is both the determinant of American identity and is restricted to 'native' Americans.
39. On the Greek and Roman authors engaged in this novel see A. Baker; Dennis; Hall, 'Migrant'; Hughes; Lake and Levy; Morley, *Modern*; Morley, 'Willa'. My own discussion here is the first to explore the intertextual relationship with Ovid.
40. See *Professor's House* 112.
41. The line Tom quotes is *Aeneid* II.3, which is translated in the Loeb edition as 'Too deep for words, O Queen, is the grief you bid me to renew'. Compare Cather's 1922 novel *One of Ours*, in which the doomed ship carrying the American troops to fight in World War I is named, for Aeneas's father, the *Anchises* (265). See Vandiver for

discussion of classical allusions in English First World War poetry – an interesting comparison.

42. Compare *Aeneid* I.166–8.
43. Ryder suggests Tom's experience is equivalent to that which Keats describes in 'On First Looking into Chapman's Homer' (225); see Ryder 223–5 on parallels between Cretan and Anasazi settlements. Hall interestingly argues that 'Outland is associated with the pre-classical, Minoan-Mycenean world' ('Migrant' 155), that is with a civilisation prior to the Athenian world which Godfrey invokes through Euripides.
44. See also Lake and Levy 18 and Morley, *Modern* 19 on Cather's implied equivalence with the looting of the Elgin Marbles; see Lake and Levy 19 on Napoleon's plundering of Egyptian artefacts.
45. Note that Tom doesn't correct Father Duchêne when he refers to 'your tribe' (218) and 'your people' (220), and he tells Roddy, 'You've gone and sold your country's secrets' (242).
46. For one of numerous examples see *Aeneid* I.220.
47. See also 235.
48. For Envy's attack on the jealous sister see *Met.* II.736–832; for Midas see *Met.* XI.92–145.
49. See for example Hall, 'Migrant' or Morley, *Modern.*
50. See Carlyle's Lecture V: 'The Hero as Man of Letters: Johnson, Rousseau, Burns' (143–80).
51. '. . . he had been christened Napoleon Godfrey St Peter. There had always been a Napoleon in the family' (161). Godfrey's comparison of himself to 'Monsieur Bergeret' (20) alludes to Anatole France's 1897 novel, *Le Mannequin d'osier* (*The Wicker Work Woman*), in which Bergeret is a classics professor who discusses the nature of heroism with his student (see editorial note in *Professor's House*, 302).
52. See *Met.* X.243–98.
53. In a strikingly non-heroic detail, his family buy him more 'brilliant rubber casquettes' while on their holiday in France (269).
54. See *Professor's House* 124, 154.
55. In *Georgics* IV.176, during his well-known extended meditation on the social organisation of bees, Virgil asks 'if we may compare small things with great'. The comparison between two things that contrast in terms of size or scale (so, in *The Professor's House*, Godfrey and Euripides) is both a feature and a theme in epic poetry.
56. See *Aeneid* VI.883, where Aeneas's father Anchises prophetically laments the early death of his distant descendant Marcellus, heir to Augustus. Interestingly, of her 1902 trip to Arles, Cather comments on statues in the amphitheatre that include a 'head' of 'the little Marcellus, erected before his death, when he was still the hope and pride of the empire' (Curtin 950–1). See also Thurin 280–1, n. 19.

57. Thurin's discussion is likewise one of his shortest, spanning only 344–52.
58. For an (anonymous) contemporaneous review that is critical of the epilogue see O'Connor 520. On Demeter and Persephone in this novel see Wolff; on allusions to this myth throughout Cather's work see Ryder; also Donovan.
59. This manuscript (housed at Drew University) is listed as 'Cather 10' in my Works Cited. On the textual history of the novel see Mignon et al.'s 'Textual Essay' in Cather, *Sapphira* 554ff; for a photograph of the first page of this version of the epilogue see illustration 52 in this same scholarly edition of the novel.
60. 'The Battle of Marathon' was written in 1820 when Elizabeth Barrett Browning was still Elizabeth Barrett and only fourteen years old. On Confederate memorialising practices see also discussions of Faulkner and Morrison in this book.
61. See Blight 1–5.
62. On the engagement with antiquity by both abolitionists and defenders of slavery see Hall et al.; also Malamud, *African Americans*.
63. Cather deploys classicism in exploring the perspectives of both sides of the war, for example in commemorating her Confederate uncle in her poem, published in 1903, called 'The Namesake' (*April* 83–4), and in focusing on a Unionist soldier in her 1907 story of the same title (see also p. 21).
64. For a discussion of the architecture of Mount Vernon, with its 'Tuscan columns', see *Sapphira* 425; for a photograph of the historical Mill House see illustration 6 in this Nebraska edition of the text (np).
65. See the 'Cather 10' manuscript, 1–2.
66. Compare my discussion of names in Faulkner's 'The Bear' (p. 105).
67. See *Sapphira* 95, 72.
68. See *Sapphira* 180, 189–90. In his 1845 *Narrative* Frederick Douglass famously initiates his life of resistance by fighting back against the abusive white farmer Covey.
69. See Wolff 222–3.
70. See Ovid, *Met.* V.391ff (for Proserpina/Persephone) and *Met.* I.452ff (for Daphne). Compare also Milton's brief allusion to both these myths in *Paradise Lost* IV.268–75.
71. Morrison herself also uses the Proserpina/Persephone myth in her representations of characters who are raped, for example in *The Bluest Eye* (1970) and in *Love* (2003).

Further Reading

Arnold, Marylin. 'The Allusive Cather'. *Cather Studies* 3 (1996): 137–48.
Hokom, Matthew. 'Pompeii and the House of the Tragic Poet in *A Lost Lady*'. *Cather Studies* 10 (2015): 349–73.

Knoll, Robert E. 'A Golden Era: 1891–1900'. *Prairie University: A History of the University of Nebraska*. Lincoln: University of Nebraska Press, 1995. 28–40.

Sutherland, Donald. 'Willa Cather: The Classic Voice'. *The Art of Willa Cather*. Ed. Bernice Slote and Virginia Faulkner. Lincoln: University of Nebraska Press, 1974. 156–79.

Wolff, Cynthia Griffin. 'Time and Memory in *Sapphira and the Slave Girl*: Sex, Abuse, and Art'. *Cather Studies* 3 (1996): 213–31.

CHAPTER 2

F. Scott Fitzgerald (1896–1940)

Fitzgerald and the Classics

In June 1916, when he was nineteen years old, F. Scott Fitzgerald published a parody of Keats's 'Ode on a Grecian Urn' in Princeton University's *Nassau Literary Magazine.* Entitled 'To My Unused Greek Book', this witty poem epitomises the young Fitzgerald's paradoxical relationship with the classical tradition – indeed, with intellectual culture as a whole. Ostensibly, the piece is a self-mocking admission of his failure to learn Greek: due to its 'uncut' and unannotated pages, the Greek book itself replaces Keats's urn, as a 'still unravished bride of quietness'. Yet at the same time the poem's references to 'dactyls' and 'caesura', its strikingly apposite language and its profound understanding of Keats testify to Fitzgerald's incipient expertise as both a reader and a writer of literature (*Spires* 123).[1]

Compared with the overt enthusiasm for all aspects of classical antiquity expressed by Willa Cather, in his extensive autobiographical record – including his letters, essays, *Note-books* and *Ledger* – Fitzgerald (at least until the 1930s) fashions himself as indifferent to and sometimes even hostile towards classical languages, literatures and culture. He is notoriously rude about the city of Rome both during and after his two visits there (in 1921 and 1924).[2] Yet this author's oeuvre (both non-fiction and fiction) bears witness to his traditional and privileged education at St Paul Academy (in St Paul, Minnesota), at the elite Newman School in Hackensack, New Jersey, and at Princeton University, between the years of 1911 and 1917. Fitzgerald was not a 'good student', but his writing was indubitably influenced by his five years of formal Latin studies (as well as those in ancient history, philosophy, and English and French literature), and by a voracious reading habit which became increasingly highbrow after he left Princeton. Unlike Cather, Fitzgerald seldom invokes classical authors by name; unlike T. S. Eliot, he does not splice his English with quotations in Latin and Greek. An insistence on the significance of antiquity to this writer known as a chronicler of his own 'Jazz Age' may appear counter-intuitive or contrary to the conventional wisdom. Yet subtle and often-complex classical allusions in fact play a key role in his four published novels, in many of his numerous short stories, and in a range of his posthumously published texts.[3]

The three novels selected for close analysis in this chapter – *This Side of Paradise* (1920), *The Great Gatsby* (1925) and *Tender Is the Night* (1934) – all enact significant dialogue with the genres of epic and of pastoral in the versions of American experience in the 1910s and 1920s that they explore. While sometimes sincere, the frequently ironic engagement with these classical modes often merges into the satire that informs both the light-hearted irreverence of the first novel, and the darker vision of the later two. In being centred on the unambiguous downfalls of the potentially heroic but flawed Jay Gatsby and Dick Diver respectively, *Gatsby* and *Tender Is the Night* are also structured on a conventional Aristotelian tragic arc. But by far the most striking aspect of Fitzgerald's classical allusiveness – not just in these three texts but across his oeuvre – is his lifelong preoccupation with ancient Rome and Romanness.

As I discuss in the section below, numerous scholars have explored the relationship between the *Satyricon* and *The Great Gatsby*, and several have considered the importance of Rome as a setting in *Tender Is the Night*. Yet critics to date have paid insufficient attention to the many and conflicting meanings of every aspect of Roman culture – its literature, mythology, history, politics and lifestyles – in Fitzgerald's depictions of America and Americans during the Gilded Age, the First World War and the mercurial 1920s. In his perception of ancient Rome's analogousness, the author is of course very much in line with his times: in the United States in the later decades of the nineteenth century and the first few decades of the twentieth century, different aspects of Romanness were invoked to bolster conceptions of virtue, republicanism, heroism, war, imperialism, capitalist wealth and consumerist luxury; decadence; decline; and ruin.[4] Roman antiquity informed the highly contested politics of gender, race and class, as well as nostalgia for a lost Golden Age. Fitzgerald's writing is both indelibly shaped by, and indelibly shapes, these multifaceted, often-contradictory but always-significant American constructions of Rome.

While scholars disagree on the extent to which Fitzgerald was or was not 'intellectual', the numerous critics and biographers who have documented his formal schooling and extra-curricular reading testify to his broad familiarity with the literature, history and languages (Greek excepted) of 'Western civilisation'.[5] Matthew Bruccoli notes Fitzgerald's recollection of his twelve-year-old self writing stories in the back of textbooks that included his 'first year Latin' (*Epic* 28). Presumably this is the 'Collar and Daniell's First Year Latin' mentioned in *This Side of Paradise* (16) – a textbook (first published in 1901) notable for its numerous striking photographs and evocative ink drawings of Roman sites and life. Fitzgerald's transcript from his next educational establishment, the Newman School, records that his Latin studies there included grammar, composition, Caesar, Cicero and Virgil; his marks in all these ranged from the poor to the mediocre, and his only A grade was in ancient history.[6] At Princeton Fitzgerald's Latin studies (according to his transcript) included 'the historical literature of Rome: Livy, Sallust, Cicero', followed by Roman comedy (Plautus and Terence), and then Horace and Catullus (Bruccoli, *Epic* 45, 54–7). Alongside courses in the history of philosophy and in ancient art, he also studied French seventeenth-century literature, English Renaissance literature and English Romantic poetry. It's noteworthy that nearly all the prescribed French and English writers – such as Racine, or Marlowe, or Keats – were themselves immersed in antiquity.

Although during his years at Princeton Fitzgerald was certainly no scholar – reading tastes included middlebrow contemporaneous novelists such as Compton Mackenzie and Booth Tarkington – he had several scholarly friends at this time. These included the erudite priest Monsignor Fay, the Catholic novelist Shane Leslie and, among his fellow students, the future renowned literary critic Edmund Wilson, and the studious poet John Peale Bishop. Each of these friends played a key role in the direction of Fitzgerald's reading, which was to include (alongside prescribed Renaissance and Romantic authors) Victorians and Decadents ranging from Samuel Butler and William Makepeace Thackeray to Oscar Wilde and Algernon Swinburne; contemporaneous poets such as Rupert Brooke; masters of the 'modernising' novel such as Henry James, Joseph Conrad, Marcel Proust and Anatole

France; classically informed realists such as Theodore Dreiser; and modernists such as Joyce, Eliot and Cather.[7] While the undergraduate Fitzgerald probably aspired more to social, athletic and creative (especially theatrical) stardom than to scholarly heights, it's important to note as well that the non-intellectual culture at Princeton (as in the elite English private schools and universities at this time) was itself, paradoxically enough, informed by the classical tradition. The prevailing cultivation of heroes and heroism in both sport and war was derived from the perceived ideals of antiquity.[8]

While in a 1922 interview Fitzgerald claims to be 'still shy on the classics' – 'I have never read the *Iliad*, the *Odyssey*, the *Divine Comedy*, the *Cid* or *Faust*' (Bruccoli and Baughman 37) – in a letter of May 1924 he vows to read 'nothing but Homer and Homeric literature' while living in France (Bruccoli, *Letters* 69). Perhaps these good intentions were inspired by his somewhat daunting father-in-law, Judge Sayre, who read Homer and Hesiod (alongside Sallust and Juvenal) 'in the original, for pleasure' (Bruccoli, *Epic* 92). In the 1930s, meanwhile, the letters Fitzgerald wrote to his daughter reveal his concern that she should adopt scholarly seriousness at school and university alongside his regret at not being a more diligent student (including, specifically, of Latin) during his own undergraduate days.[9] And in the last years of his life, when Fitzgerald directed his new partner Sheila Graham in a semi-formal reading programme, it is perhaps unsurprising that his purchases for her included Edward Gibbon's *History of the Decline and Fall of the Roman Empire* (published 1776–89).[10]

This author's interest in Henry Adams's *The Education of Henry Adams* (1918) and Oswald Spengler's *The Decline of the West* (first published in English in 1926) further testifies to his penchant for 'the "decline" school of historical thought' (D. Brown 6). In their drawing of frequent analogies between Rome and the modern West (and specifically modern America, in Adams's case), these influential authors took their place alongside critiques ranging from Guglielmo Ferrero's *Ancient Rome and Modern America* (published in English in 1914) to Lothrop Stoddard's *Rising Tide of Color* (1920) and the ironic cultural commentaries of H. L. Mencken. All of these variously warned about the corruptions of contemporary America by invoking the fate of Rome.[11] It is important to note, however, that this 'decline school' co-existed with a euphoric, ubiquitous Romanness that celebrated America's analogous imperialism, evident as much in the neo-Roman architecture of New York's Pennsylvania and Grand Central Stations (completed in 1910 and 1913) as in the decadent social habits of New York City's Gilded and Jazz Age plutocrats.[12]

From the classical allusions that pepper his undergraduate juvenilia to the sense of classical downfall and ruin that informs his 1930s writings, then, Fitzgerald's fiction is informed by the powerful classical presences in the material culture and competing ideologies of the worlds he inhabited, as well as those in his extensive reading.[13] He once claimed that he and Zelda decided to move to Rome for the autumn and winter of 1924 because Zelda had been reading *Roderick Hudson* (the 1875 novel by Henry James in which that city is key (Bruccoli, *Epic* 211)). Although this is not wholly convincing, it is indicative of the complexity of the relationship between the imaginary Europe(s) of literature and the geographical Europe in which Fitzgerald (often unhappily) lived and travelled for a significant part of his life. In his letters and journalism, the author's writing about France and Italy in particular is both deeply conflicted and blackly comic. In his 1921 article 'Three Cities', for example, he says of his fortnight spent in Rome that he could 'see the fascination of the place' but that he 'could have left in two days' (*Last Kiss* 392). In 'The High Cost of Macaroni' he reflects with a deceptively light touch on the troubled months he and Zelda spent there in 1924–5: he notes among the many details about hotels and socialising that the couple 'plodded through the ruins', and dismisses Italy's history as 'one long epic of ravage and destruction' (*Last Kiss* 349, 348).[14]

Despite days spent in the Riviera (in particular during 1922 and 1926) being among the happiest of his life, Fitzgerald (unlike Cather) is frequently disappointed and disgusted by Europe. For him the ruins of antiquity do not constitute a continuing ideal, but rather prophesy America's imminent doom. In a letter to Edmund Wilson of July 1921 (to which I will return in my discussion of *Gatsby*), he explodes thus from London:

> God damn the continent of Europe. It is of merely antiquarian interest. Rome is only a few years behind Tyre + Babylon. . . . My reactions were all philistine, anti-socialistic, provincial + racially snobbish. You may have spoken in jest about N.Y. as the capitol [*sic*] of culture but in 25 years it will be just as London is now. . . . We'll be the Romans in the next generation as the English are now. (Bruccoli, *Letters* 46–7)

These angry, anguished and paradoxical lines resonate in their complexity throughout his work. While geographical, historical Rome is for Fitzgerald an irredeemably fallen and impure dystopia, he nonetheless urges on the time when New York will be a new Rome, and when New Yorkers will become the new Romans in their rich cultural productiveness.

The Critical Field and Scholarly Debate

There is to date no full-length study of Fitzgerald's engagement with the classical tradition. While this absence is to some extent surprising, it perhaps testifies to the comparatively unobtrusive or indirect nature of Fitzgerald's allusiveness. There is also an unsurprising imbalance in the texts and subjects chosen for critical study: for example, there is now a whole cluster of illuminating essays (dating from 1950 to 2011) on the relationship between Petronius's *Satyricon* and *The Great Gatsby*, but not a single one specifically on antiquity in *This Side of Paradise*, even though in that novel Fitzgerald namechecks Aeschylus, Heraclitus, Plato, Suetonius and Petronius alongside a veritable crowd of more recent classically allusive authors.[15]

Considered separately and together, the articles on *Gatsby* and the *Satyricon* are invaluable for the range of different perspectives and approaches they constitute. The expertise of their authors is diverse: some are classicists (Briggs, MacKendrick, Sklenar, Slater), some scholars of modern literature whose interests include classical reception (Endres, Kumamoto) and others pre-eminent Fitzgerald specialists (Bruccoli, West). Reflecting this, these discussions cumulatively bring to the table invaluable information about Petronius, the Latin text and the Roman contexts of Petronius's own time; insightful readings of Fitzgerald's (often ambivalent) dialogue with this author; analysis of the translated work's status in the 1920s; and close textual comparison of the 1924 *Trimalchio in West Egg* (the draft of what was to become *The Great Gatsby*) with the published 1925 novel.[16] Christa Daugherty and James West have also discussed the two sentences invoking Petronius in Fitzgerald's 1931 story 'Babylon Revisited', analysing their excision (by the magazine's editors) before its appearance in the *Saturday Evening Post*.[17] While David Cowart's earlier essay on 'Babylon Revisited' examines this story's 'affinity with tragedy', most scholarship on Fitzgerald's deployment of tragic and heroic conventions focuses on *Tender Is the Night*.[18]

In a 1985 article, 'Fitzgerald's Daisy', Glenn Settle reads Daisy Buchanan (in particular her voice) in terms of the literary genealogy of the sirens of classical mythology. Settle rightly cites 'Plato . . . Aristotle, Ovid, Dante, Shakespeare, and Sir Thomas Browne', and Homer and Apollonius alongside Keats and T. S. Eliot, as prior texts in which sirens are a significant presence (115). Some might find Settle's approach problematic, however, in that he makes no attempt to consider which of these texts Fitzgerald himself actually knew or read. Adopting the opposite approach, the extensive scholarship on Fitzgerald's intellectual formation and on the relationship between his reading and his general literary allusiveness serves usefully as one entry point into the subject of this author and classicism. In particular, Kuehl's extensive study, 'Scott Fitzgerald's Reading', is invaluable, and includes an account of the books Fitzgerald actually owned and annotated. Both Dorothy Good and John Kuehl separately begin their analyses by refuting the views of Edmund Wilson, Malcolm Cowley, Arthur Mizener et al. about Fitzgerald's 'lack of intellectual ability' (Kuehl 58) and poor education (Good 36). These polarised opinions about the author's intellect (or lack thereof) may have arisen from the paradoxical fact that Fitzgerald, who always read widely and always dreamed of being a writer, was nonetheless as wary of overt scholarliness as he was attracted to the glamours of social, athletic, military, financial and literary success. It is perhaps this author's ambivalence about 'academic-ness' that has led many critics to overlook or underestimate the significance of classical allusions in his consistently intertextual work.

In addition to his 1984 article on the literary source texts of *Gatsby*, in 1978 Richard Roulston published an important essay on the significance of Rome in *Tender Is the Night*.[19] There he focuses as much on the context of Roman Catholicism as on Roman antiquity in Fitzgerald's deployment of the Italian capital both as the site of Dick's nadir and as the epitome of 'the pathology of Western civilization' (85). His fruitful analysis of Fitzgerald's transformations of his own personal experiences in that city is an approach continued by Caterina Ricciardi in her extensive article, 'F. Scott Fitzgerald and Rome' (1999). Ricciardi lays autobiographical details about Fitzgerald alongside his non-fictional accounts of his experiences there; his readings and rewritings of

Henry James; and the city's significance as the place in which the author revised *The Great Gatsby*. She also notes the deployment of Rome as both the past and future destination in *The Beautiful and Damned* (1922), as a significant referent in *This Side of Paradise*, and, of course, as a critical locus in *Tender Is the Night*.[20] Both Roulston and Ricciardi implicitly pave the way for (but do not themselves make) a crucial shift in scholarly focus from analysis of 'Rome' to analysis of 'Romanness'. A book on Romanness in Fitzgerald is long overdue. This could and perhaps should be a full-length study of this author's engagement not just with Romanness in Italy but with Romanness in the Europe and the USA of the 1890s to the 1930s: decades seen by many as characterised by reckless decadence, inevitable decline and spectacular collapse.

This Side of Paradise (1920)

In this autobiographical first novel Fitzgerald imbues the young male protagonist's first night out in New York with intricately wrought significance. In his junior year at the (fictional) St Regis' School, Amory Blaine and his friend attend a performance of the musical *The Little Millionaire* (35). Both the plot of this work and the two schoolboys' passion for a member of its cast are among this text's numerous nods to Oscar Wilde's classically allusive novel, *The Picture of Dorian Gray* (1890–1).[21] Creating a narrative of artistic apprenticeship (a *Kunstlerroman*) that is mainly satirical but occasionally sincere, Fitzgerald sets up the Wildean theme of the relationship between the hedonism of modern wealth and imperial Roman decadence through Amory's observation on the way to the theatre, that 'romance gleamed from the chariot-race sign on Broadway' (35). As West explains in his editorial notes, this 'chariot-race sign' was a huge and extravagantly electrified advertising hoarding inspired by Lew Wallace's bestselling novel of 1880, *Ben-Hur: A Tale of the Christ* (*This Side* 225).[22] In referencing this landmark Fitzgerald exploits the contradictory meanings and uses of ancient Rome in America at this time; while Wallace's novel is a pro-Christian critique of Roman imperialism, its iconic imagery here connotes the apogee of capitalist consumerism. The reference is an easily missed detail that epitomises the complex, ubiquitous presence of Roman antiquity throughout *This Side of Paradise*. Fitzgerald constructs an interplay between the classical and/or classically allusive literature to which Amory constantly refers and the broader relationship between the Progressive-era America and Roman antiquity. These interactions are central to the text's key themes: the usefulness or otherwise of the protagonist's education; the nature of heroism; the male quest for viable identity and for romantic and sexual fulfilment; and the cataclysmic nature of the transition from the 'Victorian' to the modern era, both in ethical and in aesthetic terms.[23]

The author follows the *Little Millionaire* section with one entitled 'HEROIC IN GENERAL TONE' (37). Here Amory's new-found prowess as a football player makes him 'the eternal hero, one with the sea-rover on the prow of a Norse galley, one with Roland and Horatius, Sir Nigel and Ted Coy' (37). This list of heroes from a range of cultural realms typifies Fitzgerald's oeuvre-wide predilection for incongruous allusive combinations. In this, and in thereby deploying the classical tradition to irreverent, ironic and comic effect, he has much in common with both Eliot and Joyce. It is interesting, furthermore, that the story of Horatius defending the bridge against the Etruscans is one of the few prose pieces (complete with illustration) in *Collar and Daniell's First Year Latin*, the textbook in which the young schoolboy Amory drafts his reply to his first love interest, Myra, and which was in all likelihood also Fitzgerald's own.[24] The inscribed textbook symbolises an unlikely conflation of Latin grammar and romantic encounter, and thereby articulates the ambivalence about formal education that animates this novel as a whole. While an early working title for this text was *The Education of a Personage*, clearly inspired by Henry Adams's *Education of Henry Adams* (1907), in its penultimate section Amory tells his companion (with truly Wildean irony) that 'in spite of going to college I've managed to pick up a good education' (255).[25] And the fact that in his *Note-books* Fitzgerald refers to the novel as 'A Romance and a Reading List' indicates his anxiety about the value of the schooling that both the author and his protagonist undergo (*Crack-Up* 176). It is significant that in two of the novels that most influenced Fitzgerald while he was writing *This Side of Paradise* – namely, *Sinister Street* by Compton Mackenzie (1913) and *The Research Magnificent* by H. G. Wells (1915) – education in Classics plays a somewhat fraught role in the protagonists' lives. In his own coming-of-age novel, in turn, Fitzgerald's continuous intertextuality with both Latin literature and classically allusive modern texts enables him to explore the comparative merits of athletic, military, romantic and intellectual prowess, to examine the meanings of the First World War, and to scrutinise both the Decadent and the modernist aesthetic.

On its very first page, this novel tells us about Beatrice Blaine's 'educational extravagance': her schooling at a convent in Rome combined with her socialising there in circles that were au fait with 'the latest gossip of the Older Roman Families' (*This Side* 11).[26] On the one hand, Fitzgerald here invokes what Vance (discussing Wilde and George Moore) terms 'the essentially Catholic notion of benign Roman continuity', in which a virtuous Rome leads on to a virtuous Christianity (121–2). This idealistic reading of history (in the vein of nineteenth-century English theologian John Henry Newman) might to some extent explain the enthusiasm for antiquity exhibited by both Fitzgerald's mentor, Monsignor Fay, and the fictional Monsignor Darcy in *This Side of Paradise*. On the other hand, through Beatrice's lavish lifestyle Fitzgerald hints at the decadent privileging of the aesthetic and the pleasurable over the moral in the antique Roman–Roman Catholic continuum. The novelist's scathing observation that the 'culture rich in all arts and traditions' in which she was immersed is 'barren of all ideas' articulates a *Waste Land*-like sense of the corrupt sterility of European civilisation, and it reinscribes the irony of his observation that 'her youth passed in renaissance glory' (11). The unmitigated disdain for European Renaissance culture expressed here is somewhat surprising, however, given the fact that Renaissance English literature (involving primarily Edmund Spenser, Philip Sidney and Christopher Marlowe) was one of Fitzgerald's preferred courses at Princeton.[27] While it is true that Renaissance texts are not among those explicitly invoked in the novel, Marlowe's 1604 play *Dr Faustus* (as well as Goethe's overtly namechecked *Faust*) presumably shaped the representation of Amory's hallucinatory encounter with the devil. With a notable lack of subtlety on Fitzgerald's part, in the section of the text labelled 'DEVIL' he names one of the women accompanying Amory 'Axia Marlowe', and thereby gives an ironic nod to the Elizabethan playwright (*This Side* 244, 106). The novelist also conveys contempt for the 'renaissance glory' that was so problematically formative for Beatrice (11). This last may say more about Fitzgerald's misogynistic perception of women's education as futile, however, than about his true opinion of Renaissance culture and learning.

Marlowe's significance to Fitzgerald is important not least because it may explain the subtle presence of Ovid – at once unnamed and tangible – throughout this first novel. Fitzgerald did not formally study Ovid in any of his Latin courses, but given that Marlowe's long poem *Hero and Leander* (1598, written with George Chapman) was inspired by Ovid's *Heroides*, and that the Elizabethan also translated Ovid's *Amores*, his oeuvre may well have constituted one of the ways (alongside Shakespeare and Wilde) through which the American encountered the Roman poet. Indeed, the name 'Amory' (containing the Latin word for love, *amor*) was perhaps inspired by the *Amores*, Ovid's witty love elegies that express a young man's romantic and sexual misadventures. The Latin love-elegy tradition, as well, may well have determined the Latinate first names of Fitzgerald's female characters such as Myra, Phoebe, Phyllis and Clara.[28] Above all, Ovid's *Metamorphoses* is surely an implicit intertext throughout the novel. This is evident through apparently minor details such as the comparison of Amory with Narcissus, which irreverently echoes Wilde's allusions to the same Ovidian figure in *Dorian Gray*. The power of Clara ('of the ripply golden hair' (130)) to 'metamorphose' material through her conversation (132), and of Kerry to 'transform' things through the same art (78), also brings this Latin poem on the theme of change to mind. And finally the *Metamorphoses* resonates in the broader themes of the cataclysmic effects of desire, of the transitions characterising Amory's life at Princeton, of change in America, and of change in Western culture as a whole. While Amory overtly invokes Heraclitus to express his sense of the incipient dramatic change that his last night at Princeton involves, Ovid's subsequent assertion (voicing Pythagoras) that 'all things are in a state of flux' (*Met.* XV.177) also echoes throughout this text.[29]

Of his initial encounter with Thomas D'Invilliers – the intellectual student who first introduces Amory to *The Picture of Dorian Gray* – the protagonist remarks on the precious rarity of finding a fellow student who could discuss Keats fluently 'yet evidently washed his hands' (54). Keats is of course central to any consideration of classical allusiveness in *This Side of Paradise*, and it is probably no coincidence that two of the three poems to which Amory alludes – 'To a Nightingale' (84) and 'Ode on a Grecian Urn' (246) – are among those most profoundly in dialogue with antiquity in the Romantic poet's oeuvre.[30] Yet, for the most part, Keats's elegiac earnestness is antithetical to the parodic and always-shifting tone of Fitzgerald's novel. It is perhaps unsurprising that the *fin de siècle* British and Irish writers commonly grouped as the 'Decadents' – Ernest Dowson, Algernon Swinburne, Arthur Symons, Walter Pater and Oscar Wilde – are a far more significant referent than the Romantic poets in this work. Amory first encounters Swinburne and Dowson after his conversation with D'Invilliers; the work of both these writers, admired by Fitzgerald himself, is suffused with classical allusions. As Vance has argued, Decadent writers often invoke the ancient world, paradoxically enough, to critique Victorian assumptions about art's necessarily instructive qualities, and Wilde (along with George Moore) deployed 'Franco-Roman decadence' to 'subvert ... the empire of England' (121). Wilde's comedies of manners such as *The Importance of Being Earnest* clearly influenced the nature of 'The Debutante', the playscript inserted into *This Side of Paradise* that is reworked from an earlier, more overtly classical version of a text Fitzgerald originally wrote in 1916.[31] Yet it is indubitably the 'Franco-Roman decadence' element of Wilde's work that is most significant in this American novel.

Amory's most intense encounter with this cultural and aesthetic moment follows from his crucial exchange with Monsignor Darcy at which the priest explains the crucial role of tangible achievements in becoming a 'personage' (101). Ironically it is at this point that Amory 'delved further' into 'the misty side-streets of literature: Huysmans, Walter Pater, Theophile Gautier, and the racier sections of Rabelais, Boccaccio, Petronius, and Suetonius' (103). In these lines Fitzgerald points to the complex set of interactions between the most famous Decadent writers and the decadence of late imperial Rome, as it is recorded in the Latin literature of its time. In his 1884 novel *À rebours* (*Against Nature*), long feted as a defining text of Decadence, the French writer J-K. Huysmans, for example, is famous for disdaining the Golden Age Latin poets such as Virgil, praising only Lucan and Petronius, who recorded the excesses of the era of Nero.[32] In *Dorian Gray*, in turn, the protagonist is preoccupied by a novel which closely resembles Huysmans's work: Wilde adds details from his readings of Suetonius to this unnamed novel-within-his-novel, describing a chapter in which its author fancies himself to be a succession of corrupt Roman emperors ranging from Tiberius and Caligula to Nero and Elagabalus.[33] As Shushma Malik argues, this section of *Dorian Gray* epitomises Wilde's Decadent reading of Nero and Tiberius as artists, as (in Wilde's words in an 1889 essay) 'the puppets of a play', a tendency which is itself part of a broader

Decadent tradition (Malik 313, 311).[34] In turn, then, when Amory invokes Huysmans, Petronius and Suetonius, Fitzgerald experiments with positioning both his protagonist and implicitly himself within this tradition.

After his dalliance with the Decadents, Amory alights upon 'the collected poems of Rupert Brooke' amongst his classmates' reading (*This Side* 103). Associated with heroic athleticism and idyllic English hedonism, Brooke also of course connotes the First World War. Amory's subsequent proper engagement with that war – when he is stationed in a military camp on Long Island – marks a change in the nature of the text's classical allusiveness. The italicised elegy to Princeton which marks the end of the novel's Part I and of Amory's undergraduate life stands out in this text for being more plangent than parodic. In the Interlude that follows, moreover, Fitzgerald lets Monsignor Darcy get away with invoking the *Agamemnon* and with comparing the American soldiers in Europe to 'Roman legions, miles from their corrupt city' (149). Somehow this letter is sincere and genuinely heroic in its tone. Yet at the same time, the reality of the war speeds up the development of the modernist consciousness that has been incipient in the novel thus far.

Amory's sense of self-irony in relation to the global conflict contributes to his very modern sense of multiplicity and contradiction. In a moment of nativist prejudice, he resents the presence of foreigners on his train, and thinks 'how much easier patriotism had been to a homogeneous race' (139). On a metaphorical level, the protagonist here confronts the complexity of the heterogeneous culture that defines the modern age. In 'the pageantry of his disillusion' he senses a 'world-old procession of Prophets, Athenians, Martyrs, Saints, Scientists, Don Juans, Jesuits, Puritans, Fausts, Poets, Pacifists' (243). He is disappointed with the entire eclectic cast list of his *Bildung* so far. Like Eleanor he is 'hipped on Freud' (220), while his conviction that 'there were no more heroes' and that he had 'grown up to a thousand books, a thousand lies' expresses a prototypical modernist disaffection with the times and with past and present literary forms (242). Yet it is in articulating this malaise, in reflecting the dissonant multiplicities of the traditions in which he was educated and of the world around him, that Fitzgerald (through Amory) creates his own distinctive aesthetic. In so doing, the author exemplifies the paradox of profoundly creative disillusionment that defines all modernist writing.

While 'convalescing' from his failed affair with Rosalind, Amory claims to have been 'puzzled and depressed' by Joyce's *Portrait of the Artist as a Young Man* (195). We know that Joyce's 1916 text was one of Fitzgerald's favourite books, however, and to some extent the capitalised, journalistic section titles in *This Side of Paradise* even anticipate the 'HEART OF THE HIBERNIAN METROPOLIS' ('Aeolus') sections of *Ulysses*. In its depiction of post-war New York City, moreover, the novel expresses a disaffection with modern urban life that certainly anticipates *The Waste Land*.[35] Thus while it is comic that Amory inserts himself in the line of artists who don't 'fit' – 'the Rousseau, the Tolstoi, the Samuel Butler, the Amory Blaine' (249) – Fitzgerald's first novel can certainly be understood as his portrait of himself as an artist, and as a young man mining antiquity in order to address his own times.

The Great Gatsby (1925)

'It was an age of miracles, it was an age of art, it was an age of excess and it was an age of satire' (*Crack-Up* 14). Fitzgerald's 1931 reflection on the 'Jazz Age' of the 1920s perfectly distils the shifts and contrasts – in subject matter, in mood, in tone and in form – within his iconic 1925 novel, *The Great Gatsby*. While this sentence also parodies the opening of Dickens's *Tale of Two Cities* (1859), arguably the two cities on Fitzgerald's mind here are New York and ancient Rome, not Paris and London. Critics have long discussed the relationship between Fitzgerald's novel and the Latin work the *Satyricon*, probably written during the reign of Nero (54–68 CE), by Petronius.[36] This rich mini-field of *Gatsby-Satyricon* studies has arisen from the American author's referencing of Petronius's decadent protagonist, Trimalchio, within his text, and his wish (in 1924) to name the novel *Trimalchio in West Egg*.[37] Yet Fitzgerald's engagement with antiquity in this text is not confined to its identification with and/or divergence from the *Satyricon*. Besides *Gatsby*'s ludic engagement with the genres of tragedy, epic and pastoral, there is a wider and widespread play with the ancient Rome/modern America dynamic that consistently fascinated Fitzgerald. The author's conscious 'Romanness' in turn has implications for the novel's politics, particularly those concerned with racial and ethnic identity.

There are significant Homeric resonances in *The Great Gatsby*. At times these are ironic, for example when, on his first visit to the Buchanans' mansion, Nick compares a 'wine-colored rug' to the sea in a mock-heroic twist both on Homer's 'wine-dark sea' epithet and on Joyce's use of it in *Ulysses* (10).[38] The Odyssean theme runs through the novel's fascination with the sea and with both actual and metaphorical sea-voyaging, while the most sincere evocation of Homeric homecoming is perhaps Nick's lyrical memory of the 'returning trains' that took him back to the Midwest of his youth (137). The underlying structure of Gatsby's quest or mission to achieve a return to perfect happiness with Daisy recalls the *Aeneid* as well as the *Odyssey*, and is also, as Ward Briggs has argued, replete with echoes of the Virgilian Golden Age in a manner that recalls Willa Cather's work.[39] Numerous critics besides Briggs, meanwhile, have explored Fitzgerald's deployment of the pastoral and counter-pastoral modes, including his allusions to Keats.[40] And while Gatsby's rise and fall to some extent follows a conventional Aristotelian tragic structure, Fitzgerald also undercuts the nobility of his own tragedy with the melodramatic description of Myrtle's death. While the car accident's 'principal witness' being a 'young Greek' may invoke the witnessing role of the Attic chorus, Nick's bitter reference to Myrtle's 'tragic achievement' (121) and the details about her undignified physical injury correspond to the ironies inherent in her name: that in Greek and Roman mythology the myrtle plant was sacred to Aphrodite/Venus, and was often worn at weddings.[41] Fitzgerald here realises Amory Blaine's observation in *This Side of Paradise*, that 'All tragedy has that strain of the grotesque and the squalid' (86).

It is in its rendering of the 'grotesque and the squalid' that Fitzgerald makes use of the *Satyricon* in his illumination of the excesses and hypocrisies of the Jazz Age plutocracy. There are several theories about why the text captured Fitzgerald's interest when he was writing *Gatsby* between 1922 and 1924. Briggs reminds us that Eliot's famous 'Sibyl of Cumae' epigraph to *The Waste Land* is from Petronius; this poem was itself published in 1922 and had immeasurable influence on Fitzgerald ('Petronius' 227).[42] In that same year, moreover, a new unexpurgated translation of the *Satyricon* was subject to a censorship case in which a friend of Fitzgerald's was involved, and which was covered by *The New York Times*; the text would thereby have attracted Fitzgerald's attention.[43] It is important to remember, though, that Fitzgerald has Amory list Petronius among his newfound 'side-street' authors in *This Side of Paradise* (103), published two years earlier, and that the first Loeb translation of the text appeared as early as 1913. Interestingly, the original Loeb translator writes of the *Satyricon* that 'Men become millionaires with American rapidity, and enjoy that condition as hazardously in Cumae as in Wall Street' (Heseltine xiv). Once again, we see that Fitzgerald's perception of America's Romanness is itself part of a tradition.

The American author's only direct invocation of the Latin novel is Nick's observation at the start of the seventh chapter, when Gatsby stops giving his lavish parties, that 'his career as Trimalchio was over' (88). Yet, pointing out the primary connection between Gatsby's parties and the famous 'Trimalchio's Feast' section of the ancient text, scholars illuminate numerous further parallels: in the music, the extravagant food and lavish décor (MacKendrick); in Fitzgerald's symbolic deployment of the eggs that feature in the Petronian feast (Tanner); in the fact that both Trimalchio and Gatsby are *nouveau riche*, and are both prey to a horde of parasitic guests.[44] Niall Slater demonstrates that Gatsby and Trimalchio are similarly preoccupied by time and its passing, while Nikolai Endres emphasises the common focus on theatricality and artifice and the literary allusiveness that characterises each work. Carraway's first name, Nick, may be inspired by Trimalchio's guest named Niceros (Drennan), while there are affinities between Fitzgerald's narrator and the narrator of the *Satyricon*, Encolpius (Endres; Slater). These narrators' aspirations to personal greatness mirror the ambitions of both Fitzgerald and Petronius (Endres); this point connects to Briggs's observation that Fitzgerald is more interested in positioning himself as the American Petronius than in casting Gatsby as the American Trimalchio. Indeed, as Endres points out, Gatsby is only *posing* as Trimalchio during that brief 'career', and is an observer of rather than a partaker in the decadence of his parties (123).[45] While Robert Sklenar in turn documents a whole host of ways in which Gatsby's novel is *not* like the *Satyricon* (or is 'anti-Petronian'), it is perhaps Paul MacKendrick's astute summary that best articulates the core of the texts' relationship: both constitute 'a literature of protest' about a society in which 'ethics fail to control economics' (314).

Scholars frequently quote the letter from Max Perkins (Fitzgerald's editor at Scribner's) in which Perkins explains that 'various gentlemen' in the publishing house don't like the title Fitzgerald chose for the October 1924 draft of the novel, *Trimalchio in West Egg* (Fitzgerald, *Trimalchio E.V.* 185).[46] In a rarely discussed line in this letter, the editor writes, 'none like it but me. To me, the strange incongruity of the words in it sound the note of the book' (*Trimalchio E.V.*185). Here Perkins detects the simultaneous resonance and dissonance between Rome and America, rooted in (but by no means restricted to) the engagement with the *Satyricon*, that Fitzgerald subtly keeps in play throughout the novel. The six-paragraph-long list of names of the guests at Gatsby's parties in the fourth chapter, for example, both parodies the contemporaneous media's obsession with celebrity and, as Briggs observes, 'reads like a parody of the epic record of early noble families of Greece and Rome' ('Petronius' 231). The eclectic nature of the names and their combinations epitomises exactly the conscious 'incongruity' (between 'Trimalchio' and 'West Egg') that Perkins values in the novel's rejected title. Antiquity maintains an understated yet powerful presence through Fitzgerald's inclusion of a 'Ulysses Swett', for example, a 'Claudia Hip' and a 'Faustina O'Brien' (*Gatsby* 49–51). This last, of course, recalls and ironises the notorious Faustina, wife of Marcus Aurelius, the 'most decadent of Roman empresses' whom Swinburne made famous in his poem 'Faustine' (Prettejohn 162–3).[47] At such moments, Fitzgerald's comic satire reaches its zenith, itself audaciously placed alongside sincere engagements with Roman culture such as the echoes, in the novel's elegiac ending, of Virgil's meditation on the human struggle against decay that Briggs meticulously parses.[48]

The changes the author made to the *Trimalchio in West Egg* version – while actually living in Rome in 1924–5 – reveal his attentiveness to maintaining the difficult balance between subtlety and significance in the novel's Roman atmosphere.[49] For example, in *Trimalchio* Nick hopes to discover in his books on finance 'the shining secrets that only Midas and Morgan and Rothschild knew' (*Trimalchio E.V.* 7). In *Gatsby* this is changed to 'Midas and Morgan and Maecenas' (7), which takes advantage of alliteration to invoke the wealthy (and decadent) patron of Roman writers who died in 8 BCE.[50] Of the changes made to chapter 6 of *Trimalchio*, meanwhile, Bruccoli notes how in *Gatsby* the author eliminates the 'detailed description of the party' that Tom attends with Daisy, and which (in *Trimalchio*) 'was a costume affair' (Bruccoli, Afterword 10). Critics have yet to discuss one crucial detail about this 'costume affair', however: Fitzgerald's interest in Roman pastoral and his conflicted anxieties about race in America converge within it in significant ways. The theme of the fancy dress party in *Trimalchio* is rustic: 'it was a harvest dance with the immemorial decorations—sheaves of wheat, crossed rakes, and corncobs in geometrical design' (*Trimalchio E.V.* 81). Lest we imagine Gatsby has recreated a Midwestern agrarian scene here, however, Fitzgerald writes that there was 'a negro dressed as a field hand serving cider, which nobody wanted' (*E.V.* 81). Through this half-sentence alone the author conjures the uncomfortable paradoxes of Thomas Jefferson's Roman-modelled slave plantation, Monticello. He also invokes the entire tradition of 'Old Southern' pastoral, which is characterised by a nostalgia for a lost agricultural idyll undergirded by race-based slavery.[51] Of course, Fitzgerald himself by no means definitively endorses the ideology of this invocation. After all, everything about this particular party is ill-judged and disastrous; the fact that 'no one wanted' the cider served by the 'negro field hand' suggests the guests' rejection of this distasteful throwback; and, anyway, all of these details are cut from *The Great Gatsby* itself.

By contrast, Tom Buchanan's much-discussed racist views are preserved in the final text. These include his excitement about Lothrop Stoddard's 1920 work, *The Rising Tide of Color* (renamed in the novel as 'The Rise of the Coloured Empires' by 'Goddard' (14)); his belief in the superiority of the 'Nordic' race (14); and his later comparison of Daisy's relationship with the non-patrician, not-wholly-American Gatsby to miscegenation.[52] Tom's gloss of Stoddard does not include the fact that Stoddard, like many race theorists of his time, reinforced his alarmist views about the embattled nature of the white 'race' of his own era by suggesting that the racial mixing that occurred in late imperial Rome was a key factor in that city's decline. Stoddard argues that 'hybrid stocks' in Latin America, for example, 'show remarkable similarities to the mongrel chaos of the declining Roman empire' (Stoddard 116), and that the threat from 'brown and yellow Asia' had begun 'with the Huns in the last days of Rome' (146). This use of the hybridisation of Rome as a cautionary tale is widespread: it appears in Spengler's *Decline of the West* but also, among other places, in the more overtly racist polemics of Gobineau's *Inequality of the Races* (published between 1853 and 1855).[53] Tom is thus 'doubly Roman' here: a self-indulgent, morally compromised plutocrat who worries about his empire's imminent demise through immigration and racial mixing. Fitzgerald's addition of the word 'empires' to Stoddard's original title reinforces the idea of imperial conflict, both ancient and modern.

The fact that Fitzgerald gives these views to the novel's most noxious character, and that Nick refers to Tom's ideology as 'stale ideas' (19), suggests the author's critical distance from this perspective. Yet the reality is a little more complicated and is illuminated by a continuing focus on Rome. As Bert Bender has argued, Stoddard's theories clearly made a great impression on Fitzgerald himself, and spoke to an interest in eugenics that the author had cultivated during his time at Princeton. Appropriately enough, it was the author's first unhappy trip to Rome that precipitated his most explicit written outpouring of 'Stoddardian' thinking, in the letter to Edmund Wilson of July 1921:

> God damn the continent of Europe. It is of merely antiquarian interest. Rome is only a few years behind Tyre + Babylon. The negroid streak creeps northward to defile the nordic race. Already the Italians have the souls of blackamoors. Raise the bars of immigration and permit only Scandinavians, Teutons, Anglo Saxons + Celts to enter. (Bruccoli, *Letters* 46–7)

Although here Fitzgerald sounds like his later creation Tom Buchanan, in the three years between this personal letter and the published novel he separates himself from the views of that objectionable character. Yet Nick himself (who is much less readily distinguished from Fitzgerald) is in turn not without his anxieties about the changing racial dynamic of New York, and himself intertwines those anxieties with a complex pastoral and counter-pastoral.

The first two of Nick's three momentous trips to the city (the afternoon at the apartment where Myrtle and Tom conduct their affair and the awkward lunch out with Gatsby) are structurally linked by the narrator's half-ironic, half-sincere depiction of New York as an idyllic wonderland. On the first visit, Nick claims that Fifth Avenue is 'so warm and soft, almost pastoral', and that (in a nod to Marlowe, Virgil and Theocritus) he 'wouldn't have been surprised to see a flock of white sheep turn the corner' (*Gatsby* 25).[54] On the second visit, the view of the city 'from the Queensboro bridge' appears 'in its first wild promise of all the mystery and the beauty in the world' (55). The wonderland becomes wackier as he encounters first some funeral-goers 'from south-east Europe' and then 'three modish Negroes' who are driven by a white chauffeur (55). 'Anything can happen' in that city,

Nick muses, 'anything at all' (55). Nick's incredulity at the sight of non-Nordics and wealthy black people is expressed through his associating them with the non-real pastoral mode. Implicitly, therefore, by suggesting that the idea of a changing ethnic and racial make-up of the city is itself as unlikely as the sudden appearance of a flock of sheep, both Nick and the novel as a whole diminish the potentially threatening power of this scenario. In this light the novel's racial politics become more ambiguous, and pastoral is shown to serve ignoble as well as noble ends.[55]

Given the widespread significance of Rome throughout *The Great Gatsby*, it is perhaps no surprise that Toni Morrison chooses to invert the significance of that city and culture in *Jazz*. In this 1992 novel Morrison takes issue both with Fitzgerald's marginalisation of black people and their centrality in 1920s New York, and with the older author's deployment of pastoral to serve racist ends. Small wonder, then, that Morrison's Virginian black protagonists – who ultimately triumph in that northern city – have survived and escaped the violence of white Southerners 'in a mean little place called Rome' (Morrison, *Jazz* 138).

Tender Is the Night (1934)

In a 1921 interview in the *St Paul Daily News*, having just returned from his first visit to Europe, Fitzgerald frankly expresses his disenchantment with that continent. 'France and Italy represent a decaying civilization,' he says. He describes 'the house where Keats died' in Rome as 'a close, dismal hole which looked out on a cluttered, squalid street' (Bruccoli and Baughman 9). Thirteen years later, writing of his visit to the French southern city of Arles in 1929, he recalls that 'following the festering waters of a stagnant canal we came to the ruins of a Roman dwelling house. There was a blacksmith shop installed behind the proud columns and a few scattered cows ate the gold flowers off the meadow' (*Crack-Up* 50). Each of these descriptions constitutes an authorial perception and construction of Roman corruption and decline that are nearly ubiquitous in *Tender Is the Night*. As his editors note, the Piazza di Spagna in Rome that the Keats house overlooks is not, in fact, 'a slum' (Bruccoli and Baughman 9). And the 1934 piece risks a tautology ('festering' and 'stagnant') to maximise the irony of the once-grand but now-ruined architecture, where cattle now feed on once-glorious golden flowers. Fitzgerald's use of this ironic Romanness to contrast past aspiration, potential and greatness with present fallenness is far more widespread than scholarship to date has recognised.[56]

Critics persuasively read *Tender Is the Night* as a 'tragic action' depicting the downfall and dissipation of the once-heroic protagonist, Dick Diver (Merrill 597), and argue rightly that Fitzgerald conceives of Dick as 'a hero born in a post-heroic age' (Foster 108). Scholars have, of course, emphasised the significance of the protagonist's nadir – his unsatisfactory affair with Rosemary, and his drunken night in the police cell – taking place in the city of Rome. These brief four chapters at the end of the novel's second book draw heavily on Fitzgerald's negative personal experience: while in Rome in December 1924 his fighting over a taxi fare led to his arrest, police beating and detainment overnight.[57] But we should also recognise that while the geographical site of Rome in the novel is the epitome of ruin, it is not juxtaposed with but rather on a continuum with other key sites in the novel – Paris and across the south of France – in which ironic, ruined Romanness is a constant and important presence. And in his explorations of each of the novel's central themes – wealth, style, luxury, consumerism, decadence, art and artifice, individual aspiration and decline, psychological and moral collapse, the relationship between people and places, the transition to modernity and the role of the First World War therein – Fitzgerald for the most part connects rather than contrasts America with his European settings through his homeland's own complex relationship to Rome.

Caterina Ricciardi's study of the Italian capital's lifelong importance in Fitzgerald's oeuvre argues that through Dick's 'catastrophe in Rome' the novelist both engages with Henry James's 1879 novella, *Daisy Miller*, and rewrites the earlier author's 1876 novel, *Roderick Hudson* (*Tender* 273).[58] One of the many ways in which *Tender Is the Night* differs from the novels that precede it, however, is that it is for the most part strikingly non-allusive to prior literature, especially to the 'highbrow' kind. Keats's 'To a Nightingale' – in its classically referent explorations of intoxication, oblivion and immortality – is of course (alongside James) a constant intertext in the 1934 work.[59] But compared with the hyper-allusiveness of *This Side of Paradise* and the numerous allusions in *Gatsby*, the paucity of named authors or textual echoes in this longer novel is conspicuous.[60] Instead, setting and place assume a quasi-textual significance, and the author inscribes landscape, architecture, archaeological sites and apparently minor features of contemporary urban environments with multiple Rome-inflected meanings. The invested nature of location in the novel testifies to the fact that the years of its completion constituted the convergence of the Great Depression in America, economic crises across Europe, Zelda's first three psychiatric episodes, the Fitzgeralds' extensive sojourns in France (as well as stays in Switzerland and North Africa), and Fitzgerald's first two spells of working in Hollywood (in 1927 and 1931). While Foster argues that the story of Dick's 'deterioration' is analogous to 'the novel's larger action', so that (like an epic hero) he is symbolic of 'a "mythic" interpretation of history' (92), the inverse is equally true. Fitzgerald mirrors Dick's deterioration, and both his and Nicole's compromised selves, in a range of symbolic settings in which antiquity is often key.

On her first visit to the beach in front of Gausse's Hotel, Rosemary has little to say in response to the avowed cultural passions of one of the couples that she meets there: the McKiscos. Albert McKisco declares himself a fan of 'Antheil and Joyce' (*Tender* 16), while Violet boasts not only that her husband 'wrote the first criticism of Ulysses that ever appeared in America' (16), but also that his own first and nearly completed novel is 'on the idea of Ulysses', focusing on a 'decayed old French aristocrat' over the timespan of 'a hundred years' (17). While Fitzgerald here mocks the couple's pretentiousness and its dissonance with the relative simplicity of sea bathing in a beautiful setting, Rosemary herself is soon (albeit unwittingly) to encounter complex and paradoxical connections between modern and classical cultures that are themselves Joycean in their incongruity. On her train ride to Cannes, she notices the advertisements directed at tourists for 'the Pont du Gard at Remoulins, the Amphitheatre at Orange, winter sports at Chamonix' (20). Here Fitzgerald recasts two of France's proudest monuments that remain from the Roman occupation – the three-tier bridge of the Nîmes aqueduct at Remoulins near Arles, and the vast amphitheatre near Avignon – as signifiers of contemporary consumerist pleasure.[61] Rosemary has found French life generally to be thus far 'empty and stale' (21), and immerses herself in the *Saturday Evening Post* as a means to reconnect with American perception and with its 'clamor of Empire' (20). The 'Mediterranean world' only appears 'less silent' to her once she has visited the Hollywood-like Gaumont film studio at La Turbie (32).[62] Yet although in her mind southern France and the United States are worlds apart, linked only by the Los Angeles-like atmosphere of the film set, Fitzgerald's unusual word choice in these lines emphasises proximity between the locales, not distance. In referring to the United States as 'Empire', and to this region of France as the 'Mediterranean world', the author exploits the analogous relationship between modernity and ancient Rome.

At the end of their driving tour of the area, Rosemary and her mother notice that 'the moon already hovered over the ruins of the aqueducts' (22). Here Fitzgerald begins the lyrical, Keatsian pastoral – idyllic and yet imbued with a sense of foreboding – in which he describes the Divers and their lifestyle from the fourth chapter of the novel onwards. When we encounter Nicole in the 'lovely grassless garden' of the Villa Diana – a name that will prove ironic in that it recalls the sometimes-cruel Roman goddess of chastity – she is presented as a conscientious nurturer of lemon and eucalyptus, peonies, lilac, nasturtiums, irises and roses (34). Ominously enough, the path in that same garden on which Rosemary waits for Dick after the dinner party is lined with 'myrtle and fern' (44); Fitzgerald again ironises the myrtle's classical association with love and marriage (as he does with Myrtle Wilson in *Gatsby*).[63] After Violet's inadvertent witnessing of Nicole's episode in the bathroom (a kind of accidental voyeurism that recalls the mythical Actaeon's intrusion on the bathing Diana), the repeated detail about the guests carrying lamps up to the house associates them parodically with the Vestal Virgins of Rome (45).[64] And the fragile, ambiguous idyll that is brought to an abrupt end by Nicole's illness is shattered once and for all by the 'farce' of the duel (59), which stars McKisco as 'the tragic clown' (57).

In the scenes set in northern France, Fitzgerald contrasts the superficial decadence of Paris with the sombre, heroic and elegiac atmosphere of the First World War battlefield and cemetery. Yet even that war is to some extent commodified and trivialised: Dick has simplified its history until 'it bore a faint resemblance to one of his parties' (70). The fact that on one of her extravagant Parisian shopping sprees, moreover, Nicole buys for her son 'Greek and Roman soldiers, a whole army of them, costing over a thousand francs' (112) suggests capitalism's corruption of heroic and epic military tradition. Consistently, Paris in this novel is a site in which the classical past functions only ironically: Rosemary's unrequited suitor Collis Clay stays at the Lutetia Hotel, named for the Gallo-Roman city that preceded Paris (82); the night of Rosemary's first wild party involves a 'quick Odyssey over Paris' that Fitzgerald compares to 'slapstick comedy' (89); and her resemblance to a 'Tanagra figure' (nineteenth-century figurines modelled on ancient Greek originals) in the film *Daddy's Girl* is undermined by the title's reminder of the historical incestuous abuse perpetrated by Nicole's father (80). Through the somewhat farcical plotline of Rosemary discovering on her bed the body of the black African Jules Peterson, murdered at the hands of African Americans, and through the fact that the sheets stained with his blood provoke Nicole into a psychotic episode, Fitzgerald deploys what Toni Morrison would call an 'Africanist' strategy to contrast a thoroughly impure, corrupt and morally bankrupt Paris with the pure, morally and racially white heroic city it purportedly once was.[65]

In the scenes set in the Swiss clinics – both at Professor Dohmler's in 1919 and in the new venture that Dick starts up with Franz – Fitzgerald creates a culture and ethos that are distinct from those of the Mediterranean world through a relative absence of classical allusions. While the author describes Dick's early training as the 'heroic period' of his life (134), and while Franz later confesses to feeling pressured by a 'pantheon' of 'heroes' from Swiss history (152), Fitzgerald's depiction of the Swiss work ethic and way of life is entirely free from any association with the decadent, corrupt and decaying classicism that is so pervasive in other locales. Noticeably, it is the Americans who visit Switzerland, in particular the various members of the notoriously wealthy Warren family, whom the author describes in pointedly Roman terms in this setting. For example, he deploys imagery resonant of Ovid to describe the wealthy Baby Warren's awareness that her 'very name . . . caused a psychological metamorphosis in people, and in return this change had crystallized her own sense of position' (183). When discussing whether or not to commit to the new clinic, Dick speaks ambivalently of Nicole's wealth in comparison to his lack of it: 'Nicole and Baby are as rich as Croesus,' he tells Frank (201). The American psychiatric patients in the new clinic are also described in classical terms – the woman with syphilitic eczema is described as a 'sarcophagus', while the self-harming teenaged girl is called 'Helen' (212). And during the post-Rome clinical visit to Lausanne (a location inevitably evocative of *The Waste Land*),[66] Dick counts the dissipating, alcoholic Devereux Warren among the many visitors to that region and hotel who, living 'on the derivatives of opium or barbital', are 'rich ruins' (279). Prior to this, Fitzgerald has prepared the reader for Dick's own imminent downfall by emphasising his lack of awareness and insight on his flight from Zurich to Munich. While Dick compares post-Edwardian England to a remorseful Trimalchio (it is 'like a rich man after a disastrous orgy' (222)), he muses complacently on the 'pleasures' of the 'incorruptible Mediterranean' (223). Yet Fitzgerald stages the protagonist's moral collapse in Rome itself because it constitutes the apogee of the Mediterranean world's corruption.

Throughout the scenes set in that city, the author on the one hand conflates America and Rome, making them interchangeable with each other, and on the other makes Dick's Americanness (and non-Italianness) key to his survival. For example, the 'façade' of New York harbour (233), in its double resonance as an architectural phenomenon and an artificial, superficial construction, is thematically linked to the 'huge set of the Forum, larger than the Forum itself' (241), in which Rosemary is making her film in Rome. Fitzgerald's decision to interweave his plot's turning point, Dick's infidelity to Rosemary, with the filming of an epic Roman movie was presumably influenced by his and Zelda's encountering the filming of *Ben-Hur* in Rome during their stay in the city in 1925.[67] Furthermore, contemporaneous American films that used ancient Rome to explore the Depression, such as *The Sign of the Cross* (dir. Cecil DeMille, 1932) and *Roman Scandals* (dir. Sam Goldwyn, 1933), were hugely popular at this time.[68] That Fitzgerald elects to call his fictional movie 'The Grandeur that Was Rome' probably constitutes an overstatement of his case, however; this overdetermination also characterises the detail that he and Rosemary dine in the 'Castello dei Cesari, a splendid restaurant . . . overlooking the ruined forum of an undetermined period of the decadence' (242). In addition, there is an unresolved contradiction about the affinities or lack thereof between the United States and Rome in the author's account of Dick's release from prison. The narrative becomes something of a semi-comic adventure story when Baby Warren musters Collis Clay and the American vice-consul to secure the (erstwhile) hero's freedom and safety, but the irony is not directed at the American codes – of wealth, influence, ethnicity, diplomacy – that enable the success. At one point the sign for the 'American Express Company' bureau even serves as the landmark by enabling Baby's escape from the 'labyrinth' of Roman alleys (261). America's Romanness, it would seem, can be cast off when it needs to be.

When Dick runs into a former dinner-party guest, Royal Dumphry, in Lausanne, Dumphry recalls the long-ago evening at Villa Diana as 'the most civilized gathering of people I have ever known' (277). That Fitzgerald chooses to stage the collapse of the Divers' marriage back at Villa Diana and on the nearby beach at Gausse's lays bare the 'uncivilized' realities of that household and that world. Dick's observation (before starting the new clinic) that 'the pastoral quality down on the summer Riviera is all changing anyhow' proves to be something of an ironic understatement (205). After they have sold their interest in the clinic, the Divers' wealth becomes more overwhelming and corrupting than ever, and in depicting Nicole as '*curator* of it all' Fitzgerald suggests the replacement of classical aesthetics by commodification and consumerism (290, my italics). The pervasive mode of the novel's closing chapters is a bitter mock-heroic: the equally vinous Dick and his cook engage in absurd 'gladiatorial combat' (298); the distasteful social scene includes the farcically decadent English woman Lady Caroline Sibly-Biers, and Dick humiliates himself by failing in his attempted swimming acrobatics, in contrast to a younger swimmer who resembles a 'statue of glory' (317). When Dick says to Nicole, 'You ruined me, did you? Then we're both ruined' (306), the full symbolic weight of 'ruins', as it accumulates throughout the text, comes into play.

Perhaps predictably, Fitzgerald's depiction of the newly confident and sexually predatory Nicole as embodying the dangerous and callous aspect of the Roman deity Diana is tinged with the misogyny underlying many of the novelist's presentations of women in this novel. Back at the villa named for this goddess, 'No longer was [Nicole] a huntress of corralled game,' he writes (335); while she is able to seduce Tommy, this detail implies that she can also turn Dick into an Actaeon who will be devoured by his own demons or hounds. The association between Nicole and specific classical deities (at the start of her marriage to Dick she imagines herself as a very different entity, 'Pallas Athene' (184)) is symptomatic of the author's tendency to essentialise women, to reduce them to an essence about which he generalises, in a way that he never does for the male characters.[69] While Dick is once described as 'godlike' (121) he is never identified with a specific classical deity, and in this he exists as an individual rather than an essence representative of qualities purportedly ubiquitous in his gender. It is his preserved individuality, with which readers can so readily identify, that ensures the genuine pathos of the novel's devastatingly 'low-key', unadorned and allusion-free closing chapter.

It is interesting that, in the penultimate chapter, Dick dismisses Mary North's well-intentioned advice to him as 'one of Dr Eliot's classics' (350). In belittling both her moral wisdom and Charles Eliot's Harvard Classics series of canonical literary works, Dick suggests that the literary greats of Western civilisation are of no use to him now.[70] Indeed (as Bruccoli notes), although Fitzgerald named the novel's 'Gausse's Hotel' after his French professor at Princeton, Christian Gausse, French literature is presumably valueless to Dick once his Riviera world has collapsed. In the unlikely event of the itinerant Dick furnishing his home in upstate New York with classic books, they would most likely remain uncut, like those in Gatsby's library, or like Fitzgerald's own Princeton Greek book.

The relocated Dick perhaps might, however, tolerate the ironies of *Ulysses*, so disparaged at this novel's opening, or the postmodern-sounding 'pastiches' with which McKisco has now gained success (234). *Tender Is the Night* itself gestures towards a postmodern aesthetic, in its fascination with the simulated and pastiche qualities of the worlds it describes. Fitzgerald's sense of his own prescience may have been one reason why he anticipated this novel's reviewers with trepidation: 'I expect a lot of good pokes from the wise boys', he said in a post-publication interview, 'for not having written the *Odyssey*' (*Last Kiss* 422).

Notes

1. The poem was published in *The Nassau Literary Magazine* 72 (June 1916) when Fitzgerald was not yet back at Princeton (he returned in September that year); see Bruccoli, *Epic* 65.
2. See Bruccoli, *Epic* 149–51, 211. I draw here on several biographies of Fitzgerald: D. Brown (2017); Bruccoli, *Epic* (1981); Turnbull, *Scott* (1962).
3. For chronologies of Fitzgerald's life and work see Bruccoli, *Epic* xxv–xxxi, 545–69. Fitzgerald's previously unpublished work is now available in the recent Cambridge editions: see for example the collections *Spires and Gargoyles* (2010) and *Last Kiss* (2017). Short stories by Fitzgerald that engage the classical tradition include 'The Diamond as Big as the Ritz', 'Winter Dreams', 'Absolution', 'The Sensible Thing', 'Dice, Brassknuckles and Guitar', 'Babylon Revisited' and 'The Third Casket' (see Briggs, 'Ur-Gatsby' 582).
4. See Malamud, *Ancient Rome and Modern America* (2009).

5. On Fitzgerald's Princeton education (besides the standard biographies) see Daniel; Gillin. On his reading and personal library see Kuehl; on his intellectual context see Berman. On the literary allusions in *This Side of Paradise* see Good; on the same in *Gatsby* see Roulston, 'Something Borrowed'. On Fitzgerald's knowledge of Classics in particular see Briggs, 'Petronius'; Endres; MacKendrick.
6. See Bruccoli, *Epic* 38–9.
7. In the 1920s and 1930s Fitzgerald frequently made and disseminated eclectic lists of books that he perceived to be important and/or neglected – see for example *Last Kiss* 130, 401, 422.
8. See the first chapter of Vandiver for an account of a similar culture in Britain's private schools at this time. On Fitzgerald's predisposition to hero worship see Bruccoli, *Epic* 35; D. Brown 4.
9. Note the much-quoted letter to Scottie of February 1938 in which Fitzgerald recalls Princeton's Dean Wist intoning Horace, while expressing his own regret at his failure to understand the lines (Turnbull, *Letters* 22).
10. See Kuehl 60 and n. 20.
11. I return to Stoddard at more length at pp. 6–45.
12. See Malamud, *Ancient* 161–80.
13. Fitzgerald's classically allusive juvenilia include 'The Debutante', 'The Spire and the Gargoyle' and 'Tarquin of Cheapside', all reprinted in *Spires and Gargoyles*. On the relationship between his time in Europe and his short stories see Kennedy.
14. On Rome see also Turnbull, *Letters* 171, 176; also, in *The Crack-Up*, 'Show Mr and Mrs F to number ___'.
15. Existing articles on the *Satyricon* in *Gatsby* include: Briggs, 'Petronius'; Briggs, 'Ur-Gatsby'; Drennan; Endres; MacKendrick; Sklenar; Slater.
16. In 2000, two editions of this 1924 draft were published: *Trimalchio: An Early Version of 'The Great Gatsby'* (Cambridge edition), ed. West; and *Trimalchio: A Facsimile Edition of the Original Galley Proofs*, ed. Bruccoli.
17. See Daugherty and West.
18. See for example Foster; Merrill.
19. Roulston, 'Dick Diver's Plunge'.
20. As Ricciardi notes (29–30), Anthony Patch has just returned from Rome at the start of *The Beautiful and Damned*, and he and Gloria are to return to Italy at the novel's end. Classical allusions in that text include Anthony's father's name ('Ulysses'), and the ironic comparison between Gloria and a siren.
21. On the plots of this 1911 musical by George M. Cohan see West's note in *This Side of Paradise*, 325. On Wilde's classicism (including in *Dorian Gray*) see Riley et al.

22. The stage production of this novel ran in New York between 1899 and 1920, and it was made into a film in both 1907 and 1925 (Malamud, *Ancient* 133, 187). Fitzgerald also references the chariot-race sign in 'My Lost City' (*Crack-Up* 24). *Ben-Hur* was being filmed in Rome when Scott and Zelda Fitzgerald were there in 1924 (Bruccoli, *Epic* 211; see p. 71).
23. On this novel's literary allusiveness see Good. See also James; Raubichek; Sklar; Van Arsdale for relevant readings.
24. See *This Side* 16. Although the story of Horatius is originally from Livy's *Histories* (II.10), it is paraphrased (in Latin) in Collar and Daniell 223–4 (and illustrated on 85).
25. On Henry Adams's influence on Fitzgerald see Powell.
26. On Rome in this novel see Ricciardi 30–1.
27. See Bruccoli, *Epic* 61; Kuehl 59.
28. 'Phyllis' is one of several named young women in love-elegy by Virgil, Propertius and Horace.
29. See *This Side of Paradise* 145. On Fitzgerald and Heraclitus (via the pragmatism of William James) see Gillin.
30. The third is 'La Belle Dame Sans Merci' (*This Side* 55). On Fitzgerald and Keats see Kuehl 61–2; McGowan (on *Tender Is the Night*). Fitzgerald's allusions to Keats in this first novel are more ironic than those in the later ones.
31. Wilde's dramatic writing was influenced by the Roman comic playwrights Plautus and Terence – authors whom Fitzgerald also studied at Princeton (Bruccoli, *Epic* 54). In the 1917 version of 'The Debutante' the character named Rosalind in the later novel is called Helen Halcyon (*Spires* 144–54); see Bruccoli, *Epic* 69–70.
32. See Malik 308–9.
33. See *Dorian Gray* 120–1; references here are to the 1891 text.
34. On Wilde and Nero see also Vance 122–4.
35. See *This Side* 235–8.
36. The Petronius who authored the *Satyricon* is possibly/probably identical with the Petronius who was a politician, courtier and 'arbiter of elegance' in Nero's court, although some uncertainty about this persists (see Harrison, 'Petronius Arbiter'). For the scholarship on *Gatsby* and Petronius see Chapter 2, note 15.
37. For analysis of the title of the Latin work, and of its possible relation to the Latin word *satura* (medley), to 'satyr' and to 'satire', see Heseltine xii, xxxvi; also Harrison, 'Petronius Arbiter'.
38. See for example Homer, *Odyssey* I.178 for the phrase 'wine-dark sea'. It is quoted by Buck Mulligan in *Ulysses* (3), and alluded to by Cather (see p. 25).
39. Briggs, 'Petronius' 226–35.

40. For invocation or reworking of Keats's 'To a Nightingale' see *Gatsby* 16, 74. On the pastoral mode in *Gatsby* see Giltrow and Stouck; Kuhnle.
41. See also discussion of Marlowe's use of the myrtle plant, discussed in note 54 here.
42. Briggs notes that no copy of the *Satyricon* is in Fitzgerald's personal library ('Petronius' 229, n. 13).
43. Briggs, 'Petronius' 227–9.
44. The account of Trimalchio's feast runs from sections 29 to 79 of the *Satyricon*.
45. In *Gatsby*, the truly debauched Dan Cody in fact has more in common with Trimalchio than Gatsby does.
46. Perkins's letter is dated 18 November 1924. Parenthetical references to *Trimalchio: An Early Version* (ed. West) will be cited '*Trimalchio: E.V.*'; references to *Trimalchio: A Facsimile Edition* (ed. Bruccoli) will be cited '*Trimalchio: F.E.*'. In their accompanying editorial discussions, West and Bruccoli both usefully illuminate the key revisions that distinguish *The Great Gatsby* from this draft.
47. See also Vance 114.
48. See Briggs, 'Petronius' 233 on the resonances of the rowing-boat imagery in *Georgics* I.199–203.
49. Slater argues the *Trimalchio* text is more Petronian than is *Gatsby*.
50. In Fitzgerald's story 'The Diamond as Big as the Ritz', the two young male protagonists attend the comically named 'St Midas's School' (*Flappers* 173). E. L. Doctorow continues the comparison between Morgan, Midas and Roman wealth in his 1975 novel, *Ragtime* (see Roynon, 'Ovid, Race').
51. I discuss this tradition (exemplified by D. W. Griffith's 1915 film, *Birth of a Nation*) in relation to Cather, Faulkner, Ellison and Morrison in Chapters 1, 3, 4 and 5.
52. On Stoddard's work in relation to Tom Buchanan's views see Michaels 23–5; also Bender.
53. See Losemann 230ff in the deployment of Rome's hybridity in later Nazi thought.
54. Christopher Marlowe's pastoral lyric 'The Passionate Shepherd to his Love', written in the late sixteenth century, thereby becomes an ironic subtext to Tom and Myrtle's affair. Marlowe's shepherd promises to make for his lover 'A cap of flowers and a kirtle / Embroidered all with leaves of myrtle' (109–10).
55. Kuhnle's essay on the pastoral in this text illuminates that mode's deployment to different ends: he argues that in its association with Nick's less compromised Midwest, pastoralism is invoked as a critique that advocates social justice.

56. My discussion is based on the 1934 text of *Tender Is the Night*, following standard practice. On the publication history of the novel, and the now largely discounted 1951 version, see West's account in Fitzgerald, *Tender* xx–xxxvi.
57. Roulston, 'Dick Diver's Plunge' 86–7; Ricciardi 35–43.
58. See Ricciardi 39.
59. See P. McGowan on Keats in this novel.
60. Exceptions to this include Fitzgerald's references to *Ulysses* that I discuss, and those to the handful of authors that are documented and explained by West in his notes (see *Tender* 361–90).
61. The Pont du Gard was built in 19 BCE, and the amphitheatre in the first century CE under Augustus. Both are UNESCO World Heritage sites. Compare Cather's strikingly different response to Arles and the Roman sites throughout this region (see p. 22).
62. Although Fitzgerald does not explicitly mention it, this town is itself famous as the site of the Roman Trophy of Augustus (a monument to his victory over the villages of the Alps).
63. In describing Nicole and Dick's early relationship, Fitzgerald uses classically resonant plants to symbolise total devotion: 'Nicole brought everything to his feet, gifts of sacrificial ambrosia, of worshipping myrtle' (158).
64. See Ovid, *Met.* III.155–252. Nicole's later bad episode in Paris (into which Rosemary intrudes) also takes place in a bathroom.
65. See Morrison's *Playing in the Dark* for her exposition of the surrogate uses to which black characters are put in American literature by white authors.
66. Eliot wrote the last section of the poem, which includes the line 'These fragments I have shored against my ruins', while living (and recovering from psychiatric collapse) in Lausanne (*Waste Land* l. 430).
67. See Bruccoli, *Epic* 211; Ricciardi 38.
68. On the 'Roman' films that were most popular during these years see chapter 7 of Malamud, *Ancient*, especially 187. Fitzgerald himself worked in Hollywood in 1927 and in 1931–2 (for MGM).
69. For examples of generalisations about women see *Tender* 69 or 325–6; also, women who don't understand the vulnerability of men's pride are therein referred to as 'emergent Amazons' (203). For different views on Fitzgerald's representation of women see Stern 109–16; Sanderson.
70. As West explains in his editorial notes, the Harvard Classics collection was compiled by Charles W. Eliot and published by P. F. Collier and Son in 1910 (*Tender* 388). The fifty-one-volume set includes both ancient and modern European classics; for the titles see <https://www.gutenberg.org/wiki/Harvard_Classics_(Bookshelf)> (last accessed 6 May 2020). See also my introduction here.

Further Reading

Briggs, Ward. 'Petronius and Virgil in *The Great Gatsby*'. *International Journal of the Classical Tradition* 6.2 (1999): 226–35.

Kuehl, John. 'Scott Fitzgerald's Reading'. *Princeton University Library Chronicle* 22.2 (1961): 58–90.

Malamud, Margaret. 'Screening Rome During the Great Depression'. *Ancient Rome and Modern America*. Malden, MA: Wiley-Blackwell, 2009. 186–207.

Ricciardi, Caterina. 'F. Scott Fitzgerald and Rome'. *RSA Journal* 10 (1999): 29–46.

Turnbull, Andrew, ed. *The Letters of F. Scott Fitzgerald*. London: Bodley Head, 1964. 3–104 (letters to Scottie).

CHAPTER 3

William Faulkner (1897–1962)

Faulkner and the Classics

In the crib to *The Sound and the Fury* (1929) that William Faulkner published in 1945 (known as 'the Compson Appendix'), the novelist tells us that Quentin Compson's father used to sit 'all day long' in his law office, 'with a decanter of whiskey and a litter of dogeared Horaces and Livys and Catulluses' (*Sound* 207). An engagement with classical antiquity is an unmissable feature of the entire Faulknerian oeuvre, from his earliest poetry collection *The Marble Faun* (1924) up to and including his last novel *The Reivers* (1962).[1] Yet classicism in Faulkner's work has too often dazzled critics, who, perhaps blinded by its ubiquity and its resonances with the classicism inherent in certain constructions of 'Southern' culture as a whole, sometimes overlook its complex and always-shifting ideological effects. The bewildering convolutions and intensity of Faulknerian plots and syntax should not beguile us into simply acknowledging the presence of a Caesar or a Clytemnestra or a Cerberus, or into dutifully documenting the invocation of Ovid or Josephus or Thucydides. As this chapter shows, a close and undeferential attention to the aesthetic and political processes at work in these allusions yields rich rewards.[2]

In his introduction to the 1946 compendium, *The Portable Faulkner*, editor Malcolm Cowley stresses the significance of Faulkner's autodidacticism. 'He had less of a formal education than any other good writer of his time,' Cowley writes, and 'he traveled less than any of his writing contemporaries' (2). Although the Harvard-educated, New York-based editor is invested here in the construction of Faulkner as a kind of autochthonous genius springing from the soil of the Deep South, it is certainly noteworthy that the novelist dropped out of high school in 1915, without completing the eleventh grade.[3] His only taste of higher education was taking a few classes (in English, French and Spanish) as a special student at the University of Mississippi in his home town, Oxford, in 1919–20. In terms of the seven authors that are the focus of this book, Faulkner's level of formal educational attainment is certainly the lowest, and he without doubt travelled less in Europe than did either Cather or Fitzgerald. As all his biographers note, however, from an early age he was an avid reader who relished his grandparents' library (Blotner, *Biography* 93).[4] His brother Murry notes of their childhood that it was 'Mother who gave us our love for literature' and mentions her encouraging them to read Defoe and Twain alongside 'Kipling, Poe, Conrad, Shakespeare, Balzac, Hugo, Voltaire, Fielding and many others' when they were very young (Falkner 17). Joseph Blotner corroborates this memory, noting that William's mother, Maud, herself read 'Plato and Aristotle', and that his paternal grandmother was an active member of the 'Women's Book Club' (*Biography* 110, 101). Reflecting in adulthood on his early teenage years, Faulkner himself claimed to have enjoyed browsing in the books of Roman law belonging to his recently qualified Uncle John.[5]

Faulkner never formally studied either Latin or Greek. The individual who was his primary intellectual influence during his formative years, however – his friend, mentor and fellow Oxford, Mississippian Philip Stone – had acquired a high level of expertise (at 'Ole Miss' and Yale) in both of these, as well as in French and German.[6] According to Blotner, during the summer of 1914 when the friendship between the two young men blossomed, the literature that Stone lent to Faulkner from his own family's vast library included Socrates, Plato, 'and volumes by Roman philosophers, dramatists and poets' (*Biography* 169). Faulkner 'liked to hear his friend recite Greek poetry' (Stone had studied seven years of Greek), including lines from Sophocles's *Oedipus Rex* (169). Significantly, Stone also introduced William to the work of Keats, of Swinburne and of Housman; just like Cather and Fitzgerald, Faulkner loved all of this classically allusive English poetry. And in 1916 Faulkner gained another friend who shared his passion for literature: Ben Wasson, who was an undergraduate at the university and whose memoir, *Count No 'Count* (1983), recalls William's enthusiasm for Verlaine, Rimbaud and Wilde, as well as Coleridge and Milton.[7] Meanwhile, when staying with Stone at Yale in 1918, Faulkner befriended Stephen Benét, a precocious student who had already published a series of his own classically allusive poems

(Blotner, *Biography* 205). William was also acquainted at this time with an older Oxford author, Stark Young, who was now a professor at Amherst College and was to become known for plays such as his 1924 work, *The Colonnade*.

Young's *The Colonnade*, which follows the fortunes of the genteel Dandridge family, is informative here because it serves as a reminder of the classically dependent nature of traditional Southern culture as a whole. Its set includes the highly symbolic and much-referenced Roman architectural style of the family home (including the eponymous colonnade); its cast includes the classically named Dandridge ancestors such as 'Leonidas' (Young 40); and it is replete with references to fauns, to Lucretius and so on. The intense friendship between Faulkner and Stone, which peaked during 1914–15, was characterised by a similar tendency to connect antiquity with the modern and the contemporaneous: the pair talked of 'aesthetics, the Greeks, the Civil War, and Mississippi politics' (Snell 82). Their habit of drawing such analogies was widespread in the environment in which they were raised, and to recognise this context is to see the extent to which Faulkner, with his texts strewn with classically named characters, allusions to myth and neoclassical architectural backdrops, is representative of, rather than exceptional within, the literary and cultural production of this time and place. To recap from my introduction, there was a sustained, strategic identification with ancient Greece and Rome on the part of the slaveholding South, a strategic recourse to antiquity in pro-slavery arguments, and a deployment of mythic, epic and tragic conventions in the discourse of the Confederate cause during the Civil War and its aftermath.[8] While Willa Cather in *Sapphira and the Slave Girl* invokes this worldview, recalling the Virginia of her early childhood, Faulkner grew up and made his long-term adult residence in a world that reflected this ideology: witness the columned and porticoed style of nearby plantations and of the Stones' family home; and the distinctive neoclassicism of many buildings on the University of Mississippi campus, or of the Lafayette County Courthouse in Oxford's main square.[9]

Faulkner's own home from 1930 onwards, Rowan Oak, was itself a classic antebellum mansion built in 1844; his naming it 'Rowan Oak' after a Scottish myth he had been reading about in Frazer's *The Golden Bough* indicates his own predisposition to mythologising (Blotner, *Biography* 651, 661).[10] From the style of

Confederate memorial statuary to the first names of people encountered daily (William and Estelle Faulkner's first cook was called Narcissus, for example), a motivated engagement with antiquity was self-evident in the culture in which Faulkner lived and wrote. He came of age in a world that revered *Birth of a Nation* and which gave rise to the Southern Agrarians' *I'll Take My Stand* (1930). Perhaps, therefore, one of the most striking aspects of Faulkner's classicism is not his depiction of white traditionalists such as the Latin-literature-loving Mr Compson or a myth-obsessed Reverend Hightower, but rather the way he deploys classical tradition to explore the experiences of black or mixed-race characters such as Charles Bon or Lucas Beauchamp. In such moments it is arguable that he writes very much against the dominant local grain.

During his year of classes at the University of Mississippi and his brief periods working in a New York City bookstore (in 1921) and as Oxford's postmaster (1921–3), Faulkner published a number of individual poems which were unambiguously classical in their frames of reference: most famously 'L'Apres-Midi d'un Faune' in the *New Republic*, but also 'Sapphics' and 'Naiads' Song' in the university's *The Mississippian*.[11] His verse of this period was indebted to Conrad Aiken, whom he greatly admired and read with Stone and Wasson, as well as to Pound's imagism and Eliot's 'Prufrock'.[12] He continued to read and admire American authors who themselves engaged with antiquity, such as Dreiser, Cather and Eugene O'Neill.[13] His own verse-play, *Marionettes*, written in 1920, testifies to the influence of Ernest Dowson, Walter Pater, Oscar Wilde and the Decadent art of Aubrey Beardsley (Blotner, *Biography* 295). It shares its title with the theatre group to which Faulkner belonged at the university, and shares its thematic conception with Helen Haiman Joseph's *Book of Marionettes* (1920), which maps out the history of the marionette art form 'from its beginning in ancient Greek and Oriental cultures' up to the present (Blotner, *Biography* 284). The idea of ancient Greece as a fruitful source or origin was becoming something of a theme for Faulkner himself, who in his review of Aiken's 1916 work, *Turns and Moves*, praised that poet's style for 'completing a cycle back to the Ancient Greeks again' (Blotner, *Biography* 301).

As Blotner has documented, Phil Stone's own purchases at his favourite New Haven bookshop during the early 1920s – at least some of which would have found their way to Faulkner – include translations of Euripides, Plato and Sophocles, as well as Appian, Catullus and Horace. One transformative gift from Stone, in 1924, which Faulkner certainly read, was a copy of the fourth printing of *Ulysses*.[14] Bowled over by Joyce, during his travels in Italy and his two-month stay in Paris in 1925 he began composing and then working hard on a novel, entitled *Elmer*, that was heavily indebted to the Irish work. Although the book never saw publication, the architectural and artistic treasures of Milan and Paris that he encountered while working on it affected him profoundly. His letters to his mother in these months include his waxing lyrical about the carvings on Milan Cathedral, where among the Christian iconography there are 'beautiful naked Greek figures that have no significance whatsoever', and about seeing the *Winged Victory* and the *Venus de Milo* in the Louvre: the 'real ones' (Blotner, *Letters* 9, 13).[15] These letters express neither the boundless enthusiasm for Europe that is Cather's, nor Fitzgerald's perception of that continent's corruption and decay, but rather an admiring and empathetic identification with its history and aesthetics.

The extensiveness of Faulkner's personal library at Rowan Oak suggests that during the late 1920s and throughout the 1930s, when he wrote and published the key novels of his career, he was also intensively both buying and reading books. The Rowan Oak collection included, in addition to numerous American authors, a 1927 edition of Apuleius, Robert Graves's *Claudius* novels in editions of 1934 and 1935, Andrew Lang et al.'s 1935 translations of Homer, and a 1931 translation of Suetonius.[16] It's also notable, however, that many of the classical or classically focused volumes in this library post-date Faulkner's major productive years: for example, his edition of Euripides is dated 1958, of Virgil is dated 1956; his copy of Gibbon's *Decline and Fall of the Roman Empire* is published in 1947, and his Herodotus in 1942. As Joan Serafin catalogues, some of Faulkner's in-text allusions of the late 1940s deploy an association between such classical texts, alcohol and dissipation, thereby suggesting the decaying and corrupt nature of the South: witness Mr Compson in the 'Compson Appendix', or the none-too-subtly-named Mr Backus in *Knight's Gambit* (1949), with his 'weak toddy and Ovid and Horace and Catullus' (Serafin 5). But during 1957–8, when Faulkner is writer-in-residence at the University of Virginia, he articulates in his lectures and speeches the converse, a sense of antiquity's enduring power. His trips to Rome (in 1954 and

1955) and to Athens (in March 1957), together with an impulse to position his public, literary self as analogous to classical authors, perhaps account for this quasi 'restoration of faith' in classicism.[17]

It is interesting to compare Faulkner's deployment of Greece, in his talks at the University of Virginia, before and after his travel to Athens. Before the visit, he references Greek tragedy with reference to 'The Bear' (1942) and *Absalom, Absalom!* (1936).[18] He discusses free will in relation to 'a Greek background of fate', and muses that the 'old simple clear Hellenic tradition' may be 'obsolete' or 'may come back, if life goes in cycles' (Gwynn and Blotner 38, 42). After his trip to Athens, speaking in May 1957, he mentions having seen 'the Hellenic light' and 'Homer's wine-dark sea'; that he was struck by a sudden view of Parnassus; that he sensed the presence of the gods, and that 'the people seem to function against that past that for all its remoteness in time was still inherent in the light' (Gwynn and Blotner 129–30). Three weeks later, the enduring impact of his Athenian sojourn was evident when he gave a much-quoted explanation for the title of *Light in August* (1932): in Mississippi in August, Faulkner declared, 'there's a luminous quality to the light, as though it came not from just today but from back in the old classic times. It might have fauns and satyrs and the gods . . . from Greece, from Olympus in it somewhere' (Gwynn and Blotner 199). Critics tend not to emphasise the retrospective nature of this framing, the fact that this was twenty-five years after the novel's publication and in the wake of a trip to Athens. But it is arguable that Faulkner's sense of an analogy between the South and classical antiquity, and between his own work and classical literature, did not diminish but became ever stronger as his life progressed.

The Critical Field and Scholarly Debate

There is more published commentary on Faulkner than on any other anglophone writer besides Shakespeare.[19] Unsurprisingly, therefore, there are more published analyses on his engagement with the classical tradition than on that of any of the other six authors discussed in this book. In a rough estimate, there are around eight books and at least thirty scholarly articles or book chapters on the subjects of classical myth, tragedy and other engagements with antiquity in the Faulknerian oeuvre.[20] Carvel Collins's 1957 article on *The Sound and the Fury* and *As I Lay Dying* paved the way for numerous subsequent studies of Faulkner's allusiveness by identifying the source of the later novel's title as lines spoken by Agamemnon in a specific translation of the *Odyssey*, while Cleanth Brooks was probably the first to discuss the centrality of 'the problem of tragedy' in *Absalom, Absalom!*.[21] Yet despite the extensiveness of published analyses of Faulkner's classicism – a field in its own right with a particular flowering in the late 1950s to early 1970s – there is a great deal of scholarship in this area still to be done. This is a subject ripe for revisiting, with the caveat that contemporary readings might usefully focus on classical engagements not as an end in themselves, as the older scholarship preoccupied with the so-called 'mythical method' has tended to do, but as significant dimensions within the newer politicised interpretations, such as feminist, race studies, global and postcolonial approaches.

In 1983, Joan Serafin published the useful and exhaustive study based on her 1968 PhD thesis, *Faulkner's Uses of the Classics*. Rigorously categorising the novelist's allusive methods into sections such as 'Rhetoric', 'Imagery', 'Symbols' and 'Mythology', it includes a meticulous catalogue, over 150 pages long, of references in all the novels, in the poetry and in a range of interviews. While not literary criticism in the conventional sense, the book is an invaluable resource to anyone interested in Faulknerian classicism. In her introductory essay, meanwhile, Serafin makes claims for the effects of Faulkner's allusiveness as a whole that typify the 1950s–1960s scholarship on this subject:

> In Faulkner's view the South's condition was partly analogous to the disintegration of the ancient classical world, which, like the South after the Civil War, left behind only remnants of cultural luxury and, consequently, tattered, floundering spirits. Such a view afforded his fiction epic dimensions, for he depicted a 'doomed' and 'accursed' people who continued to cling to a lingering, anachronistic cultural structure and mentality. (2)

As do his use of regional and biblical materials, Serafin continues, 'the classical allusions contribute to an overall rhetorical and structural pattern' (2).

The detection (correct but perhaps self-limiting) of this novelist's construction of analogy between his heroes and the classical heroic tradition, or between the downfall of the Old South and the downfall both of individuals and of great houses/families in Greek tragedy, informs many of the key works documented by Robert Hamblin in his survey, 'Mythic and Archetypal Criticism'. Constituting the first chapter of his and Charles Peek's *Companion to Faulkner Studies* (2004), Hamblin's overview identifies Walter Brylowski's *Faulkner's Olympian Laugh: Myth in the Novels* (1968), Richard Adams's *Faulkner: Myth and Motion* (1968) and Lynn Gartrell Levins's *Faulkner's Heroic Design* (1976) as exemplary of the 'mythical method' approach to Faulkner. These studies are influenced by Freud and Jung, by the anthropological theories of the Cambridge Ritualists, and of course by Eliot's famous 1923 essay, '*Ulysses*, Order, and Myth', on the 'mythical method' in Joyce (165). While Brylowski works out intricate systems of mythical 'levels' in the Faulknerian oeuvre, he, Levins and Adams all position classical mythological references alongside those from the Bible, Buddhism, medieval romance, Gothicism and so on. Though Hamblin does not mention John Lewis Longley's *The Tragic Mask* (1963), this critical predecessor shares with the later studies an endorsement of Faulkner's own investment in the 'heroic' as an end in itself, and in his creation of a mythology of Yoknapatawpha that is analogous to the mythology of the classical past.

There are clear limitations both to the approaches of Longley, Brylowski et al. and to Hamblin's decision to compartmentalise all readings of Faulkner's classical allusiveness within a single 'mythical and archetypal' school. Hamblin thereby implicitly suggests that all studies of this novelist's classicism have commonalities sufficient to constitute, together, a parallel to the categories of 'historical', 'formalist', 'biographical', 'feminist and gender' and 'postmodern' which define the subsequent chapters in this *Companion*. As Eliot's theory about Joyce's use of myth to order history in *Ulysses* has long been viewed as an oversimplification, however, to apply the same theory to Faulkner's classical allusiveness inevitably also approaches oversimplification. Moreover, each of these authors (along with Hamblin himself) gives uncritical credence to Faulkner's own statements, in interviews and elsewhere, both about his sense of an analogy between the South and antiquity, and about his sense of myth's relationship to the 'universal'.

Faulkner's words on these subjects are fascinating and important, but they are not an unproblematic key to his fiction. Hamblin quotes Faulkner's observation at the University of Virginia in 1957, for example, that 'the verities that these people [in his novels] suffer are universal verities' (Hamblin 6). While the ideal of universal human experience and shared humanity is of course the basis of emancipatory theory and human rights (and Faulkner himself here goes on to mention both his black and his white characters), politicised literary studies have taught us to be aware of the New Critical concept of a purported universalism. Indeed, the 'myth and symbol school' that defined the first (or 'old') 'American studies' itself, as it emerged in the 1950s, and which has played a formative role in these mythical/archetypal readings of Faulkner's classicism, has long been problematised for its falsely oversimplifying impulses, its erasure of specificity and diversity, and its appeal to a fabricated 'universalism' that in fact privileges white male subjecthood.[22]

To conceive of Faulkner's engagement with antiquity exclusively in terms of a 'mythical/archetypal' preoccupation is to contribute to a dangerously tight web of 'myth and symbol' connections, Faulkner's own constructions of his classicism, and a critical predilection for deploying classical references and analogies within scholarly discourse itself. This widespread critical practice is exemplified by contemporaneous reviewers of the novels such as Lyle Saxon, who said of *The Sound and the Fury* on its publication that it was 'worthy of the attention of a Euripides' (Blotner, *Biography* 632), or Julia Baker, who in 1931 likened the world of *Sanctuary* to the world of the same Athenian dramatist (Blotner, *Biography* 686). There is a reciprocity here, a mutually reinforcing and endlessly reiterable perspective common to author, reviewers and scholars that reduces the complexity and conceals the instability of Faulkner's work. Moreover, in its assumption (a prerequisite of most 'analogical' reading) about a stable, fixed classical world in which myths and history have objective meaning and unitary interpretation, it falsifies the contested and always-changing nature of antiquity itself.

As Hamblin notes, Donald Kartiganer's reading of the novelist in *The Fragile Thread* (1979) is a persuasive critique of 'mythical method' analyses of Faulkner in that it stresses the incompatibility of that approach with Faulkner's modernism (Hamblin 8–9). In Kartiganer's view, *Light in August* and *Absalom, Absalom!* constitute 'a sense of the novel still going on, its author still fumbling through the fragments of character and event'; they embody not a system or a worldview but an author always aiming 'to attend to their fragments' (xvii); and are in a state of 'constant becoming' (xviii). The observation about 'constant becoming' applies equally well to antiquity itself, in that scholarly discoveries about and reframings of classical culture's inevitable fragmentedness and constructedness keep it in a permanent state of evolution. While Kartiganer's emphasis on the 'self-deconstructing' readings within Faulkner's texts could potentially lead to postmodern *aporia* (xvii), however, my intention is that reading Faulkner's classicism in light of new currents in classical scholarship (such as 'black classicism') can bring to it a new political specificity.

Kartiganer's challenge to the mythical/archetypal readings may have enabled two sophisticated studies of Faulknerian classicism that appeared in the late 1980s: Warwick Wadlington's *Reading Faulknerian Tragedy* (1987) and Dinnah Pladott's article of 1985, 'The Tragic Enigma'. Other than Susan Donaldson's brief reassessment of Faulknerian pastoralism in 2007, however, there have been regrettably few attempts to analyse Faulkner's classicism within or as a feature of specific political perspectives.[23] In my own readings that follow here – of *Light in August*, *Absalom, Absalom!* and *Go Down, Moses* (specifically 'The Fire and the Hearth') – I analyse these texts' diverse classical allusiveness as a strategy, as a resource on which ideologically complex representations depend.

My discussions of *Light in August* and *Absalom, Absalom!* include exploration of the novelist's allusions to Ovid's *Metamorphoses*, and thereby reveal a new direction in the analysis of the classicism within these two texts. While there is no copy of the Latin poem in Faulkner's library, prior critics have attributed many of his allusions in *Soldier's Pay* (1925) and in *The Hamlet* (1940), in particular, to this Roman poem.[24] But, as is the case with nearly all of the seven authors who are the central focus of this book, Ovid's profoundly significant presence in Faulkner's major works has been insufficiently discussed until now.

Light in August (1932)

Joe Christmas 'didn't know what he was . . . and that to me was the tragic, central idea of the story,' observed Faulkner at the University of Virginia in 1957 (Gwynn and Blotner 72). The Reverend Gail Hightower's 'waking and sleeping life', as the novelist writes towards the end of the text itself, was haunted by 'phantoms who loomed heroic and tremendous against a background of thunder and smoke and torn flags' (*Light* 469). Critical discussion of the classical tradition in *Light in August* tends to invoke these two quotations, together with Faulkner's claim that the titular 'light' recalls that of 'the old classic times', complete with 'fauns and satyrs and the gods . . . from Greece' (Gwynn and Blotner 199).[25] In order to get beyond the significance of Joe Christmas and Hightower as doomed protagonists – the one whose actions are inevitably catastrophic, and the other who is trapped in a mythologised past – it is useful to focus less on Faulkner's deployment of tragedy and myth, and more on his engagement with the related but distinct genre of epic. A range of epic and mock-epic conventions, both stylistic and thematic, contribute significantly to what Alexander Welsh has called the 'subtle, modernist redaction of traditional kinds of heroism' in this text (144).

John Lewis Longley's influential discussion (in *The Tragic Mask*) of Joe Christmas as a 'modern tragic protagonist' (195), one comparable with Oedipus who is at the same time a 'modern Everyman' (203), is politically problematic not just for its part in his wider claims about the 'universal echoes' of Faulknerian tragedy (173).[26] *Light in August* indubitably constitutes a dialogue with Greek tragedy, not least in its focus (resonant of Aeschylus) on 'old spilled blood and old horror and anger and fear' (47); on characters' 'fury' (206); through explicit deployment of a 'messenger' (323) or through Byron and Mrs Hines explaining events to Hightower in a comic 'strophe and antistrophe' (376). Yet Faulkner's depiction of a 'doomed and cursed' society (252) – peopled by doomed and cursed races and individuals trapped in a doomed and cursed history – might just as well be questioned as valorised.[27] The novelist's focus on 'fate' or on the 'infallibility' of the drastic actions of Joe Christmas or Percy Grimm, and his implication that the South's past, present and future are inevitably disastrous, erases the role of human agency in Southern history. The configuration of racism and racial conflict as predestined catastrophe, enacted on the South's 'tragic and inescapable earth' (*Light* 60), ultimately serves a reactionary agenda because it obscures human responsibility for a race-based slave economy and its consequences.[28] To acquiesce in this account of the country's racial crisis, as Longley implicitly does when he describes Joe Christmas as 'saddled with a terrible, inevitable curse' (194), is implicitly to endorse the moral and political escapism or denial that much of Faulkner's engagement with tragic conventions in this novel involves.

It may appear counter-intuitive to assert that epic informs an alternative, resistant construction of Southern history and individual experience in *Light in August*. In their concerns with the celebration of heroic individuals and powerful civilisations, epic poems such as the *Iliad* and the *Aeneid* do not immediately strike us for their emancipatory or resistant potential.[29] Indeed, while Faulkner exposes Hightower's entrapment in a constructed epic of the Southern past, the very representation of 'wild bugles and clashing sabres and the dying thunder of hooves' (493) may well seduce the reader into a nostalgia for (or at least an admiration for) bygone glory days. And 'Fate' often plays a powerful, ideologically invested role in many epics: as Toohey explains of the *Aeneid*, for example, Aeneas is 'motivated . . . by the demands made by a Fate (*fatum*) intent upon the establishment of the Roman empire' (126). Yet there are also certain conventions or preoccupations of classical epic – many of which eventually evolve into key features of the *Bildungsroman* – that make radical or counter-hegemonic readings of *Light in August* possible. While the *Iliad* and the *Odyssey* (in Toohey's account) 'chart the development of an outstanding individual to hard-won maturity' (45), and are concerned with 'a hero's response to crisis' (10), Faulkner depicts not one but a range of characters who are subjected to (and, to a varying degree, fail at) this trajectory. From its outset to its end the text signals its relationship to epic through deploying a range of the classical genre's formal aspects: the epic present tense (often used in battle scenes in the *Aeneid*, for example); the narration of events through individual characters' retelling of what they have seen, heard or personally undergone (a trademark of the *Odyssey*'s narrative technique); and a deployment of the extended or epic simile, occasionally in a formulaic way.[30] Crucially and perhaps paradoxically, it is the ubiquity of epic conventions in this novel – the fact that Faulkner does not reserve them for one privileged character or plotline only, but applies them almost indiscriminately – that therein underpins a conception of equality between human beings.

It is a critical commonplace to remark on the unconventional separateness of the Lena Grove plotline and the Joe Christmas plotline in this text.[31] Yet Faulkner implicitly connects them through the fact that their life experiences are both depicted in the Odyssean terms of a journey: Lena's quest to find Lucas Burch, 'alone and afoot' (16), resolves into 'just travelling' at the novel's close (506), while the defining metaphor used to describe Joe's trajectory is a 'street' (114, 223), with all its 'imperceptible corners of bitter defeat and bitter victories' (230). While classical epic tends to privilege one hero (his exceptionalism defining his heroism), Faulkner measures several of his characters by the standards of epic humanness, and indeed borrows a trope from the mock-epic epic, Ovid's *Metamorphoses*, to do so. At the end of the creation myth in Book I, Ovid defines man's distinction from other animals by his ability to walk on two limbs and to hold up his head: 'though all other animals are prone, and fix their gaze upon the earth, [the god] gave to man an uplifted face and bade him stand erect and turn his eyes to heaven' (*Met.* I.84–6).Throughout *Light in August*, Faulkner applies exactly these criteria of humanity-defining dignity to his central characters, frequently using the specific Ovidian emphasis on uprightness. For example, when Hightower sees the unheroic-looking Byron approaching his house on the Sunday night, the former minister muses on human walking, 'animals balanced on their hinder legs', as 'that cleverness of which the man animal is so fatuously proud' (76). When McEachern moves to beat the young Joe Christmas for not learning his catechism, on this day in which he '*became a man*' (146, original italics), the boy 'walked erect and in silence, his head up' (148). During Byron and Hightower's long conversations, first it is Hightower who is 'sitting a little more than erect' (300), while during the next night's talk Faulkner repeatedly, almost obsessively, uses the same word again of Byron's walk.[32] Rather than single out one exceptional character, therefore, Faulkner deploys the Ovidian definition of human dignity to assert parity among humans, to assert that (as Joanna Burden's grandfather preached) 'the Negro and Moses and the children of Israel were the same' (251).[33]

Hightower himself appears not to share Ovid's and Faulkner's conception that an upright gait signifies a species-defining achievement: he thinks that the 'unhorsed figure' of the walking Byron is 'puny' and, preoccupied as he is with Confederate cavalry, 'he thinks quietly how right the ancients were in making the horse an attribute and symbol of warriors and kings' (76). Faulkner deploys the classical conception of horses and skilled horsemen as noble and heroic – praised by Homer and depicted in the friezes on the Parthenon, as noted by Xenophon – to bestow on Joe Christmas not heroism but its absence.[34] When Joe rides and beats McEachern's horse to collapse and death in his pursuit of Bobbie, Faulkner compares the man and beast to 'an equestrian statue strayed from its pedestal' that has 'come to rest in an attitude of ultimate exhaustion' (210). Here the novelist invokes classical, Renaissance, neoclassical and American Civil War commemorative practice to mock his undignified protagonist. Ulrich Raulff's recent history of the horse (2018) testifies to the preponderance of the European tradition of 'equestrian monuments' that resonate ironically in Faulkner's image: from the 'cities of the Roman empire', to Bernini's sculpting of Louis XIV on horseback, and to Napoleon's predilection for being painted in the saddle (for example by David in 1800 (Raulff 235–6)). A more immediately obvious resonance and counterpoint, of course, are the Confederate equestrian statues in the American South, such as those of General Lee on his horse, the much-mythologised Traveller, which were erected in Charlottesville, Virginia, and on Monument Avenue in Richmond, in the same state.[35] Faulkner inverts this long heroic tradition to depict Joe Christmas's total abjection and debasement at this point, both horse and man frozen or 'carved' in their brokenness (*Light* 211).

According to Welsh, *Light in August* displays not so much an absence of heroism as 'the futility of the heroism that it would praise' (145). Perhaps one reason for the futility of individual heroism in the world of this novel is the influential and maleficent role of society (or the community) therein. In his essay 'The Closed Society and its Subjects', André Bleikasten rightly corrects Cleanth Brooks's depiction (in 'The Community and the Pariah' (1963)) of Joe, Hightower, Joanna and Byron as pariahs whose error is their separateness from society. As Bleikasten points out, Faulkner in fact depicts the community as pack-like adherents to a 'Southern ideology' that involves racism, sexism and Puritanism (91). Significant here is Faulkner's little-discussed deployment of classical models of 'rumour' in his depiction of destructive gossip that is the catalyst to violent group behaviour. While in the *Iliad* and the *Odyssey* 'rumour' is depicted as a messenger of Zeus,[36] in the Roman epics *fama* (rumour or report) is personified as a dastardly monster. In the fourth book of the *Aeneid*, for example, Fama (provoked by the love affair between Dido and Aeneas) is the 'swiftest of all evils', a winged and feathered beast, a 'foul goddess' that 'affrights great cities' (*Aeneid* IV.174–97).[37] Faulkner's extended personifications of gossip or rumour punctuate the novel, and appear to be particularly indebted to Ovid's depiction of Rumour and her always-open house in the *Metamorphoses*:

> The whole place resounds with confused noises, repeats all words and doubles what it hears. . . . And yet there is no loud clamour, but only the subdued murmur of voices, like the murmur of the waves of the sea if you listen afar off . . . Crowds fill the hall, shifting throngs come and go, and everywhere wander thousands of rumours, falsehoods mingled with the truth, and everywhere confused reports flit about . . . (*Met.* XII.47–55)

During the sleepless night in which he contemplates murdering Joanna Burden, Joe hears 'voices, murmurs, whispers', and in the black neighbourhood of Freedman Town he feels enclosed by 'bodiless voices murmuring, talking, laughing' (*Light* 105, 114). In Mottstown, some time later, Christmas's name 'flew up and down the street, and the boys and men . . . began to run' (334); in Jefferson, meanwhile, as the idea of lynching gains momentum, 'the talk' is an animate force that 'clotted', along with groups of people, in front of the jail (339).[38] In an extended simile here, 'talk' is 'like a wind or fire' in its 'dying and borning again' (340), recalling the way rumour about Hightower's wife is 'blown from mind to mind' at the beginning of the novel (71). These descriptions also bring to mind the Homeric Aeolus, god of winds, whom Joyce engages to symbolise the compromised language of 'news' in *Ulysses*.[39] As the mob mentality intensifies, Faulkner again presents rumour as an independent force – 'the voices came and went, in quiet question and answer' (458) – until by the end of the novel we are almost too familiar with the phenomenon that Hightower describes as 'rumour with a thousand faces' (484). While the novelist may ultimately overplay this classical analogy, however, recognising its role in his critique of Southern culture and ideology is key to understanding the 'protesting' or resistant aspects of the text.

One further possible debt to Ovid's *Metamorphoses* supports the reading of the novel as an emancipatory text, and so strengthens the idea that epic can play a subversive role therein. Both Faulkner's much-discussed tendency to arrest time through images of the statuesque or carving, and his interest in flux and permeable boundaries (for example in the much-quoted passage about the 'spaces of light and dark' that had 'long lost their orderliness' (*Light* 333–4)), are indebted to Ovid's poem.[40] They recall the many moments in the Roman epic in which humans transform into fixed and inanimate objects, or when the poet discusses and depicts fluidity and shifting parameters. While there is not space here to explore that rich topic in any detail, to acknowledge it is to see the extent to which the classical presences, particularly those derived from epic, can work as oppositional forces in these texts. Some of antiquity's legacies inform the impulses in *Light in August* that are reactionary and elegiac, those which lament (for example through the tobacco-stained 'stone columns' of the porticoed courthouse (415)) a lost age of heroism and justice. Other classical legacies here, however, are those in which the capacity for radical change is key, and which therefore enable subversive readings of the text.

Absalom, Absalom! (1936)

When imagining Sutpen's improper proposition to Rosa Coldfield, Shreve suggests that in place of being 'a widowed Agamemnon to her Cassandra', Sutpen behaves as 'an ancient stiff-jointed Pyramus to her eager though untried Thisbe' (*Absalom* 144). The simultaneous arbitrariness and absurd inappropriateness of the Ovidian analogy here undercuts the grandiosity of Mr Compson's earlier claim: that although Sutpen had named Clytie 'Clytemnestra', in reference to his 'own ironic fecundity of dragon's teeth', Compson himself 'had always liked to believe that he intended to name her Cassandra' (48). These quotations epitomise not only the ubiquitous and unmissable allusiveness of Faulkner's ninth novel, but also the more significant point that each allusion is the specific construction of the specific narrator that utters it. To analyse patterns within a single narrator's classical allusiveness, therefore – as I do here with reference to Mr Compson's representation of Ellen and Judith, and to Shreve's representation of Eulalia, Charles Bon and their Haitian provenance – is to reveal the specific narratorial motivations and ideologies that shape each speaker's version of events.

Despite Faulkner's emphasis in this text on the total unreliability of his four narrators (Rosa, Quentin, Mr Compson and Shreve), the extensive scholarship on *Absalom, Absalom!*'s engagement with antiquity has focused more on the existence of allusions than on their invested constructedness, or, in other words, than on the implications of who alludes to what and why. This is particularly the case in most discussions of the novel's relationship with Greek tragedy – a critical tendency perhaps rooted in the paradigmatic nature of Sutpen's rise, hubris-induced errors in the pursuit of his 'design', and subsequent downfall. In addition, the sheer number of direct classical invocations in this text (running to seven pages in Serafin's catalogue (22–31)) constitute an allusiveness that has an initial obviousness about it that obscures its instability and complexity. It is certainly easy enough to be merely impressed by Faulkner's relentless roll call of Greek and Roman names, ranging from 'Cerberus' and 'Choris' to 'Juno' and 'Penelope', and by the reiteration (from earlier novels) of the 'mask in Greek tragedy' (49), of the 'strophe and antistrophe' (24), of 'fury' (31), 'fate' (57) and 'doom' (61).

Ilse Dusoir Lind exemplifies this reverential or endorsing consensus in her 1955 article, in which she proclaims that 'events of modern history, here viewed as classic tragedy, are elevated through conscious artistry to the status of a new myth' (887). Even though she rightly points out that 'the heroic enlargement . . . and the aura of relentless doom are endowed by the narrators who create it' (891), she herself arguably reinforces this 'heroic enlargement' through listing many of the novel's classical references and its 'atmosphere of doom' to support her often-repeated claims about the text's 'grand tragic vision' (888–90, 887). Meanwhile, Longley sums up Sutpen's story as 'the tragedy of aspiration' (206), in which the protagonist's 'downfall is symbolic of the downfall of [Southern] culture' (217). Even Brooks, who rightly points out that 'Sutpen is an imaginative construct, a set of inferences—a hypothesis put forward to account for several peculiar events' ('History' 31), takes this character's 'tragedy' to be a given, one caused by an 'innocence' comparable to that of 'Sophocles's Oedipus' ('History' 18–19).[41]

Critics to date have paid insufficient attention to the fact that, at the novel's outset, both Quentin's and Rosa's reimagining of events are informed as much by Ovid's *Metamorphoses* as by Greek tragedy.[42] For example, Quentin imagines Ellen as a 'Niobe without tears' (8). Given that (unlike the Ovidian prototype) Ellen dies before any of her children do, we find Faulkner already signalling an inaptness of analogy which is to be repeated in many of Mr Compson's and Shreve's allusions. (By contrast it is Rosa whose allusions are often apt: in describing Judith's hysterical reaction to the 'phaeton' carriage (17), for example, she powerfully expresses the girl's anxiety about her father through the implicit resonances of Ovid's tale of Phaethon.[43]) This is of course ironic, since of the four narrators Rosa is allowed to say the least, and she is also in all probability the one least well-versed in Classics. Indeed, if we are to believe the 'Compson Appendix' to *The Sound and the Fury*, a lack of familiarity with antiquity is not one of Mr Compson's deficiencies: as mentioned above, he memorably sits in his office 'all day long with a decanter of whiskey and a litter of dogeared Horaces and Livys and Catulluses' (*Sound* 207).

Mr Compson punctuates his narration to Quentin (which takes up most of the first half of the novel) with nearly all of the comparisons between Sutpen's life story and Greek tragedy and/or myth that have captured scholarly attention to date. But equally important is the obsessive way he represents Ellen in particular (and Judith on occasion) in terms that invoke both Ovid's *Metamorphoses* and the 'Cupid and Psyche' story from a later Roman text, the novel *The Golden Ass* (also itself known as *Metamorphoses*), by Apuleius.[44] Somewhat surprisingly, Mr Compson at times exhibits an awareness of the restrictedness of Southern womanhood, and even to some extent critiques the way that Sutpen, Henry and Charles Bon constrain and reduce the lives of Ellen and Judith. Yet the classical allusiveness of his narrative, which insists on their constant tearfulness and obsessively compares them to butterflies, is itself both confining and diminishing of these women's agency and stature.[45]

In the third and fourth chapters of *Absalom, Absalom!*, which constitute nearly all of Mr Compson's account, this narrator describes the violent transformations undergone by the South and Southern families – the Coldfields and Sutpens in particular – during the Civil War and its aftermath. In so doing, he engages deeply (though never explicitly) with the doctrines of Pythagoras as set out in Book XV of Ovid's *Metamorphoses*. In often-cited lines, Ovid 'quotes' at length Pythagoras's words on the inevitability and ubiquity of change: 'there is nothing in all the world that keeps its form. All things are in a state of flux, and everything is brought into being with a changing nature. Time itself flies on in constant motion, just like a river' (*Met.* XV.177–80).[46] Mr Compson's recounting of how, on the outbreak of war, Ellen's father 'seemed to change overnight' (64); of Henry's earlier 'transference, metamorphosis, into the body which was to become his sister's lover' (83); and of the 'fluid' physical changes undergone by Judith in adolescence and Sutpen when gaining weight (53, 63) all bring this section of Ovid's *Metamorphoses* to mind.[47] Faulkner signals the Roman source of his allusions through Mr Compson's claim that 'Ellen went through a complete metamorphosis, emerging into her next lustrum with the complete finality of actual re-birth' (50).[48] While Pythagoras (according to Ovid) cites the butterfly as one of numerous examples of constant and inevitable change in nature – 'worms that weave their white cocoons on the leaves of trees . . . change into funereal butterflies' (*Met.* XV.372–4) – Mr Compson compares Ellen to a butterfly at least six times over the two chapters, and does so in increasingly grandiose and extended terms.[49] Ironically, although Mr Compson comments wryly on the ideology of Southern womanhood, 'an untroubled code in which females were ladies or whores' (91), and on Charles Bon's and Henry's reprehensible reduction of Judith to 'just the blank shape, the empty vessel' on to which they projected their own agenda (94), his own relentless casting of Ellen as a butterfly serves only to erase her individuality and her selfhood.

The other striking feature of Mr Compson's descriptions of Ellen in these chapters is a concurrent preoccupation with her 'weeping' and being 'in tears' (34). While this crying purportedly begins at her wedding, this narrator mentions her 'tears' and 'intermittent weeping' at least once on every single one of the remaining nine pages of that chapter, one that ends (of course) with the fact that she is 'weeping again now' (37–45; 45). This representation of a figure constantly crying recalls Ovid's Niobe again, and interestingly contradicts Quentin's assertion that Ellen was 'Niobe *without* tears' (8, my emphasis). Yet a weeping bride and wife, especially combined with butterfly imagery, also brings to mind Apuleius's 'Cupid and Psyche' – the tale that is embedded within *The Golden Ass/Metamorphoses* about the often-weeping young woman, Psyche, and told to another weeping bride-to-be, Charite, who has just been abducted on her wedding day. While one meaning of the ancient Greek word 'psyche' is 'butterfly', Psyche herself cries with noticeable frequency throughout the course of her turbulent relationship with her sisters and with her lover and eventual husband, Cupid.[50] The shadowy presences of Apuleius's text in this section of Faulkner's novel make a significant contribution to its confused and confusing gender politics. Mr Compson's description of Ellen's bearing children 'in a shadowy miasmatic region something like the bitter purlieus of Styx' before rising 'like the swamp-hatched butterfly' (*Absalom* 54–5) recalls the final dangerous task that Venus forces the pregnant Psyche to perform in Apuleius's Book VI, which involves a journey across the Styx into Hades.[51] While Apuleius's story of Cupid and Psyche has been deployed and revised and reinterpreted by countless writers and artists over time, one feminist understanding of the tale reads Psyche as an icon of resilience and heroic action.[52] To tune into such connotations is to see that Mr Compson (unwittingly?) undercuts the simultaneous anti-feminist mythologising which is a recurring feature of his highly allusive account.

Turning now – as does the novel, after Rosa's italicised letter – to the account as it is taken up by Quentin and Shreve, it is evident that the classical allusiveness of Shreve, in particular, burdens the narrative with a whole further set of ideologies. Shreve, who presumably studies Classics as a significant part of his Harvard degree, imagines that the lawyer who persuades Charles Bon to attend the University of Mississippi does so on the grounds of 'the scholarship, the culture, the Latin and the Greek that would equip and polish him for the position which he would hold in life' (*Absalom* 248). This construction of Classics as a means to membership within the powerful establishment is one affirmed in Charles Bon by Compson's earlier comparison of this character arriving at Sutpen's Hundred as a sophisticated 'young Roman consul' among rural 'barbarian hordes' (74). Yet this is not Shreve's only conception of classicism. He and Quentin also configure Charles Bon as a Decadent, a pleasure-seeking 'sybarite' who lives a lifestyle inspired by Roman decadence akin to that of Oscar Wilde and his Dorian Gray (256), and whose grave the narrator imagines as 'a scene by the Irish poet, Wilde', when it is visited by the unnamed 'octoroon' and their son (157).[53] And in a third construction of classical tradition, Shreve includes in his imagining of events a number of details or allusions that harness moments of friction, oppression or resistance/subversion in Roman history, and that contribute importantly to disruptive, potentially radical discourses within the novel.

When the Canadian narrator resumes his telling at the start of chapter 7, he remarks to Quentin that 'the South is fine, isn't it. It's better than the theatre, isn't it. It's better than Ben Hur, isn't it' (*Absalom* 176).[54] While *Ben-Hur* (Lew Wallace's 1880 novel and the play and film that followed it) is often invoked in popular culture to symbolise a celebratory kind of Romanness – as Malamud has documented, and as we have seen in relation to Cather and Fitzgerald – *Ben-Hur* is in fact a story of resistance to Roman rule: the initially Jewish Ben-Hur refuses to join the Roman army; undergoes life as a galley slave as a punishment; and becomes a Christian in a final subversive move.[55] Given the frequent analogies in this novel between the Southern slave economy/culture and Roman rule – witness Rosa's reference to Judith, Ellen and herself as a 'triumvirate' (133), or Shreve's comparison of Sutpen's scythe to a 'symbolic laurel of a caesar's triumph' (145) – this *Ben-Hur* reference is noteworthy for its introduction of the idea of resistance by an oppressed or enslaved group.

It is not dissimilar in effect to Shreve's casting of Eulalia, Charles Bon's Haitian-born mother, as 'the old Sabine', an epithet he uses twice on consecutive pages (243–4). The Sabine people – who, according to legend, were colonised by the earliest Romans, leading to years of war and the well-known rape of their women, and who then assimilated with their oppressors (under Romulus and Tatius) – have conventionally symbolised accommodation and integration rather than subversion.[56] Shreve's very conscious association of Haiti with the Sabines nonetheless draws attention to the history of oppression, colonisation and the mixing of races that Haiti constitutes and that both American history and Sutpen's dynasty involves. And even the name of this character (Charles Bon's mother), which is not stated by any of the narrators but is recorded in the 'Genealogy' as 'Eulalia' (307), is significant. It recalls the Spanish saint, Eulalia of Merida, who was a Christian persecuted and killed for refusing to renounce her faith in around 304 CE, under the rule of the Roman Emperor Diocletian (Farmer 184–5). As a well-buried subtext, the name 'Eulalia' in *Absalom, Absalom!* speaks as much of native and enslaved African resistance to oppression in Haiti as it does to Spanish colonial rule of the first-annexed Santo Domingo.

As Gayle Rogers notes, in recent years (as part of the wave of postcolonial and global readings of Faulkner) critics have paid considerable attention to this novelist's significant deployment of Haiti as the birthplace of the fictional Sutpen's first wife, first son and the slaves who build his house. Critics such as Aliyyah Abdur-Rahman, Richard Godden ('*Absalom*') and especially Hugues Azérad have explored both the resonances within the novel of the Haitian Revolution or slave revolt of 1791 (led by Toussaint L'Ouverture and leading to Haitian independence in 1804), and the fact that Faulkner is anachronistic in his suggestion that the men building Sutpen's house in the 1830s were people enslaved in Haiti. As Rogers summarises,

'Haiti' in *Absalom, Absalom!* encodes a 'duality . . . as a possible site of both degeneration and regeneration, possession and dispossession' (240). Shreve's casting of Eulalia as a 'Sabine' reminds us that the complexities of Haiti's relationship to antiquity contribute significantly to its paradoxical associations with both oppression and emancipation within the novel.

Relevant to any theorisation of Faulkner's use of Haiti as a site of radical resistance is the fact that C. L. R. James's study of the 1791 revolution, *The Black Jacobins*, was first published in 1938, just two years after the appearance of *Absalom, Absalom!*. Of equal significance is James's far less well-known stage play, *Toussaint Louverture: The Story of the Only Successful Slave Revolt in History*, written in 1934 and first performed in London in 1936 – the very year in which Faulkner's novel was published.[57] While James's writing is itself replete with classical allusions, in both the historical account and the play he gives great emphasis to Toussaint's own classically informed self-fashioning.[58] In the words of the publisher's 'blurb' about the play, 'In *Toussaint Louverture*, James demonstrates the full tragedy and heroism of Louverture by showing how the Haitian revolutionary leader is caught in a dramatic conflict arising from the contradiction between the barbaric realities of New World slavery and the modern ideals of the Enlightenment.'[59] While I am not suggesting that James's writing was a direct influence on Faulkner's, its 'black classicist' representations of an Enlightenment-inspired resistant black Haitian hero may well shape and attune readers to the disruptive and unstable role of Haiti within *Absalom*.[60] So, for example, in Rosa Coldfield's outwardly demeaning description of Sutpen's Haitian slaves as 'half tamed to walk upright like men' (4), we can be attentive to the buried echo of Ovid's equation between humanness and uprightness that is so key in *Light in August*, and we can hear both oppression and imminent insurrection contained within this phrase.

A black classicist context also contributes importantly to Abdur-Rahman's suggestion that Shreve's closing vision of Jim Bond is an emancipatory prayer rather than a vision of doom. It is possible to read the Canadian's much-quoted assertion – that 'in a few thousand years . . . I who regard you will also have sprung from the loins of African kings' (302) – as a deployment of the Afrocentric and classical abolitionist arguments about the African origins of Greek and Roman civilisation.[61] According to the theories of black American activist intellectuals such as David Walker and W. E. B. Du Bois, the European heritage to which the Canadian (abolitionist) Shreve refers – the mythical past that 'happened long ago across the water' (289) – is itself derived from Africa, and so is inextricably connected with it. This might mean that America itself, the nation within which Sutpen so desperately wants to excel, is neither as 'white' nor as 'pure' as he would wish. In 'a few thousand years', Shreve suggests, humans might recognise the complexities of their provenance and their genealogy, and hence might both acknowledge their true identity, and realise true equality.

Go Down, Moses (1942)

In a discomforting passage towards the end of 'Delta Autumn' – the sixth section of Faulkner's thirteenth novel, *Go Down, Moses* – Ike McCaslin is shocked by what Roth Edmonds's 'woman' reveals about her identity. He launches into a tirade against interracial mixing, ranting about '*this land*', where '*Chinese and African and Aryan and Jew all breed and spawn together until no man has time to say which one is which nor cares*' (*Moses* 347, original italics). The act of miscegenation and incest that this encounter forces Ike to confront is one of several so-called 'contaminating' relationships that punctuate this text. As Eric Sundquist argues, the (white) L. C. Q. McCaslin's sexual relationship with his own mixed-race daughter, Tomasina (as revealed in 'The Bear'), is the first of several couplings in which the narrowly avoided catastrophe in *Absalom, Absalom!* (interracial incest) becomes reality (Sundquist, *House* 132). As a symbolic 'antitoxin' to this 'toxin' (101), in 'The Fire and the Hearth' section of the novel, Faulkner deploys the classically derived conception of the hearth as a sacred site, connotative of purity. The hearth, resonant here of the Greek goddess Hestia (or Roman equivalent, Vesta), as well as of the communal hearth of the ancient Greek city-state, represents throughout the novel all that is antithetical to the many 'impurities' that define the McCaslin/Edmonds/Beauchamp dynasty. Reading Toni Morrison's 1998 novel *Paradise* alongside Faulkner's text, moreover, illuminates the extent to which ancient Greek paradigms of the hearth – both domestic and civic – inform the earlier novelist's treatment of racial and sexual 'purity' and 'impurity'.[62]

Scholarship has paid more attention to the gold-hunting and bootleg-whisky-making elements of 'The Fire and the Hearth' than to Lucas's anxiety and rage about the fact that his wife, Molly, had

had to live in Zack Edmonds's house and nurse his baby alongside her own.[63] Critics' focus on the comic and burlesque elements of this section – labelling Lucas a 'buffoon', for example (Clark 68) – erases the brief but significant moments in which the black protagonist is a psychologically realised near-tragic hero, agonised by the possibility of a white man sleeping with his wife.[64] In just a few pages focalised on Lucas in the second section of the first chapter, and a few pages focalised on Roth in the first section of the third, Faulkner explores with great seriousness and poignancy the unclarified and inevitably painful domestic situations to which the racially hierarchical Southern economy has given rise. These involve confused maternity and fraternity, and ubiquitous 'shame' (*Moses* 109).[65] At these times the novelist suffuses his account of Lucas and Molly's embattled marriage – one which epitomises the way that black women's sexual fidelity and black men's paternity and masculinity have historically been threatened – with a classically heroic texture. For example, Faulkner describes the transitional moment of Lucas's passage through the dangerously flooded river to fetch the doctor for Zack Edmonds's wife as if it were a life-changing *katabasis* (descent to the underworld) comparable to that undergone by Odysseus, Aeneas or Orpheus: 'as though [Lucas] had crossed and then re-crossed a kind of Lethe' (46).[66] The novelist ensures that Lucas is more anti-hero than hero by the novel's end, for example through the misfiring gun and the ludicrous non-hearing about the non-divorce. But there is no resolution to the profound pain that this character feels about the interwoven families, or about the historical 'stain' on his relationship with Zack Edmonds (111). Lucas's unease articulates the catastrophic nature of the corrupt sexual relationships, the incestuous miscegenation, that – figuring comically in 'Was' and traumatically in both 'The Bear' and 'Delta Autumn' – unify this text as a whole.

In depicting the agonised Lucas's almost-obsessive preoccupation with the fire in the hearth of his home, Faulkner invokes both the sacredness of the hearth in the ancient Greek and Roman domestic sphere, and the way that the *koine hestia* – the communal hearth in a city's centre – came to symbolise civic pride and ethnic purity in ancient Athenian life. As Lucas casts his mind back to the night forty-three years ago when Roth was born (and his birth mother died), the black protagonist recalls that he was 'keeping the fire going in the stove' of his own house while Molly was serving as the midwife (*Moses* 45); that he was 'keeping alive on the hearth the fire he had lit there on their wedding day and which had burned ever since' (46); and that he was 'himself alone keeping alive the fire which was to burn on the hearth until neither he nor Molly were left to feed it' (46). He recalls finding Molly back in their home after he has demanded her return, 'sitting before the hearth where the supper was cooking', in 'the room where he had lit the fire two years ago which was to have outlasted both of them' (49). He even muses on the 'solidity of heat' in the hearth's bricks, which is a 'condensation not of fire but of time' (50).

The way the constantly burning hearth fire symbolises the health and vitality of Lucas's home and marriage recalls the fact that in ancient Greece 'each family had its own hearth where small offerings were placed at meal times', and 'Newborns, brides, and new slaves were initiated into the family by various rituals at or around the hearth' (Mikalson 701). In Lucas's close attention to the hearth fire he displays something of the respect for that site that Hesiod demands in *Works and Days*, in which the ancient writer's instructions for living include a very specific injunction to 'avoid' the 'hearth-fire' after sexual intercourse (*Works* l. 733).[67] These revered domestic hearths mirrored the *koine hestia* or communal hearths in public buildings, such as the *prytaneion* instituted by Theseus in Athens, where 'the flame that burned perpetually on Hestia's altar symbolized the vitality of the civic unit' (Pantel and Zidman 93), where important dining took place, and from where religious processions began.[68]

While in Athens 'the *prytaneion* seems to have served also as a quasi-archives', housing 'the laws of Solon' and 'statutes . . . of both historical and allegorical significance for the community' (Miller 16–17), Lucas houses the certificate of the secret marriage between George and Nat 'hidden under the loose brick in his fireplace' (*Moses* 70). And Faulkner deploys all of this symbolic power not just through Lucas's reverence for his and Molly's own hearth fire: through repeating the detail that Wilkins does not have 'a cook-stove' (67), the author indicates the unlikeliness of Nat's marriage to George Wilkins working out well. In 'Pantaloon in Black', meanwhile – the tragic tale of Rider's downfall that follows on from 'The Fire and the Hearth' – Rider mourns his wife by remembering how he had 'built a fire on the hearth on their wedding night', just as 'the tale told . . . Uncle Lucas Beauchamp' had done 'forty-five years ago' (134).

Toni Morrison's *Paradise*, in its depiction of 'the Oven' as the defining civic monument in the all-black Oklahoman town of Ruby, constitutes a dialogue both with Athenian conventions about the public and the domestic hearth, and with the classically influenced symbolic fireplace in 'The Fire and the Hearth'.[69] Morrison writes that the fire in the Oven was 'alive . . . always' (*Paradise* 16), and that in the settlement's earliest days, the site functioned 'as the meeting place to report on what done or what needed; on illness, births, deaths, comings and goings' (111). Through the Founding Fathers' obsession with their unsullied pure blackness, however, and with perpetuating the original families without external 'contamination', Morrison reveals the dangers to which an extreme reaction to the situation Faulkner's Lucas finds himself in can lead. Playing on the ancient Greek analogy between an oven and a woman's body that Page duBois documents in her 1988 study *Sowing the Body* (110–29), Morrison connects the men of Ruby's fetishising of the Oven with their paranoid protectiveness of their women. Interestingly, the 'field' and 'furrow' that, as duBois explains (39–85), were earlier Greek metaphors for the female body in classical antiquity also resonate in both 'The Fire and the Hearth' and in *Paradise*. Faulkner includes a detailed description of Lucas's ploughing 'each furrow' of the field allotted to him after demanding that Zack return Molly to his home (*Moses* 47), while George Wilkins's illicit 'ploughing and chopping and picking cotton' on state-owned land suggests his sexual incontinence (33–4). In *Paradise*, the dispute about whether the Oven's motto reads 'Be . . . ' or 'Beware the Furrow . . .' indirectly invokes the same classical metaphor (Morrison, *Paradise* 93).

In Morrison's text, motivated by the desire to prevent exactly the white sexual encroachment on black marriage and family life that must historically have been the Rubean Fathers' (or forefathers') experience, the town of Ruby becomes dangerously introverted and obsessed with its own purity. It thereby ironically mirrors the racism and injunction against interracial mixing that white America had perpetuated (while also violating) for so long. The analogy with the Greek *prytaneion* holds up here in that in ancient Greece, over time, exclusivist notions of Greek identity and 'true blood' became associated with the communal hearth: 'Herodotus restricts the "most true-blooded Ionians" to those who had "set out from the Prytaneum at Athens"' (Parker, *Religion* 26). While in 'The Fire and the Hearth' Lucas's anxiety is legitimate (and whether or not Zack Edmonds has slept with Molly is never revealed), in *Paradise* the Rubean Fathers create an endogamous culture that ironically but inevitably ends in incestuous interbreeding and sickness in children. This incest is not of course the interracial kind practised by L. C. Q. McCaslin and by Roth Edmonds in *Go Down, Moses*; rather it is its opposite, the kind of incest within white families that Walter Benn Michaels describes in *Our America* as the logical outcome of the 'effort to prevent half-breeds' (49).[70] Ironically, the Rubean Fathers' attempts to maintain racial purity end in the impurity of incest instead, making a mockery of the ideals embodied in the hearth or by Hestia. In *Go Down, Moses*, meanwhile, the interracial incest initiated by white men across the generations constitutes an even greater corruption of or falling away from the Greek-derived ideal of constancy and purity to which Lucas, doggedly tending his own hearth fire, so heroically aspires.

In Morrison's *Paradise*, Patricia Cato burns in disgust the family trees – the complex and too-closely-interwoven genealogies of Ruby's founding families – on which she has been working for a very long time. In Faulkner's 'The Bear', when Ike McCaslin reads the ledger (account book or record) of the family plantation, he discovers not only the horrifying truth about his grandfather's sexual relationship with Tomasina, but also the fact that his ancestors' 'spelling did not improve' as they listed the family's slaves and their descendants (*Moses* 252). Named in aspirational invocation of a classical slave economy perceived (from a considerable distance of time and space) to be ideal, the black human property 'Roscius and Phoebe and Thucydides' are listed by his own father as 'Roskus' and 'Fibby' and 'Thucydus' (252–4). Meanwhile Lucas Beauchamp has eliminated all traces of his transgressive ancestor, 'Lucius Quintus', from his own name (269).[71] Faulkner uses these anti-classical names to convey the inevitable corruption and impurity of the non-heroic South, just as he does with the tobacco-stained portico of the courthouse in *Light in August* (415) and the 'rotting' and 'sagging' portico in *Absalom, Absalom!* (128, 173). Lucas Beauchamp, however faithfully he tends the fire on his hearth, cannot guarantee the purity of his marriage and family – moral or otherwise – that the classical Hestia connotes.

Notes

1. On Apuleius in *The Reivers* see Provencal.
2. See Serafin (discussed at p. 85) for an invaluable catalogue of classical allusions in Faulkner's fiction, non-fiction and poetry.

3. See Parini 33. Other biographies on which I draw in this chapter are by Blotner (which includes a useful chronology of Faulkner's life and publications) and by Gray. See also Towner, whose *Introduction* includes a list of Faulkner's novels (11).
4. William may have been influenced by his grandparents' copy of Samuel Goodrich's *Pictorial History of Greece: Ancient and Modern* (1874; Blotner, *Library* 114).
5. See Blotner, *Biography* 12.
6. On Stone's classical education see Snell 54–64; for his intellectual influence on Faulkner see (besides Blotner) Gray 78–80 and Parini 30–3.
7. See Wasson 41, 33.
8. See the discussion in my introduction here.
9. See Wasson 34. The fiction of Eudora Welty (who was profoundly influenced by Faulkner) similarly engages with this 'Southern classical' tradition.
10. Faulkner read this work in New Orleans in 1935 (Blotner, *Biography* 396); see also Blotner, *Biography* 651, 666.
11. See Blotner, *Biography* 246, 253, 263.
12. On Faulkner's debt to Eliot, and struggle to escape his influence, see Blotner, *Biography* 241, 307–10, 399.
13. In 1924 Faulkner reviewed O'Neill's *The Emperor Jones* (1920), which centres on a black protagonist named Brutus (Blotner, *Biography* 331).
14. See Blotner, *Library* 123–5; Blotner, *Biography* 352. On Faulkner and Joyce/*Ulysses* see Blotner, *Biography* 429, 461, 520–1, 569, 824.
15. He repeats the exact phrase used of Milan Cathedral in describing the carvings on Notre Dame in Paris; see Blotner, *Letters* 12. He commends the Gallo-Roman walls remaining in the north-western French town of Senlis (see Blotner, *Biography* 472).
16. See Blotner, 'Library' 79–80.
17. On his love for Rome see Blotner, *Biography* 1487–8. For his trip to Athens see Blotner, *Biography* 1645ff.
18. See Gwynn and Blotner 10, 35.
19. See Towner 95.
20. Key books are by Adams; Brylowski; Levins; Longley; Serafin; Wadlington. Articles on classicism in two or more texts include those by Park and by Holland-Toll.
21. The title for *As I Lay Dying* is taken from Sir William Marris's 1925 translation of the *Odyssey*, published by Oxford University Press (see Collins 123). When asked about the source of the novel's title, Faulkner quoted 'the speech of the ghostly Agamemnon to Odysseus, which includes the words, "As I lay dying . . ."' (Blotner, *Biography*

634–5). See Homer, *Odyssey* XI.421–6. For further discussion of *As I Lay Dying*'s allusiveness see Hays; Schleiner. On *Absalom, Absalom!* see Brooks, 'History'.

22. Stavrou's 1959 article on the Promethean archetype in Faulkner's work (which ignores the potential of any non-white Prometheus) exemplifies the 'myth and symbol' approach. For useful essays on the changing nature of American studies see Maddox. See Chapters 4, 6 and 7 here for discussions of Prometheus in Ellison, Roth and Robinson.
23. Crowell's article on Charles Bon and Oscar Wilde is a notable exception.
24. Brylowski writes of the 'excessive "myth-dropping"' of *Soldier's Pay* – which includes references to Atalanta and to Narcissus, among many others – that 'Faulkner had evidently come to the novel fresh from a reading of Ovid' (45). On Ovid and *The Hamlet* see Mortimer.
25. For prior critical discussion of classicism in this novel see Taylor, besides the works listed on pp. 86–9.
26. For a useful critique of the problematic nature of much scholarship on Faulkner and tragedy see Wadlington 15–16.
27. Compare *The Sound and the Fury*: 'Theres a curse on us its not our fault is it our fault' (100; *sic*).
28. For Toni Morrison's resistance to this tendency in Faulkner see pp. 159 and 161–5, and Roynon, *Morrison* 99–101.
29. Toohey writes that Roman epic in particular is concerned with power and history (as compared with Greek epic, which centres on family, community, gods) (90). The *Aeneid*, as he writes, 'justifies colonialism' in its valorisation of the founding of Rome and the Roman Empire (122). The *Odyssey* and *Metamorphoses* are, of course, more obviously open to subversive readings.
30. On the use of the present tense in the *Aeneid* see Quinn 77–8; on the formulaic (and other) aspects of epic form see Toohey 11–18.
31. See for example Kreiswirth.
32. See 311 and 317; compare also 217 and 370.
33. For discussion of the same Ovidian trope in Marilynne Robinson see pp. 213–14. On dignity in the context of tragedy in *Light in August* (and in Faulkner generally) see Wadlington 52.
34. On horses in antiquity (including epic tradition) see Anderson; Forrest 121 (on Homer). See also Forrest 89–91 for discussion in Xenophon's *Peri Hippikes (On Horsemanship)* about carvings of horses and equestrians on the Parthenon's frieze, and of horses in ancient Rome.
35. The Charlottesville march and protest resulting in one woman's death in 2017 was rooted in controversy over the statue of General Lee on horseback in the former Lee Park. On the heroic equestrian monument in Boston that depicts Colonel Robert Gould Shaw (commander

of the Union Army's 54th Massachusetts (all black) regiment) see Blight 338; compare p. 140 n. 37 here (on *Invisible Man*).

36. See *Iliad* II.93; *Odyssey* XXIV.412.
37. On classical rumour/*fama* and its reception (though not in American literature) see Hardie.
38. The voices of the baying hunting dogs are represented in a similar way (328); this implicitly suggests that the people are like dogs.
39. See *Odyssey* X.1–80; Joyce, *Ulysses* 147–89.
40. For processes of transformation into fixedness, the statuesque or carving within the novel, see *Light* 34, 65, 125, 150, 163. On flux in the *Metamorphoses* see my discussion of *Absalom, Absalom!* at pp. 96–7.
41. For further discussions of tragedy in this novel see Markowitz; Schwartz; Wadlington.
42. For an overview of Faulkner's engagement with Ovid see my discussion at p. 88.
43. For discussion of Phaethon (and the 'phaeton') in Ellison and in Morrison see respectively pp. 127–33 and 162.
44. Faulkner owned a copy of this Apuleius text, in a 1927 edition (Blotner, *Library* 79).
45. Compare Brooks, 'History', on Judith's heroic resilience.
46. See Chapter 4 here for discussion of the same passage of Ovid in Ellison's work.
47. Compare Rosa's observation that the men who returned from the war had been 'transformed' (126). Cather uses a similar trope to describe returning soldiers in *Sapphira and the Slave Girl* (see Chapter 1).
48. The 'lustrum' is the ancient Roman term for the five-year period in between each census.
49. See *Absalom* 54–5, 58, especially 66–7, and 77.
50. Charite is weeping in IV.24, while Psyche is weeping in IV.34, IV.35, V.5 and VI.2.
51. See Apuleius VI.17–21.
52. For the reception history of the 'Cupid and Psyche' tale see May and Harrison.
53. For a fascinating discussion of Faulkner's engagement with Wilde in this novel see Crowell.
54. See Gwynn and Blotner 285 for Faulkner's memory of seeing a production of *Ben-Hur* in his childhood.
55. See Malamud, *Ancient* 135–6.
56. See Cornell.
57. The play was published for the first time in 2012; see Høgsbjerg.
58. As Girard notes, L'Ouverture liked to cast himself as the rebel slave Spartacus (see Girard 1, 20).

59. See <https://www.dukeupress.edu/toussaint-louverture> (last accessed 7 May 2020).
60. For discussion of black classicism see my introduction here, as well as Chapters 4 and 5. For an overview of recent theorising of Haiti in Faulkner's text see Rogers 238–41.
61. For discussion of the 'Africanness of classicism' and Martin Bernal's work see my introduction here. See also Malamud, *African Americans* 146–64.
62. See n. 69 of this chapter for the extensive scholarship on Morrison and Faulkner.
63. Essays specifically on 'The Fire and the Hearth' include Duvall, 'Silencing'; Clark; Godden, 'Agricultural'. Relevant discussions of race relations in the novel as a whole (beside Sundquist's *House*) include Matthews, 'Touching'; Gwin.
64. On the tension between Lucas's heroic individualism and his communal responsibilities here see Zender 120–2.
65. See Sensibar on the significance of the African American servant Callie (to whom this novel is dedicated) in William Faulkner's life and in this text.
66. For Odysseus's underworld encounter with Tiresias see *Odyssey* XI; for Aeneas's with his father, Anchises, see *Aeneid* VI; for Orpheus's attempted rescue of Eurydice from Hades see *Met.* X.1–105. Faulkner's self-conscious classicism in this section includes the detail that the Edmonds house has a 'portico' (44), and that Molly's face is a 'tragic mask' when Roth calls round there (111).
67. Parker explains, 'it is the hearth that [Hesiod] seeks to protect. This is partly due to respect for fire, a pure element, which is liable to contamination by this particular form of dirt' (*Miasma* 77).
68. See Mikalson; also Parker, *Religion* 26.
69. For a detailed discussion of the analogy between the Oven in *Paradise* and the Athenian *prytaneion* see my *Toni Morrison* 70–4. Comparative scholarship on *Go Down, Moses* and Morrison includes MacKethan on 'The Bear' and *Song of Solomon*, and Duvall on *Song of Solomon* and *Go Down, Moses* as a whole. There is no published commentary on *Paradise* and 'The Fire and the Hearth'.
70. On incest in *The Sound and the Fury* see Michaels 1–12.
71. Compare Cather's use of corrupted classical names in the final section of Chapter 1.

Further Reading

Collins, Carvel. 'The Pairing of *The Sound and the Fury* and *As I Lay Dying*'. *Princeton University Library Chronicle* 18.1 (1957): 114–23.

Faulkner, William. *As I Lay Dying* (1930).

Kartiganer, Donald M. *The Fragile Thread: The Meaning of Form in Faulkner's Novels*. Amherst: University of Massachusetts Press, 1979.

Rogers, Gayle. 'American Modernisms in the World'. *The Cambridge Companion to the American Modernist Novel*. Ed. Joshua Miller. Cambridge: Cambridge University Press, 2015. 227–44.

Serafin, Joan. *Faulkner's Uses of the Classics*. Ann Arbor and Epping: UMI Research Press, 1983.

CHAPTER 4

Ralph Ellison (1913–94)

Ellison and the Classics

Towards the end of Ellison's best-known work, *Invisible Man* (1952), when the narrator tries to create light in the coal cellar by burning the documents in his briefcase, the first thing he sets fire to is his high school diploma. This subversive act at once resonates and contrasts with the novelist's own perspectives on formal education and on intellectual traditions. For while Ellison's school and college grades were never stellar, he was a formidable auto-didact throughout his long and productive life. His work was indelibly shaped by his energetic and eclectic reading in both modern and ancient European literature (translated where necessary) as well as in classically dependent disciplines such as psychology and anthropology. Ellison's synthesising of European cultural material with the African American traditions, both intellectual and vernacular, in which he was also expert is a definitive feature of his fiction from his short stories of the 1930s and 1940s (now collected as *Flying Home and Other Stories* (1996)) onwards. It characterises both *Invisible Man* and the unfinished second novel which was published posthumously in 2010 as the vast series of manuscripts entitled *Three Days Before the Shooting* . . . . This conscious hybridisation is also significant in his essays, letters and interviews, wherein he sets outs his perspectives on American identity, history, culture and society; on the definitive role of black Americans within these; and on the function of the novel and the novelist in modern democratic life.[1]

Across the decades of his writing career, the texture of Ellison's work develops from the highly crafted but restrained idiom of the early stories, via the exuberant multi-tonality of *Invisible Man*, to the highly wrought rhetoric of *Three Days.* Classical myth and mythological archetypes, together with motivated engagement with classical literary genres, feature variously but always significantly in all of these. The alert reader will tune into Ellison's playful use of Homeric epic and Greek tragedy in *Invisible Man*: in this text the author deploys figures as various as Odysseus, Proteus, Prometheus and Icarus to explore black male American identity and the viability (or non-viability) of the black male hero. To recognise these mythical heroes' role in the 1952 novel is to see that Ellison's preoccupation with flight and flying in many of his earlier short stories is engaged as much with the Daedalus/Icarus myth as with West African and African American folkloric tradition about flight.[2] And while *Three Days*, in charting the rise and fall of Bliss/Adam Sunraider, mirrors the structure of Greek tragedy, it is perhaps the indistinct but tangible echoes of classical mythological figures such as Phaethon in the work's Part I (see pp. 127–33) and of Daedalus and Pygmalion in the work's Part II (see pp. 134–8) that best reward close scrutiny.[3]

Ellison's widespread engagement with classical tradition is fundamental to his exploration of three key recurring themes: first, the hero's struggle to survive and/or thrive in a racially discriminatory nation (a subject that encompasses the hero's relationship to society or the group); second, the rapid change, fluidity and instability that characterise modernity; and third, the elements of tragedy, sacrifice and ritual scapegoating that define both America's past and its present. Homer, Aeschylus, Sophocles, Euripides, Aristotle, Seneca, Virgil and Ovid all play their subtle but significant part in Ellison's imagined worlds. As this last poet's *Metamorphoses* is an important influence largely neglected by critics, it constitutes the focus of much of my own discussion here.[4]

The author's non-fiction is much more forthright than is his fiction about his indebtedness to the classical tradition. In letters, essays and interviews Ellison insists that classicism is as significant a cultural inheritance for African Americans as it is for those of European descent. In both his analyses of (African) American history and his literary criticism, he draws frequent analogies between modern figures and classical archetypes, comparing Huckleberry Finn to both Oedipus and Prometheus, for example, and the black folk hero John Henry to Hercules.[5] He also often explains his own literary technique or the aesthetic principles he values most in terms of classical metaphor or equivalence: witness his implication in 'Beating that Boy' (1945) that the Negro writer must perform a kind of *katabasis* (descent to the underworld) to encounter 'the ghosts of his former selves' (*Collected* 150); or in his National Book Award acceptance speech of 1953 that 'Proteus stands for both America and the inheritance of illusion through which all men must fight to achieve reality' (*Collected* 154). Throughout the non-fiction Ellison reiterates his perspectives on tragedy and the tragic, as well as repeatedly invoking the Ovidian-inflected concepts of 'chaos', 'transformation' and 'metamorphosis' to describe personal, historical or societal and aesthetic processes all at once.

Ellison's most famous non-fictional identification with a figure from antiquity perhaps explains why his classicism has been a significant factor in many black writers' hostility towards him: 'I knew the trickster Ulysses just as early as I knew the wily rabbit of American lore,' he has said, 'and I could easily imagine myself a pint-sized Ulysses but hardly a rabbit' (*Collected* 112). Some have understood this comment, made in the 1958 essay 'Change the Joke and Slip the Yoke', as a privileging of European- over African-derived tradition.[6] Ellison's own stated view of his use of the varied cultural resources available to him, however, articulates less a sense of hierarchy and more that of energetic eclecticism – a modernist yoking together of intellectual and vernacular cultures, or a synthesis of apparently disparate resources or forms. For example, in his introduction to the 1964 essay collection, *Shadow and Act*, where he famously refers to himself and his peer group as identifying with the 'Renaissance man' (*Collected* 50), he holds forth on the 'surreal incongruity' with which they had venerated as heroes both 'gamblers and scholars' and 'figures from the Italian Renaissance, both classical and popular . . . combined with the virtues of some bootlegger' (53). Of course, in this beautifully crafted retrospection we must take into account Ellison's predilection for self-fashioning; indeed, such conscious and motivated hindsight may well also inform his claim that 'reading Lord Raglan's *The Hero*' was the catalyst for his creation of *Invisible Man* (*Collected* 76).[7] Yet there is no doubt at all that, during the formative years of his youth in Oklahoma City, growing up without a father (who had died in 1916) and in straitened financial circumstances, this writer-in-the-making found that reading was an essential escape. Books were always both a refuge and an adventure.

During his childhood, Ellison's mother passed on to him magazines such as *Vanity Fair* (which ran articles about the modernist art and music of the day), handed on from the homes of the white people for whom she worked. Family friends, meanwhile, allowed him to read widely in their own book collections, including in the European novels curated as the 'Harvard Classics', which he recalls in his 1964 autobiographical address, 'Hidden Name and Complex Fate' (*Collected* 200). Ellison makes no mention of encountering translations of classical epic or tragedy at this stage, either here or in the 'Dunbar branch' of the public library (an improvised provision for black residents that emerged when the main city library enforced a whites-only policy (Rampersad 29)); he instead records a passionate devotion to American epic novels such as *The Adventures of Huckleberry Finn* (1884) and *The Last of the Mohicans* (1826). He relished the writings of the Southerner Albion Tourgée (who, interestingly, was acutely attuned to the Old South's ideologically motivated deployment of classical tragic and epic traditions in its nostalgic representations of its 'lost cause'), and loved George Bernard Shaw's prefaces to his plays.[8] He also encountered both Freud and Nietzsche at this early age, through whom he would have come across classical archetypes, ritual and myth.[9]

At high school Ellison didn't flourish in English, but he did enjoy four years of Latin with a teacher, Henry Berry, who also knew Hebrew and Greek (Jackson 71; Rampersad 30–1).[10] Jackson suggests that it was perhaps because Ellison spent so much time on his music – learning trumpet and performing it in classical, jazz and musical theatre contexts – that he failed to graduate until 1932, a year after his peer group. Yet his musical training would surely have shaped both his reading and his writing in important ways. First, the widespread cultural controversies and his own personal conflicts about the comparative merits of classical and/or popular music were mirrored in the juxtapositions he encountered – and consistently subverted throughout his writing life – between high and low (or classical and popular) literary/cultural traditions. Second, his immersion in all types of music taught him about the nature and value of tradition itself. This insight may well have enhanced his receptivity to Greek and Roman tradition once he moved on to undergraduate studies, at the Tuskegee Institute in Alabama, in 1933.[11]

Though financial constraints prevented Ellison from completing his fourth year at Tuskegee, and so from completing his degree, the significance of his intellectual development at the Institute (between 1933 and 1936) cannot be overstated. Although his central focus was music, key intellectual influences included the brilliant English professor Morteza Sprague, who both in and out of the classroom introduced him to a vast range of literature, and the college librarian, Walter Bowie Williams, for whom the novelist-to-be worked in the library from 1934 onwards (Rampersad 60–1).[12] It was in 1935, in that library, that Ellison first encountered *The Waste Land*, in what was to be perhaps the most significant intellectual discovery of his career. As Jackson writes, the young man was 'ripe for transformation at the hands of Eliot's masterpiece' (150), and the epiphany that the poem constituted for this young student is something to which he returned again and again, in personal reflections, over the decades.[13] Crucial was the treasure hunt that Eliot's footnotes entailed: as Ellison himself has said, 'looking up their references' was the beginning of his 'conscious education in literature' (*Collected* 203). Eliot's footnotes directed him to Weston's *From Ritual to Romance*, to Frazer's *Golden Bough*, and even inspired him to 'revive his dusty Latin skills . . . in order to understand a generous Ovid quote' (Jackson 152).[14] Ellison was struck not just by Eliot's juxtaposition and synthesising of unalike cultural resources – high and low, classical and (black) American – but also by his use of improvised and jazz-like rhythms.[15]

In time for his relocation to New York in 1935, Ellison had been led by Eliot to other modernist writers – including Pound, Joyce and Faulkner – to whom a complex engagement with antiquity was key, and who may well in turn have accelerated Ellison's own recourse to Greek and Roman texts. His observations in 1965 about Eliot's 'ruthless assault upon the literature of the past' could almost serve as a blueprint for his own perspective and technique from the 1940s onwards (Graham and Singh 91), as he continued his voracious reading in classical literature and culture during this decade. His vast personal book collection, now housed at the Library of Congress, includes many works annotated in his own hand that in all likelihood constituted part of his 'apprenticeship' in the years preceding *Invisible Man*: these include (in addition to Raglan's *The Hero*) anthologies of translated tragedies by Sophocles (1905), Aeschylus (1907) and Euripides (1936), Jane Harrison's *Themis* (1927), Aristotle's *Poetics* (1943), George Thomson's *Aeschylus and Athens: A Study in the Origins of Social Drama* (1946), and Joseph Campbell's *The Hero with a Thousand Faces* (1949).[16] Interestingly, his marginal commentaries on his classical texts – for example his notes on the pages of Aeschylus's *Seven Against Thebes* or *Prometheus Bound* – often highlight moments where either a group or an individual takes action against a state or dominant power.[17] Ellison was profoundly interested, too, in Erich Fromm's theories about the emergence of the individual during the (European) Renaissance; his copy of Fromm's *Escape from Freedom* (1941) is one of the most heavily annotated in his library. It is also significant that the *Life* magazine pictorial essay series on 'The History of Western Culture' (1947–8) preserved in his archive includes a very well-thumbed copy of its 'Renaissance Man' piece, published in March 1947.[18] This *Life* essay implicitly holds up the polymathic character, classical education and self-fabricated individualism of Aeneas Silvius Piccolomini (who was to become Pope Pius II in 1458) as an exemplum for all good Americans to follow. It would doubtless have made a great impression on the highly cultured Ellison in late-1940s New York.

Following the publication of *Invisible Man*, during the decades spent working on the novel that was to become *Three Days*, on university teaching, guest lecturing and travelling, Ellison continued to read intensively in classical, mythological and related fields, and he grew his personal library significantly. Many works in his collection that were published in the 1950s speak to his ever-growing interest in comparative mythology and archetypal approaches: Otto Rank's *The Myth of the Birth of the Hero* (1952), W. B. Stanford's *The Ulysses Theme* (1954), Paul Radin's *The Trickster* (1956), and R. W. B. Lewis's *The Picaresque Saint* (1959).[19] His ownership of two works by Gilbert Murray in new editions published in this decade – *Five Stages of Greek Religion* (1951) and *The Classical Tradition in Poetry* (1956) – indicates his ongoing study of the work of the Cambridge Ritualists.[20] The author's two-year residence at the American Academy in Rome, from 1956 to 1958, inevitably provoked several fascinating pronouncements about antiquity on the part of this author.[21] For example, in his first letter from Rome to his friend Albert Murray, in October 1955, he waxes lyrical about the fact that in that city the 'Renaissance' is 'around you everywhere you turn', and that 'some of the classical people around here are snobbish about this mess, but it belongs to anyone who can dig it' (*Trading* 98–9).

It is notable that the two translations of the *Odyssey* (1951 and 1961) that Ellison owned, as well as his only translation of the *Iliad* (1962) and his 1959 edition of Moses Finley's *World of Odysseus*, all post-date the composition of *Invisible Man*. The relative lateness of these purchases suggests these epics' continued importance during the decades in which he laboured over *Three Days*. Ellison also owned an *Aesop's Fables* published in 1982, and a 1981 translation of Bakhtin's classically wide-ranging *Dialogic Imagination*; this last is extensively highlighted and dated '1986' in Ellison's hand. Well into his eighth decade, then, he was still pondering the classical tradition, still underlining passages that both expressed and shaped his always-complex engagement with antiquity, and with its legacies in the cultures of modernity.

The Critical Field and Scholarly Debate

Although several initial reviews of *Invisible Man* make a brief comparison between Ellison's text and the *Odyssey*, developed scholarly discussions of his classical allusiveness did not appear until 1969.[22] While in her article published that year, 'Negro Literature and Classic Form', Nancy Tischler explored the prize-winning novel's Voltaire-like debt to classical comedy and satire, critics of the early 1970s emphasised instead its relationship with epic and tragedy. First off the mark in this regard was Archie Sanders, who in 'Odysseus in Black' argues that the novel is 'cast in the Homeric mold' and who (like John Stark three years later) maps the structure of *Invisible Man* on to the structure of the *Odyssey*. Both Sanders' and Stark's discussions are simultaneously illuminating and reductive, in that while each delineates several persuasive parallels, both attempt to define a much tighter, systematic relationship between the two texts than Ellison's playfulness and his avoidance of orderly or ordering analogies allow.

Charles Scruggs's 1974 discussion of Ellison's use of the *Aeneid*, therefore, is an invaluable corrective and supplement to the prior critical preoccupation with the *Odyssey*. It suggests, for example, that through the lascivious character named Sybil (claimed by Stark as a misnamed Homeric Circe), who precipitates the narrator's passage through the Harlem riots and subsequent move underground, the novelist parodies the role of the Sibyl, the chaste prophetess who enables Aeneas's knowledge-gathering descent into the underworld. Notably, none of these early articles move significantly beyond the mere identifying of allusions and inversions to analysis of the implications (for example, in terms of the thematics of racism) of doing so. Each thereby avoids asking the political questions about what's at stake in Ellison's classicism. Tischler's and Scruggs's discussions probably come closest to politicised analysis without explicitly saying so: the former discusses classical comedy's role in the healing of 'psychic wounds' (Tischler 365), while the latter links the novelist's engagement with Virgil to his parodic invocation of D. W. Griffith's white supremacist epic film, *Birth of a Nation* (1915).

Why, after Scruggs's discussion of 1974, is no scholarly work on Ellison's classical allusiveness published for sixteen years? Until 1990, and the appearance of Kenneth Goings and Eugene O'Connor's reading of *Invisible Man* in terms of the paradigm of a 'trickster/hero' (219), there is more than a decade and a half of critical silence on this topic. While the late 1970s brought with them the waning of the Black Arts Movement, with which Ellison existed in a much-documented mutual antipathy, the 1980s saw both the emergence of numerous works defining the recently institutionalised field of African American studies, and the prevalence of post-structural and postmodernist literary readings of the Euro-American canon. It is surely not a coincidence that in these specific political and intellectual contexts no fresh examinations of Ellison's classicism emerged. Indeed, while his self-avowed indebtedness to Greek and Roman tradition was central to what Justine McConnell has labelled his 'humanist, integrationist' stance ('Invisible' 172), it at the same time indubitably fuelled the hostility that has become known as the 'Ellison animus', the suspicion and contempt in which he has been held by numerous artists, intellectuals and students over several decades. To exemplify this negative reception, Jerry Watts quotes Clifford Mason's claims, in a 1970 issue of *Black World*, that while 'Black literature deserved its own references, its own standards, its own rules', Ellison's references are a 'disabling psychosis' that are 'based on a white substructure' (Watts 31).[23] In the minds of many, his classicism has been seen as of one accord with his hostility to Pan-Africanism and black nationalism expressed through the satirical depiction of Ras the Exhorter in *Invisible Man*, through his refusal to identify with the Black Power and Black Arts movements, and through his explicit distancing of himself from Africa. In other words, as some saw it, his engagement with Greek and Roman antiquity was just one more factor in his purported 'Uncle Tom-ism'.[24] His investment in European traditions was seen by some as an adherence to a cultural hierarchy in which Western culture was privileged.

Ellison himself, however, staunchly and consistently defended his right to an aesthetic and political freedom which included the right to be classically allusive as and how he chose.[25] Yet although he would state clearly his belief that 'the imagination is integrative', deliberately twinning his insistence on combining African American and European traditions in his writing with his political stance as 'an American integrationist' (Graham and Singh 235), he never engaged with specific accusations about the motives behind or the effects of his classicism. While his reticence may have contributed to critics' avoidance of the controversial subject of his allusiveness during the 1980s, it may also have contributed to scholars' overlooking and underestimating the subversiveness of his classicism for a surprisingly long time. For it was not until the new field of 'Black Classicism' emerged in the early 2000s – a movement that I outline in the introduction to this volume – that the work of acknowledging and exploring the political radicalism of this novelist's engagements with antiquity began in earnest.

As late as 1999, in her article entitled 'Invisibility and Recognition', Martha Nussbaum compellingly advocates the reading and teaching of *Invisible Man* alongside Sophocles's *Philoctetes*, but does not suggest that the modern text consciously engages the ancient one.[26] Just a few years later such an approach would have seemed glaringly divorced from its rightful intellectual context, for (to recap from my introduction to this book) it was in 2005 that Michele Ronnick published her paradigm-shifting definition of 'Classicism, black' in the *Encyclopedia Africana*. Indeed, Ronnick's work in the 1990s in what she then termed 'Classica Africana' was a catalyst in Patrice Rankine's groundbreaking study of Ellison, *Ulysses in Black* (2006). Rankine analyses the political implications of *Invisible Man*'s relationship with the *Odyssey* within the context of black classicism, reading the novelist's frequently shifting deployments of both the Odysseus figure and the Cyclops figure as sophisticated acts of subversion and resistance. His discussion paved the way for studies of further aspects of Ellison within black classicist frameworks: for example, the 'polyphony' that William Cook and James Tatum explore in the 'Invisible Odyssey' chapter of their study, *African American Writers and Classical Tradition* (2010), Justine McConnell on the invisible man as both Homeric hero and anti-hero (2010), my own comparisons of Ellison with Morrison (2013), and Bryan Crable's recent explorations of the novelist's engagement with Lord Raglan and with Cambridge Ritualists as a whole (2018, 2021).[27] The position of Rankine's work – hence that of Ellison's too – within that of black classicism more generally was consolidated by Emily Greenwood's invaluable survey article of 2009, on 'new directions' within that field.

Even though there is little trace of any explicit interest on the part of Ellison himself in prior black writers' classical allusiveness, there are two dimensions of black classicism that are particularly relevant to his own engagements with antiquity.[28] The first is the fundamental role of the classical tradition in both the pro- and anti-slavery debates of post-Enlightenment and antebellum America, which has been quite recently excavated by scholars such as Edith Hall, Margaret Malamud and John Levi Barnard, and which resonates in all classically allusive American fiction of more recent centuries. The second dimension is the important genealogy of ideas about the interconnectedness of Greece and Rome both with North Africa (particularly Libya, Egypt and Ethiopia) and with West Africa, which became well-known with the publication of Martin Bernal's *Black Athena* (1987), and with the controversy that followed it.

Ellison himself is rarely categorised among those authors invested in the interconnectedness of classical and North/West African cultures. He is not commonly associated with the idea that, to quote Paul Gilroy, 'the roots of European civilization lay in African sources' (*Black Atlantic* 130), and his non-fictional disavowals of Africa have perhaps dissuaded his many readers from pursuing such interpretations of his work. Yet his texts in fact offer rich readings in this regard. In a 2012 essay comparing Ellison with Wole Soyinka and Derek Walcott, for example, Rankine illuminates significant ways in which all three authors force a reassessment of the nature of classical antiquity itself by emphasising its elements of darkness and chaos. In addition, the fact that Ellison owned a copy of Soyinka's 1976 essay collection, *Myth, Literature and the African World*, in which the Nigerian author attests to 'persuasive parallels' between Greek and Yoruban culture' (14), may well explain Ellison's comparison of Bliss/Sunraider in *Three Days* to both Icarus and Eshu-Elegba.[29] Here, as well as in his association between this protagonist and the ill-fated Phaethon (see below), Ellison joins the subversive genealogy of those claiming an African stake in the classical past. Arguably, then, in this and in numerous other ways, his classicism does not diminish but rather intensifies his radical political stance.

Invisible Man (1952)

When Brother Jack excoriates this novel's narrator for working the crowd at Tod Clifton's funeral, not only does his rage cause his glass eye to pop out of his head, but he then proceeds to 'squint' at the invisible man 'with Cyclopian irritation' (474). This comparison between the Brotherhood leader and the cyclops Polyphemus (the one-eyed, cannibalistic giant whom the eponymous hero eventually defeats in Book IX of the *Odyssey*) stands out in Ellison's text as an allusion that is unusually overt. It's a parallel that is uncharacteristically neat. As numerous critics have explored, the novelist deploys complex, often inexplicit and usually ironic echoes of the Homeric epic in his depictions of the invisible man's quest for identity, home and belonging; in his refusal to reveal his name; his journeying both across the United States and within New York City; his dubious sexual encounters with women; and his resilience and capacity for self-reinvention in the face of obstacles and defeats. While in *Ulysses in Black* Rankine identifies the protagonist's survival of three prototypical cyclopic encounters – during the Battle Royal and in the hospital as well as with Brother Jack – as key to this text's critique of white racist oppression, Cook and Tatum explore profound affinities in narrative technique and structure between Ellison's novel and the ancient Greek poem. Yet readers should not allow the critical preoccupation with the novelist's Odyssean engagements to blind them to other equally significant aspects or ramifications of Ellison's classicism in *Invisible Man*. These include intertextual relationships with several other classical and/or canonical European texts (such as Ovid's *Metamorphoses* and Dante's *Inferno*) and with other genres and paradigms besides epic; the consciously imitative modernist nature of Ellison's allusiveness; his subversive depictions of American dominant cultural classicism; and his implications that American culture itself is ripe for transformation.

In his 2012 article, Rankine builds on Scruggs's 1974 essay to elucidate the politics of the novel's engagement with the *Aeneid*. He suggests that the epic's depiction of Rome melding diverse customs 'provides a model for how the chaos of cultures can produce unity' (465–6). In their discussion of Ellisonian 'polyphony', meanwhile, Cook and Tatum build on Robert Butler's work to re-emphasise the echoes of Dante, illuminating the 'numerological play' that recalls the nature of the *Divine Comedy* as a whole (173). Yet Greek tragedy is arguably just as important as epic to Ellison's explorations, in this text, of the power and the limitation of heroic individualism, and of the relationship between the individual and the group. It is surely significant that the teacher who 'made [the narrator] read Greek plays' at the Southern college – one Professor Woodridge – also sums up the 'task' of education and pedagogy as 'that of making ourselves individuals' (40, 354). Ellison draws inexplicit but significant analogies between his protagonist and archetypal tragic heroes such as the self-blinding Oedipus or the wound-nursing Philoctetes. He may thereby be constructing a further analogy: one between the post-Reconstruction emergence of 'the individual' in African American society and culture (as theorised by Lawrence Levine) and the idea that the evolution of the Greek tragic hero reflected the emergence of the individual from archaic communal structures in the Athenian society of its own beginnings.[30] In staging the invisible man's trajectories as a series of downfalls and/or 'reversals' (*Collected* 220), Ellison writes in conventional Aristotelian mode while simultaneously mocking that mode. Furthermore, the author's interest in the apparent inevitability of scapegoating or sacrifice (the narrator realises that in the Brotherhood he is 'both sacrificer and victim' (506)), and in non-rational rituals (such as the crowd behaviour at Tod Clifton's funeral or during the Harlem riot), speaks to his attentiveness to the chaos and Bacchic fury of pre-Enlightenment Greece.[31]

It's significant that one of the two texts from which the novelist elects to quote as an epigraph – T. S. Eliot's 1939 play *The Family Reunion* – is itself a work informed by the Aeschylean *Oresteia*. Ellison chooses as an epigraphic author not Homer, Sophocles or even Ovid, but instead positions this densely allusive modernist poet alongside the equally classically engaged Herman Melville. Here and through the allusiveness in *Invisible Man* as a whole, the African American writer seeks equivalence not with the authors of ancient epics, tragedies or comedies, but rather with modernist forebears – primarily Eliot and Joyce of course – in whose own work classical references are key. In a much-quoted passage in his *Paris Review* interview of 1955, Ellison observes that he had known, as a novice, 'that in both *The Waste Land* and *Ulysses* ancient myth and ritual were used to give form and significance to the material', but that 'it took [him] a few years to realize that the myths and rites which we find functioning in our everyday lives could be used in the same way' (*Collected* 216). In this mini-manifesto (one in which Eliot's essay '*Ulysses*, Order, and Myth' surely resonates), Ellison claims both Joyce and Eliot as his aesthetic ancestors, and explains the rationale for the mixing of classical and vernacular, academic and folk, or 'high' and 'low' traditions that are a trademark of *Invisible Man*.[32]

In *Dedalus in Harlem: The Joyce-Ellison Connection* (1982), Robert List not only testifies to the African American author's deep and wide indebtedness to the Irish one, but also shows how Joyce and Ellison share a predilection for a relationship with antiquity that is dissonant and syncopated rather than harmonious or neat. These authors' allusions are often conscious 'comic near-misses' (List 283), deliberately incongruous juxtapositions between antiquity and modernity.[33] In *Invisible Man*, for example, Ellison's choice of the name 'Sybil' for the inebriated white woman who begs the narrator to stage an assault constitutes (as Scruggs has argued) a parodic dialogue with the *Aeneid*.[34] Unlike the Sibyl in Book VI of that epic, who directs Aeneas to the golden bough, thus ensuring the success of his fact-finding mission to the underworld, Sybil has 'no information' for the narrator (*Invisible* 517), and instead is the catalyst to his involvement in the Harlem riots and his descent into the coal cellar. But an equally important prior text here is *The Waste Land*, in which Eliot's epigraph quotes Trimalchio's description, in Petronius's *Satyricon*, of the caged, aged and suicidal Sibyl of Cumae, which is itself described in Ovid's *Metamorphoses*.[35] Just as Ellison riffs on Joyce's heroic/mock-heroic ending to *Portrait of the Artist*, changing that narrator's commitment to the 'uncreated conscience of [his] race' to that of the '*uncreated features of his face*' (Joyce, *Portrait* 365; *Invisible* 354, original italics), here he riffs on Eliot's anti-heroic invocation of an unedifying detail in an ancient text. The 'classical tradition' for Ellison involves the complex palimpsests of modernist reception as much as it involves the writers of antiquity themselves.

When the narrator attempts to part from Sybil, the couple memorably 'tottered before an ancient-looking building' decorated with 'huge Greek medallions', 'a dark labyrinthine pattern' and a stoop boasting a 'carved stone monster' (*Invisible* 529). Scruggs rightly points out the echoes here of Daedalus's carvings of the Cretan labyrinth on the walls of Apollo's temple, described by Virgil in the *Aeneid* VI, just before the hero meets the Sibyl. But through these details Ellison surely also draws attention to the often-ironic fact that so much American architecture is neoclassical in style. Here and at other key moments in the novel, Ellison anticipates Morrison in juxtaposing the ill-fated actions of his characters, and the indignities and/or brutalities to which they are too often subject, with the heroic classicism which dominant American culture has always made fundamental to its civic ideals and identity, and has expressed through its art, architecture and so on. This interplay forms a crucial backdrop to Ellison's explorations of the struggle for civil rights.

Critics to date have paid surprisingly little attention to the details, in *Invisible Man*, about the neoclassical (perhaps an Egyptian-inspired art nouveau) style of the Wall Street building in which the employment-seeking narrator looks up Mr Bates: it is made of 'white stone' with a 'sculptured bronze façade' (166). Inside Mr Bates's office, the narrator is overwhelmed by the signifiers of classical, humanist education and the concomitant *imperium* of such 'men of power' (168): the 'ceiling-high bookcases' and the 'portraits' of figures who exude 'assurance and arrogance' (167). It is no coincidence that from the 'marble hall' of these offices the invisible man can see 'the Statue of Liberty' (165), the ultimate neoclassical expression of an ideal from which he is excluded.[36] In a later but equally dissonant juxtaposition, when the narrator is on the bus that takes him away from Sybil and into the rioting Harlem, he refers somewhat cryptically to passing 'the hero's tomb' and recalls a significant previous visit there (532). This detail presumably references the actual, historical tomb – housed in a neoclassical-style mausoleum on Riverside Drive – of the epically named and much-mythologised Unionist general Ulysses S. Grant. The narrator here appears nostalgic for a time 'long past', when he adhered more innocently and less ambivalently to the values it embodied (532).[37] No less conflicted, however, is his youthful response to the ambiguous 'bronze statue' of the revered Founder of his college, depicted holding the veil of a kneeling slave (36). Ellison alludes to and critiques the motivated classicism of the dominant American built environment just as he does the many literary traditions that he inherits.[38]

The author shows, throughout the sequence of college chapters, that the South shares with the North a commitment to the 'Great Traditions' that are embodied in Mr Norton and that are rooted in classically inflected ideology (37). During the 'ritual' service in the Chapel (a building 'vine-covered' in a nod to the Theatre of Dionysus? (110)), the students must participate in the 'black rite' of the much-mythologised 'Horatio Alger', while their blind guest speaker glories in the overdetermined name of 'Homer A. Barbee' (111, 133). Yet at the same time, and with great incongruity given that this is an all-black college, Ellison depicts a campus and a culture saturated in Southern pastoralism, one of the key classically derived modes (along with the sense of tragedy) that underpins Confederate memorialisation of and nostalgia for their lost cause. Ellison subverts the very same heroic, pastoral sublime that Cather indulges in *Sapphira and the Slave Girl*, for example, and that entraps Hightower in Faulkner's *Light in August*. The author first introduces the college by referencing every clichéd symbol of the mythological Old South: 'honeysuckle', 'wisteria', 'magnolias' and 'mocking birds' (34). His rhetoric in the style of a classical ode – 'Oh, long green stretch of campus' – is ultimately exploded, however, through the obvious pastiche of Eliot's *Waste Land* that follows it (36–7). Those who find fault with Ellison in the belief that his classicism compromises him politically should perhaps look again at such passages in this novel, where he himself exposes that tradition's often-treacherous ideology.

In the address given at West Point in 1969 (published as 'On Initiation Rites and Power' in 1974), Ellison reflects once again on his epiphanic discovery, while at Tuskegee, of *The Waste Land* and its source texts. The studied, stylised language he uses here, as he talks about reading the 'books' that Eliot references in his footnotes, is particularly interesting for the way it implies the crucial role of Ovid's *Metamorphoses*, without ever naming that author or his text. This reading 'was the beginning of my transformation (or shall we say, metamorphosis)', Ellison says, 'from a would-be composer into a novelist' (*Collected* 525). Few critics have taken the novelist's hint here about Ovid's importance in his work, but to do so is to recognise the full implications of his preoccupation, in *Invisible Man*, with 'transformation' and 'chaos' and with the 'merging fluidity of forms' (both political and aesthetic) that the Rinehart-like narrator's sunglasses enable (*Invisible* 491).[39] Although (as with Virgil) no copy of Ovid's text survives in Ellison's personal collection, he would have encountered this Latin poem not just through Eliot's footnotes, but also through Dante; through Joyce's allusiveness in *Portrait* (including its epigraphic quotation from Ovid); and through his copy of Joseph Campbell's *Hero with a Thousand Faces* (which mentions the *Metamorphoses* twelve times). He would have also encountered Alain Locke's optimistic discourse of Ovidian transformation in his introductory essay to *The New Negro* (1925), where Locke states that the black man had undergone a 'metamorphosis', and that a 'transformed and transforming psychology permeates the masses' (3, 6–7).

Ellison anticipates Morrison in engaging sceptically with this discourse of both the individual's and the dominant culture's capacity to change: the narrator of *Invisible Man* celebrates, tries out and discards one 'new identity' after another as the plot of the novel unfolds (310). On arrival in New York City, for example, he notes the 'change that was coming over him' and that he was 'subtly changed' (178); in his successful speech on the 'dispossession' he tells the audience that '*something strange and miraculous and transforming is taking place in me right now*' (345, original italics) and afterwards declares that he 'had been transformed' (353). Ellison creates a kind of dramatic irony as the reader loses faith in the narrator's endless declarations of self-reinvention and rediscovery. The narrator's sexual liaison with Hubert's wife has undertones of Wilde's Ovidian-derived *Picture of Dorian Gray* (witness Hubert's air of 'sophistication, decadence, over-civilization' (418)), and the myth of Icarus resonates in the 'plunge' outside of history undergone by both Tod Clifton and the narrator (434, 438, 447). Yet the most Ovidian of all figures in *Invisible Man* is, of course, Bliss Proteus Rinehart. While critics rightly trace his shapeshifting changeability to both Odysseus and Proteus in the Homeric epic, his malleability and the vision of a boundarylessness, in terms of both selfhood and society, reflect a 'chaos' profoundly reminiscent of the language and imagery of the pre-creation Chaos that Ovid depicts in his opening to the *Metamorphoses*.[40]

When the invisible man perceives through Rinehart 'a vast seething, hot world of fluidity', in which 'the world seemed to flow before [his] eyes' (498–9), he realises 'the notion was frightening', and from the 'possibilities posed by Rinehart's multiple personalities', he 'turned away' (499). Chaos is not the future that either the narrator or his author seeks. Yet while Ellison stops short of Morrison's speculative envisioning of societies and cultures that have been transformed, he does nevertheless insist in this novel that the capacity for transformation, the potential for change, is inherent in American culture. After Tod Clifton's death, musing on the three African American boys recently arrived in New York from the South, he notes that they 'speak a jived-up transitional language' and 'think transitional thoughts' (441). It is this moment of transition, of change in *process*, that both Ovid's poem and Ellison's novel capture so well. While for Ellison the outcome of such transitions is not yet certain, any vision of a fairer, more democratic future is significantly indebted to what he can 'forge' from Ovid (*Invisible* xvii), as much as from Virgil, from Homer, from the Greek tragedians and from their modernist inheritors. While Ellison's 1981 introduction risks overdetermining the Ovidian resonances – in its emphasis on the author's own 'wild star-burst of metamorphosis', for example (xxii) – political change, in 1952, is still very much a possibility.

Three Days Before the Shooting . . . Part I (2010)

Ellison's 'classical exuberance' – to borrow an attribute he ascribes to one of his characters – is a striking feature of the hefty and unfinished series of manuscripts that were published six years after his death, as *Three Days Before the Shooting . . .* (*Three* 193).[41] My analysis of the classicism in Part I – McIntyre's account of events leading up to Senator Sunraider's shooting (Book 1), and Hickman and Bliss/Sunraider's stream of consciousness/call-and-response recollection in the hospital (Book 2) – opens with a brief overview of this widespread and complex allusiveness. It then explores the importance, throughout both Books 1 and 2, of the mythological figure of Phaethon, the son of the Sun who, in Ovid's *Metamorphoses*, crashes his father's sun-pulling chariot and thereby sets fire to the world.[42] Phaethon, I contend, resonates both in the depiction of Bliss/Sunraider and in the accounts of the black protester, Lee Willie Minifees, who haunts the senator's consciousness.

In the essay 'Tell It Like It Is, Baby' (published in 1965 but begun in Rome in 1956), Ellison implies that the 'pattern of classical tragedy' he detects in Abraham Lincoln's heroic rise and horrific assassination is mirrored in the trajectory of Sunraider in his own second novel (*Collected* 46).[43] As Timothy Parrish has observed, 'Bliss's story cannot escape Lincoln's shadow', and '*Three Days* insists on the enduring, even foundational meaning of Lincoln's tragedy' ('Aesthetics' 210). The novelist depicts both Hickman and Bliss/Sunraider wrestling in different ways with historical circumstances, with fate and with Aristotelian tragic flaws such as hubris and partial-sightedness. Ellison thus implies that the downfall and/or the as-yet-unrealised potential of America itself may be ascribed to similar contrary forces and shortcomings. Although no clear relationship exists between this work and any single classical text – Ellison does not here repeat *Invisible Man*'s prolonged call-and-response with the *Odyssey*, for example – the arc and atmosphere of tragedy co-exist with characteristically eclectic classical references. These range from Hickman's sermonic comparison of scattered, enslaved Africans to diasporic 'dragon's teeth' to invocations of Demosthenes (318, 328), Prometheus (302), Amazonians (346) and, of course, of Odysseus and Polyphemus (388).[44] As in his first novel, furthermore, Ellison makes great play of the classicism of America's civic environment (which co-exists symbiotically with the epic nature of its history): the eagle and the Latin motto in the 'Great Seal' (242); the 'laurel wreaths of antiqued bronze' on the elevator doors (28); the 'pillars' and 'becolumned lobby' gracing many houses (317, 30). Above all, Ellison emphasises the classical ideals expressed in the architecture of the Lincoln Memorial itself, and the 'ancient story' that the 'colossus' of this statue tells (420). The disparity between the heroic aspirations encoded in the architectural and decorative style of Washington DC and its social, racial and economic realities suggests that this city, in Minifees's words, is a 'fool's paradise', fraught with 'the difference between what it *is* and what it's *supposed* to be' (41).

Ellison uses the nouns 'transformation' and 'metamorphosis' (and the verbs derived from these) with an almost-obsessive frequency in *Three Days.* Explicit invocations of figures who are key in Ovid's *Metamorphoses* such as Narcissus, Pygmalion, the much-discussed Icarus and the never-discussed Actaeon suggest that this epic poem is if anything a more significant presence in *Three Days* than in *Invisible Man.*[45] After 1952 (and the first novel's publication) Ellison would have continued to encounter invocations of Ovid in his reading, for example in new works by Joseph Campbell (particularly volume 4 of *The Masks of God* (1968)) and in Dante's *Divine Comedy*, two further copies of which Ellison acquired after 1952. Malraux, meanwhile, who rarely invokes Ovid's name explicitly, was himself preoccupied with the concept of metamorphosis. He used the word and idea repeatedly in works such as *The Walnut Trees of Altenburg* (1945) – which Ellison owned in its 1952 translation – and titled one of his non-fiction works *Metamorphosis of the Gods* (1957).[46] Ellison's preoccupation with 'chaos' and with the fluid unpredictability of history – in both the past and the present – reiterates the echoes of Ovidian flux and instability that punctuate *Invisible Man.*[47]

And the changes undergone by both the work's central characters – Hickman's from jazzman to preacher, and Bliss's from black preacher's protégé through 'movie man' to white supremacist statesman – speak to mid- to late-twentieth-century American readings of the Roman poem that find within it the discourse of self-transformation.[48] Bliss/Sunraider's beloved cinema, like many technologies in this work, is an art form that enables numerous metamorphoses. And Hickman's transition (precipitated by Bliss's birth) from being a trombonist to being one of 'god's trombones' (a preacher) is described with an Ovid-like attention to the physical process of the change: 'my trombone mouthpiece had grown to my lips and my good right arm changed into a slide' (471). Ovid's epic would appear to be invaluable, in complex and various ways, to Ellison's simple but all-defining conviction in this text, that 'men change and have wills and wear masks' (421).[49]

When Hickman and Deacon Wilhite visit Jessie Rockmore's house in Book II, the elderly man and those around him are disgusted by the police officer's apparent belief that by changing his 'accent and manner' he could 'transform himself from white to black', and thereby exert power over his 'out-maneuvered black audience' (*Three* 438–9). In Ellison's exploration of the unstable and shifting nature of racial identity throughout this work as a whole, the myth of Phaethon is a significant intertext because it constitutes a mythological 'Just So'-type story about how African people's skin became black. In Ovid's account, it is thanks to the global fire that burns when Phaethon crashes the chariot belonging to his father, the Sun, that 'the peoples of Aethiopia became black-skinned' (*Met.* II.236).[50] Yet the story's resonances with the central themes of *Three Days* go much further than that.

In Ovid's unusually long and psychologically detailed tale, Phaethon is anxious about whether the Sun (here called Phoebus) is really his father, and asks that Phoebus allow him to drive the chariot that pulls the sun as a proof of his paternity.[51] Fearful of and already grieving the anticipated catastrophe, Phoebus expresses 'fatherly anxiety' and 'a father's cares' (*Met.* II.91–2, 94), but reluctantly agrees. Phaethon is at first delighted to be entrusted with the magnificent chariot, every splendid feature of which Ovid describes in painstaking detail. When he is soaring through 'the top of heaven', however, disaster soon strikes: the horses run wild, Phaethon cannot control them, and the chariot goes off course before 'plunging headlong down' into the Earth. The ensuing worldwide conflagration is described over sixty lines of the poem.

When Jupiter at last ends the chaos, by striking Phaethon dead with a thunderbolt, the youth's body follows the scorched and scattered 'fragments of the wrecked chariot'. It is 'hurled headlong and falls with a long trail from the sky'. 'Though he greatly failed', his epitaph reads, he 'more greatly dared' (*Met.* II.179–228).

In its themes of an ultimately doomed relationship between a father and a son; of filial insecurity and paternal grieving; of a young man overreaching himself; of a flight that ends catastrophically for the whole world as well as for these protagonists; and in its preoccupation with darkness and light, the Phaethon myth possibly surpasses the Icarus/Daedalus myth in speaking to the central themes of *Three Days*.[52] It clearly speaks to Ellison's novel-wide concern with 'an array of absent fathers' and with the 'flights and falls of . . . questing figures' (Conner, 'Father' 167, 175). Its aptness very possibly explains why tropes of both the chariot and the fire recur, in various forms, throughout Ellison's depictions of both Bliss/Sunraider and Lee Willie Minifees, and of the combustible political background of their lives. In his sonorous speech in the Senate, just before he is shot, Bliss/Sunraider notably declaims that 'it is in our nature to soar', and that 'by following the courses mapped through the adventurous efforts of our fathers we affirm and revitalize their awesome vision' (238). Though Bliss himself appears oblivious to the Phaethon-inflected irony of his discourse – and indeed of his acquired name, 'Sunraider' – Ellison punctuates his account of Bliss/Sunraider's consciousness, as well as others' perceptions of him, with vignettes and symbolic objects that contribute to the power of this myth as a kind of theme tune accompanying this character's life. In Book I, McIntyre's own narrative consciousness develops the mythical dimensions of Bliss/Sunraider's life by bestowing great significance on various events that explicitly involve the senator and/or implicitly reflect on his life and times. Minifees's burning of his Cadillac is the most obvious of these, but the focus on the elevator 'car' that appears to be out of control, gliding and plunging (28–9), and the 'unforeseen combustibility of the sports car at Le Mans' (73) also bring Phaethon to mind. In this first book, McIntyre's own mythologising tendencies are clearly on display in his depictions of a protagonist who, the narrator claims, 'lived with fire and with ice, with sun and with lightning' (30).

In Book II, meanwhile, Ellison's exploration of Bliss/Sunraider's and Hickman's present and past itself intensifies the dialogue with the myth of the son of the Sun. The senator's rhetorical flourish about 'the darkness in lightness and the lightness in darkness' is made only too real by Severen's shooting of the chandelier, which the fallen senator perceives as 'a watery distortion of crystal light, a light which seemed to descend and settle him within a ring of liquid fire' (214). If these words are reminiscent of the lengthy description of the conflagration caused by Phaethon's misguided ambition in the *Metamorphoses*, then Bliss's preaching of a sermon by 'John P. Eatmore' is even more so (302). This 'fire sermon' of course alludes to a vast range of texts – from *The Waste Land* to the preaching on hell in *Portrait of the Artist* and to Milton's chaos in *Paradise Lost*.[53] But, while Sundquist compares Sunraider to Prometheus at this point, the line from the sermon that he quotes – 'For man was beseeching the Lord for warmth when it was the *sun* itself he coveted' (*Three* 305, original italics; 'Labyrinth' 134) – brings Phaethon to mind just as much as the fire-stealing titan. The sermonic account of Man's 'headlong plunge, in hectic heathen flight' in the 'volcanic fire', and of humanity's 'charred flesh' (305–6, 309), echoes Ovid's long description of burning volcanic mountains, of the Earth's singed hair and ashy eyes, and of Phaethon's burning face as he falls. Bliss/Sunraider's sickbed hallucinations (or memories?) of his 'flying' from a train on which he was hobo-ing recalls Phaethon's fate just as much as Icarus's in its preoccupation with the sun and sunlight (308–9). And his befuddled recollection of a car that flies, the '*mirage-like image of black metal agleam with chrome*' that he watched '*floating away*', once more suggests the airborne chariot of the Sun (411, original italics).

Just before Bliss/Sunraider is shot, he raises a laugh in the Senate by referring to the 'wildest black man behind the wheel of a Cadillac' (243). Although he dismisses it as a comic trifle here, his sickbed hallucination of the flying car perhaps indicates how Minifees's burning of his convertible Cadillac has disturbed and now haunts the senator more than he has been prepared to admit. Yet it is striking that critics to date have paid very little attention to the Cadillac-burning incident: in *The New Territory*, for example, which contains five detailed analyses of *Three Days*, there is only one passing reference to Minifees (Parrish, 'Aesthetics' 212). This episode's lack of appeal or interest to scholars is possibly due to the fact that it is already highly interpreted (if not over-interpreted) within the text by several characters. Yet in McIntyre's telling us that the scene was 'unbelievably wild' (46) and that the immolation was 'a crude and most portentous gesture' (47); in McGowan's later assertion that the 'nigra' was 'trying to politicize the Cadillac' (59); and in Minifees's own declaration that he had burnt his car 'to answer that half-assed senator' (223), there is a linguistic flatness or obviousness that obscures as much as it reveals. My contention is that to read the act of Cadillac-burning in relation to the Ovidian myth that reverberates within it, and to interpret Minifees himself as a kind of 'anti-Phaethon', is to understand more fully the political significance of this event.

Speaking with McIntyre in the psychiatric ward, Minifees refers to his incendiary action as his 'Sunraider riff' (222). We might also understand it as his 'Phaethon riff', as Ellison creates a connection, or rather an associative disconnection, between Phaethon's ill-fated driving of the chariot of the sun and Minifees's burning of his car. McIntyre's reference to the 'gleaming' white Cadillac as a 'shining chariot' (37) is echoed by Ellison in a 1976 interview, in which, in attesting to black elegance, he cites 'the way the dedicated worshipper of the Cadillac sits at the steering wheel of his chariot' (Graham and Singh 329). Ovid's detailed description of the beautiful gold and silver mechanics of Phoebus's chariot resonates in the 'gleam' of Minifees's vehicle, and Ellison further emphasises the classical and archetypal elements of the scene through Sunraider's broadcasted insults about the 'neopagan comfort' of Cadillacs, and the 'fiery metamorphosis of the white machine' once it has been set alight (47, 39). McIntyre's description of the spectacle of the 'flaming convertible' being 'distorted by heat' constitutes that same Ovidian eye for the physical process of transition or transformation that Ellison so often displays (40, 39). Minifees's assertion that the senator's insults made him feel that his 'brain was on fire' – although driving the Cadillac had entailed that 'good old familiar feeling of flying' (43, 42) – compels us to think further about what the relationship between this black man and Phaethon, or between this black man and Bliss/Sunraider-as-Phaethon, might mean.

Ovid's tale of Phaethon is about both a son's anxiety that his father proves his paternity, and that son's desire to impress and to equal his father in greatness and prowess. Perhaps Minifees's burning of his own 'shining chariot' (37), then, his ultimate rejection or inversion of Phaethon's heroic aspiration and catastrophic downfall, is also a rejection of the white patriarchal power that

Senator Sunraider and American dominant culture symbolise. In his committee session remarks on the Cadillac that had so angered Minifees, the senator mocks African American 'desire' for wealth and power, asking whether they want 'a jet plane on every Harlem rooftop?' (47). This particular black American man, however, rejects both the power of white men and the chance to equal their purported greatness and prowess, by destroying what those white men have made desirable. While disaster and destruction strike Phaethon because he loses control, inadvertently wreaks havoc, and is laid low by Jupiter's thunderbolt, Minifees conversely asserts control, deliberately creates havoc, and does not wait for some omnipotent force's weaponry to bring him down. Even though Minifees has to 'hit [him]self' to 'hurt' Sunraider (224), and even though he is subsequently institutionalised by the powers that be, he is left with his autonomy and self-determination intact.

Understanding Bliss/Sunraider as a neo-Phaethon and Minifees as an anti-Phaethon has one further important implication. If the fire caused by Phaethon led to the 'Aethiopians' becoming black-skinned, then Minifees's subversion of the Phaethon role is also a subversion of this idea; Ellison thus rejects the idea of the primacy and priority of white people in power. In her 1998 novel, *Paradise*, Toni Morrison 'out-Ovids Ovid' by inverting the Phaethon myth to suggest that black Africans are the 'original' members of the human race.[54] Ellison's mythical resonances in the Minifees episode anticipate that move. They can be read as a subtle 'black classicist' intertextuality that roots the origins of human existence in Africa, and that thereby asserts not black equality with whites, but black priority.

Three Days Before the Shooting . . . Part II: 'Hickman in Washington DC' (2010)

In the pages of 'Hickman in Washington DC' that rewrite the visit to the Lincoln Memorial (first described in the prologue of Part I), Hickman is disturbed by his congregation's ensuing silent melancholy.[55] He had hoped that their encounter with this monument 'would mark the high point of their tour through the shifty hall of mirrors called "history"' (579). Part II of *Three Days* as a whole is profoundly concerned with the 'shifty hall of mirrors called "history"' – with transformed and transformative representations of, and understandings of, the past. Throughout this 'Washington

DC' section of the manuscript, Ellison makes significant recourse to Ovidian mythology about artists and artistry. These resonances inform his explorations, through Hickman's consciousness, of the power and the limitations of literature, of music, of the visual arts and of preaching to narrate the past, to account for the present, and to shape the future.

Ellison's account here of the quasi-pilgrimage to Lincoln's shrine surely constitutes some of the most intensely determined reading of America's architectural and decorative classicism in his oeuvre. The sculpture of the racist nineteenth-century statesman John C. Calhoun that now adorns the foyer to Bliss/Sunraider's senatorial office – a 'pedestal-mounted white marble bust' (508) – is soon eclipsed by the lyrical account of the neoclassical monuments on the National Mall at cherry blossom time. The stunning view that Hickman takes in from the Lincoln Memorial steps is freighted with both painful history and ambiguous promise:

> the banks of the basin were accented by trees whose branches were pale pink with blossoms, and above the curve of its southernmost bank the Jefferson Memorial loomed majestic and white in the sunlight. . . . he looked beyond the reflecting pool to the Washington Monument and on to the far distant dome of the Capitol. (579)

For a brief moment here, the tone is one of genuine idyllic pastoral, in sharp contrast to the ironic, burlesqued 'Old Southern' pastoral through which the invisible man describes the flawed arcadia of his Southern college. Yet the 'shifty hall of mirrors' that Hickman's perception involves soon takes over, complicating the serenity with a near-postmodern fluidity, instability and meta-awareness: 'Reflected in its pool Lincoln's marble-clad memorial rippled and swayed, and the reflections of visitors arrayed on its steps were bobbing and weaving in the breeze-ruffled water like figures in a dream sequence from a historical movie' (578). This passage exemplifies the way that classical structures are rarely frozen or motionless in Ellison's text. They may be corrupted and decayed, like the scarred bronze door of the storefront church, with its 'off centre' laurel wreath (562), but their meanings are always in process and always being made new.

As Hickman meditates on the statue of Lincoln itself – on the implications of its 'great sculptural form' and the 'voiceless eloquence of impermeable stone' (575, 574) – he believes that he is witnessing a remarkable transformation. 'The stone seemed to come alive,' Ellison writes, 'the great chest appearing to heave as though stirred at last by the aura of acts unfinished and promises unkept which [Hickman] and his flock brought into its presence' (576). The novelist here implicitly associates Hickman with two artists in Ovid's *Metamorphoses* who have the power to change stone or sculpture into living humanity. The first of these is Deucalion, who appears in *Metamorphoses* I as a key player in the Ovidian creation myth. Together with Pyrrha, Deucalion is ordered by Themis to recreate human beings (after their destruction in the flood) by throwing stones, which 'lose their hardness and stillness', initially resembling 'statues just begun out of marble' before being 'changed to flesh' (*Met.* 1.401–8). The second is Pygmalion, the Cypriot sculptor whom Ellison briefly invokes explicitly, with reference to Sippy Brown, in the 'Georgia and Oklahoma' section of his work (*Three* 699). Ovid's Pygmalion famously creates a statue of a woman that is so realistic that it seems 'living' (X.250), and so beautiful that he loves and prays to marry it. Venus grants his prayer by bringing the statue to life.[56] Through recasting these Ovidian tropes of vivified stone as a momentary revivification of Abraham Lincoln, the novelist of course seeks to revivify Lincoln's vision of racial justice and equality, to restore those ideals both to the incipient Civil Rights era in which Hickman visits DC, and also to the racially fraught Reaganite era in which Ellison was now revising his work. Crucially, however, the Ovidian echoes also reinscribe the significance of Hickman himself, as a powerfully generative artist figure akin to Deucalion and Pygmalion, one whose creative thinking and passionate faith may well transform the apparently set-in-stone racial conservatism characterising the American culture he inhabits.

As I have already discussed, throughout *Three Days* Ellison connects Lincoln and Bliss/Sunraider through the paradigm of the tragic hero, and his essay 'Tell It Like It Is, Baby' articulates a tragic conception of Lincoln's life and legacy that illuminates the tragic conception of the second novel.[57] Yet this essay is also striking for its Ovidian sentiment, its palpable engagement with Ovid's structuring principle of metamorphosis. Through repeated references to his own location in Rome as he writes the piece, Ellison implicitly draws attention to the thematic resonances of Ovid's poem – an epic written during a time of great change, instability and transition, as ancient Rome was still coming to terms with the establishment of

Augustan imperial rule a generation earlier. Ellison refers, for example, to the 'Roman dark', 'the hushed Roman night' and 'the bright Roman day' (*Collected* 32, 44).

An Ovidian spirit or dynamic, therefore, constitutes a significant second link between the essay and *Three Days*.[58] For example, while in the novel Hickman believes the statue of Lincoln is coming to life, Ellison notes in the essay that in being transported through his dream back to that president's assassination, it was 'as though a book of nineteenth-century photographs had erupted into vivid life' (*Collected* 34). While witnessing the desecration of Lincoln's corpse, the essayist expects to be changed, himself, into a beast with 'hairy paws' (38), and he describes the desecrated body as 'the Happy Hooligan transformation' (40). In the essay, Ellison only finds consolation and the restoration of order through remembering a scene from a film in which actor Charles Laughton recites the Gettysburg Address: in this reiteration Lincoln's words are 'transformed into a most resonant image of the American's post-Civil War imperative of conscience and consciousness achieved' (45). Within *Three Days*, meanwhile, it is arguably Hickman's encounter with the temporarily revivified statue of Lincoln that transforms that memorial into a similar symbol of political and historical 'conscience and consciousness achieved'. Both in the essay and within 'Hickman in Washington DC', then, Ellison's deployment of Ovidian transition-in-progress is fundamental to his representations of the American past and present.

In both the prologue and epilogue to 'Tell It Like It Is, Baby', which were added by the author in 1965, Ellison mentions the fact that at the time of his bad dream about Lincoln he had 'fallen asleep while reading *The Classical Tradition in Poetry*' by Gilbert Murray.[59] The point of this self-fashioning is presumably to direct the reader to the connections between Murray's work and Ellison's own. While the essay is explicit about parallels in the realm of the tragic, linking Lincoln's trajectory to Murray's discussion of Hamlet and Orestes, there is a less obvious but equally significant connection between Murray's and Ellison's deployment of Ovid's *Metamorphoses*. Murray notes that the theme of creation out of chaos – which is of course a defining preoccupation of Ellison's work – is a central theme of Milton's *Paradise Lost*, and that it also features in 'Hesiod, in Apollonius, in Vergil, of course in Lucretius, even in Aristophanes and Ovid' (10). For Ellison, the creator who makes sense of the chaos – the artist figure – is every bit as significant as his creation. This conviction is evident in the illuminating reflection on his own creative process with which he brings 'Tell It Like It Is, Baby' to a close: past and present 'collide within his interior life', he writes, 'either to be jumbled in the chaos of dream, or brought to ordered significance through the forms and techniques of his art' (*Collected* 46).[60]

Ellison's claim that he heard a 'nightingale' during his sleep-disturbed but productive 'Roman night' brings to mind not just Keats's famous ode, but also the mythical Philomel (or Philomela). In the *Metamorphoses* Philomela is turned into a nightingale having been raped by Tereus, who also cut out her tongue. Ellison would have encountered this gruesome tale while still at Tuskegee, of course, through Eliot's allusion in *The Waste Land* to 'the change of Philomel', as depicted on the wall of the lady's boudoir in 'A Game of Chess' (*Waste Land* l. 99).[61] It is perhaps the fact that Ovid's Philomela manages to convey her traumatic experience through weaving a tapestry, as well as the powerful painting depicting her in Eliot's poem, that inspires the *ekphrasis* on the tapestry in the 'Fall' section of 'Hickman in Washington DC'. Here, in the lounge of the Longview Hotel, the eponymous character meditates on the enormous wall-hanging or tapestry in which Brueghel's *Landscape with the Fall of Icarus* is bordered by 'miniature portraits' of heroic American 'inventors and scientists', along with numerous technological inventions (*Three* 598). Critics have rightly emphasised the intended parallels here between Icarus and the 'high-flying senator' Bliss/Sunraider (592): Sundquist, for example, illuminates this relationship while going on to elucidate the way Ellison interweaves the Icarian flying myth with the 'Ibo Landing story'; this folkloric tale about enslaved Africans flying out of the sea back to Africa is a cultural survival that has been central within African American resistance ('Labyrinth' 132). Sundquist's point sits well alongside my own, above, about the ways in which Ellison in both books of *Three Days* exploits the Greek, Roman and African interconnections inherent in the myth of Phaethon.

Equal in significance to the Bliss/Sunraider-as-Icarus dynamic here is the concomitant construction of Hickman, the father figure, as Daedalus: as the artist-engineer who created both the Cretan labyrinth and the wings that enabled both his son and himself to fly. Resonating within Hickman's meditation on the woven version of the Brueghel is not just Joyce's invocation of Daedalus in Stephen's obviously allusive surname. We also detect the Irish author's epigraph to *Portrait of the Artist*, where he quotes (in Latin) Ovid's account of how Daedalus, hating his exile in Crete, 'sets his mind at work among unknown arts' (Joyce, *Portrait* 174; Ovid, *Met.* VIII.188 – sometimes translated as 'to new inventions'). Indeed, both this 'Fall' episode and 'Hickman in Washington DC' as a whole might well be understood as Hickman's portrait of himself as an artist, as a young man but also as an aging man. He ruminates on the way he has shaped Bliss/Sunraider's life ('we cast him as a hero' (*Three* 527)), but also embarks on long reflections on his own past both as a jazz trombonist and as a preacher. He meditates not just on his change from one to the other, but on the transformative, generative and regenerative powers of both of those arts. He notes that the 'ancient landscape' in the tapestry reminds him of a 'game' in jazz, recalled in great technical detail (595), and he remembers how his jazz playing had given him 'power to control . . . [the] most intimate moods and emotions' of others (589), and how he thereby changed the course of their lives.

Gilbert Murray states unequivocally, in his *The Classical Tradition . . .*, that 'Poetry, in the old, commonplace Aristotelian view, is an "artifact" . . . it is a thing made' (243). Throughout 'Hickman in Washington DC', Ellison depicts a changing and unstable America as it is experienced, reflected and shaped by at least three 'artificers', to use Joyce's wonderfully ambiguous term for the composite of his own father, God and Daedalus whom he addresses at the end of *Portrait*. This author makes Ovidian metamorphic tradition his own in positioning Hickman, Bliss/Sunraider and ultimately of course himself within a tradition of artists akin to both Daedalus and Pygmalion. The extent to which he shares Joyce's ambivalence about the power of the artist, and about whether or not the artist is ultimately noble and heroic, is a complex question that has yet to be fully explored. But while he certainly exploits to the full the ironies inherent in dominant American classicism, he appears unambivalent to the end about the classical tradition itself, and about its usefulness as an infinitely rich resource.

Notes

1. See *Collected Essays* (2003); for correspondence see *Trading Twelves* (2001) and Callahan and Conner (*Selected Letters*); for interviews see Graham and Singh. For a useful chronology of Ellison's life and

publications (until 2005) see Posnock, *Cambridge* xi–xiv. My discussion draws on the two full-length biographies of Ellison: Jackson (2002) and Rampersad (2008); also Callahan, Introduction to *Flying Home* (1996).

2. See Sundquist, 'Labyrinth' 132–5.
3. There are of course numerous other classical heroic presences in *Three Days* that are beyond the scope of this chapter.
4. See Roynon, 'Ellison and the *Metamorphoses*' for a fuller discussion, including of allusions to the Diana/Actaeon myth in *Three Days*.
5. See *Collected Essays* 87–8, 395; Graham and Singh 92, 250.
6. See for example H. Baker 174–5, discussed in McConnell, 'Invisible' 171.
7. On Raglan's 1936 work see *Collected* 218, 528; Graham and Singh 14; Crable, 'Who?'.
8. On Tourgée see Blight 219; Roynon, *Morrison* 82.
9. On Ellison's reading see Rampersad 29ff; Jackson 48, 70.
10. Ellison described his teachers as 'dedicated products of New England classical education' (Graham and Singh 370). On his archived schoolboy copy of Caesar's *Gallic Wars* see my introduction to this book, and the illustration that precedes the preface.
11. For Ellison on 'tradition' see *Collected* 216, 496ff; Graham and Singh 213, 255.
12. See also Jackson 110–11: Ellison was wowed by a visiting lecturer who used excerpts from the *Iliad* and Minoan frescoes to advance his arguments about black history.
13. See for example Graham and Singh 65, 361.
14. Eliot footnotes line 218 of the poem by quoting *Met.* III.320–38, about the hermaphroditic Tiresias.
15. See Graham and Singh 90–1.
16. Parenthetical dates here refer to the publication dates of the specific editions owned by Ellison. For a full list of Ellison's books see 'The Ralph Ellison Collection', <http://hdl.loc.gov/loc.rbc/eadrbc.rb016001> (last accessed 11 May 2020). For Ellison's own reflections on the critical role his reading played in his self-formation during the 1940s see Callahan and Conner 190–6 (letter to Richard Wright, August 18, 1945); Callahan; *Collected* 57.
17. On Ellison and Prometheus see B. Foley, especially 7–8, 86–7. For details of these and Ellison's further annotations within his own books see Roynon, 'We Are Individuals'.
18. This issue of *Life* is available at <https://books.google.co.uk/books?id=8EkEAAAAMBAJ&dq=Renaissance+Man&source=gbs_navlinks_s> (last accessed 11 May 2020). See Roynon, 'Individuals' for further discussion of this *Life* series, Fromm and Burckhardt.
19. On Ellison's interest in Campbell (including his ownership of the four-volume *Masks of God*) see Roynon, 'Ellison and the *Metamorphoses*'.

20. See Crable, 'Ellison's Appropriation'.
21. See pp. 135–8 for further discussion of the connections between Gilbert Murray's *Classical Tradition*, Ellison's 'Tell It Like It Is, Baby' and his time in Rome.
22. See Stark 63, n. 1; also Schallück.
23. For analyses of critical hostility to Ellison see Watts 30–3; also Posnock, 'Mourning and Melancholy' (2016). Percival Everett's 2001 novel *Erasure* constitutes incisive comment on the Ellisonian predicament.
24. See Watts 30, quoting Mason.
25. He did so most notably in his essay 'The World and the Jug' (1963; *Collected* 155–88).
26. Nussbaum may be unaware that Ellison's 1905 collection of Sophocles's tragedies includes *Philoctetes*.
27. Shreve's essay on *Three Days*, 'Implicit Morality', is unusual as a recent exploration of Ellisonian tragic structures that does not reference black classicism.
28. See my introduction for an essential overview of the black classicist scholarship.
29. See Sundquist, 'Labyrinth' 129.
30. See Levine 223–4; Roynon, *Morrison* 135–6. For mid-twentieth-century classical scholarship that links the tragic hero to the increasing significance of the individual in Greek society see Little 12, 50; Dodds 46, 76.
31. See Rankine, '*Black*' 460–1; Crable, 'Ellison's Appropriation'.
32. See also 'The World and the Jug' (especially *Collected* 164, 185), where Ellison first conceptualises his literary 'ancestors'.
33. List is quoted in Cook and Tatum 184. On Ellison and Joyce see also Conner, 'Father'.
34. *Aeneid* VI.42–155; see Scruggs 369–70. Ellison may also have in mind the 'Sybil who tore up the leaves of prophecy' in Shaw's preface to *Pygmalion* (Shaw 197).
35. Eliot quotes the *Satyricon* (*Waste Land* 124, including n. 1); see Petronius, *Satyricon* section 48; Ovid, *Met.* XIV.101–53. See Chapter 2 on Fitzgerald and Petronius.
36. Ellison here anticipates the prologue of Paul Beatty's *The Sellout* (2015) (see my introduction here).
37. Compare Ellison's recollection of finding a plasticine 'frieze' of the African American soldiers 'depicted on Saint-Gaudens's monument to Colonel Robert Shaw and his 54th Massachusetts Negro Regiment' (*Invisible* xvii). Compare the Shaw monument in Chapter 3, n. 35 here.

38. See Nadel on Ellison's subversion of Lewis Mumford's once-iconic account (itself entitled *The Golden Day* (1927)) of American literature's purported tragic fall from its mid-nineteenth-century greatness.
39. See Roynon, 'Ellison and the *Metamorphoses*' for a fuller discussion, including of Ellison's echoing the Pythagorean worldview that 'all is flux' (*Met.* XV.178).
40. See *Met.* I.5–20 on Chaos; *Met.* VIII.731–7 on Proteus.
41. For invaluable explanations of the plot and themes of *Three Days* see Conner and Morel, Introduction; also Callahan and Bradley's introduction to the text itself.
42. See Chapters 3 and 5 for Phaethon in Faulkner and Morrison respectively.
43. See Conner, 'Father' for analysis of its relationship to *Three Days*.
44. Ellison also describes lynching as a ritual that is akin to classical scapegoating: 'like old Greek folks emptied of sin' (463). See Crable, 'Ellison's Appropriation' on lynching as ritual.
45. For Narcissus see *Three* 393, and the text-wide thematic interest in echoes and echoing; for Pygmalion see 699 (in Part II), but also pp. 134–5. See also Roynon, 'Ellison and the *Metamorphoses*'.
46. In *Three Days*, McIntyre attributes the word 'metamorphosis' to 'one of the more intriguing French writers' (87). See De La Piedra 138 for the source of the name 'Vannec' here: Malraux's *The Royal Way* (1930).
47. Compare *Invisible* 491, 499; *Collected* 343–4; *Three* 587.
48. For example Doctorow's *Ragtime* (1975) or Eugenides's *Middlesex* (2002); see also Roynon, 'Ovid, Race' on these novels.
49. On cinema and transformation in *Three Days* see Lindenberg.
50. When Ovid was writing this poem (in around 8 CE), the term 'Aethiop' or 'Ethiopian' was often used to mean any black man or black slave, and/or any African.
51. *Met.* II.1–355.
52. Dante's several references to Phaethon – for example that his story 'still makes fathers wary of sons' (*Paradiso* XVII.1) – may well have suggested the myth to Ellison. Notably, in *Inferno* XVII.106–11, Dante compares Virgil's fear of flying to that of both Phaethon and Icarus at the moment of their downward plunges back to earth.
53. See Devlin.
54. See Roynon, *Morrison* 175.
55. My discussion here focuses only on this small section of Part II; for an overview of Part II see Callahan and Bradley's introduction to the computer sequences (Ellison, *Three* 485–98). My thanks to Lena Hill for emphasising, in our conversations, that the European contexts and

references ebb away in 'Hickman in Georgia and Oklahoma', wherein African American and Native American folklore predominate.

56. See Lateiner for a discussion of all the key artist figures (including Pygmalion) in the *Metamorphoses*.
57. See Conner, 'Father'.
58. See Roynon, 'Ovid, Race' on this 'Ovidian dynamic'.
59. Ellison owned a 1956 edition of this eminent classical scholar's 1927 work; see p. 116.
60. Ellison also uses the central Ovidian term to describe his own authorial formation: his 'odd metamorphosis as a writer' (*Collected* 29).
61. In his footnote Eliot references 'Ovid, Metamorphoses VI, Philomela' (*Waste Land* 141). See *Met.* VI.438–674.

Further Reading

Ellison, Ralph. 'Tell It Like It Is, Baby'. *Collected Essays*. New York: Modern Library, 2003. 29–46.

Ellison, Ralph. 'The World and the Jug'. *Collected Essays*. New York: Modern Library, 2003. 155–88.

Greenwood, Emily. 'Re-rooting the Classical Tradition: New Directions in Black Classicism'. *Classical Receptions Journal* 1.1 (2009): 87–103.

Rankine, Patrice. '*Black is, black ain't*: Classical Reception and Nothingness in Ralph Ellison, Derek Walcott and Wole Soyinka'. *Revue de littérature comparée* 344 (2012): 457–74.

Roynon, Tessa. 'Ellison and the *Metamorphoses* of Ovid: Transformative Allusions'. *Global Ralph Ellison: Transnational Aesthetics and Politics*. Ed. Tessa Roynon and Marc Conner. Oxford: Peter Lang, 2020/21.

CHAPTER 5

Toni Morrison (1931–2019)

Morrison and the Classics

In Toni Morrison's final novel, *God Help the Child* (2015), Booker recalls the first time he set eyes on the woman who was to become his lover. He remembers Bride as 'a midnight Galatea always and already alive' (132). This novel is something of an anomaly in the Morrisonian oeuvre in that it has not, for the most part, been rated highly either by readers or by critics. The revisionary allusion to Galatea (the statue-turned-woman created by Pygmalion in Ovid's *Metamorphoses*), however, which is both explicit in this quotation and implicit throughout the novel as a whole, exemplifies the complex dialogue with the classical tradition that has been a consistent feature of Morrison's literary output over the last fifty years.[1]

Morrison's classical allusiveness ranges from the invocations of *Moirai* (the Fates) and the resonances of the myths of Demeter/ Persephone and of Tereus and Philomela in *The Bluest Eye* (1970) to the profound engagement with both the *Odyssey* and the *Iliad* in *Home* (2012). It includes the engagement with Greek tragedy that is central to *Beloved* (1987); with classical epic and pastoral in *Jazz* (1992); and with the Miltonic Latinisms that resonate throughout *A Mercy* (2008).[2] This author always avoids straightforward parallels or too-ready analogies between ancient and modern figures; as McConnell argues, Morrison refuses 'to provide easy frameworks that gratify the traditionally-elite readers who have classics at their fingertips' ('Postcolonial' 145). For example, she gives names to many of her characters and places that are simultaneously non-schematic, misleading and significant in relation to the classical tradition: these include Ajax (or A. Jacks) in *Sula* (1973); Circe in *Song of Solomon* (1977); Valerian in *Tar Baby* (1983); Seneca and Pallas in *Paradise* (1998); and the town of Lotus in *Home*. Although it is crucial to recognise that classicism is just one among the many cultural resources on which her work draws (and that, unlike in Willa Cather's work, for example, the classical world is not privileged over others), the legacies of Greece and Rome are indubitably a powerful, often-subversive presence in the Morrisonian oeuvre.

In strikingly different ways, each of this author's eleven novels strategically alludes to Greek and Roman history, mythology, literature and social, cultural and/or religious practice. In so doing, they together challenge and rewrite the prevailing narratives of American history and ideology which, as I outline in this book's introduction, have themselves harnessed the classical tradition to hegemonic ends. Through engaging both the ancient world and the ways that dominant American culture has capitalised on antiquity's legacies, Morrison not only protests racial discrimination, violence and injustice. She also takes issue with American individualism (through choric structures that represent the community or society) and challenges both patriarchy and American exceptionalism (through the affinity between the Oven and the Athenian *koine hestia*, or communal hearth, in *Paradise*, for example). Her classicism enables her to fulfil her own imperative that 'the past has to be revised' (Taylor-Guthrie 264).

There is to date no full-length or authorised biographical study of Morrison on which to draw, and neither do we have a comprehensive catalogue of her personal book collection, as we do for Faulkner and for Ellison.[3] We know from her interviews and other self-reflections, however, that she was always both a voracious reader and a good student: she has described books as 'major' and as a 'driving thing' in her childhood (Denard 100). While she grew up immersed in the African American storytelling, folk and musical traditions of her close-knit family, as well as in the rhythms and cadences of the King James Bible, her formal education primarily involved the canonical works that have come to define 'Western civilisation'. Her favourite authors as a teenager were not African American, but rather canonical novelists such as Tolstoy, Dostoevsky, Austen and Dreiser.[4] She never learned Greek, but she did study four years of Latin while at high school in Lorain, Ohio, and has subsequently commented on the brilliance of her Latin teacher there.[5] As a frequent reader at the public library of her home town Lorain at this time, moreover, she may also have read the early editions of Edith Hamilton's *The Greek Way* (1930), *The Roman Way* (1933) and *Mythology* (1942), all of which were in this institution's holdings. That library's early-twentieth-century editions of *Aesop's Fables* may have led, eventually, to her own revised versions of Aesop in her children's series, *Who's Got Game?* (2003–4).[6]

The author attests frequently in interviews to the fact that she was a Classics minor (while majoring in English) at Howard University, where she was an undergraduate from 1949 to 1953. She has also often discussed – for example in her crucial essay of 1989, 'Unspeakable Things Unspoken' – her admiration for Greek tragedy and her sense of 'its similarity to Afro-American communal structures . . . and African religion and philosophy' ('Unspeakable' 369).[7] She has expressed some ambivalence about her time at Howard itself, however. She encountered there a very traditional English department, in which 'the things [she] studied were Western' and where her wish to write a paper on 'Black Characters in Shakespeare' caused 'alarm' (Taylor-Guthrie 174–5). The Classics department's 'class bulletin' or syllabus description for the years that she minored in the field reflects a similar intellectual culture, typical of 1950s conservatism, in its declaration that 'the important contributions which classical antiquity has bequeathed to Western civilization . . . cannot be ignored in a liberal education, for this heritage lies at the root of our own civilization' ('Howard' 85). Such language resonates interestingly in the scathing depiction of I Corinthians's college education, and her subsequent unemployability, in *Song of Solomon*.[8]

Yet although one of the Classics courses that Morrison presumably took, 'Greek Drama in English', is highly conventional in its 'discussion of the definition, origin, and development of tragedy and comedy based on the *Poetics* of Aristotle' ('Howard' 86), it is notable that her instructor would have been the then Head of Department, Frank M. Snowden. Snowden is himself a politically nuanced figure. As early as 1948, he published an article on 'The Negro in Ancient Greece' in the journal *American Anthropologist*, and his major works went on to include *Blacks in Antiquity* (1970) and *Before Color Prejudice: The Ancient View of Blacks* (1983). Yet he also published (in 1996) an outspoken critique of Afrocentric scholarship, as part of an essay collection (edited by Lefkowitz and Rogers) which takes issue with Martin Bernal's *Black Athena*.[9] Morrison may well be indebted to Snowden both for her sense of the analogies between the ancient world and the United States (on which his *Blacks in Antiquity* draws) and for her ambivalence about Classics and their politics. Indeed, Morrison's conflicted perspective on canonical, 'great books' liberal education as a whole arguably has affinities with the invisible man's worldview at the end of Ellison's novel: 'I condemn and affirm, say no and say yes, say yes and say no' (*Invisible* 579).

Alongside her studies, moreover, Morrison was a member of two renowned drama groups: the Howard Players and the Washington Repertory Players. Although the archives record her playing key parts in Shakespeare's *Richard III* and *Taming of the Shrew*, there is no evidence that she herself performed in Greek tragedies. Greek dramatic productions staged at Howard during her years there, however, include Euripides's *Alcestis*, in 1952, and, in 1959 and 1961 (during the years when she had returned to campus as a teacher), *Medea* and *Antigone* respectively.[10] As Dana Williams argues, Morrison may well have been influenced by the work of significant figures in the Drama department such as Owen Dodson, who exemplified the art of a politically engaged 'black humanism' (4). How might such figures, Williams asks, 'have influenced Morrison's willingness and ability to envision and see the value of revisions of traditional mythologies and humanities themes?' (46).

In completing her MA in English at Cornell University, where she studied from 1953 to 1955, Morrison famously wrote her thesis on 'Virginia Woolf's and William Faulkner's Treatment of the Alienated', in which she identifies Greek tragic elements of Faulkner's novels in unambiguously Aristotelian terms. Readers often discuss the resonances of T. S. Eliot in her writing, and it is clear that canonical European and Euro-American modernism, in all its classical allusiveness, played a key part in her intellectual formation. It is important to note, however, her hesitancy as well as her acquiescence in discussions about the influence, or lack thereof, of the classical tradition on her work. She declared in 1981, for example, that she 'wrote in what [she supposed] should be called the tragic mode in which there is some catharsis and revelation', but that 'there's a whole lot of space in between' (Taylor-Guthrie 125). This sense of resistance is also tangible in her discussions of her work's relationship with Greek myth. In 1976, she invoked W. B. Stanford's now-canonical work of 1954, *The Ulysses Theme*, in describing *Song of Solomon* in terms of 'the traveling Ulysses scene, for black men . . . that going from town to town or place' (Taylor-Guthrie 26). Yet in 1979 she draws a distinction between peripatetic black men, who are chastised by society, and the child-abandoning Ulysses, who is 'considered a hero' because he is 'a classic' (Taylor-Guthrie 65).

Throughout her non-fiction Morrison demonstrates her familiarity with the key classically informed texts that underpin Enlightenment thought, and also with those that critique that thought.[11] In *The Bluest Eye* she stages a fictionalised critique of an Enlightenment-derived Linnaean worldview through the compulsively classificatory behaviour of the intra-racist Pauline Breedlove, who liked to arrange household objects 'according to the size, shape, or gradations of color' (86–7). Morrison exposes the same tendency through the more ominous Soaphead Church in that same novel; through Schoolteacher's violent rationalism in *Beloved*; and through the purity-obsessed voyeurism and violence of the Morgan twins in *Paradise*. Her interest both in antiquity and in the Enlightenment projects of empire and colonialism that it bolstered is particularly evident in her work at the Musée du Louvre in Paris, where she was Guest Curator in the autumn/winter of 2006 to 2007. Focusing her programme there on the theme of '*L'Étranger chez soi*', or 'The Foreigner's Home', she commissioned a series of responses to Géricault's painting *The Raft of the Medusa*, and the mapping out of three *parcours* (itineraries or pathways) through the Antiquities collection. As the leaflet guide on these *parcours* explained, they highlighted three groupings of objects in accordance with three specific themes, all related to 'the experience of otherness in ancient civilisations': 'Figures of the foreigner in the land of Egypt'; 'Foreignness in the Greek city: Images of women in ancient Greece'; and 'Foreigners in the Assyrian Empire'.[12] Her interest in this subject at the Louvre – the 'othering' effected both during antiquity and during the Enlightenment – reflects her critique of canon formation and her championing of Martin Bernal's *Black Athena* in 'Unspeakable Things Unspoken'. It also anticipates the essays in one of her most recent collections, *The Origin of Others* (2017), where she returns again to some of her time-honoured themes: to the futile inefficacy of exclusion, categorisation and hierarchy, and to the horror of the violence done in their name.

The Critical Field and Scholarly Debate

In their study, *African American Writers and Classical Tradition* (2010), William Cook and James Tatum mention Morrison only in passing. In their implicit justification for omitting any detailed study of this author, they claim that 'some novels of Toni Morrison . . . consistently downplay . . . classical connections' (4). But to interpret her 'downplaying' of classicism as evidence of its insignificance in her work is surely to misread her conscious ambivalence about it. In March 2012, I witnessed Morrison expressing her sense of conflictedness about the classical presences in her work when I delivered a lecture on this topic at Princeton University, which she attended. She was asked by an audience member whether she intended all the allusions (and their implications) that I had discussed. Memorably, she replied that 'Nothing is deliberate, you know . . . Nothing is deliberate. But I've read all those things, and they were beautiful, and everything I have read seeps in.'[13] To my mind this paradoxical reply, this stance of a simultaneous 'yes and no' in relation both to classical allusiveness and to the wider but no less vexed question of authorial intention as a whole, epitomises Morrison's strategy in her fiction itself. She resolutely has it both ways, insisting that classicism is at once crucial and not nearly as significant as cultural history would have us believe. Over the decades, this is a tension that has both troubled and (at times) misled critics.

As we have seen in the case of Ralph Ellison, both an African American author's engagement with the classical tradition in her/his writing and a critic's focus on that dimension of his or her work are inevitably highly politicised and controversial processes. Authors of the earliest essays and articles on aspects of Morrison's classicism – which did not start to appear until 1985, and which focus on *The Bluest Eye*, *Song of Solomon* or *Beloved* – tend to express anxiety about their approach. Marianne Hirsch, for example, notes in her 1989 study that the presence of 'classical Western structures' in *Beloved* is 'surprising' (29), while Shelley Haley begins her 1995 comparison of *Medea* and that novel by expressing her 'unease' (178).[14] Writing before Michele Ronnick's just-emerging formulation of 'Classica Africana' had gained widespread traction, and so before the explicit naming of 'black classicism' as a theoretical concept, these critics doubtless took heed of Morrison's own anxieties about comparisons between black and Western literature.[15] 'Finding or imposing Western influences in/on Afro-American literature has value,' she has said, 'but when its sole purpose is to place value only where that influence is located it is pernicious' ('Unspeakable' 376). Rightfully demanding that we pay attention to the political and cultural specificities of black expression, she guards against the 'incipient orphanization' of a work which a politically blind focus on European traditions can involve ('Unspeakable' 376). Morrison has stated that she 'does not intend to live without Aeschylus or William Shakespeare' ('Unspeakable' 371). At the same time, however, she has vehemently resisted receptions of her work that conflate her too easily with the European classically allusive modernist canon: 'I am not *like* James Joyce; I am not *like* Thomas Hardy; I am not *like* Faulkner; I am not *like* in that sense,' she famously declared in 1983 (Taylor-Guthrie 152). Her emphasis on how black writing is 'not *like*' its canonical white forebears and contemporaries has crucial implications not just for her own writing, but for black diasporic literature as a whole.

Patrice Rankine's *Ulysses in Black* (2006), a study primarily of Ellison that also discusses Milkman Dead in *Song of Solomon* 'as a New Negro Ulysses' (83), and Tracey Walters's *African American Literature and the Classicist Tradition* (2007), which studies the classical intertexts for Morrison's explorations of motherhood (primarily the myths of Demeter/Persephone and of Medea), are both fully attentive to the political ramifications of their subject. In so doing, and in positioning Morrison within a tradition (either alongside Ellison, or in Walters's case in a genealogy stretching from Phillis Wheatley through Pauline Hopkins to Rita Dove), these two pioneering works established the black classicist approach within American literary studies. It is worth noting that both Rankine and Walters focus exclusively on black literary lineages, and that in this respect both continue the approach of the identity-centred works of African American studies (such as Susan Willis's *Specifying* of 1987, or Henry Louis Gates's *The Signifying Monkey* of 1988) which were critical landmarks in the 1980s.

In my monograph *Toni Morrison and the Classical Tradition* (2013), I both develop and diverge from the readings of Rankine and Walters. Focusing on all ten of the novels published at that time (up to and including *Home* (2012)), I position her within the all-important black classical tradition but also examine her work's revisionary dialogue with classically informed white authors ranging from Milton and Cotton Mather to Cather and William Carlos Williams. Each chapter centres not on a specific novel but on a key period or process in America's past, thereby illuminating how Morrison's ambivalent allusiveness critiques the prevailing narratives of American history that themselves deploy the classical past, and how it also engages antiquity to imagine alternative realities. In this respect, I suggest, her oeuvre transforms or reconfigures American culture itself. In his recent study,

Empire of Ruin: Black Classicism and American Imperial Culture (2017), John Levi Barnard builds on what he terms my 'essentially dialectical reading of African American cultural production in relation to dominant American cultures of classical monumentalism and public historiography' (11). He positions Morrison alongside David Walker, Charles Chesnutt and others, to illuminate a tradition of nineteenth- and twentieth-century black American authors who have 'apprehended [the] proliferation of classical monumentalism as evidence of national hypocrisy and hubris' (11). He significantly develops discussion of *Song of Solomon*, in particular, and by including Morrison in a genealogy that includes visual artists such as Kara Walker he testifies to her significance as a radical voice in American cultural and intellectual history.

Much of the radicalism of Morrison's classicism is rooted in her insistence on what I have called its 'Africanness'.[16] In 'Unspeakable Things Unspoken' she celebrates Martin Bernal's first volume of *Black Athena*, and valorises his argument that the African origins of ancient Greek culture have been strategically erased, terming it a 'stunning investigation of the field' (373). She laments his powerful thesis that (in her words) it took 'seventy years to eliminate Egypt as the cradle of civilization . . . and replace it with Greece', and admires his account of both the '*process*' and the '*motives*' for the 'fabrication' of ancient Greece as a white, pure entity that is entirely distinct from Africa (374, original italics). She engages these ideas in many of her novels: in both *Sula*, for example, which pre-dates Bernal's book by some fourteen years, and *Paradise*, which postdates it, she configures within the texts themselves exactly the kinds of fabrication Bernal describes. Sula's imagining of her lover Ajax (or A. Jacks) as a statue whose white layers she chips away, thereby revealing the black 'loam' within, epitomises this process (*Sula* 135). Prior scholarship considering Morrison in light of the *Black Athena* debates includes Justine Tally's *'Beloved': Origins* (2008), which comprises a detailed exploration of the interconnected Greek and Egyptian traditions that resonate within this single novel, and La Vinia Delois Jennings's *Toni Morrison and the Idea of Africa* (also 2008), which locates several moments in the Morrisonian oeuvre in which the author exposes 'Western' superimpositions on originally African cultural forms. My own work diverges from these studies by reading Morrison as concerned less with origins and more with syncretism. She is not invested in an 'either/or' approach to the controversy about whether African or classical culture has greater validity and authenticity, but in a 'both/and' perspective, in which much of what the dominant culture claims as Western or classical is also at the same time African.

Recognition of Morrison's complex classical allusiveness has played an important role in critics' sense of her fiction as itself doing theoretical work. Her literary practice irrefutably demonstrates that aesthetic choices are always political ones, and makes age-old questions concerning the 'aesthetic versus the political' (as applied to Ellison, for example) appear almost nonsensical. While her classicism is an important dimension of her own transnationalism, of her own interventions in the politics of race, gender and class, and also of her own negotiations of modernism and postmodernism, it has also contributed significantly to our general understanding of those concepts in general. The sheer diversity of her work's cultural references, a hybrid allusiveness that makes her at once 'like' and completely 'unlike' T. S. Eliot or William Faulkner, for example, is testament to the viability of her own theories, interwoven with those of Paul Gilroy, about the black diaspora's prior claim on modernism.[17] Meanwhile Justine McConnell, in her 2016 article on *Sula* and Wole Soyinka's *Bacchae of Euripides*, illuminates the scattering of fragments of the Sophoclean Ajax (and *Ajax*) throughout Morrison's novel, labelling it a 'postcolonial *sparagmos*', and proffering *sparagmos* as a metaphor for, or theory of, classical reception studies itself (133).

Much work remains to be done on the implications of Morrison's classicism in a range of contexts. Indeed, as a later generation of writers – such as Jesmyn Ward and Robin Coste Lewis – publish novels and poems that are clearly indebted to Morrison in their own subversive classical allusiveness, new intertextualities emerge that compel us to reconsider that of the earlier author.[18] The commonalities between Morrison's perspectives on the classical tradition and those of visual artists such as Fred Wilson (for example in his 2016 exhibition, 'Wildfire Test Pit'[19]) testify to her ongoing influential position in cultural production that involves radical revisions of the past.

Song of Solomon (1977)

This novel – an exploration of black masculinity that Morrison wrote in the aftermath of her father's death – is in essence the tale of a flawed hero whose quest for gold leads him to discover his family's history instead. In her 2005 preface, Morrison describes the text as 'A journey, then, with the accomplishment of flight . . . All very saga-like. Old school heroic, but with other meanings' (*Solomon* x). The fascination of her consciously conflicted classicism in this text lies in those unspecified 'other meanings'. For while Morrison's own words on her fiction cannot and should not always be a reliable guide to it, of course, there is something of the saying 'yes and no' to European tradition, the strategic 'having it both ways', in this statement that anticipates her ambiguous reflections at Princeton on her non-deliberate yet significant allusiveness. It exactly captures *Song of Solomon*'s fraught and unstable relationship with classical precedents.

While the highly ambiguous Circe is the only character to bear an explicitly classical, Homeric name, Morrison's depiction of Milkman's travels from his fictional home town in Michigan to Danville, Pennsylvania, and to Shalimar, Virginia, involve, in critic Rankine's words, 'fragmented images of Ulysses' journey and return' (*Ulysses* 113). Numerous scholars have charted Morrison's ludic engagement with classical myth in creating this mock-epic epic, this mock-heroic heroic account of Milkman's error-and-setback-strewn path to enlightenment.[20] The author configures Milkman's convoluted trajectory as a darkly comic anti-*Bildungsroman*, one which involves stealing a bag of bones that he thinks is gold and being arrested in his home town; ruining his clothes and nearly being defeated by the wilderness surrounding the Butler place; and being beaten up in small-town Virginia. Morrison thus not only imagines her protagonist as a hapless version of Odysseus (or Ulysses), but simultaneously creates an intertextual relationship both with Ellison's invisible man and with Joyce's Stephen Dedalus. While Milkman exists in an uncomfortable relationship to mythical American heroes such as the self-making Horatio Alger, and to biblical heroes such as Moses, Morrison also (with tangible irony) imbues him with qualities that recall and revise the Sophoclean Oedipus: he walks with a limp; the faint suggestion of incest taints his relationships with his mother and his sister; and he is utterly deluded about the nature of his past and his ancestry until they are revealed to him.

Though the action of *Song of Solomon* is set primarily during the Civil Rights era of the 1950s and 1960s, Milkman's discoveries about his grandfather's post-slavery farming successes, which ended brutally when he was shot dead by white landgrabbers, enable the author to confront and depict the brutal realities of African American experience since the end of the Civil War. Through the memories of Milkman's father about the catastrophic fate of 'Lincoln's Heaven' (*Solomon* 51), which is replete with farm animals named for heroic figures in American history, the novelist not only exposes the inaccessibility of the American dream and of idyllic pastoralism to black Americans. She also mocks the hagiographic, individualistic 'cult of the hero' that is informed by antiquity (typified by the Founding Fathers' classicism, for example), and that is itself such a powerful force in dominant American historiography. Indeed, through Milkman's interactions with the townsfolk of Danville, who build him up into a hero via their collective memories of his grandfather, Morrison wonderfully dramatises the dynamics of the relationship between the individual and the community, or between the hero and society. The old men of Danville function as a kind of chorus whose praise and adulation for the lineage of the hero, the protagonist Milkman, makes him 'fierce with pride' (236).[21] Yet Milkman's affinity with tragic heroism includes both hubris and downfall (in his case a bathetic one), in that he becomes utterly dependent on Circe for his rescue and his future.

As Kimberly Benston has argued, it is in the depiction of Circe as problem-solver that Morrison clearly diverges from Ellison, Joyce and Homer. Rather than depicting women as domestic or seductive ensnarers, through the eminently capable and infinitely enduring Circe and Pilate (as well as the long-suffering and undervalued Ruth and I Corinthians), Morrison constructs a feminist revision of classical myth and of the European literary tradition that is indebted to it. Milkman gradually revises his conception of the heroic through his slow acknowledgement of women's power: Circe's capacity to avenge the white murderers of his grandfather, the resilience of his mother, and the value of Pilate as a wise and nurturing ancestor figure. Eventually even he begins to realise the limitations of individualism, materialism and patriarchy.

It is through Circe and the Butler place, too, that Morrison revises many of the classically informed dimensions of William Faulkner's depictions of the 'Old South'.[22] As I discuss in Chapter 3, Faulkner emphasises the decaying neoclassical features of Southern architecture (such as the 'rotting portico' of Sutpen's house in *Absalom, Absalom!*

(128)) to depict the decline and fall of the Confederacy and of slave-holding Southern culture. Morrison parodies this tendency not just in her gothic depiction of the columned and porticoed Butler place as 'dark, ruined, evil' (*Solomon* 238), but also in setting her scene of racist crime and guilt not in the South but in supposedly liberal Pennsylvania. She thereby refuses to exonerate the northern United States from its part in the nation's past and ongoing racial injustice. Moreover, as Barnard argues, Circe's proud presiding over the conscious ruination of the Butler place, her refusal to counteract that decay in any way, constitutes a 'retribution' through ensuring 'the progressive deterioration' of the 'ideological pillars of white power' (163). In these details, Morrison positions herself within a tradition of resistant black representation of the 'ruins of empire' that includes writing by William Wells Brown, Pauline Hopkins and many others.

As Jennings demonstrates in *Toni Morrison and the Idea of Africa*, *Song of Solomon*'s Circe possesses many qualities of the traditional West African *banganga* (specialist) figure, a kind of medicine woman or priestess who recurs in Vodun cosmology. Jennings argues that 'Circe's placement in the narrative subtextually interrogates the Hellenic appropriation of select African divinities for select inclusion in the Greek mythic pantheon' (140). In her reading, Morrison's naming of her priestess figure 'Circe' is part of her authorial insistence on the Africanness of classicism that I have already outlined.[23] 'The naming is an act of cultural excavation,' Jennings contends, 'of once again exposing the African palimpsest on which Western culture superimposes itself' (162). Morrison herself certainly attests to the simultaneity of African and classical resonances in this text, even if not to African priority in this specific case. In a 1981 interview, she speaks tellingly about the mythical sources of Milkman's great-grandfather, Solomon (or Shalimar), who flew back to Africa and whose heroic status is evident in the children's rhyme to which the novel's title alludes. Of the text-wide motif of flying and flight, the author observes, 'If it means Icarus to some readers, fine. I want to take credit for that. But my meaning is specific. It is about black people who could fly' (Taylor-Guthrie 122). Once again, Morrison's perspective here articulates the 'yes and no', the 'both . . . and', and the refusal to be drawn on the exact provenance or identity of her cultural resources. In suffusing her novel both with paradigms of Icarian flight and with the African (American) emancipatory mythology of the flying African, she anticipates the syncretism of Ellison in the 'Fall of Icarus' tapestry sequence in 'Hickman in Washington DC'.[24]

While Circe brings about her revenge on the Butler family and white society through non-violent means, the way she allows the *miasma* or pollution of ruin to take over the mansion exemplifies characters' novel-wide preoccupation with these concepts that in themselves are at once West African and ancient Greek.[25] In *Song of Solomon* (and also in *Beloved*, *Paradise* and *Love*), Morrison deploys a discourse of pollution that recalls the Aeschylean *Oresteia* in her exploration of the themes of justice, injustice and black vengeance.[26] Guitar is motivated by the horrendous (true historical) facts of the lynching of Emmett Till in 1955 and of the murder of four schoolgirls in the 16th Street Baptist Church in Birmingham, Alabama, in 1963. In his despair at America's unjust laws and prejudicial criminal justice system, he rationalises the tit-for-tat violence of his guerrilla group, the Seven Days. While Harris has correctly described this group as a 'Fury-like society' (72), she does not discuss the activists' concomitant invocation of blood as a pollutant. When Guitar observes that 'the earth is soggy with black people's blood', for example (*Solomon* 145), his words recall the preoccupation of the chorus, in Aeschylus's *Libation Bearers*, with blood that has been spilled on and soaked into the ground.[27] At the same time, Guitar's conviction that reciprocal attacks on whites are justified by the need to maintain 'Balance. Numbers. Ratio' (156) recalls the insistent choric imagery of the *Agamemnon*, in which the old men of Argos claim that 'Justice turns the balance scales' (trans. Fagles, l. 250). Through the irony that Guitar speaks the language of Enlightenment rationalism in his desire to 'keep the numbers the same' (154), Morrison at once critiques the hypocrisy of that purportedly orderly worldview and exposes the futility of imitative revenge.

As David Cowart has argued, in this novel Morrison questions not just the radical violence of the Seven Days, but also the problem of the gender inequality and misogyny that characterised militant black groups during the Civil Rights decades.[28] There is one notable, multi-layered classical allusion by which she draws attention to the patriarchal attitudes of male activists: when I Corinthians returns home from her liaison with Porter, she is surprised to find a group of men (the Seven Days) holding a meeting in her kitchen, and she wonders 'if it was a secret hour in which men rose like giants from dragon's teeth and, while the women slept, clustered in their kitchens' (203). Morrison alludes here to the myth that the House of Cadmus (Oedipus's lineage) arose from sown dragon's teeth, and also to the different myth in which Jason plants teeth which grow up into men who fight each other.[29] Her invocation of the dragon's teeth simultaneously resonates with prior literary allusions to this trope by a range of American authors (such as Henry Adams, Ezra Pound, Frances Ellen Harper and W. E. B. Du Bois), each of whose allusions is invested with his or her own specific ideological commitments.[30] Corrie in turn repurposes the allusion to her own feminist ends: the concept of armed men 'clustering' in a woman's kitchen (which is always a sacred, creative space in Morrison's work) is a threatening one that protests the usurpation of women by male civil rights activists, as well as women's general lack of power and autonomy in this era.

The author's critique of self-aggrandising masculinity and female disempowerment – one of the principal means by which Morrison diverges from the allusive modernism of Joyce, Ellison and Faulkner in this text – also engages Ovid's *Metamorphoses*. During the hunting episode in the Virginia woods, through associating Milkman with Narcissus, and Ryna (his abandoned great-grandmother) with 'Echo' (274), the novelist comments implicitly but brilliantly on the protagonist's narcissism. Indeed, in the novel's indeterminate ending, whether Milkman ever achieves true heroic status remains as ambiguous as the outcome of his leap through the air, and as his relationship with classical tradition as a whole.

Beloved (1987)

Some of the earliest criticism to be published on Morrison and the classical tradition has explored the relationship between *Beloved* and Euripides's *Medea*.[31] The fact that both Sethe and the eponymous protagonist of Euripides's play commit infanticide has made the comparison an obvious one. It is made more persuasive by late-nineteenth-century artistic and literary representations of Margaret Garner – the historical slave woman from northern Kentucky who did kill her child, and whose story was Morrison's inspiration for her novel – as 'the modern Medea'.[32] Yet Morrison herself has resisted the connection on numerous occasions, pointing out that the conflation with the scorned lover, Medea, erases the political specificities of enslaved motherhood that both Margaret Garner's and Sethe's predicaments protest. 'Margaret Garner didn't do what Medea did and kill her children because of some guy,' Morrison tells Paul Gilroy in 1993 (Gilroy, 'Living' 180); 'this is not Medea who is mad at some dude and is going to get back at him', she said in 1987 (Smith 51). Sophocles's Oedipus, whose life-changing actions come back to haunt him, is in some ways a more nuanced parallel, and it is this figure who certainly resonates in Paul D's comparison of Sethe's face to 'a mask with mercifully punched-out eyes' (*Beloved* 10). Yet although this novel's most significant dialogue with a specific Greek text (or texts) is probably its deployment of ideas and imagery from the *Oresteia*, it is arguable that equally important dimensions of Morrison's engagement with tragedy in *Beloved* are those not concerned with any individual Greek author or play. Of great note is the way she both uses and revises, to radical effect, the general Aristotelian conventions of the tragic in her rewriting of the history of slavery and its aftermath.

The author's articulations in her MA thesis about the influence of Greek tragedy on William Faulkner clearly attest to the importance of Aristotelian conventions in her own intellectual formation. 'The fall of a once great house,' she writes therein, 'old family guilts inherited by an heir; the conflict between individual will and fate and the self-wrought catastrophe are all immediately recognized traits in Greek tragedy' (Morrison, 'Virginia' 24). In *Beloved*, Morrison strategically harnesses tragic forms in the service of protest and resistance by negotiating key Aristotelian (or quasi-Aristotelian) paradigms and concepts – such as the 'tragic hero', 'the downfall' and 'the chorus' – that were reified in the 1950s scholarship prevalent during her years at Howard and at Cornell.[33] The casting of Sethe as a tragic hero – one who exercises agency (and thereby brings about her own downfall) through her decision to kill her own child – is one means by which Morrison claims and insists on true freedom for her protagonist.[34] In facing up to the different ways in which she must lose her child – to captivity or to death – Sethe confronts a dilemma akin to that faced by tragic protagonists such as Antigone. Her actions are morally complicated, and escape easy judgement. We may or may not be persuaded by her rationale that in cutting Beloved's throat she 'took and put [her] babies where they'd be safe' (193), but our response is likely to be similar to that of Baby Suggs, who 'could not approve or condemn Sethe's rough choice' (212). Morrison complicates the idea of 'self-wrought catastrophe' by writing a kind of 'resistant' tragedy, one in which Sethe's outrageous action protests the multivalent outrageousness of the institution of slavery. As Otten has argued, her attack on Beloved precipitates 'a fall wrought with destruction but one that is still morally superior to . . . sterile accommodation' (285). For this reason, while Morrison certainly depicts Sethe as hubristic ('was her head a bit too high? Her back a little too straight? Probably,' the onlookers decide as she is arrested after the murder (179)), the author is also deeply invested in her hero's heroism. As the scar on her back testifies, Sethe's resilience and powers of endurance are way beyond the ordinary: as Denver records, her mother is the one who 'never looked away' (14).

As in *Song of Solomon*, however, Morrison at the same time engages the paradigm of the Greek chorus to revise the Enlightenment-derived American ideal of the isolated hero, the heroic individualist who (in the words of R. W. B. Lewis in *The American Adam*) is 'an individual standing alone, self-reliant and self-propelling' (5). As the communal exorcism of Beloved at the end of the novel shows, Sethe is reliant on the community, who quite literally sing in chorus on her behalf, for her salvation. Conversely, when Morrison depicts Sethe's, Denver's and Beloved's repeated falling down on the ice, in the skating scene that initiates their nadir, she emphasises the absence of community in their lives: 'nobody saw them falling' (205). With devastating irony, the author draws attention to the dangerous absence of a chorus or community in the struggling women's lives by deploying this line as a choric refrain, repeated three times. In assigning an active, significant role to the community-as-chorus in *Beloved* (though one that is by no means always benign, of course), Morrison both critiques individualism and revises conventional assumptions about the inactive or non-participatory role of the chorus in Greek tragedy.[35]

The author's conception of nineteenth-century African American experience as tragedy 'writes back' to conventional articulations of the history of the Old South, and the Confederate 'Lost Cause', in tragic, epic and pastoral terms. As I discuss in preceding chapters, much of Faulkner's work, as well as Cather's in *Sapphira and the Slave Girl* (and in the scenes involving Blind d'Arnault in *My Ántonia*), is informed by these conventions, while Ellison's writing often takes that same classically dependent 'Old Southernness' to task. To borrow historian David Blight's words on the tragic vision of W. E. B. Du Bois, *Beloved*'s appropriation of tragic conventions to express the black perspective on slavery and its aftermath ensures a focus on the 'cause lost' rather than the 'Lost Cause' (252). Morrison's depiction of African American suffering in tragic terms is, moreover, a crucial part of her dialogue with Faulkner. While both of them deploy the classical concept of the fallen *oikos* – both household and building – to indicate emotional and moral collapse, Morrison counteracts Faulkner's decaying Compson Place or Sutpen's Hundred with her haunted, 'spiteful' and 'loud' 124 Bluestone Road (3, 199), thereby significantly redressing a political imbalance. Similar in effect, in terms of a revisionary dialogue with Faulkner, is Morrison's decision to stage the central violent action of *Beloved* during the time of 'August sunlight' (177); she thus wrestles racial violence out of the mythical and mythologising Greek-inspired light of the 'old classic times' that Faulkner claims as the source of the title for *Light in August* (Gwynn and Blotner 199). And in repeatedly associating Sethe's violent acts with the 'hummingbird' inside that character's consciousness (192, 308), the African American author challenges the validity of pastoralism, in which (in Crèvecœur's *Letters from an American Farmer* (1782), for example) the hummingbird is the epitome of the rural idyll.[36] As *Beloved*'s depictions of the ironically named 'Sweet Home' lay bare, the beauty of natural and agricultural settings in the American South is bound up with realities that are far from idyllic.

The theme of revenge is central in *Beloved*, in both the murdered Beloved's quest to avenge herself on her mother, and the black community's quest to avenge itself for centuries of white oppression and brutality. In configuring this theme, Morrison (in this work and in its companion novels in her trilogy, *Jazz* and *Paradise*) continues and develops *Song of Solomon*'s intertextual relationship with Aeschylus's trilogy about cyclical murder and revenge within the House of Atreus. The ghost of the murdered child, in Morrison's novel, is at once a contaminant and a vengeful spirit: the house on Bluestone Road is 'palsied by the baby's fury' and Sethe cannot forget the 'baby blood that soaked her fingers like oil' (6). Denver goes to great lengths to clean up after her sister's visitations – in other words, to conceal the fact that her presence is a polluting one – but the living girl's 'tears' that she 'dripped into the stovefire' bring to mind the 'hearth soaked in sorrow' that the Chorus of *Libation Bearers* bewails (*Beloved* 20; *Libation Bearers*, trans. Lattimore, l. 49).

The closing vision of the novel's main text, by contrast, largely rejects the revenge paradigm. It replaces the viability of both the Aeschylean Furies and the West African concept of the *abiku* (the wandering unquiet child spirit) with an implicitly Christian ritual of exorcism, atonement and (self-)forgiveness that both gets rid of the ghost and enables a rebirth or fresh start for Sethe.[37] While the graduate student Morrison observes of *The Sound and the Fury* and *Absalom, Absalom!* that 'an atmosphere of doom pervades these novels' (Morrison, 'Virginia' 99), it is significant that she does not transfer this 'atmosphere of doom' on to *Beloved*. The author's ultimate eschewal of a calamitous ending for Sethe – which can be read as a resistance to tragic catastrophe itself – reflects the fact that, as she said in a 1983 interview, 'she is interested in survival, in who survives and who does not, and why' (Taylor-Guthrie 145). As I discuss below in relation to *Jazz*, Morrison frequently configures the anti-tragic in her work, thereby staking a politically crucial interest in African American survival. It is perhaps for this reason that she revises both Ovid's depiction (in the *Metamorphoses*) of the hubristic mother, Niobe, and Phillis Wheatley's already-revised version of that myth. While Shields points out that Wheatley's poem 'Niobe in Distress' changes the hubris of Ovid's Niobe into an admirable rebelliousness that is entirely the later poet's invention, in her depiction of Sethe Morrison transposes exactly Wheatley's sense of maternal resistance, and also her sense of excessive maternal love.[38] In Ovid's version of the myth (followed by Wheatley), Niobe weeps so much at the loss of her children that she becomes a dripping rock or statue. This process of petrification may inform Morrison's depiction of a rigidified Sethe, when she is driven away from the murder scene by the sheriff, in a dress that is covered in blood: 'The hot sun dried Sethe's dress stiff, like rigor mortis' (180). Yet, crucially, Sethe here does not weep at all, and turns into neither a stone nor a statue. This hero survives, in all her flawed humanity, and looks ahead to 'some kind of tomorrow' (322).

The novel's epilogue, however, unsettles the equilibrium of the main text's optimistic ending by reintroducing (in a consciously haunting and elusive manner) the historical African American stake in revenge. Morrison's present-tense meditation here tells us that Beloved's 'footprints come and go, come and go'. Our feet 'will fit' if we step into them, but 'take them out and they disappear again as if nobody ever walked there' (324). Here the author tentatively reconfigures the famous 'recognition' scene in the *Libation Bearers*, to which the fact that Electra's foot fits into Orestes's print is pivotal. At Agamemnon's grave, Electra says:

> . . . Footprints are here.
> The feet that made them are alike, and look like mine.
> . . . I step
> Where he has stepped, and the heelmarks, and the space between his heel
> and toe are like the prints I make. (*Libation Bearers*, trans. Lattimore, ll. 205–10)

In *Libation Bearers*, the reunited siblings go on from here to plot their murders of both Clytemnestra and Aegisthus; in engaging with this moment, *Beloved*'s epilogue acknowledges the pain of the wronged who can never be avenged. The emergence of the Black Lives Matter movement in 2013, and the repeated police murders of black people which precipitated it, make Morrison's use of the present tense in this epilogue unhappily prescient.[39]

Jazz (1992)

Why does Violet Trace come from a 'mean little place' in Virginia 'called Rome' (*Jazz* 138)? Morrison's second novel in her trilogy – arguably her masterpiece – rarely features in scholarly discussions of her classical allusiveness. Yet this tale of Joe and Violet's participation in the great black migration from the rural South, and their experience of urbanisation in Harlem (which includes Joe's ill-fated love affair with the teenaged Dorcas), does not draw merely on epic and mock-epic traditions. Morrison engages profoundly with both classical and classically derived American traditions of pastoral (particularly of the 'Old Southern' variety that she has already invoked in *Song of Solomon* and *Beloved*) in her configurations of the Reconstruction and Jim Crow era South, and in her construction of counter-pastoral in New York City.[40] The author explores the complex meanings of freedom and self-determination as Joe, Violet and Dorcas confront them in a culture in which racism and injustice continue. In so doing, Morrison deploys tragic tropes – including a continuing dialogue with the *Oresteia* – before finally claiming a viable anti-tragic mode.

Many critics have discussed Morrison's parodic dialogue with Faulknerian epic and baroque in the brief 'Golden Gray' section of *Jazz* (165–80). Herein the author depicts this elegant, mixed-race young man's journey through rural turn-of-the-twentieth-century Virginia: his quest to locate and confront his black father involves the reluctant rescue, en route, of the injured, woods-dwelling and heavily pregnant Wild.[41] There is an overt satirical classicism in these pages. In picturing Golden Gray that August day – a month that, as in *Beloved*, brings Faulkner's Olympian-Mississippian August light to mind – the narrator adopts a present tense that irreverently recalls that convention in classical epic. 'I see him in a two-seat phaeton,' says the narrator. 'He is a long way from home' (143). As Faulkner does through Judith Sutpen's dramatic response to the phaeton carriage in *Absalom, Absalom!*, Morrison (though in a mock-epic mode that undercuts the Faulkner) imports from Ovid's tale of Phaethon both the anxiety about paternity and the racial dynamics of that myth.[42] She continues this mock-heroic mode by bestowing on Golden Gray's father the name of 'Henry Lestory or LesTroy or something like that' (148). Through the fact that 'LesTroy' sounds like 'Less Troy', the none-too-subtle invocation of the definitive war of classical mythology suggests Morrison's wish to diminish the epic and dramatic importance that the dominant (and in particular Southern) culture attributes to racial purity and to racial mixing. At the same time, the name 'LesTroy' suggests the twelfth-century poet famous for his courtly romances, Chrétien de Troyes. Morrison thereby parodies the way Southern mythology blends the traditions of both chivalric romance and classical antiquity to legitimise its slave economy.

The historian Margaret Malamud has explored how, as it did in ancient Greece and Rome, slavery in the American South provided the slave-owning master class with *otium*, or leisure, and hence with the freedom required to cultivate the arts (*African Americans* 134). An emphasis on leisure is certainly one of the hallmarks of the American pastoral canon, from the writings of Crèvecœur or the classically obsessed Thomas Jefferson to the epic movie *Birth of a Nation* (1915): freedom from working in the fields is a prerequisite, of course, to the capacity to eulogise works in literary writing. Leisure is also fetishised in the reactionary manifesto of the Southern Agrarianists, *I'll Take My Stand* (1930).[43] In *Jazz*, Morrison deconstructs the insidious matrix of slavery, leisure, pastoralism and romance through the resolute anti-pastoralism of her scenes set both in the South and in the North. She does this first and foremost by paying close attention to the brutal realities of the agricultural labour, and of the total absence of leisure, in the impoverished rural life that Violet Trace and her family lived. The author documents Violet's heroic endurance in chopping wood, picking cotton, hauling hay and driving the mules behind the plough for hours (a detail that rebukes the Agrarianists' celebration of Cincinnatus and his plough), and records her subsequent total exhaustion. Morrison also depicts Joe, who 'loved the woods' (106), as a would-be pastoralist rather than a true one. In his heartbreaking search for his mother, Morrison initially creates for him a highly contrived pastoral setting that bears no resemblance to the reality of Virginia forests: he hears 'the music the world makes, familiar to fisherman and shepherds' that 'woodsmen have also heard' (177). But Morrison discredits Joe's perception of a rural paradise and ethereal sounds as soon as she describes them – when this character at last discovers the cave where his mother lives, he encounters an odour that is 'a mixture of honey and shit' (177). This is no pastoral idyll, and Joe is ultimately alienated from that tradition.

Morrison effects not just a general challenge to the Virgilian celebration of life (in the *Georgics*, for example) that so appealed to Jefferson et al., but also specifically engages that Roman poet's first Eclogue. In his 1964 study, *The Machine in the Garden*, Leo Marx identifies Virgil's *Eclogues* as 'the pure fountainhead of the pastoral strain in our literature', and states that 'it is in them that the political overtones of the pastoral situation become evident' (19). He also notes that the first Eclogue, on account of its subject matter, is sometimes referred to as 'The Dispossessed'. As I discuss at length in my 2013 monograph, Meliboeus and Tityrus's conversation in that first Eclogue (which is about the former shepherd's eviction from his home by the authorities in the imperial city of Rome) resonates powerfully in Morrison's repeated accounts of 'the dispossession' of Violet and her family from their rural Virginian home near the 'little depot called Rome' (177). In a scene that implicitly revisits the eviction in *Invisible Man*, Morrison depicts in stark detail the white men's turfing the family out and stealing their belongings. While Virgil's Meliboeus laments that he is to be 'driven from his home place', and wonders when he 'will see his native land again' (Virgil, *Ecl.* trans. Lewis, I.4, I.67), Morrison suggests that the African Americans are doubly dispossessed, in that they have already been uprooted from their native Africa, and that for them the concept of *patria* (fatherland or homeland) is fraught with complexity.

Jazz continues its challenge to pastoral conventions in its depiction of the Traces' journey north. In its often though not always joyful representations of the life and culture of Harlem, the novel exemplifies Morrison's theory that black writing about urban life is not founded on an aversion to 'the mechanization of life' ('City' 38). While Leo Marx identifies Hawthorne's encounter with a train as the moment of crisis that defines the agricultural/industrial tension in a rapidly modernising America, Morrison has observed that 'the horror of industrialization seems . . . mostly an elite preoccupation' ('City' 38). In her exuberant and formally exquisite depiction of Joe and Violet's 'train-dance' to the North, she celebrates the train as a means to black freedom, and places 'the wave of black people running from want and violence' firmly within a counter-pastoral tradition (*Jazz* 33). This counter-pastoral also plays a significant part in her novel's dialectical relationship to *The Great Gatsby* and to Fitzgerald's conflation of pastoralism with an exclusionary racial politics.[44] It is important to note, however, that Morrison's indictment of Southern pastoral and its inapplicability to black life does not result in an uncritical celebration of the urban North, nor of the freedoms and responsibilities that this entails. Joe Trace, finding his way in New York City, inherits much from Ellison's invisible man in his seemingly endless quest for a viable identity, and in the implicit critique of Alain Locke's euphoric rhetoric of the Negro 'metamorphosis' ('The New Negro' 3).[45] Joe's observations that he 'changed once too often' (129), that he 'changed into new seven times' and that he had 'been a new Negro all his life' (129) constitute a sceptical comment on Locke's distinctly Ovidian discourse.

In Harlem Joe takes ownership of his self. He tests the limits of his autonomy in an environment that constrains him – in which the past may be 'an abused record with no choice but to repeat itself at the crack' (220), and Morrison hereby stages a classic struggle between free will and its absence. Importantly, however (in yet one more divergence from the Faulknerian conflict that she outlines in her MA thesis), she substitutes the Greek concept of an anonymous 'Fate' with specific historical oppressions wrought by one people against another ('Virginia' 24). And in terms of engagement with Greek tragedy as a whole, Morrison develops in *Jazz* the configuration of violence and revenge in the terms of the Aeschylean *Oresteia* that, as I have discussed, she initiates in *Song of Solomon* and continues in *Beloved*. For example, while in the *Agamemnon* Calchas describes the dead but unappeased Iphigenia as a polluting presence ('the terror returns like sickness to lurk in the house / the secret anger remembers the child that shall be avenged' (*Agamemnon*, trans. Lattimore, ll. 154–5)), in the Traces' home after Joe has murdered Dorcas, not dissimilarly, 'the girl's memory is a sickness in the house' (*Jazz* 28). Dorcas's aunt, Alice Manfred, is meanwhile possessed by a 'trembling fury' towards Joe (76).

Morrison does include some forms of non-violent atonement in this novel, however, such as the peaceful but powerful Fifth Avenue protest march. This prepares us for the ultimate anti-tragic resolution of the novel's plot, for which the narrator builds up our expectations by acknowledging the problematic nature of her own predilection for the tragic. 'I was so sure one would kill the other,' she says of the Joe-Violet-Felice trio (220); she observes that she has 'a kind of sweet-tooth' for 'pain' (219), and a penchant for 'spots of blood' (128). As in the pre-epilogue ending of *Beloved*, in Morrison's insistence on a reunion between Joe and Violet and a renewal of their love, in Felice's implicit rejection of the role of sacrificial victim, and in the persistence of these characters as 'original, complicated, changeable – human' (111), Morrison stakes out her interest in black survival. Indeed, it is arguable that this time around, where there is no qualifying epilogue in place, she even champions black triumph.

There is not space here to map out this novel's extensive engagement with Egyptian traditions and with the African American emancipatory tradition of Ethiopianness, which ranges from the author's use of the *Harlem Book of the Dead* as a source text for the story of Dorcas, to the significance of the beauty products that Joe Trace sells being the 'Cleopatra' brand.[46] It is important in closing, however, to make some mention of Morrison's use of lines from the Nag Hammadi library as her epigraphs to both *Jazz* and *Paradise*. Several critics have explored the politically radical implications of the author's epigraphic quotation, in *Jazz*, from the Nag Hammadi text entitled 'Thunder, Perfect Mind', and of its associations with Morrison's narrator.[47] Of equal significance to Morrison's project is the African-Greek hybrid nature of these Coptic Gnostic texts, which were discovered in upper

Egypt in 1945, but which were written in the third and fourth centuries CE.[48] Culturally, there could hardly be a less 'pure' body of work than this collection, which (according to scholar James Robinson) consists of texts 'originally composed in Greek' but which were then translated into Coptic. Given that Coptic is 'the Egyptian language written with the Greek alphabet' (J. Robinson 12–13), the very existence of these Coptic manuscripts testifies to what Bernal calls 'the triangular relationship between Ancient Egypt, Ancient Greece and Christianity' (30), and to the cultural syncretism to which first Greek and then Roman conquests of Egypt gave rise. They are just one testimony to the African/classical interactions that European imperialist culture was (and is?) so anxious to erase. Morrison's engagement with Coptic Gnosticism in *Jazz*, then, constitutes a powerful writing against the 'fabrication' of ancient Greece. It exemplifies the restoration of Africa to the classical tradition in which her oeuvre is so profoundly invested.

Notes

1. For the Pygmalion and Galatea story see Ovid, *Met.* X.243–98. Scholarship that does engage seriously with *God Help the Child* includes Eaton et al. (which contains Montgomery's essay on Galatea); G. McGowan; Wyatt.
2. For a detailed study see my monograph, *Toni Morrison and the Classical Tradition* (2013).
3. Morrison's papers are archived at the Firestone Library, Princeton University; currently these include only a fraction (six boxes) of her personal book collection: <https://findingaids.princeton.edu/collections/C1491/c3972> (last accessed 18 May 2020).
4. See Denard 100; Conner, *Aesthetics* xx; Cowart, 'Faulkner' 88–9.
5. Discussion with the author following my lecture, 'Parsing the Classical Toni Morrison', Princeton University, 7 March 2012.
6. This series, co-written by Morrison with her son Slade, includes *The Ant or the Grasshopper?* and *The Lion or the Mouse?* of 2003 and *Poppy or the Snake?* of 2004, all published by Simon & Schuster.
7. See for example, in interviews, Taylor-Guthrie 16, 101, 125, 176–7. Further interviews are collected in Denard.
8. See Roynon, *Morrison* 13–14.
9. See Snowden, 'Bernal's "Blacks" and the Afrocentrists'.
10. See Muse; Roynon, *Morrison* 108.

11. See *Playing in the Dark* 38; and her essay, 'The Site of Memory', in *What Moves at the Margin* 108.
12. See the museum leaflet, *Le Louvre Invite: Toni Morrison; Étranger Chez Soi' : Parcours dans les trois départements archéologiques, 13 octobre – 15 janvier 2007.*
13. See Roynon, *Morrison* vii.
14. The first article on Morrison's classicism was Bessie Jones's, appearing in 1985, on *Song of Solomon*. For a fuller list of scholarship see Roynon, *Morrison* 8, n. 5. Particularly recommended (besides essays on *Beloved* and *Solomon* discussed later in this chapter) are Demetrakapoulos and Holloway, Miner (both on *The Bluest Eye*); Traylor (on *Tar Baby*).
15. See my introduction here for discussion of Ronnick's 2005 *Encyclopedia Africana* entry on 'Classicism, black', and for an overview of the foundational works in the field of black classicism.
16. See Roynon, 'Africanness of Classicism'; Roynon, *Morrison* 162–84 for detailed discussion of Greek, Roman and African intersections in the oeuvre.
17. On Morrison, Gilroy and black modernism see Roynon, *Cambridge Introduction* 111–14.
18. See for example Jesmyn Ward's *Salvage the Bones* (2011), discussed in my conclusion, and her 2017 novel *Sing, Unburied, Sing*. See also Robin Coste Lewis's long poem, *Voyage of the Sable Venus* (2015).
19. See <http://www2.oberlin.edu/amam/WildfireTestPit2.html> (last accessed 18 May 2020).
20. See for example essays by Awkward; Benston; Cowart, 'Faulkner'; Freiert.
21. See Roynon, *Morrison* 57ff, and 135ff on the chorus/protagonist paradigm in Greek tragedy.
22. See Cowart, 'Faulkner'. On the extensive scholarship comparing Morrison and Faulkner see Roynon, *Cambridge Introduction* 119–20; on their relationship in terms of classicism see also Roynon, *Morrison* 77–101.
23. Jennings includes a photograph of a *skyphos* dating from the fourth century BCE, found in Thebes, now in the Ashmolean Museum in Oxford, which depicts an 'African Circe' with Odysseus (Jennings 163).
24. Although, as discussed in Chapter 4 here, Icarus features throughout Ellison's work, this specific syncretism occurs only in the manuscript written in the 1980s, 'Hickman in Washington DC'.
25. On *miasma* in ancient Greece see Parker, *Miasma*.
26. See Roynon, *Morrison* 142ff.
27. See for example *Libation Bearers*, trans. Lattimore, ll. 47, 66–7.

28. See Cowart, 'Faulkner' 96. Civil Rights-era patriarchy and misogyny are recorded in Angela Davis's *Autobiography* (1974), which Morrison edited, and are documented by Michele Wallace in *Black Macho* (1978).
29. See Ovid, *Met.* III.95–114.
30. See Roynon, *Morrison* 153ff.
31. See for example Haley; Walters.
32. See Morrison's foreword to *Beloved*; also Roynon, *Morrison* 81 on Thomas Satterwhite Noble's painting of Garner, 'The Modern Medea'; also Malamud, *African Americans*; Weisenburger.
33. See Roynon, *Morrison* 61.
34. On Sethe's heroic dilemma see also Phelan.
35. Morrison comments frequently in her non-fiction on the idea of the community as chorus; for discussion see Roynon, *Morrison* 135–42.
36. See Roynon, *Morrison* 90–1.
37. See Jennings on how the *abiku*, the *bandoki* and *kanda* inform the representation of the vengeful Beloved.
38. On Niobe in Wheatley see Shields 222. Perhaps not coincidentally, at Sweet Home Sethe longs for advice from a midwife called 'Aunt Phyllis' (*Beloved* 187).
39. For an account of this movement see <https://blacklivesmatter.com/about/herstory/> (last accessed 19 May 2020). The movement gained new momentum in 2020 following the murder of George Floyd.
40. See Roynon, *Morrison* 92–111. On *Jazz* and the pastoral see Conner, 'Wild Women'.
41. See for example Duvall, 'Morrison'; Dimino.
42. On Phaethon (and the phaeton) in *Light in August* see Chapter 3, and on Ellison's *Three Days* see Chapter 4. On the dramatic use of the present tense in classical epic see Quinn 77–8.
43. See for example John Crowe Ransom's piece in this collection, discussed in Roynon, *Morrison* 94–5.
44. See Roynon, *Morrison* 106–7.
45. The action of *Jazz* takes place primarily in 1925, the year in which both *The Great Gatsby* and *The New Negro* were published.
46. See Roynon, *Morrison* 172–5.
47. See for example Conner, 'Wild Women'; Conner, 'Modernity'; Roynon, *Morrison* 175–8.
48. For an English translation of the Nag Hammadi library see J. Robinson; also <http://gnosis.org/naghamm/nhl.html> (last accessed 19 May 2020).

Further Reading

Barnard, John Levi. *Empire of Ruin: Black Classicism and American Imperial Culture*. Oxford: Oxford University Press, 2017.

McConnell, Justine. 'Postcolonial *Sparagmos*: Toni Morrison's *Sula* and Wole Soyinka's *The Bacchae of Euripides: A Communion Rite*'. *Classical Receptions Journal* 8.2 (2016): 133–54.

McGowan, Grace. '"I Know I Can't Change the Future, but I Can Change the Past": Toni Morrison, Robin Coste Lewis, and the Classical Tradition'. *Contemporary Women's Writing* 13.3 (2019): 339–56.

Morrison, Toni. 'Unspeakable Things Unspoken: The Afro-American Presence in American Literature'. *Within the Circle: An Anthology of African American Literary Criticism from the Harlem Renaissance to the Present*. Ed. Angelyn Mitchell. Durham, NC: Duke University Press, 1994. 368–98.

Roynon, Tessa. *Toni Morrison and the Classical Tradition: Transforming American Culture*. Oxford: Oxford University Press, 2013.

CHAPTER 6

Philip Roth (1933–2018)

Roth and the Classics

In Roth's 1998 novel, *I Married a Communist*, narrator Nathan Zuckerman records Murray Ringold speaking disparagingly of the melodramatic style in which Eve Frame, the unloving wife of his brother, Ira, executes her attack on her husband. 'Under the pressure of her rage', Murray recalls, 'Eve was quite the neo-classicist'. The three-page letter in which she expresses her hatred to Ira 'might well have concluded in a fanfare of heroic couplets' (268). A subversive perspective on the classical tradition and its uses is indubitably one feature of Roth's vast oeuvre.[1] In both his fiction and his non-fiction, he frequently glories in an irreverence for high culture and its institutions, at times performing a certain kind of anti-intellectualism. A parodic take on classical literature and its cultural legacies is often key to his mock-heroic conceptions of both himself and his characters. Although the liberal education he received as an undergraduate and postgraduate student was characterised by a 'Great Books' approach typical of the 1950s, one which begins its syllabus with Greek epic and tragedy in translation, in a 1983 interview Roth described his years at the University of Chicago as a time of learning 'how to talk back to all those great books' (Searles 143).[2] Yet many of Roth's novels – in particular the 'American trilogy' (*American Pastoral* (1997), *I Married a Communist* (1998) and *The Human Stain* (2000)) which is my focus in this chapter – deploy heroic, epic and tragic traditions with great earnestness. Alongside their moments of ironic allusiveness, these texts – which even in their trilogic structure mirror the *Oresteia* – often reverentially invoke an intense and grand/grandiose version of the classical past that is ultimately a 1950s neo-Aristotelian construction.[3]

Over the course of a literary career that ran from 1959 to 2010, Roth published over thirty books. His output was an always-evolving, experimental trajectory that has involved 'high seriousness, . . . low humour, . . . expansive monologue, . . . elliptical dialogue, . . . spare realism, . . . and grotesque surrealism' (Brauner 1), as well as the sustained ethically, historically and politically engaged texts ranging from *Sabbath's Theater* (1995) to *The Plot Against America* (2004), and the sparer final phase. My discussion here does not, therefore, attempt to give an account of this author's classicism across the whole oeuvre. Roth references the ancient word in numerous texts and in contrasting tones and modes, ranging from Zuckerman's surreal conception, in *The Ghost Writer* (1979), of Amy Bellette (or 'Anne Frank') as 'the Pallas Athene of Athene College' (89), to the implicit engagement with Ovidian transformation and in particular with the myth of Pygmalion in *The Humbling* (2009).[4] His allusiveness includes the hilarious mock-epic self-fashioning of Portnoy in *Portnoy's Complaint* (1969), which joyfully invokes the 'house of Atreus' and includes an exuberant deployment of the condom brand name 'Trojans' (306, 392), as well as the sombre title of his final novel, *Nemesis* (2010). His classicism is as varied in its nature, and often (though not always) as slippery in its meanings, as it is nearly-ubiquitous in its presence.

An account of the role of the classics in Roth's intellectual formation is no more straightforward, moreover, for several intersecting reasons. First, although he died in 2018, his authorised biography (by Bill Bailey) is not scheduled to appear until 2021, and so is still in progress as I write this book. While his personal book collection has now been donated to Newark Public Library, it will not be made available to researchers until fully catalogued (which is also projected for 2021). Second, due to Roth's by-now-notorious predilection for blurring the boundaries between his own 'real' experiences and the fictional experiences of his created characters, much of the information he has given us about his studies at high school and university is unreliable to an unusual degree. In David Brauner's terms, *The Facts* (1998) typifies Roth's penchant for 'fictional autobiography', while Zuckerman's various reflections on his experiences at the University of Chicago (in *I Married a Communist*, for example) speak to the author's predilection for 'autobiographical fiction' (Brauner 9).[5]

The facts we are certain of are these: that Roth (in his own words) was 'raised self-consciously as a Jew' (Searles 127), in a family and community descended from late-nineteenth-century immigrants, and attended Weequahic High School in Newark, New Jersey, from 1946 to 1950. As a member of the first generation in his family to go to college, he spent 1950–51 at the Newark extension of Rutgers University. He viewed the 'liberal-arts studies' he began at Newark Rutgers as a means to social and ethnic mobility (Roth, *Facts* 37), even as he was desperate to get 'away' (35–6). After transferring to Bucknell University, from which he graduated in 1954 with a BA in English, he completed his MA degree at Chicago in 1955. He returned there in 1956 to begin the PhD programme, with the intention of writing a dissertation on Henry James (Hayes, 'To Rake' 97). Although he dropped out of that programme after only one semester, he stayed on at Chicago as a teacher (primarily of freshman composition) until 1958. It is interesting that, among the seven authors who are the subject of this book, he is the only one who appears never to have studied any Latin, either at high school or afterwards.

In *The Facts*, Roth locates the beginnings of his conscious, significant reading in his encounters with his brother's copies of *Winesburg, Ohio* and *A Portrait of the Artist* when he was aged 'fifteen and sixteen' (40).[6] In that account, he does make the odd passing mention of the books he read while at the colonial, spired and colonnaded, predominantly Christian campus of Bucknell that, as he says, had 'beguiled' him (*Facts* 45–6). In contrast to several of the other authors that I discuss here, however, he does not depict his formal intellectual pursuits as the central adventure of his life at this time. He does note that at Bucknell he studied 'Literary Criticism, Modern Thought, Advanced Shakespeare, and Aesthetics' (56), and that he was 'earnestly reading [his] way from Cynewulf to *Mrs Dalloway*' (59). At that time he saw no possible way of bridging the gap, as a creative writer, between the cultural specificities of his upbringing and the elevated preoccupations and style of the canonical literature that constituted his degree course. Formative experiences for his later literary output were his acting in college productions of '*Oedipus Rex*, *School for Scandal*, and *Death of a Salesman*' (69), and his role as the occasionally notorious editor of the often-satirical student magazine, *Et Cetera* (57). Roth would have discovered satire not just via Sheridan but also as a classical and neoclassical form documented in the *Literary History of Modern England* by Albert Baugh (1948), which he studied as part of his senior year special seminar (67).[7] While in a 1981 interview Roth suggests that being Jewish in the Christian culture of Bucknell made him 'take on the role of a Houyhnhnm who had strayed on the campus from *Gulliver's Travels*' (Searles 126), the fact that he made the dean's list, was elected to Phi Beta Kappa and graduated 'magna cum laude' suggests that despite his sense of his own difference, he succeeded there in most if not all of the conventional ways (Parrish, *Companion* ix).

In his self-fashioning in *The Facts* and in interviews, Roth is alternately restrained, low-key and even at times glib about his years as a graduate student and young instructor at Chicago. His throwaway line, in 1983, that his Master's year involved 'bibliography by day, women by night' (Searles 142) anticipates Coleman Silk's experience of 'the legs of a girl walking in front of him' distracting him from 'the world of antiquity' once he had enrolled at NYU (*Human* 111). Even in the 1991 interview about Chicago with Molly McQuade, in which he describes this period of his life as 'exhilarating' and 'wonderful' (Searles 280, 284), Roth is reticent about specific ways in which that period of his life shaped both his intellectual formation and his literary output. He tells McQuade that he 'took the standard master's degree program in literature', which involved 'good courses' with professors 'Elder Olson, Morton Dauwen Zabel, and Napier Wilt' (Searles 281), but he does not (here) mention what he studied with them.[8]

As Kasia Boddy documents in her discussion of the 'Great Books' tradition and *The Human Stain*, Elder Olson was a 'neo-Aristotelian' (42): he, in the decade following Roth's Chicago years, was to publish books on both Aristotelian influence and tragedy. Olson exemplified the 'Chicago school' of 1950s Aristotelianism which philosopher Richard McKeon and university president Robert Maynard Hutchins (chancellor and president at Chicago until 1951) also espoused.[9] As Boddy has discussed, moreover, David Grene – from whose translation (in the standard Chicago series) of *Oedipus Rex* Roth quotes in his epigraph to *The Human Stain* – was one of the most famous professors in Chicago's Classics department during the novelist's time there. Although it is Zuckerman in the fiction rather than Roth in the non-fiction who is explicit about studying both Aristotle (see *Zuckerman Unbound* (1981), for example) and Greek and Roman mythology (in *The Human Stain*), the 1950s liberal conception of the Aristotelian tragedy, with its emphasis on the primacy of the individual, and of (purportedly) non-ideological infinite dialectic, is arguably the single most important influence on this author's work.[10]

In his accounts of life after Chicago, Roth has frequently identified himself with a series of locations that connote high culture and intellectual elitism: 'I've lived in Rome, London, Iowa City and Princeton,' he states in a 1981 interview (Searles 126), and he repeats this same list in *The Facts* (136). Yet about Europe as a site of the classical past, he is for the most part surprisingly silent – a silence that may or may not reflect inner conflicts about classical literary and cultural traditions and legacies themselves. Of the seven months he spent on a Guggenheim Fellowship in Rome, from 1959 to 1960, he is noticeably unforthcoming about any impression that being in that city might have made on him. Although Rome features intermittently in *Letting Go* (1962) – the novel he wrote while based there – and is the setting for a few notorious pages of *Portnoy's Complaint*, the contrast between Cather, Fitzgerald or Ellison and himself in terms of interest in this city or any other ancient European site is stark.[11] We can perhaps attribute this reticence to the fact that these months spent in Rome were simultaneously the first year of his disastrous first marriage. It may also be because the primary meaning of Europe itself, for any Jewish American coming of age in the 1950s, was not a classical age of ruins and mythology, but the unspeakable realities of the Holocaust in its all-too-recent past.[12]

Roth endorses modern European (and European-American) writers even though he engages very little with sites of ancient European civilisation. In 1973, while he looks back half-mockingly to his 'twenties' as a time in which he 'declared [himself] *for* art – the art of Tolstoy, James, Flaubert, and Mann' (Searles 65), the author he mentions with notable frequency in his non-fiction is Henry James. While he specifies his admiration for *The Wings of the Dove* and *The Golden Bowl*, his invocations of James are for the most part concerned with that author as the epitome of dominant cultural elite intellectualism.[13] He refers repeatedly to the frisson he caused in the classroom by being '*a Jew*' who '*knows Henry James*' (Searles 21, original italics); documents his wariness about the role of literary studies as a means to assimilation (Searles 283); and talks in *The Facts* of the '"civilizing" function' of James as 'tempting' (115). Yet at the same time Roth clearly relished the process of becoming an intellectual and an expert in the canon, testifying to Molly McQuade about the 'pleasure' that he and other Jewish classmates at Chicago took 'in having humble origins and high-minded pursuits' (Searles 283). James Joyce, perhaps, for Roth, both best exemplifies an ambivalence about canonicity within his own pages and plays a fundamental role in Roth's own intellectual ambivalence. That the American author calls the second chapter of *The Ghost Writer*

'Nathan Dedalus' speaks volumes about this half-serious, half-comic relationship. His choice of the 'bound/unbound' pun for the first four Zuckerman works (collected as *Zuckerman Bound* in 1985) – with its simultaneous irreverent invocations of the Aeschylean *Prometheus Bound* and of Shelley's assertion of romantic/artistic/political freedom in *Prometheus Unbound* (1820) – creates a similar effect. Roth's allusiveness configures his characters and himself as at once imprisoned and set free by books, and by the classical tradition as a whole.

The Critical Field and Scholarly Debate

Although Roth is one of the most widely and deeply analysed American writers of the late twentieth and early twenty-first centuries, among the innumerable studies of his work there is to date no full-length exploration of his classicism as a subject in its own right. Critics seldom fail to notice and to comment on his allusiveness, although from the mid-1980s to the start of the new millennium there was a prevailing tendency towards uncritical, reverential illumination of classical references rather than analytical enquiry into those references' effects or their cultural and political work. It may well be the sophisticated approaches of classical reception studies, which established itself as a dynamic discipline in the early 2000s, that have led to the more nuanced analyses of recent years, and to many readings which position Roth's engagements with classical antiquity in relation to the intellectual histories of both his own work and the wider culture. It is of course *The Human Stain*, with its Classics professor protagonist and its explicit engagement with the 'culture wars' and identity politics, that has generated most of the readings of this nature. But recent articles also range from Patrick Hayes's 2013 reassessment of Roth's negotiations of Jamesian tragedy in *Letting Go*, to Nicholas Stangherlin's analysis, in 2016, of Judaic and Greek syncretism evident in invocations to the tragic figures of Job, Prometheus and Oedipus in *Nemesis* (2010). These exemplify the rich rewards that a focus on classical dimensions can yield across much of this novelist's oeuvre.

Mainstream reviewers and Roth's publishers were the quickest to endorse and extend rather than analyse the tragic frameworks of the novels in the American trilogy, labelling them 'American tragedies' in a nod to Dreiser's 1925 novel *American Tragedy*. Such a process confers an immediate validation, a muscular pedigree, upon the more recent texts, and just a few scholarly assessments of the three novels together have adopted the same oversimplified and oversimplifying approach.[14] Important critical studies of classical dimensions of the trilogy that complicate the 'genre-spotting' tendency include David Brauner's *Philip Roth* (2007) and the fourth chapter of Catherine Morley's *The Quest for Epic in Contemporary American Fiction* (2008). Brauner meticulously maps the correspondences between the trajectories of Ira Ringold, Seymour Levov and Coleman Silk and that of the prototypical Aristotelian tragic hero. He demonstrates that Roth's deployment of the Aristotelian heroic downfall and his subversive engagements with the genre of the pastoral and the motif of purification enable the novelist to critique specific moments in American history.[15] Morley, meanwhile, analyses the novels in the light of Northrop Frye's and Harold Bloom's respective theories of epic, identifying the trilogy's 'literary patrimony' as one that includes (alongside Homer and Virgil) John Milton, the epicists of the nineteenth century's 'American Renaissance' era such as Nathaniel Hawthorne, and James Joyce (86). Particularly useful are her exploration of the epic concepts of 'wrath and return' in *I Married a Communist* (109–12), her analyses of the ways in which Roth uses the epic genre to make specific individuals representative of national experience and consciousness, and her illumination of this novelist's epic inheritances as an important part of his transnationalism.

American Pastoral, treated as a stand-alone text, has generated only one article – Gustavo Canales's – that focuses exclusively on its 'classical motifs', while *I Married a Communist* has generated none.[16] Due to both the frequency and the unmissable presence of the allusions in *The Human Stain*, by contrast, scholarly articles on classicism in that text alone now constitute something of a minor industry. Since Elaine Safer's 2002 study of 'tragedy and farce' in this novel, there have appeared at least eight further essays on its classical dimensions: in order of their publication these include those by Geoffrey Bakewell (2004), Patrice Rankine (2005), Gustavo Canales (2009), Sam Bluefarb (2010), Kasia Boddy (2010), Adam Kelly (2010), Alan McCluskey (2014) and Michael Kalisch (2016). Happily, these articles for the most part complement and (implicitly) complicate each other. Bakewell and Rankine separately explore the ways in which Roth's complex engagement with *Oedipus Rex* and the Oedipus myth enables his serious explorations of the modern

American individual and national consciousness (Bakewell) and of racial passing as a tragic experience (Rankine). Safer and Bluefarb contrastingly emphasise the comic and/or farcical elements of certain classical engagements in this text, ones that co-exist with tragic elements and that enable Roth's satire of political correctness and of contemporary academia. While Canales identifies the significant presences of the Euripidean tragedies, *Alcestis* and *Hippolytus*, exploring their role in that same satire, Kelly highlights the ways in which the text functions as a 'reflection on the genre [of tragedy] and an examination of its processes and assumptions' (189). Boddy's landmark essay reads Roth's rewritings of Greek tragedy and of the *Iliad* in terms of his own relationship to the 'Great Books' tradition in which he was schooled. New directions include McCluskey's reading of the tragic elements through the lens of cosmopolitanism, and the completely fresh focus, by Kalisch, on Roth's indebtedness to classical paradigms of friendship in depicting the relationship between Zuckerman and both Murray Ringold and Coleman Silk.

Readings such as Boddy's and McCluskey's are invaluable for the ways that they move between close readings of the classicism in a single text and wider debates both about Roth and about contemporaneous literature, culture and politics, but there remains much work to be done on this important interplay. For example, while Brauner usefully sets out the always-shifting conflicts between 'Jewish Americanness' and 'American Jewishness' that this author and his work embody (11), critics have yet to address in full the implications of the relationship between the Judaic or Hebrew and the Graeco-Roman traditions in his writing.[17] In addition, it may well be true that it is only with his most overtly classically allusive texts, the American trilogy, that Roth's own position within that canon and his status as a 'Great American novelist' (published from 2005 onwards in the prestigious Library of America series, no less) became assured. While Brauner argues that Roth is at different times and in different guises both a 'radical conservative' and a 'conservative radical' (15), from the American trilogy in particular he often emerges as an unambiguous conservative in his perspectives on the political and cultural dynamics of late-twentieth-century America. Does his classicism straightforwardly undergird his conservatism in these novels? In other words, does it unambiguously reinforce his attack on the recalibrations of the canon and of academic syllabi that identity politics demands? In contrast to Morrison, then, who deploys the classical tradition to radical political ends, does Roth's classicism always bolster what he depicts in *The Human Stain* as the much-beleaguered 'I', the (implicitly white male) individual now beset by the tyrannies of the all-engulfing 'we'? (*Human* 183).

One pluralised constituency with which Roth's writing inevitably exists in fraught antagonism is that of feminism. While Deborah Shostak has argued that 'Roth's work can appear as much a prescient critique of misogynist attitudes as a purveyor of them' (112), few feminist readers and critics will agree with her.[18] Many important feminist close readings, not least on the relationship between this author's classicism and his patriarchal and misogynistic perspectives, have yet to be done. In the discussions of the novels in the American trilogy that follow, I illuminate this novelist's widespread engagement with Ovid in each of these texts, involved as they are with multiple transformations both of the self and of American culture. In so doing, I also explore the politics of his invocations of Ovidian myths about sexual violence and male predatoriness in particular. In *The Ghost Writer*, the Rabbi Wapter is mocked for asking the aspiring young author, Zuckerman, why he insists on privileging the 'cheap' and 'slimy' in his writing over the 'noble' and 'sublime' (66). It is arguable that Roth uses the classical tradition as a way of dignifying, or making respectable, some 'slime' that is highly questionable in terms of power relations between women and men.

Given the extent of the metafictional dimensions in Roth's writing, and (in all of the Zuckerman novels) of the endless interplay between the unreliable narrator and the author himself, some critics have argued that it is impossible to ascribe any stable meanings to his fiction. Any analysis of the politics of his classicism, for example, is of course open to the charge of conflating Zuckerman with Roth. It is true that, both in *Zuckerman Bound* and in the American trilogy (especially *The Human Stain*), the narrator is incorrigibly and at times ludicrously allusive to the classical tradition. And in *The Facts*, it is Zuckerman who, in his letter to Roth at the work's end, indulges in invocations of 'pastoral' (169), 'Pandora's box' (174), 'mythology . . . and Greek drama' (185) and 'Cicero' (190), in marked contrast to the relatively un-allusive author who has preceded him. Yet while it is never possible to equate Zuckerman with Roth, the inverse is also true: we can never be certain that Zuckerman is *not* Roth. It is noteworthy that in June 2017 (only months before his death), Roth published a short piece in the 'Life and Letters' column of *The New Yorker*. Therein he wrote, ostensibly as himself, of his 'mytho-historical conception of [his] own country', of its 'grandiosity', of 'the American adventure' that was 'one's engulfing fate', and of the 'drama and destiny' of the American moment ('I Have Fallen' 46–7).[19] This is an insistently classicising Roth, one who sounds a great deal like his Zuckerman.

American Pastoral (1997)

Reflecting on his various encounters at his high school reunion, near the beginning of this novel, Nathan Zuckerman observes that 'Destiny had become understandable' (52). In recalling his own study of the topic in 'freshman Greek and Roman Mythology', he remembers writing down that 'the Fates are three goddesses called the Moerae, Clotho who spins, Lachesis who determines its length, and Atropos who cuts the thread of life' (52). This unattributed paraphrase of a paragraph on the *Moirai* in Edith Hamilton's *Mythology* (1942) is interesting for several reasons.[20] First, it suggests the influential role of Hamilton's book in both Zuckerman's and Roth's own educations. Second, it draws attention to Zuckerman's self-conscious deployment of the classical framework through which he tells the unhappy tale of Seymour Levov. This narratorial classical obsessiveness is just as important as the fact that the spirit of Sophocles's *Oedipus Rex*, from which its epigraph quotes, pervades the novel's central concern with the conflict between self-determination and uncontrollable historical and cultural forces. Likewise, Zuckerman's disarmingly honest rumination on the interest that Seymour's catastrophic fate holds for him as a writer – 'to imagine yourself into his bad luck, to implicate yourself . . . in the bewilderment of his tragic fall—well, that's worth thinking about' (88) – is at least as significant as the fact that he (and Roth) configure this protagonist in the tragic mode.

Brauner and (separately) Canales have meticulously and usefully mapped out the cultural nuances and implications of the depiction of Seymour – a successful Jewish American businessman who, by the mid-twentieth century, has assimilated to the extent that he appears to be living the idyllic, privileged WASP dream – as an unseeing, erring, hubristic Aristotelian tragic hero who undergoes a prototypical Aristotelian downfall before that century's end.

Brauner also illuminates the complexities of the ubiquitous theme of purity/impurity and purification (themselves derived from classical, Jewish and Puritan traditions), while Morley elucidates the synthesis of Judaeo-Christian, classical and recent European and American traditions that the novel's epic conception and scope enact. And Zuckerman himself observes to us of Seymour's fate, in a statement that recalls Arthur Miller's manifesto about the 'tragedy of the common man', that 'the tragedy of the man not set up for tragedy – that is every man's tragedy' (*American Pastoral* 86).[21] We do not wonder about the rationale behind the novel's title, given that, in Zuckerman's words, Merry is 'the daughter who transports [Seymour] out of the longed-for American pastoral into everything that is its antithesis and enemy, into the fury, the violence, and the desperation of the counterpastoral—into the indigenous American berserk' (86). Similarly, we can hardly fail to notice that Seymour is 'the household Apollo of the Weequahic Jews' (4); that moments of passionate intensity (such as the cheerleaders' dancing, which is 'ecstatically discharged' (4)) are often described in Nietzschean Dionysiac terms; or that the second bomb blast with which Merry is involved destroys a 'most elegant Greek revival house' (149).

Canales makes the provocative point that Merry 'displays the same tragic flaw as her father and mother', in that she, like them, has 'spent her life creating new identities for herself' ('Bomb Blast' 213). Although Brauner reads the novel as a near-allegory that censures Seymour for assuming a false WASP identity and lifestyle, it is impossible to determine whether the protagonist's tragic error is his changing of his identity, or his violation of emotional and sexual taboos (in mimicking Merry's stutter and kissing her). What exactly are we being asked to lament in this text? Do we pity the fact that Seymour cannot make the American dream a reality, and cannot sustain an idyll that is genuinely desirable; or are we instead being shown the flimsiness and hypocrisy of the dream and the idyll that so many deludedly pursue? The politics of these two perspectives could not be more different: one reinforces dominant American ideology while the other critiques and invalidates it. Even Zuckerman, moreover, appears ambivalent about Seymour's self-reinvention. Early on, the narrator exhibits some mild (and rare) comic irony at his hero's expense in remembering that, while at high school, 'the Swede' had shelved a series of baseball novels between bookends which were miniatures of Rodin's sculpture *The Thinker* (7). Yet Zuckerman himself exhibits that same predilection for classically derived cultural reference points: he later compares the inscrutable Seymour to 'Michelangelo's David' (30), and in his (composed but never delivered) high school reunion speech he likens the neighbourhood Jewish boys of their shared childhood to 'well-born children in Renaissance Florence' (42).[22] By contrast, however, there is no ambiguity surrounding either the actions of or the various new identities assumed by Merry – we are encouraged to share the revulsion of her family (and its chronicler) at her every new incarnation.

While Zuckerman gently marvels at the myriad 'transformations' undergone by his former classmates, Seymour later marvels (with hostility and disgust) at young women activists' 'thirst for self-transformation' (44, 254). Although Ovid is never explicitly invoked or quoted in this novel (unlike, for example, Shakespeare or Tolstoy), the *Metamorphoses* and the 'Ovidian dynamic' inferred from it constitute important subtexts not just in the general exploration of a rapidly changing America, or in the general theme of self-fabrication and reinvention.[23] The Latin epic features very specifically in the portrayal of Merry's relationship with her father and of the sexualised violence she endures at his hands, and at the hands of other men too. As is common in Roth's novels, nearly all of the women characters in *American Pastoral* have an element of the mythological or allegorical about them; they are for the most part less 'real' and less psychologically realised than the men. While Zuckerman compares the now-wrinkled face of a female former classmate to an 'antique stone head of a Roman sovereign' that has been 'scored . . . as if with an engraving stylus' (77), the name 'Dawn' connotes the Roman Aurora, goddess of the dawn.[24] In sharing his recollections of his archetypally dysfunctional family with Zuckerman, meanwhile, Jerry Levov relishes referring to his niece as 'the monster daughter. The monster *Merry*' (67, original italics), and as 'the family's fucking monster' (71). Most significantly of all, the text enacts a specific engagement with Ovid's tales of Myrrha, who embarks on an incestuous relationship with her father (and whose name resonates in 'Merry'), and of Philomela, who is both multiply raped and mutilated by Tereus. Roth signals the engagement with Ovidian transformation through Seymour's wish, on confronting the squalid and violated Merry in her hovel, that 'she had become an animal' (238).

In her well-known essay, 'Reading Ovid's Rapes', feminist classicist Amy Richlin observes that sexual violence and sexual transgression are an obviously 'suitable scenario' for the *Metamorphoses*, a poem in which the central unifying theme is 'the dissolution of boundaries of body, genus, gender and genre' (176). Merry's trajectory constitutes a boundlessness comparable to the total transgressions with which Ovid's poem is concerned: in Jerry's words, she is/was 'out of bounds, a freak of nature, *way* out of bounds' (*American Pastoral* 71, original italics). Ovid's account of Myrrha's sustained sexual relationship with her own father in Book X – disturbing not least because it is instigated by herself – resonates not just in Merry's request to Seymour that he 'k-k-kiss' her the way he would her 'umumumother' (89). Equally significant for *American Pastoral* is the Roman's poet's emphasis on the unspeakable nature of this kind of sexual relationship (as well as on the unspeakable nature of Tereus's crimes in the Philomela story). Although his tale of Myrrah runs over 150 lines, Ovid ensures that no character – neither Myrrah, nor the nurse, nor her father Cinyras – ever names the act of incest, resorting instead to euphemism, insinuation and analogical hinting. In Roth's novel, in imitating Merry's stutter as he rejects her request with a 'N-n-no' (90), and in following up by kissing her 'stammering mouth with the passion that she had been asking him for all month long', Seymour utterly violates two taboos at once, but his actions are likewise never openly acknowledged (91). Ovid's near-untellable tale of Myrrha and Cinyras is a disturbing subtext throughout.

The Roman poet anticipates the story of Myrrha in his horrific tale of Philomela, who is abducted, imprisoned and repeatedly raped by her brother-in-law Tereus (who also cuts out her tongue): Ovid includes the scheming Tereus's wish that he himself were Philomela's 'father' so that he could then embrace her (*Met.* VI.481–2). In Roth's depiction of the stuttering Merry, violated first by her father and then raped twice during her time in exile, Ovid's myth of Philomela resonates in numerous ways.[25] In her study *The Rhetoric of the Body from Ovid to Shakespeare* (2000), Lynn Enterline argues that the Philomela narrative exemplifies how, in the poem as a whole, 'the usually separated realms of the rhetorical and the sexual most insistently meet' (1); and how Ovid's narrative 'bring[s] to light the often occluded relationships between sexuality, language and violence' (2). The power of communication and of disrupted communication are central themes in this tale – as Enterline points out, in describing Tereus's rape 'the narrator begins to stutter over the word 'unspeakable' (4), while, in a notorious passage, Ovid luridly describes the cut-out tongue of Philomela as 'palpitating' and 'faintly murmuring' on the ground (*Met.* VI.557–8).[26]

There are significant echoes of this myth in the scene in which Seymour re-encounters Merry in *American Pastoral*: the moment in which he reaches into his daughter's mouth and 'took hold of her tongue' is yet one more violation of her body, as well as of her power to communicate. 'He pried her mouth open, disregarding . . . the injunction against violence,' Roth writes; he 'pried open her mouth and with his fingers took hold of her tongue', and at the same time he illogically orders her to 'speak!' (265). Roth's descriptions here suggest a kind of violation that is if anything more egregious than Seymour's imitation of the stammer and the mouth kiss a decade earlier. The relationship between 'sexuality, language and violence' could hardly be more explicit.

An invocation of the myth of Philomela might, in the abstract, enable a powerful protest against male domination, sexual violence and erasure of the female voice. Indeed, Morrison in *The Bluest Eye* typifies the many modern writers who have deployed the myth to such feminist ends. But Roth arguably negates the possibility of such a reading in his text by his focus on Seymour's point of view. We learn about Merry's rape not via her own words but via Seymour's thoughts, in which they are a kind of reported speech and become disturbingly close to a sexual fantasy of his own. Throughout the novel, Merry has no interiority or agency that is not mediated through Zuckerman's imagination of Seymour's thoughts about her. When Seymour realises that 'the rape was in his bloodstream and he would never get it out' (270), there is a real sense in which Roth appropriates Philomela's suffering by transferring it on to that character rather than on to Merry. Seymour is at times himself lost for words: on receiving Rita Cohen's letter he realises he cannot verbalise eruptions of 'the unexpected' except as a 'thing', 'thing thing thing thing . . . but what other word was tolerable?' (176). Zuckerman confers the stutter itself upon his hero during Seymour's lengthy ruminations on his 'inexplicable' misfortune (92): 'he envisioned his life as a stutterer's thought, wildly out of his control' (93).

Lastly, Roth recalibrates Ovid's tale so that Procne and Philomela's infamous revenge on Tereus – getting him to eat his own son that they cook for him and serve at the dinner table – becomes the part to which he gives greatest emphasis.[27] The American author configures all of

Merry's actions as irrational vengeance against Seymour; at their grim reunion the father interprets even the fact that she no longer stutters as 'a great revenge to take' (250). And although the Philomela myth does not continue to resonate in any specific way in *American Pastoral*'s Part III, the dinner party in which the entire Levovian edifice crumbles can be seen as a distant, distorted echo of Philomela's serving up of Itys on the dinner table. In Roth's hands, however, the avenger is the greatest wrongdoer. The novelist's interweaving of Ovidian myths in this novel constitutes a very different kind of classical allusiveness from Nathan Zuckerman's at times heavy-handed, overly overt allusions to classical gods and to Aristotelian motifs. Ovid is a more subtle, but also more politically problematic presence than is Greek tragedy in this text.

I Married a Communist (1998)

That there are to date no critical essays that focus primarily or exclusively on Roth's engagement with classical tradition in this novel is to some extent not surprising: *I Married a Communist* is far less explicitly allusive to Greek and Roman antiquity than are its trilogic companions, *American Pastoral* and *The Human Stain*. Although the novel is motored by the Homeric dynamic of 'wrath' and 'return', the overt cultural models to which Zuckerman compares Ira are the betrayed tragic heroes of the Shakespearean oeuvre (Othello, Hamlet and Lear) and the betrayed protagonists in the Bible's Old Testament (Adam, Esau, Moses, Samson and so on).[28] The narrator makes repeated analogical connections not between Ira and the heroes of classical mythology, but between Ira and various mythologised political heroes of America's past and present: Thomas Paine, Abraham Lincoln and Paul Robeson. There is, however, a significant and in some ways problematic contrast that Roth draws between the Aristotelian and tragic perspectives that the novel valorises on several simultaneous levels, and the apparently more pragmatically or cynically deployed 'neoclassicist' tendencies of the uber-assimilationist and anti-Semitic Eve Frame and Sylphid Pennington (*Married* 268). Informing both of these outlooks is a wide-ranging exploration of the nature and impact of education, intellectualism and cultural transmission. The 'Great Books' tradition and its antitheses that Boddy illuminates as central to *The Human Stain* are arguably of equal if not greater importance in this prior text.

Although Zuckerman does not conceptualise Ira as any one specific classical hero, his account of Ira's paradigmatic rise and fall is expressed in the terms of the heroic tradition that is broadly classically derived. He associates Ira with 'heroically exaggerated ambitions' (16) and with 'heroic suffering' (25), and as a schoolboy is unashamedly awed by the athletic physiques of both Ira and Murray, remembering them as 'two big, natural men' (27). Zuckerman fuses his pantheon of classical and American demi-gods (therein taking after dominant American culture itself, of course) in comparing Ira to a local civic statue of 'Abraham Lincoln . . . cast in bronze' (91). But Murray, on the other hand, does not share the narrator's hagiographic tendencies regarding his brother; indeed, he has a sceptical awareness of the 'aura of heroic purity' that Ira exerts over others (54), and 'in general provides a counterweight . . . to Zuckerman's tendency to idealise Ira, and to Ira's tendency to mythologize himself' (Brauner 155).

Yet, as Brauner also points out, in inferring from the way his brother was 'brought down' that 'a genuine catastrophe is always personal bathos at core' (Roth, *Married* 3), Murray's account is itself an 'Aristotelian analysis' (Brauner 154). Murray laments that his brother was 'ruined' (*Married* 15), and it is he who names the grand tragic themes of 'hubris' (161) and of 'revenge and betrayal' (184). Although he refers humorously to the masseuse and prostitute, Helgi Pnär, as the 'deus ex machina' (182), his own discourse is, at times, as earnestly reliant on the age-old classical paradigms as is Zuckerman's. When narrating Ira's psychiatric breakdown, for example, he states that the 'collapse' of this 'titanically defiant' person was 'total' (283). His choice of the word 'titanically' obliquely invokes the titan Prometheus, a rebellious hero who appealed widely to the American left of the 1940s.[29]

As in *American Pastoral* and *The Human Stain*, there is no point at which we can distinguish absolutely between Roth, Zuckerman and any narrator-within-the-narrative (in this case, Murray), and so we cannot reliably attribute either the earnest classicism or the hyperbolic mock-heroism to any single authorial or fictionalised narrative voice. We cannot say for certain, then, with regard to the story of Ira's ascent and downfall, that the tragic and heroic frameworks are at any time being critiqued rather than endorsed. After all, it is Roth not Zuckerman who elects to call the protagonist of this novel 'Ira' – the Latin word for 'anger' ('Un-Iraing Ira was impossible,' says Murray (304)). There is a similar ubiquitous deployment (attributable to no exclusive voice) of other key classical tropes: the Ovidian dynamic of personal and cultural 'transformation' or 'metamorphosis' is once again widespread (301), and a conception of intense passion derived from Nietzsche and 1950s scholars such as E. R. Dodds (in *The Greeks and the Irrational* of 1951) resonates in the descriptions of Ira's 'masculine intensities' (2), in his uncontrollable temper and his 'antirational thought' (67, 98), and in the unambiguous statement that the fallen Ira was 'returned to the chaos where it had all begun' (297).

Within the novel itself, we discover that Zuckerman – like Roth – learned about Aristotle and about valorised versions of 'chaos' during his studies in literature at the University of Chicago. Zuckerman's paper on Aristotle is acceptable to his professor, Leo Gluckman, in ways that his populist-leaning play is not, presumably because while the play promotes a fixed and unambiguous left-wing ideology, the essay accords with the professor's privileging of 'nuance' and 'contradiction' and with his rejection of art as 'proclamation' or as 'pro-this and anti-that' (218). The fictional Professor Gluckman's view of literature and art clearly echoes many of Roth's own views expressed in interviews and essays. This character's induction of Zuckerman into a classical inheritance and 'culture' that is 'grander' than his 'neighborhood's' contrasts obviously with the life of radical activism exemplified by Communist Johnny O'Day (218). But the education offered to Zuckerman by the academic Gluckman and by the neighbourhood men, Ira and Murray, do not in fact differ from each other as much as the narrator implies.

On the novel's first page, Zuckerman recalls Murray's gift, as his high school English teacher, for 'dramatizing inquiry' (1). He later recollects his youthful awe at witnessing Ira and Murray's discursive approach to literature, at their 'boxing with a book' (27). As Boddy has discussed, this concept of 'boxing with books' suggests exactly the 'antagonism' and dialectic that the liberal intellectual position espoused by Lionel Trilling involves (49–50). It also has affinities with the neo-Aristotelian perspective prevalent at the University of Chicago when Roth was a graduate student there.[30] And even Ira's tutelage under Johnny O'Day, in the 'Quonset hut library' on the riverbank in Chicago (46), includes discussion of Plato's *Republic* and Machiavelli's *The Prince* – these are a step up from the utilitarian 'dictionary' that O'Day persuaded him to read in the evenings after dock work in Iran (35). Zuckerman looks back on his life as one characterised by a multivocal impulse to 'educate Nathan', but the 'book of voices' that constitute his life are in one sense more unified (even in their contradictoriness) than he suggests (222). Indeed, the novel unambivalently condemns only one kind of education and culture: that embraced by Eve and by Sylphid.

This mother and daughter's unquestionably unforgivable trait is their anti-Semitism – Sylphid's racist insult to her mother, and Eve's to her sister-in-law Doris, are all the more shocking due to the fact that both women are, technically, only passing as non-Jews themselves.[31] In the novel's fourth and fifth chapters, Roth depicts their lavish, cultured and classical or neoclassical lifestyle and tastes as their passport to a WASP identity and an elitist social scene. In this 'Jew's utopia of not being Jewish' (179), they are an extreme reincarnation of Roth's fellow Jewish students at the University of Chicago, who develop expertise in Henry James and the Western canon as a means to assimilation (see pp. 174–5). Yet in these chapters, and almost wherever Roth depicts Eve and Sylphid, the novel takes on a satirical, near-farcical tone of hyperbole and savage mockery that is unlike any of the other sections in the book. This is doubtless because Roth wrote this novel partly to avenge himself on his ex-wife, Claire Bloom, who in 1996 published her tell-all memoir that exposed her perspective on their highly dysfunctional marriage.[32] The tenor of the vitriol directed at Eve and Sylphid differs from the necessary censure of anti-Semitism. It is one which makes these passages themselves, ironically enough, the kind of polemic that Professor Gluckman, within the novel, and Roth, so often in his own non-fiction, warn against. Close analysis reveals that the repeated association of the two women with an affected, ludicrous and inauthentic classicism is a fundamental element in this contemptuous representation.

Zuckerman claims that Eve Frame's Manhattan townhouse, with its 'aesthetic harmony' and the 'hundreds and hundreds of serious books' on 'archeology, antiquity and . . . mythology', was as formative for him as his time at Chicago (118). While a reverential encounter with a bookshelf is a recurring trope in Roth's oeuvre, the depiction of the home here becomes a caricature in its inclusion of details such as the 'floodlit statuary' in the rear garden, and of Sylphid's dominating 'gold-leafed . . . harp', which is a 'symbol' invoking 'civilization's enlightened beginnings' (136, 120). There is of course a spiteful irony in Roth's decision to make Sylphid a harpist, given the comic dissonance between this ethereal-sounding instrument – which mythologically originated as the lyre of Apollo and of Orpheus – and Sylphid's unprepossessing physical appearance. (Due to her 'square trunk and stout legs' she not only 'fails to promote a man's desire', Zuckerman says, but also looks 'like a wrestler wrestling the harp' (138).) Sylphid's dress sense is of course absurdly faux-classical as well: to Ira and Eve's wedding she wears one of her 'Greek scarves' in her hair, a peasant blouse with 'Greek embroidery', and 'Greek sandals' with 'thongs' that apparently 'dig in' to her legs (110).

While Roth does parody the chorus of disapproving Jewish women who ask 'what kind of name is Sylphid?' (21), the choice is a calculated one on his part, in that this neo-mythological name (together with 'sylph') is a term for 'spirit of the air', first conceived by the German Renaissance thinker and medic Paracelsus, recurring in the title of a novel by Georgina, Duchess of Devonshire, and in poems by the Victorian writers Robert Browning and Edward Bulwer Lytton.[33] While an inappropriate faux-classical name is comic, it arguably has little to do with any serious critique of anti-Semitism, and is closely aligned with authorial contempt for the fact that Eve is well read in Victorian novels. While Ira may read Plato and Zuckerman may read Aristotle without threatening their credibility, Eve may not read conscientiously, nor have her daughter play the harp, without becoming the object of savage scorn.

Reflecting near the novel's opening on the HUAC (House Un-American Activities Committee) hearing to which Ira was subjected, Murray reflects of Bryden Grant's testimony that 'pettiness and vapidity can come on the grand scale too' (9). This observation might describe equally well the authorial perspective on Eve and Sylphid: their hatreds, squabbles and vendettas, though lethal in outcome, are to some extent versions of 'pettiness on the grand scale', or certainly pettiness depicted by Roth in a scathing mock-heroic style. Eve compiles a list of Communists, for example, 'with the autocratic sadism of Caligula' (276). Conversely, Ira's tragic fall is implicitly and sincerely associated with Arthur Miller's theory of the 'tragedy of the common man', developed in conjunction with *Death of a Salesman*, that a man who is in no social, economic or political sense grand can nonetheless achieve a dignified tragic grandeur.[34] Notably, Zuckerman references the 1948 'Broadway production' of this play in telling Ira's story (153).

Throughout the novel as a whole, Roth and Zuckerman create an Americanised version of Aristotelianism-as-rugged-individualism that somehow becomes more authentic than the 'classical, old-time, traditional education' that is belittled by the Communists in Illinois (177), and that is emulated so grotesquely by Eve and Sylphid. And while, as Kalisch has observed, classical traditions of male intimacy and friendship serve to edify Zuckerman's friendship with Murray in this novel, there is no parallel edifying classicism available to the female characters. Instead, Roth directs his energy into a mock classicism that demeans and humiliates his two central women. This is an impulse that, arguably, undermines any serious critique of anti-Semitism.

The Human Stain (2000)

Narrator Nathan Zuckerman sees Coleman Silk alive and well for the last time when they are fellow audience members at the prestigious Tanglewood Music Festival. When Zuckerman notices that his intellectual friend has brought along his under-educated and much younger girlfriend, he wonders of the unlikely pair whether 'under the auspices of Aphrodite . . . the retired classics professor [was] now bringing recalcitrant, transgressive Faunia to life as a tastefully civilized Galatea' (208). In the unsubtlety of its allusiveness to the tale, by Ovid, in which the sculpture created by Pygmalion becomes a living woman, in its simultaneous persuasiveness and provisionality, and in the problematic gender politics to which all of these dimensions give rise, this sentence exemplifies a little-discussed but highly significant aspect of Roth's classicism in *The Human Stain*.

The many critics who have explored this novel's allusiveness have understandably focused their analyses not on its Ovidian resonances but on the conspicuous tragic and epic frameworks through which Roth tells the story of Coleman's rise and fall.[35] In one sense, we as critics cannot claim any great insightfulness in our awareness of these frameworks; Roth, Zuckerman, Coleman and even his colleague, Delphine, have in common a relentless referencing of antiquity which is impossible to miss. Allusions insistently punctuate the narrative, from Roth's epigraphic quotation of Sophocles to Zuckerman's textbook Aristotelian meditations on

Coleman as 'the great man brought low' (18). Coleman habitually blends his scholarly expertise with his personal life – having once held forth in the classroom on male sexual power in the *Iliad*, he later compares Viagra to 'Zeus' (32), and wishes to live 'in a way that does not bring Philoctetes to mind' (171). And whether comparing Coleman's intense rage, indignation and desire for 'retaliation' to that of Achilles, Medea and Ajax (63), configuring the novel's central thematic concern with purity and impurity in the ancient Greek terms of *miasma* (pollution), or claiming that veteran Les Farley's 'team leader' in Vietnam just happened to be called 'Hector' (258), Zuckerman ensures that his classical liberal education is fully on display throughout this text.

Adam Kelly persuasively links the novel's self-conscious classicism to its inherent reflections on the nature of tragedy itself, while Boddy and Morley separately explore its concurrent reflections on epic. Yet critics who rightly detect elements of farce and satire here – in the novel's depictions of Delphine's emotionally, intellectually and politically confused behaviour, or of Athena College's indulgence in an extreme or ludicrous political correctness – stop short of wondering whether Zuckerman himself is at times the object of Roth's mockery.[36] This is surely a valid question, however, given the heavy-handedness and absurd disproportionality of scale that characterise some of the narrator's observations. He compares Coleman watching Faunia milk the cows to 'two leading actors and the chorus' (51), and assumes that his son, Mark, imagines his conflicts with his father as belonging 'on the southern hillside of the Athenian acropolis, in an outdoor theatre sacred to Dionysus' (314). Through such details, does Roth intend to expose his narrator as a classically obsessed and deluded mythologiser? The fact that the distinction between Roth and his fictional narrator is never clear-cut – witness in this novel the existence of the Sophoclean epigraph – undercuts the theory that the author is lampooning Zuckerman for an overzealous allusiveness. The novel instead combines narrative unreliability (and factual indeterminacy) with an unevenness of tone and mood that sees high seriousness alternate with farce and cheap humour. This creates 'epistemological uncertainty' and 'interpretive plurality' (McCluskey 8). It enables both the 'dialectic' (valorised by Lionel Trilling) and the resistance to closure that Boddy identifies as a central quality both of the *Iliad* and of *The Human Stain*.[37]

Regrettably, however, when it comes to representing gender politics in this novel, Roth appears to abandon strategies of epistemological uncertainty and interpretive plurality. The author portrays women with great certainty and singularity: through multiple layers of narrative framing, they are consistently subordinated to roles as enablers of male ascendancy, as laughable would-be destroyers, or as fulfillers of male sexual desire. And as in *American Pastoral* and *I Married a Communist*, classicism is once again key here to the eradication of female credibility and power. This is evident first of all in the classical connotations of three key female characters' names. Iris – who in mythology is a neutral and story-less messenger of the gods – is as Coleman's wife the ideal 'medium through which to make himself anew' (*Human* 132); Delphine 'is far fallen from the priestess of Delphi, from whom great leaders sought prophetic wisdom' (Safer 214); and the name 'Faunia' connotes the archaic Italian deity Faunus, who is identified with satyrs and with the sexually voracious Pan.

There is notable narrative inconsistency or unevenness of tone in the association between the women characters and classicism. Coleman and Zuckerman take Faunia (a.k.a. 'Voluptas' (35)) very seriously, whereas Delphine is herself depicted as a risibly incontinent invoker of antiquity, using the hyperbolical email address 'clytemnestra@houseofatreus.com' (289) and referring to a 'cabal' of three hostile female colleagues as 'les trois grâces/grasses' (271).[38] Yet there is no ambiguity about these women's lack of voice, agency or power. In ways that recall once again the tongue-less Philomela, communication for each of these classically named women is alternately non-existent (Iris is dead), catastrophic (Delphine sends an easily identifiable 'anonymous' letter and an erroneous self-incriminating email, and cannot speak when she reaches University Security on the phone), fraught (Faunia feigns illiteracy), and/or mediated (Zuckerman frequently imagines himself into Faunia's mind and voice).

Throughout *The Human Stain*, Roth attempts both to normalise and to dignify male subjugation of women through repeated invocations of the paradigm of rape in Greek myth, and of specific rapes in Ovid's *Metamorphoses*. He makes this process possible, or clears a space in which such a strategy can operate, through simultaneously engaging with wider debates about the classical tradition and its role in identity politics and canonical revisionism. His intra-textual exploration of the changing nature of 'Classics' and Humanities as a whole, between the 1950s and the 1990s, serves to aid and abet his anti-feminism. First, Roth discredits feminist approaches to classicism (and so the idea of gender equality) by allying them with the controversial accusation of racism levelled at Coleman. Delphine's insistence that the way we read Euripides has political implications is placed on a par with the College's reaction to Coleman's saying 'spooks'.[39] Concurrently, in his valorisation of 1950s individualistic humanism – 'the so-called humanist approach to Greek tragedy' with which Delphine takes issue (193) – Roth undermines the notions of solidarity or collectivity which are the basis for feminism and other activist movements. In representing 'the passionate struggle for singularity' against 'the tyranny of the we' as itself a heroic fight (108), one articulated in seductively grandiose, quasi-epic rhetoric, the author demeans the notion of consensus, feminist or otherwise. And he simultaneously occludes the fact that patriarchal individualism is itself merely a consensus that does not present itself as such.

The apparently universal or 'individualised' worldview that Coleman, Zuckerman and Roth reinscribe expresses itself through numerous references to sexual violence against women. Coleman's professorial discourse on the *Iliad*'s opening 'quarrel' sets the tone with its masculinist celebration of the fight between Agamemnon and Achilles over two (here unnamed) female sexual trophies of the Trojan War: Chryseis and Briseis (4). Coleman continues in this vein when referring to Faunia as 'Helen of Troy' (232), and his choice of 'Zeus' as an alternative name for Viagra references the notorious sexual predatoriness of this deity (32). As classicists such as Leo Curran and Amy Richlin have separately discussed, in Ovid's *Metamorphoses* Jupiter/Zeus is the perpetrator of a striking number of the poem's 'fifty or so occurrences of forcible rape, attempted rape, or sexual extortion hardly distinguishable from rape' (Curran 263). Later in the novel, Zuckerman takes Coleman's cue about this god's 'amorous transformations' (32), and extemporises wildly on this theme, implicitly referencing Ovid's tales of Jupiter/Zeus's rapes of both Europa and Leda: 'All Zeus ever wants to do is fuck—goddesses, mortals, heifers, she-bears—and not merely in his own form but even more excitingly, as himself made manifest as a beast', as a 'bull', a 'swan' and so on (242).

While Ovid is of course thematically useful to Roth here in illustrating one of the novel's key themes – the way humans are transformed by desire – the author also uses these allusions to dignify and validate sexual violence, to make what he calls in *The Ghost Writer* the 'slime' appear not slimy but venerable and heroic (*Ghost Writer* 66). In using the words 'amorous transformations' and 'fuck' instead of 'rape' (32, 242), the author is complicit in the practice of euphemism that characterises pre-feminist classical scholarship.[40] The critical silence among Roth scholars on these references to Zeus in *The Human Stain* suggest that the author has to some extent been successful, in this novel, in disguising male rape fantasies as classical myth. In 'Reading Ovid's Rapes', Richlin reminds us that 'theories of representation, starting with the formulation of the gaze as male, trace the link between gender and violence' (160).[41] To analyse *The Human Stain* in relation to both theories of the 'male gaze' and feminist classical scholarship is almost to wonder whether Roth might in fact have read widely in both, and has then set out to write a consciously provocative novel that exemplifies the dynamics and processes that each critiques. For example, when Zuckerman watches Coleman watching Faunia milk the cows, or when Zuckerman imagines Coleman watching Steena and then Faunia dance for him, the author constructs a multi-layered male gaze in which Coleman, the narrator, the author and the reader are complicit.

In closing, we should not overlook Roth's authorial audacity in ensuring that his female characters themselves consent to and enlarge upon the novel's validation of sexual violence. In Zuckerman's imagination, moreover, in so doing each woman implicitly alludes to an Ovidian myth of rape. Steena admires Coleman's commonalities with a bird of prey: in an insinuated invocation of Zeus-as-eagle-as-rapist that reads almost comically in the age of '#MeToo', she compliments him on his 'swooping' (24).[42] Delphine's most cherished possession is a ring given to her by her ex-boyfriend which depicts (with striking euphemism) 'Danaë receiving Zeus in a shower of gold' (186). And both Faunia's affection for the crow that she visits and the bizarre monologue, imagined by Zuckerman, in which she claims that she 'was' or is herself 'a crow' (169) identify this formerly abused woman with Ovid's Phocian princess who becomes a crow to escape being raped by Neptune.[43] Zuckerman even projects his fantasies about Zeus-as-rapist on to Faunia's consciousness, through imagining that it is her words to the unsuspecting bird sanctuary warden that include celebratory validations of 'Coleman's Greeks' and of the endlessly metamorphosing 'sensual'

Zeus (242–3). Ironically, Roth attributes to Faunia an account of Zeus's sexual violence that is less sympathetic to his victims – it ignores them completely – than are many of Ovid's own accounts.[44] The Roman poet indubitably pays more attention than does Roth to the preyed-upon women's fear, resistance and flight.

Notes

1. For a list of Roth's works see Pozorski 243.
2. On Roth and the 'Great Books' tradition see Boddy.
3. See Hayes, 'To Rake': over the course of his novelistic career, Roth diverged from (via Nietzsche, for example) and then returned to the liberal and neo-Aristotelian perspectives in which he was trained.
4. I am deeply indebted to a former Oxford student, Phoebe Scriven, who first brought Roth's widespread engagement with Ovid to my attention.
5. Pozorski categorises *The Facts* as fiction (243). Pierpont's biography does not include details of Roth's intellectual formation. See Pozorski 25–42 for a biographical account; Pozorski 239–42 and Parrish, *Companion* ix–xi for chronologies; Searles for interviews.
6. See Searles 6 for Roth on his teenage enthusiasm for the fiction of Howard Fast and Thomas Wolfe. Also in Searles, Roth mentions Twain, Cather, Dreiser, Fitzgerald, Joyce, Salinger, Bellow and, frequently (as in his fiction), Shakespeare. See also Searles 97–8 on Roth's brother's reading and artistic influence.
7. Baugh devotes a chapter to sixteenth- to eighteenth-century satire following detailed discussion of the Renaissance and Humanism. For Roth on both reading and writing satire see Searles 41, 48.
8. See also Searles 68.
9. On the primacy of Aristotle's *Poetics* and on neo-Aristotelianism at Chicago in the mid-twentieth century see scholars and writers interviewed in McQuade, 4, 19, 21.
10. See *Zuckerman Unbound* 179. See Boddy on Roth, Aristotelianism and Trilling's endorsement of Aristotle; see also Hayes, 'To Rake'.
11. See *Letting Go* 210, 297–8, 403; in *Portnoy* see 370–6, where Roth mockingly refers to the threesome as a 'triumvirate' (370) and names the prostitute 'Lina', connoting Messalina, the reputedly promiscuous wife of Emperor Claudius. On the Catholic dimensions of Rome in *Portnoy* see Gordon.
12. See Searles 127.
13. See Searles 68, 70, 143. See McQuade xii for Charles Simic's similar point on Henry James; on Roth and James see (among others) Hayes, 'Not Quite'.

14. See the cover blurb for *I Married a Communist* (Vintage edition), which also quotes Claire Messud's praise for this 'tragedy of classical proportions'. See also Iannone; Lyons.
15. Brauner 148–85.
16. Canales, 'Bomb Blast'.
17. On this subject see Glaser; Stangherlin.
18. See Morley, *Quest* 102–3.
19. The piece is adapted from Roth's acceptance speech for the National Book Foundation Medal, delivered in 2002.
20. See Hamilton 46 (she spells the word '*Moerae*').
21. Miller became a friend and neighbour of Roth in Connecticut (Searles 241). 'Tragedy of the Common Man' formed the introduction to Miller's 1958 *Collected Plays*; see Draper 165. Compare *Married* 153; see pp. 188–9.
22. Compare Ellison, *Collected* 50, 53.
23. On this dynamic see Roynon, 'Ovid, Race'.
24. On the female face or head, compare Cather's very different deployment of heroic heads in Chapter 1. See Canales, 'Bomb Blast' 209 on 'Dawn', and 211 on the resonance of 'Mars' in 'Marcia' Umanoff.
25. The first rape, on arrival in Chicago, when Merry was 'held captive and raped and robbed' (257–8), particularly echoes Ovid's account of Philomela's enforced journey, imprisonment in a cabin and rape.
26. See Enterline: 'Ovid's iterated *nefas* signals a kind of narrative impasse, a fixation on the poem's troubled failure to speak about an event that defies speech' (4). See also *Met.* VI.524–5, 540.
27. See Curran on Philomela's 'vengeance' as 'exceptional' (276).
28. See Morley, *Quest* 109–11.
29. Compare the importance of Prometheus to Ellison, and to Robinson; see Chapters 4 and 7 here.
30. Compare Hayes, 'To Rake' on Roth's early work.
31. See Brauner 152.
32. See Morley, *Quest* 109.
33. See 'sylph' and 'Paracelsus' in *Encyclopedia Britannica*. Also, Georgiana Cavendish, *The Sylph: A Novel* (1780); Bulwer Lytton, *Delmour, or, a Tale of a Sylphid* (1823); Browning, *Paracelsus* (1835).
34. For more on Roth and Arthur Miller see p. 180 and note 21 above.
35. For a discussion of this criticism see pp. 176–7.
36. See Safer; Bluefarb.
37. See Boddy 49–50.
38. Roth may have in mind the first line of Lucretius's *De rerum natura* in Silk's choice of the moniker 'Voluptas'. There, Aphrodite is described as 'hominum divumque voluptas', meaning 'pleasure of gods and men'.

39. Roth pre-empts exactly the reading of his own text that I enact here, by having Coleman declare that there is no 'feminist perspective on Euripides that isn't simply foolishness' (192).
40. Curran writes that 'rape is the dirty little secret of Ovidian scholarship' (264).
41. On the 'male gaze', Richlin references Berger, Kaplan and de Lauretis (Richlin 160).
42. See *Met.* X.155–61 for the rape of (young male) Gannymede.
43. For Danaë see *Met.* IV.611. For the crow (and the raven) see *Met.* II.566ff. Roth signals this myth by referencing ravens alongside crows: see *Human Stain* 165, 238. The raven's transformation from white to black is a reversed reflection of Coleman's passing.
44. See Lively (after Cahoon) on this tendency as common critical practice in non-feminist readings of Ovid (199).

Further Reading

Boddy, Kasia. 'Philip Roth's Great Books: A Reading of *The Human Stain*'. *Cambridge Quarterly* 39.1 (2010): 39–60.

Hayes, Patrick. '"To Rake Suburban Life over the Barbecue Coals": Cultural Criticism in Philip Roth's Early Fiction and Journalism'. *Critical Insights: Philip Roth*. Ed. Aimee Pozorski. Ipswich, MA: Grey House, 2013. 97–118.

Kalisch, Michael. 'A Late Adventure of the Feelings: Eulogizing Male Intimacy in *I Married a Communist* and *The Human Stain*'. *Philip Roth Studies* 12.2 (2016): 83–96.

Richlin, Amy. 'Reading Ovid's Rapes'. *Pornography and Representation in Greece and Rome*. Ed. Richlin. Oxford: Oxford University Press, 1992. 158–79.

Roynon, Tessa. 'Ovid, Race and Identity in E. L. Doctorow's *Ragtime* (1975) and Jeffrey Eugenides's *Middlesex* (2002)'. *International Journal of the Classical Tradition* 26.4 (2019): 377–96.

CHAPTER 7

Marilynne Robinson (1943–)

Robinson and the Classics

'It pleases me,' writes Robinson in her 2012 essay, 'Imagination and Community, 'to think how astonished old Homer would be to find his epics on the shelf of such an unimaginable being as myself, in the middle of an unrumored continent' (*When I Was a Child* 21). Later within the same essay collection, she asserts that '[her] style is more indebted to Cicero than to Hemingway' (*When* 87). Throughout her extensive body of non-fiction, this author invokes a striking range of ancient Greek and Roman authors: Sophocles, Pindar, Caesar, Virgil and Ovid, among several others.[1] Yet the fact that classical allusions are not among the most obvious features of her fiction – they are there but they are both infrequent and understated – has led most critics to overlook the significance of 'pagan' antiquity, as she calls it, in the first four novels she has published: *Housekeeping* (1980), *Gilead* (2005), *Home* (2008) and *Lila* (2014).[2]

Robinson is still alive as I write this book, and the nature of her education (as with that of Morrison and Roth) has yet to be documented within a full-length biography.[3] We know that she studied Latin at high school (in Coeur d'Alene, Idaho, from 1958 to 1962), where, she notes, 'Mrs Bloomberg . . . trudged us through Cicero's vast sentences' and 'led five or six of us through Horace and Virgil' (*When* 87). 'It was all over our heads,' Robinson claims, recalling that she and her classmates were 'bored but dogged' (*When* 87). Her reading in her 'formative years' included 'Shakespeare, the Bible, *Walden*, *The Little House on the Prairie*, *Treasure Island*, *Kidnapped*, the poetry of Emily Dickinson, the collected works of Poe, Melville, and Dickens; classical Greek and Roman literature, [and] history books about heroes like Oliver Cromwell' (Stevens, 'Chronology' xi). For her undergraduate degree at Brown University (at the now-merged women-only Pembroke College, between 1962 and 1966), she majored in American literature, with a focus on the nineteenth century. Her PhD, completed at the University of Washington in Seattle in 1977, included a dissertation on Shakespeare's *Henry VI, Part II* 'and the historiographical traditions behind it' (Stevens, 'Chronology' xii). While Robinson never formally learned Greek, her deep and broad learning in history and theology as well as literature, and her fascination with language and etymology, are evident in any one of her numerous essays.[4] The sheer frequency of her reflections therein on the significance of antiquity, together with a tangible deliberateness in the classical allusiveness of her own critical prose and spoken interviews, perhaps articulates her own sense that the significance of classicism in her oeuvre has been erroneously underestimated until now.

In her much-quoted *Paris Review* interview of 2008, the author muses on the nature of the human condition. 'The ancients are right: the dear old human experience is a singular, difficult, shadowed, brilliant experience', she says, 'that does not resolve into being comfortable in the world' ('Art of Fiction' 58). The first clause of this sentence, 'the ancients are right', is fascinating for the fact that it at first appears to be merely supplementary to Robinson's main point about the complexity of human existence. Yet in fact she is allying her own perception of that complexity to the perceptions of classical texts, thereby both valorising that tradition and, implicitly, positioning herself within that genealogy. Close study of each of her novels reveals the formative influence not just of classical philosophy and ancient religious thought, but also of classical epic and tragedy, on the 'big questions' about meaningfulness, existence, suffering, faith and salvation that these texts ask. Greek and Roman traditions are as important as Judaeo-Christian ones in these explorations, and, crucially, this author seeks to establish (or re-establish) commonality and continuity between the two.[5]

Robinson's particular intellectual passions are twofold. First, she is fascinated by the theology, history and literature of sixteenth- and seventeenth-century Europe that underpinned the Renaissance and the Reformation. She is also preoccupied with the theology, history and literature of seventeenth- to nineteenth-century America that underpinned colonisation and subsequent independence from England. She has thought deeply about how these intellectual currents informed both the religious awakenings and the movements for social reform – the abolition of slavery, the advancement of women's rights, and so on – that characterised the pre-Civil-War

United States. Her essays repeatedly emphasise the connectedness of these two eras and locales, and reiterate the fact that what happened in America was inevitably shaped by (rather than separate from) earlier European cultural, religious and political thought.[6] She also emphasises that classical culture was central to both. In her 2015 essay 'Humanism', for example, she defends the classical tradition (and the currently embattled 'Humanities') with a fervour that is palpable:

> The recovery, translation, and dissemination of the literatures of antiquity created a new excitement, displaying so vividly the accomplishments and therefore the capacities of humankind, with consequences for civilization that are great beyond reckoning. The disciplines that came with this awakening, the mastery of classical languages, the reverent attention to pagan poets and philosophers, the study of ancient history, and the adaptation of ancient forms to modern purposes, all bore the mark of their origins yet served as the robust foundation of education and culture for centuries, until the fairly recent past. (*Givenness* 4)

While repeatedly celebrating the Renaissance and its legacies, meanwhile, the author no less frequently laments a 'tendency' she detects in her and our own times, 'to give the past away' (*When* 174).

All this talk of 'civilization', 'tradition' and 'the past' inevitably shores up one common misconception about Robinson: that she is conservative and reactionary, resistant to change, nostalgic for so-called 'Victorian' and/or 'Puritanical' values and power structures, and longs for a return to a pure and 'original' monoculture. In fact, nothing could be further from the truth. What Robinson at once values and attributes to antiquity in the European Reformation and in eighteenth- and nineteenth-century American historical processes is the spirit of radical reform. She repeatedly documents and expresses her respect for the learnedness of great reforming individuals, whether these be Marguerite de Navarre or John Calvin in Europe, or the American abolitionists, preachers and educators, 'the highly cultured men committed to radical social reform' such as Charles Finney (*When* 171), or William McGuffey, who was a 'professor of ancient languages' (*Death* 132).[7] In Robinson's mind, classical learning enables rather than hinders radicalism; cultures that value literacy, books, print media and the humanities are the basis of democracy, and of a just society.[8] She is explicitly critical of an ill-founded nostalgia that in her view underpins contemporary Christian fundamentalism and conservatism: 'lacking curiosity and any general grasp of history, we have entered a period of nostalgia and reaction. We want the past back, though we have no idea what it was' (*Death* 206).[9] Indeed, if she is nostalgic for anything, it is not for an illusory time of stasis, but for the eras of radicalism and reform that an unambivalent immersion in classical learning once engendered. Unlike Fitzgerald, for example, she is not preoccupied by a sense of contemporaneous 'decline' (and even writes an essay dismissing the concept), but rather emphasises hope, potential, and what is recoverable rather than what is lost.[10]

While this author never hankers after the idea of a fixed, unchanging past, she differs from many modern and contemporary writers in that she does detect unchanging qualities or universal values in the traditions of antiquity, and she is not afraid to say so. For example, in her essay 'Freedom of Thought', she analyses the moment in *Aeneid* I when Aeneas sees the temple wall-paintings depicting the Trojan War, in Carthage, and is moved by 'lacrimae rerum, the tears in things' (*When* 14).[11] She continues: 'Aeschylus, Sophocles, and Euripides would surely have agreed with [Aeneas] that the epics and the stories that surround them and flow from them are indeed about lacrimae rerum, about a great sadness that pervades human life' (*When* 14). Although she does not say so explicitly here (she rarely comments on her own fiction in her non-fiction), Robinson presumably perceives a continuity between classical literature's depiction of human sadness and the broad and deep treatment of sadness, loss, grief and loneliness in her own novels.

It is this same sense of affinity, inheritance and direct connection with antiquity that enables this author to make such widespread use of Ovid's conception of change or transformation (and to blend it with the Christian conception of the same) within her own creative work.[12] In other words, paradoxically, the idea of change is a concept she imports, unchanged, from classical literature into her own. While in her non-fiction she rehearses the well-known fact that Arthur Golding's translation of the *Metamorphoses* (first published in 1567) was among Shakespeare's favourite sources, she couples this with the less well-known fact that this same Golding was also a translator of Calvin's sermons.[13] As the ensuing discussions demonstrate, the *Metamorphoses* is a key text in both *Housekeeping*, with its interest in liminality and border crossings, and *Home*, where the idea that (as Lila states) 'a person can change' is key (*Home* 238). Classical notions of a civil society, of justice, of human dignity and of democracy's enabling of both an individual's and society's positive change, moreover – while recalling many of the concerns of Ralph Ellison – are central to the exploration of both 'civilization' and the Civil Rights Movement that *Gilead* and *Home* constitute. Robinson has pointed out several times that she was studying for her undergraduate degree during the social activism and radical change of the 1960s. The profound connection between learning in the humanities and not elitism but its opposites – humane behaviour and human rights – is in the very texture of her novels.[14]

Staunch defences of classical culture punctuate Robinson's non-fiction. Her declaration, in 'Freedom of Thought', that the 'importance [of] the literatures of antiquity [in] the development of human culture cannot be overestimated' is a case in point (*When* 12). Here she eulogises about the sophistication of ancient city-states and the predominance of 'vivid, atemporal stories' within these civilisations (*When* 12). Equally if not more significant, however, are her more indirect and poetic reflections on the nature of her own childhood education: 'I was given odds and ends—Dido pining on her flaming couch, Lewis and Clark mapping the wilderness—without one being set apart from the other' (*When* 87). She even compares her sense that these fragmentary cultural encounters are valuable to 'a pearl diver finding a piece of statuary under the Mediterranean, a figure immune to the crush of depth, . . . its eyes blank with astonishment, its lips parted to make a sound in some lost dialect, its hand lifted to a city long-since lost beyond indifference' (*When* 87). These lines epitomise both the key aims or effects of Robinson's classicism, and several of her classically influenced methods. They express her conviction about the imperative to revisit antiquity and to locate (or relocate) much-needed value and values there. The writing here is itself evocative and beautiful, embodying the author's oeuvre-wide valorisation of classical aesthetics.[15] As she notes herself, the 'pearl diver' image is an 'extended metaphor', a key element of her own fictional style that she attributes to her high school drilling in Latin poetry's 'epic simile' (*When* 87).[16]

The effect of this, as in all Robinson's engagements with the classical tradition, is at once to protest our contemporary distance from and indifference to antiquity, and to insist on the ancient world's continuing presence. In the 'pearl diver' passage above, the lost and indifferent city to which the fragmented statue gestures might just as well be a contemporary American one as an ancient Mediterranean one. But at least it has been recovered, Robinson might well say, even if it is not yet either understood or redeemed.

The Critical Field and Scholarly Debate

At the time of my writing this chapter, no scholar has published a monograph exclusively on Robinson. The first two collections of essays – *This Life, This World* (edited by Jason Stevens, 2016) and *A Political Companion to Marilynne Robinson* (edited by Shannon Mariotti and Joseph Lane, also 2016) – constitute a range of approaches to Robinson's oeuvre, but notably no essay in either collection focuses on classicism as a subject in itself, nor do any include significant analyses of the role of classical allusions within a different subject or theme.[17] While the approaches in Stevens's volume (in his own words) include 'Romanticism, ecocriticism, medicine and literature, religion and literature, theology, American Studies, critical race theory, and feminist and gender studies' (4), Mariotti and Lane describe the themes of their collection (and so the central concerns of Robinson) as follows:

> democratic questions concerning our being in the natural world, our relationship to the ideological space of 'home', . . . our relationship with religion and access to divine authority, the limits of our abilities to recognize, respect, and live in peace with the 'other', and the challenges of living in an increasingly neoliberal world. (6)

My own contention in this chapter is that Robinson's classicism, while a subject in its own right, also functions significantly within all of the perspectives and the themes that the contributors to Stevens's and Mariotti and Lane's collections elucidate.

To date (and to the best of my knowledge) there exist only three stand-alone essays on Robinson's engagement with any aspect of antiquity. The first, by Gary Williams (published in 1991), is on the significance of Carthage in *Housekeeping*; the second, by Carol Dougherty (published in 2014), is on the relationship between the *Odyssey* and the same text (I will return to both of these); and the third (also appearing in 2014), by Aaron Mauro, is on the significance of *oikonomia* (household economy) in the first three novels. The scantiness of criticism on the classical presences in Robinson's oeuvre may be symptomatic of a broader scholarly tendency to confine her work within certain limited categories, and/or of long-view literary historians' failure to take adequate account of her significance or position. It is notable that in their *New Literary History of America* (2009), editors Greil Marcus and Werner Sollors make no mention whatsoever of Robinson or any of her work. In *The Cambridge History of the American Novel* (edited by Leonard Cassuto, 2011), meanwhile, Robinson suffers a fate not dissimilar to Cather – while the older writer is relegated to the 'regionalist' section of that *History*, Robinson is discussed solely within Amy Hungerford's brief discussion of 'Religion and the Twentieth-Century American Novel'.[18] Lawrence Buell, in *The Dream of the Great American Novel* (2014), devotes only one sentence to Robinson, and even Elaine Showalter, in her monumental 2009 study of American women writers, *A Jury of her Peers*, devotes only three pages to *Housekeeping* and a meagre single sentence to *Gilead*.[19] A long-overdue analysis of Robinson's numerous and varied classical engagements might well contribute to a better recognition of her significance, a deeper understanding of the breadth of her concerns, and a reassessment of her position within (or without) the canon. There are many key questions still waiting to be addressed. Given that many modernist novelists are classically allusive, for example, does Robinson's own allusiveness make her in any way modernist? And how exactly does Robinson's interest in Greek and Roman antiquity sit with her unambivalent Christianity?

In *Home*, we are privy to Glory's reflections on her teaching of literature in high school, and to her musing on 'Puritan Milton with his pagan muses' (22). In teaching his own children, Glory realises, her father had never doubted 'that there was a single path from antiquity to eternity' (22). It is clear from Robinson's non-fiction that she herself perceives not a conflict between the pre-Christian and Christian eras, but strong and significant continuities and commonalities. She variously states that the Bible itself 'acknowledges . . . pagan myth as analogous to biblical narrative despite grave defects', and that St Paul, Augustine, Aquinas and Calvin all 'quote the pagans with admiration' (*When* 14, 12).[20] As I shall go on to discuss in the analyses of each novel, several of the key symbols in her fiction (such as the 'wound' and 'woundedness'), together with key concepts therein (such as 'transformation'), resonate simultaneously in their classically allusive and Judaeo-Christian contexts. Mauro observes, meanwhile, that the concept of *oikonomia* is at once significant within pagan antiquity and within Christian theology.[21] Robinson does not conflate the two traditions, but she ensures their productive co-existence. This in turn contributes to the idea within her novels (one much discussed by critics) that the writing and the reading of literature is itself a religious or sacramental activity. Robinson points out that 'the Homeric narratives . . . were the basis of Greek and Roman religion', and that if 'ancient literature and religion are not the same, then certainly neither is imaginable without the other' (*When* 14, 11).[22] In the implicit claim for the sacredness of her own and others' fiction, Robinson hereby uses antiquity as a persuasive exemplum.

In *The Living Moment: Modernism in a Broken World* (2012), Jeffrey Hart includes Robinson's *Gilead* in a study of authors that includes Fitzgerald, Eliot and Hemingway, among others. His rationale is that Ames in *Gilead* is preoccupied with the fragmentary, while the novel also 'acts with unusual power to evoke in its reader the capacity for experiencing the moment' (101). Despite Robinson's oeuvre-wide interest in the 'fragmentary' – her pearl diver finds a 'fragment' of a statue – and despite the fact that her classical allusiveness is itself, inevitably, a deployment of fragments of a tradition, I would argue that Robinson's fiction is not itself modernist. In my earlier chapters I argue that the allusiveness of Cather or Fitzgerald is key to our understanding of these writers as modernist, but this is because their classicism contributes crucially to ambiguity, conflict and irresolution in their texts: they respond to brokenness with further disjunction and dissonance. By contrast, Robinson both perceives and values brokenness and fragmentariness, but responds to these not merely with a longing for reconstitution, but with unambiguous representations of wholeness and declarations of faith. Anthony Domestico labels such expressions of conviction in *Housekeeping* as 'creedal statements' and 'imperative hypotheses' (94): one memorable example is Ruth's speculation about a trawling of the lake through which every lost thing would be restored, 'till time and error and accident were undone, and the world became comprehensible and whole' (*Housekeeping* 92). Not dissimilar is Glory's increasing conviction, at the end of *Home*, that young Robert 'will come back some day', leading her to declare that 'the Lord is wonderful' (338), or John Ames's unequivocal assertion at the end of *Gilead* that 'the Lord breathes on this poor gray ember of creation and it turns to radiance' (279). These are not hopes or wishes, but convictions and statements of faith. Indeed, Sylvie's musings about the objects that would be dredged up from the lake, and about the memories embedded in our consciousness, go to the heart of the Robinsonian vision: 'what are all these fragments for, if not to be knit up finally?' (*Housekeeping* 92).

Besides the continuities between Robinson's 'paganism' and her Christian faith, there are further dimensions to or effects of her classicism that we should recognise. Acknowledging her widespread engagement with the classical tradition, for example, enables us to position her work within what she herself calls 'American high culture' (Hedrick and Robinson 1). The nation's historical and ongoing intellectual culture – that in her view is much neglected – is integral rather than antithetical to her socially radical ideals. Robinson's classicism is also part of her feminism – like Cather and like Morrison, she has (in her own words) 'appropriated traditions that in many cases have been associated with men' (Hedrick and Robinson 2). And while she comments on the internationalism that accrues to her beloved John Calvin through his own extensive scholarship and intellectualism, we can claim for the classical allusiveness in her own fiction a not-dissimilar effect.[23] Robinson once compared her brother, in his boyhood insistence that she become a poet while he became a painter, to Alexander the Great 'dividing up the world'. At one and the same time, she observed, he was still just a boy in 'this tiny town in Idaho' ('Art' 41). Her ubiquitous classicism ensures, among other things, that her own work is at once regional and global.

Housekeeping (1980)

When Lucille starts to ignore her sister, Ruth, the latter (narrator of Robinson's haunting first novel) explains that 'schoolwork itself became a sort of refuge' (136). As a respite from awkward isolation, Ruth tells us, 'it was a relief to go to Latin class, where [she] had a familiar place in a human group, alphabetically assigned' (136). Latin brings to Ruth a sense of both order and belonging. As Robinson notes in her essay 'When I Was a Child', furthermore, it also furnishes that character with the cultural resources to make the allusion that constitutes one of the best-loved and most-discussed paragraphs in the novel – the one that begins, 'Imagine a Carthage sown with salt . . .' (*Housekeeping* 152; *When* 86). Yet when Robinson claims that she gave to Ruth only the frames of reference that were available to the author herself at that character's age (*When* 86), the word 'only' here is perhaps unwarranted. This extraordinary story – one of loss and survival, of love and neglect, of the competing claims of 'home' and 'wilderness', of domesticated safety versus dangerous freedom, of feminist liberation versus erased female agency – engages widely with both Ovid and Homer (and perhaps Virgil too), in understated but highly significant ways.

Ruth asks us to 'imagine a Carthage sown with salt' when she encounters Sylvie's secret valley in the light of the midday sun (152). Her extended allusion urges us to imagine beautiful new growth and fertility in the Phoenician colony – on the North-Eastern African coast – that the Romans purportedly destroyed for ever in 149 BCE. It articulates a faith in restoration, regrowth and reconciliation: 'whatever we may lose, very craving gives it back', she states, and 'the world will be made whole' (152–3).[24] In a short but fascinating article, Gary Williams explains the significance of a defeated Carthage as a defeated culture of 'otherness', in that its destruction 'paved the way for the dominance of Greco-Roman values in Western culture' (71). The critic persuasively suggests that 'in the quiet but deeply subversive transformation described in [Robinson's] Carthage passage, we have an image of the transformation Ruth experiences as she grows to see things through her aunt's eyes' (72). In imagining a resurrected Carthage, Williams argues, Ruth implicitly imagines what an alternative, non-dominant American culture might be like. Furthermore, as Robinson herself points out, by using the word 'sown', Ruth 'combines' the historical legend of salted Carthage with the Greek myths about 'the sowing of dragon's teeth which sprouted into armed men' (*When* 86).[25] Through this hybrid allusion the character and the author reinforce the idea of imminent new life. They posit a notion reminiscent of Cather: that of strengthening a new civilisation through the recollection of an old one.

Ruth's invocation of Carthage also brings Virgil's Dido and Aeneas to mind. The faintly heard echoes of the *Aeneid* impart a heroic resonance to the plot of this novel and an epic scale to its setting. Aeneas's perception of the 'lacrimae rerum' (the 'tears' or 'sadness' of things valorised by Robinson) occurs in *Aeneid* Book I (*When* 14). But Ruth's speculation about an imagined, below-lake underworld peopled by a 'crowd' of the dead (among them her mother) recalls the crowded underworld that Aeneas encounters in Book VI of Virgil's epic. Aeneas's brief reconciliation with his father, Anchises, resonates in Ruth's imagining of her drowned mother (*Housekeeping* 92), while the association of the missionary Aunt Molly with the New Testament quotation about 'fishers of men' in the same section of the novel exemplifies Robinson's interweaving of biblical and Roman tradition (91).[26] Antiquity re-emerges a few pages later when Ruth describes the girls' trip to the disused quarry, where the remaining wooden 'shafts' are 'the height of stools or pillars' (97). 'These we took to be the ruins of an ancient civilization' (97), she recounts, in a detail that recalls the interwoven classical and Native American civilisations in Cather's *Professor's House*.

There are certainly times when Ruth's choice of analogy seems authentically adolescent in its wish to appear learned – for example when she compares her dead grandmother's hand, somewhat inexplicably, to that of 'Helen of Troy' (41), or attributes a 'Delphic niceness' to Sylvie's scattering of messages amongst the leaves in the house (85).[27] And yet at other times Ruth's narrative strikes the reader as profoundly classically allusive even when Ruth herself appears to display no awareness of her own invocations. This is particularly true of the widespread echoes, distortions, inversions and revisions of both Ovid's *Metamorphoses* and Homer's *Odyssey* that are such a striking feature of the novel. In this unselfconscious allusiveness Robinson may be configuring Ruth as the diver who finds a fragment of a statue beneath the Mediterranean in 'When I Was a Child' (*When* 87). Though the diver may never have heard of the Athenian sculptors 'Phidias or Myron', she or he may experience 'recognition' in encountering the fragment (*When* 89); likewise, though Ruth may not yet have heard the names of Ovid or Homer, she recognises and redeploys their powerfully symbolic myths.

Ovid's *Metamorphoses* surely suffuses *Housekeeping*, while neither the poet nor his text is named therein. During the epic flood in Fingerbone, which recalls the flood so vividly described in Book I of Ovid's poem as much as that survived by Noah in Genesis, Ruth observes that Fingerbone was 'strangely transformed' (73).[28] When Lucille and Ruth stay overnight on the shore, Ruth observes the lake's power (even when there is no flood) to effect 'transformations of the ordinary' (112). Later that night, her perception that 'all our human boundaries were overrun' articulates a thematic preoccupation that

Housekeeping and the *Metamorphoses* share: the instability of 'civilization' and its necessary but fragile demarcations (115). The inevitability of change is a predominant concern for Ruth. Her descriptions of her grandmother's aging – of the 'tendrils' that 'grew from her eyebrows' (26), or of the 'marbled lips and marble fingers' that a drowned-but-resurrected Sylvie might display (84) – are distinctly Ovidian in their metaphorical technique and their focus on the *process* inherent in altering and altered forms. Robinson and Ruth also distort some of Ovid's best-known archetypes to devastating effect: the snow lady that the two schoolgirls sculpt echoes Pygmalion's ivory-white Galatea, except that her 'conjured presence' becomes not a living lover but a melted 'dog-yellowed stump' (61).[29] And when Ruth, in the middle of her metaphysical musings about time and reflections, asserts that 'anyone that leans to look into the pool is the woman in the pool' (166), she transforms Ovid's tale of Echo and Narcissus, thereby claiming agency (however doomed) for the female, in place of Echo's disembodied voice.

In reflecting on the relationship between the character of Sylvie and the history and mythology of the American frontier, Robinson has stated: 'My one great objection to the American hero was that he was inevitably male—in decayed forms egregiously male. So I created a female hero, of sorts, also an outsider and a stranger' (*When* 92). Robinson's motivated deployment of female protagonists also revises the male-centredness of the classical epic tradition in which Aeneas, Achilles and Odysseus all have the leading roles. The fact that the girls' mother is called Helen (together with Ruth's invocation of Helen of Troy, discussed earlier) contributes to the novel's dialogue with Homeric tales, but the thematic connection between *Housekeeping* and the *Odyssey* is so strong that such intentional naming is arguably redundant. In its focus on whether or not 'the wanderers will find a way home' (*Housekeeping* 195) – that is to say, on its preoccupation both with wandering or journeying and with home and homecoming, and in the ubiquitous symbolic use of the lake and water – Robinson's novel inevitably brings Homer's sea-faring hero and his wanderings to mind.

The critic Carol Dougherty explores the fact that while both *Housekeeping* and the *Odyssey* centre on 'the dynamic between those who leave and those who stay', 'Robinson complicates the relationship by challenging comfortable assumptions about what makes a house a home' ('Homecomings' 281). Dougherty identifies many ways in which the American author inverts key elements of the paradigmatic epic: 'whereas the *Odyssey* thinks about home/housekeeping through travel', she writes, '*Housekeeping* turns this around to consider mobility from the perspectives of houses and housekeeping' (290). In Ruth's repeated tendency to imagine a house/home as a boat (either Noah's ark (*Housekeeping* 184) or a 'moored ship' (203)), the author reverses the *Odyssey*'s trajectory 'from ship to bed' (Dougherty, 'Homecomings' 293). Dougherty links her reading to that of Geyh, in which 'Robinson's notion of the transient female subject is one that is constituted by perpetual interaction between the settled and the transient' and 'scenes of return' are key to 'the construction of a transient subjectivity' (quoted in Dougherty, 'Homecomings' 300). These themes in *Housekeeping* of course also constitute its intertextual relationship with both *Moby-Dick* and *Huckleberry Finn*, the classic American novels that themselves engage profoundly with the *Odyssey* in their depictions of waterborne journeying, transient existence and crossing frontiers. Robinson's opening line, 'My name is Ruth' (3) – which clearly functions as a feminist revision of Melville's famous opening gambit, 'Call me Ishmael' (*Moby-Dick* 21) – is indicative of the female author's regendering of the prototypical nineteenth-century American epic.[30]

Dougherty writes that Geyh 'fails to contend with the profound sadness and sense of loss that permeates the novel's conclusion' (300). Certainly, this tangible, permeating sadness is something that Robinson not only consciously creates but also consciously values. The author perhaps strives to recapture the valorisation of that emotion that characterised her grandparents' era, a time in which (as she observes in 'When I Was a Child') 'mourning, melancholy, regret, and loneliness were high sentiments, as they were for the psalmists and for Sophocles' (*When* 89). While Robinson's grandparents express these sentiments through artwork in the classical funerary style, the novelist ensures that *Housekeeping*, with its collapsing/collapsed household and almost-personified house, recalls the tradition of ancient Greek tragedy.[31] As Mauro discusses, in engaging the ancient Greek connection between *oikos* (house/household) and *oikonomia* (economy), *Housekeeping* at once invokes Greek tragic tradition, and epitomises the way in which 'the home continues to be the site of so many literary and lived tragedies' (Mauro 152).

Perhaps the most subtle and simultaneously most powerful classically derived configuration of 'lacrimae rerum' in this novel – of the tears or sadness of things – is manifest in the descriptions of fallen and blowing leaves with which Robinson punctuates her text. For example, in the aftermath of the flood in Fingerbone, Ruth observes that 'every spirit passing through the world . . . has come to look and not to buy' (73). Everyday objects become worn but are ultimately abandoned, 'just as the wind in the orchard picks up the leaves from the ground as if there were no other pleasure in the world but brown leaves . . . and then drops them all in a heap at the side of the house and goes on' (73).[32] Her frequent and detailed descriptions of leaves recall the famous simile, in the sixth book of the *Iliad*, in which Glaucus reflects to Diomedes on the sorrow of death and of the inevitable passing of time:

> Just as are the generations of leaves, such are those also of men. As for the leaves, the wind scatters some on the earth, but the luxuriant forest sprouts others when the season of spring has come; so of men one generation springs up and another passes away. (*Iliad* VI.146–50)

As Sylvie becomes increasingly 'wilded' and eccentric, Robinson again deploys leaves to suggest both current and future loss: 'this was the time that leaves began to gather in the corners', Ruth observes of their home. 'They were leaves that had been through the winter, some of them worn to a net of veins. There were scraps of paper among them, crisp and strained from their mingling in the cold brown liquors of decay and regeneration, and on these scraps there were sometimes words' (85). In her association between leaves and written pages here, the author engages profound questions about literature's power (or powerlessness) to arrest time. In this Robinson anticipates Alice Oswald's long poem, *Memorial* (2011), which, as its subtitle suggests, is an 'excavation of the *Iliad*'. Oswald's extensive reworking of Homer's extended 'leaves' simile attests to the simultaneous meaninglessness and meaningfulness of both individual human lives and the act of writing about them. As does Robinson, Oswald brilliantly incorporates connotations of the 'leaves' of a book, and so subjects to scrutiny the very concepts of literature, of history and of cultural inheritance themselves.[33]

Gilead (2004)

After writing about the deaths of his first wife and his daughter, the epistolary narrator of *Gilead* states that he has 'been thinking about existence lately' (64). Convinced that after death humans do remember their mortal experience on earth, Ames declares, 'In eternity this world will be Troy, I believe, and all that has passed here will be the epic of the universe, the ballad they sing in the streets' (65). This configuration of human existence in terms of the foundational site of conflict in the *Iliad*, the *Odyssey* and the *Aeneid* follows immediately on from the minister's configuration of entering the Kingdom of God in the terms of St Paul: 'when we have all been changed and put on incorruptibility' (65).[34] The combining of Christian belief and classical myth here epitomises Robinson's interest not in juxtaposing the two traditions but in intertwining them. At the same time, the resonances of the brutal Trojan War and its complicated aftermaths (involving dispossession, enslavement, relocation and repatriation) undercut the sense of security and serenity that Ames's expressions of faith construct. In the hybridity of its allusiveness, this paragraph therefore distils the simultaneous moods of repose and 'unreposefulness', of being at peace and not at peace, and of feeling at home and not at home that characterise Ames's reflections on his life story and on the world around him in the novel as a whole.

Ames makes occasional ironic reference to 'the darkness of paganism' (25) and 'unredeemed paganism' (161), and continues, occasionally but significantly, to weave classical textures into his narrative. He therefore presumably shares the view of Glory and her father (in *Home*), as well as that of Robinson herself, about the confluences between Graeco-Roman antiquity and Christianity.[35] Unsurprisingly, then, we can surmise that Ames shares with Robinson an antipathy to the Enlightenment-derived separation of reason and faith, or knowledge/rationality and belief. We can assume that both author and character identify, through their convictions about interconnectedness, with nineteenth-century writers such as Emerson, Hawthorne, Melville and Dickinson. Yet this accommodating or inclusive perspective no more assures tranquillity for Ames than it does for the often-deeply-conflicted authors of the century that preceded him. About his abolitionist grandfather, for example – about that ancestor's radical emancipatory politics, his violent direct action against slavery, and his discomfort in society and in domesticity – the narrator of *Gilead* is completely unresolved. He asserts that he does not regret his decision to follow his father's contrasting stance of peaceful compromise (one that in reality becomes indifference) towards continuing racial injustice. Yet he configures his and his father's quest to find and honour the old man's grave, in Kansas, as a heroic and epic journey. His memory of his grandfather losing an eye in the Civil War makes that ancestor at once a hero and a figure who, recalling both the Homeric Cyclops and the one-eyed Jack in Ellison's *Invisible Man*, may be somewhat monstrous in the singleness of his political vision. 'The one eye he had was somehow ten times an eye,' Ames recalls (36). And there is an unresolved ambivalence in Ames's account of his parents' attempts to domesticate and civilise his grandfather: in his mother's washing of his 'stained and yellow' shirts, for example, until they looked as 'white and polished' as heroic 'marble busts' (91–2).[36]

When Robinson has Ames write of the 'stains and . . . wounds' in those shirts (92), or of Boughton favouring Jack 'as one does a wound' (271), the novelist allows the double resonances of Christ's wounds and the self-defining wounds of mythical heroes such as Odysseus and Philoctetes to play out in full. She replicates this technique in *Home*, just as she replicates in *Gilead* the Homeric association between leaves and death that, as we have seen, is so key in *Housekeeping*.[37] Indeed, it's arguable that the combination of classical and Christian perspectives constitutes one of the strongest continuities between *Housekeeping* and the much later (and very differently toned) Gilead-centred triptych. For one thing, *Gilead* reprises the first novel's echoes of the *Aeneid* that are almost indistinguishable from Christian symbolism: Ames imagines himself and his son in heaven as being 'like brothers', but then fantasises about a heavenly reunion in which young Robert's 'child self' will be 'jumping into [his] arms' (189). Here the old man imagines a reconciliation at once experienced by and denied to Aeneas: in *Aeneid* VI the hero re-encounters and speaks with his father during his visit to the underworld, but is agonised to find that his father has no physical substance that he can embrace.[38]

Just as Robinson derives her own sense of 'lacrimae rerum' from the *Aeneid* (*When* 14), Ames implicitly declares his own affinity with the expressiveness of Latin as a language. He comments on his own heart disease, 'angina pectoris', as having 'a theological sound, like misericordia' (5). In his posing as a figure named 'Moriturus' (being about to die or prepared to die), Robinson invokes a formulaic word from the *Aeneid*, and Ames comments on the 'burden' that grammar places on the word 'mutandis' (meaning a compulsory change, a change that must be made) in the phrase *mutatis mutandis* (189).[39] Robinson has Ames reflect (as well as embody the idea) that 'a lot of the newness' of 'new thinking' (such as his brother's theology and atheism) 'was as old as Lucretius' (203). At the same time, Ames (presumably unwittingly) rewrites Freud's iconic comparison of the individual human psyche, with its layers shaped by changing experiences over time, to the multi-layered architecture of the city of Rome.[40] When Ames declares that 'each one of us is a little civilization built on the ruins of any number of preceding civilizations' (224), he uses the 'civilization' metaphor to create a sense of continuity and collaboration between (rather than within) individuals throughout history. His image is one that complicates or modifies the concurrent interest in individual uniqueness and isolation.

It is no surprise that Ames treasures the 'big shell' that 'one of the Boughton boys' sent him from a trip 'to the Mediterranean' (52). In its 'susurrus' (another Latinate word beloved by the narrator (52)), it presumably whispers of both the classical and the Judaeo-Christian heritage that that region encompasses. It is Ames's immersion in both traditions, and his recognition of their intertwined nature, which informs some of his most definitive statements both about the history of Gilead, and about the human capacity for redemption and change. 'There have been heroes here, and saints and martyrs,' he says (198); Gilead is an epic site as well as a sacred one, in other words. Ames also speaks of the personal 'transformation' that his marriage to Lila involved, and expresses his faith in terms of 'transformations' that are 'abrupt', 'unsought' and 'unawaited', but that do 'occur in this life' (231). His use of the word 'transformation' on these occasions invokes both the core of the Christian message and the core of the pagan epic, Ovid's *Metamorphoses*, largely written in the first decade CE, when the Emperor Augustus was approaching the height of his powers in 'pagan' ancient Rome.

Home (2008)

When trimming her aged father's hair, Glory – the protagonist whose point of view is privileged in this novel – reflects on 'the visible human strain of holding the great human head upright for decades and decades' (177). 'Some ancient', she recalls, 'said it is what makes us different from the beasts, that our eyes are not turned downward to the earth. It was Ovid' (177). The lines that Glory dimly recollects here are from the end of the account of the creation, at the very start of the *Metamorphoses*. Ovid relates that when Prometheus made human beings out of clay, 'of his own divine substance' (*Met.* I.78), 'though all other animals are prone, and fix their gaze upon the earth, [the god] gave to man an uplifted face and bade him stand erect and turn his eyes to heaven' (*Met.* I.84–6).[41] Through this allusion to the Roman text, Robinson invokes a classical precedent for the unshakeable belief in human dignity and potential for heroism that underpins the whole of *Home*. Both the near-tragic trajectory of Jack's life, which on first reading may appear to be this novel's central concern, and the gradually emerging and ultimately key thematics of racial inequality, the Civil Rights Movement and interracial marriage are informed by a series of significant engagements with antiquity.

Given that *Home* is the longest of Robinson's novels, it is perhaps no surprise that it is also the most diverse in its allusiveness to archetypal classical figures, to specific myths, to specific texts, and to several classical genres. As a work in which characters frequently experience a complicated nostalgia, in which one protagonist undergoes a troubled return or homecoming after a twenty-year absence, and in which the other ponders, 'What does it mean to come home?' (106), it perhaps inevitably recalls the *Odyssey*. While the most obvious intertext for Jack's story is the parable of the prodigal son from Luke's Gospel, and while Robinson makes no overt reference to Homer's epic in *Home*, the Greek poem surely resonates in Glory's comparison of her just-returned brother to 'the hero in a melancholy tale' (44). The novel is thereby linked thematically with both *Housekeeping* and *Lila* – texts in which a preoccupation with wandering or transience makes the Homeric text a more obvious presence. *Home* also anticipates *Lila* in the way it engages the pastoral tradition alongside the epic: in its recurring interest in gardening and cultivation of the land, and in the attention it pays to the pleasure and significance inherent in specific flowers and produce. In line with a tradition within American novels that stretches from Cather's *My Ántonia* to Morrison's *Beloved*, however, the pastoral context by no means guarantees any idyll. In Glory's confrontation with the stark truth, at the novel's end, that her 'Gilead of the sunflowers' is to black people just one more 'foreign and hostile country' (338), Robinson exposes the reality of the paradise-based-on-exclusion that so much of 1950s America constitutes.[42]

There is no shortage of sadness (or 'lacrimae rerum') in *Home* (*When* 14). The 'endless, excruciating past', as Glory memorably puts it (249), is marked primarily by both the birth and the almost unspeakable death, as a toddler, of the daughter that the teenaged Jack had fathered with the even younger Annie. Alongside this defining catastrophe, the irrecoverable years of Jack's absence, the troubled nature of his relationship with his father, and the apparent impossibility of sharing his life with Della and their son in a racially prejudiced America take their place next to Glory's own disappointments. These include her failed career and failed romantic relationship, her loneliness, her unfulfilled maternal longing and her sense of frustration in her enforced return 'home'. The family have also endured their mother's death and their father's decline into senility. Glory reflects often on her father's 'grief' and 'despair' (58), and knows (as does Ames) that Jack is a 'wound in his father's heart' (221). Here, as she does in both *Gilead* and *Lila* as well, Robinson allows the word 'wound' to play out in its dual Christian and Greek tragic resonances.

Indeed, Jack Boughton is surely the Robinsonian character who comes closest to being a tragic protagonist. While he has affinities with the injury-nursing Philoctetes in Sophocles's eponymous tragedy, Jack is also a kind of inverted Oedipus and inverted Odysseus. While both these classical figures return home unrecognised (Oedipus not even realising he is home, and Odysseus in disguise), Jack, on the other hand, is welcomed as a returning family member while the secret of his relationship with Della and his fathering of Robert make him something of a stranger. The Boughtons' once 'staunch and upright house', now 'heartbroken' (4), meanwhile, indubitably fits with the concept of the tragic *oikos* that Mauro identifies as a unifying element across Robinson's oeuvre.[43] And Jack is if anything somewhat taken with his own tragic sense of himself. His conviction that he might be predestined to failure and sin invokes, besides its Christian context, a sense of Faulknerian and Greek tragic cursedness and *miasma*: he asks Ames whether it's possible that he 'spread a contagion of some kind. Of misfortune' (235). Glory's thoughts after his averted suicide make clear that a successful attempt would have constituted true tragedy: 'he had very nearly brought a terrible conclusion to his father's old age . . . an inexpressible, unending grief' (260).

Early in the novel, in a little-discussed moment of self-irony, Jack casts himself mockingly as the mythical titan and Aeschylean tragic hero Prometheus.[44] Mortified by having missed a phone call from Della, he says he will have to stay next to the telephone, and half-jokes, 'Jack Boughton in chains. All I need is an eagle to peck at my liver, such as it is' (85). Despite the protagonist's levity here, Robinson's allusion to the figure who creates mankind (both in Hesiod's *Works and Days* and in Ovid's *Metamorphoses*), who steals fire for humans (in Hesiod), and whose ensuing punishment at the hand of Zeus (being tied to a rock while pecked at by eagles) is dramatised in Aeschylus's *Prometheus Bound*, is of central importance in *Home*.[45] For centuries (as well as across a range of modern American literature, as this book demonstrates), this figure has symbolised the human struggle for power and freedom, and the price that some freedom fighters pay for that.[46] The identification of Jack with the iconic status of Prometheus within twentieth-century communist and anti-racist struggles emphasises that character's investment in the American civil rights struggle, and suggests his own potential for playing a heroic and reforming role in his country's future.

There are layered intertextual resonances here: for example, depending on which Du Bois text Jack and Glory are reading in *Home*, Jack may be casting himself either self-deprecatingly as the white supremacist Prometheus at the end of *The Souls of Black Folk*, or as a champion of the tormented but surviving and still-fighting 'black Prometheus' in Du Bois's 1935 work, *Black Reconstruction*.[47] Meanwhile, the fact that Shelley's *Prometheus Unbound* revises the continuing story of Prometheus as told in Aeschylus's second and now-lost play, and in so doing insists on the titan's overthrowing of Zeus and of Olympian power, imbues Robinson's analogy with a profoundly radical vision of a dominant American culture overthrown. Furthermore, the importance of Prometheus to Christian theologians such as Augustine and Tertullian – witness the latter's description of Christ as the '*verus* Prometheus' (true Prometheus) – sustains Robinson's commitment to blending Christian and pagan allusions. The Tertullian association corresponds to her own identification of Jack with Christ as well as with classical heroes.[48]

It is highly significant that Jack (and not his younger brother) was originally to be named 'Theodore Dwight Weld' after the historical abolitionist of that name (*Gilead* 214). While in the

Gilead-Home pairing Robinson associates Jack with Ames's abolitionist grandfather, she also allies him with the culture of the nineteenth-century radical reformers and anti-slavery activists as a whole. In her non-fiction, as I have discussed at the start of this chapter, Robinson repeatedly expresses her pride in the radicalism of the nineteenth-century Midwest, as well as her sense that contemporary America (particularly the now-conservative and fundamentalist Midwest) needs to remember and restore that radicalism.[49] She emphasises the learnedness of the abolitionists, their combination of classical and Christian intellectual interests, and their commitment to education through the promotion of literacy and the founding of colleges. It is relevant to this discussion that while Robinson is consciously 'tracing a lineage' from Calvin and the Reformation to the reforming zeal of the American antebellum radical tradition (*Death* 132), she also associates the seventeenth-century European reformers themselves with Prometheus, writing of 'the Promethean work of the Reformers' (*Givenness* 26). The novelist uses Prometheus, then, to trace a direct lineage from the Reformation through nineteenth-century radical reform all the way to Jack Boughton himself.

After Teddy's visit, when Jack has made the decision to leave home once and for all, and has written the letter to Della, Glory notices that 'the flesh of his face looked a little like wax, or like clay' (*Home* 281). This is a simile resonant of many key processes of transformation in Ovid's *Metamorphoses* – not just Prometheus's creation of the human race out of clay in Book I, but also Deucalion and Pyrrha's re-peopling of the earth from thrown stones after the crisis of the flood (later in the same Book), and also Pygmalion's sculpting of a statue that comes alive (in Book X). Jack is relentlessly doubtful and usually ironic about his own capacity for change – for example after being found by Ames wearing his baseball mitt, he self-mockingly comments to Glory about his 'miraculous transformation' into a 'solid citizen' (210). Yet Robinson associates him throughout the novel with both the need and the capacity to transform American society, particularly with respect to its racial politics. There is an underlying insistence on the human capacity to change both on the individual and on the societal level, expressed simply in Lila's declaration (one of the few lines replicated verbatim in *Home* from *Gilead*) that 'a person can change. Everything can change' (*Gilead* 174–5; *Home* 238).

Jack finds little to persuade him that social change in the town of Gilead is imminent or even likely – instead he re-encounters his father's reactionary, racist denial of the validity of the black struggle and Ames's indifference and apathy. But through associating Jack with Ovidian transformations (which complement Glory's own memory of Ovid's words on the dignity of humanity), Robinson invests in him the viability of a changed and improved America. In the deployment of Ovid to urge for the transformation of society itself (rather than in the ultimately fruitless quest for a changed black identity), the novelist continues the practice of Ellison in *Invisible Man* and Morrison in *Jazz* (1992). In both of these earlier texts, the idea of the black self changing itself to fit in with the dominant American society is first tried and then rejected. The invisible man and Joe Trace in turn abandon the entire concept.[50]

As a whole, *Home* narrativises Robinson's commitment to human dignity and sacredness, and to human capacity for positive change, to which she believes the academic field of the Humanities (including of course Classics) is key. In 'Reformation' she expresses her sense that 'we are now living among the relics or even the ruins of the Reformation' (*Givenness* 26). She extols 'the traditionally widespread teaching of the liberal arts, the disciplines that celebrate human thought and creativity as values in their own right and as ends in themselves', in which the 'fine colleges founded in the Middle West when it was still very much a frontier – Oberlin, Grinnell, Knox' were so exemplary (*Givenness* 26). Robinson links liberal arts education to political reform/radicalism within her own life story, mentioning more than once that her college days coincided with the Civil Rights era, and emphasising the significance of that synchronicity.[51] Glory's reflection on the value of her own teaching work expresses this same sentiment: remembering her teaching of 'Il Penseroso' (by 'Puritan Milton with his pagan muses') as equal to her father's ministry, she realises that through teaching literature she had been 'helping [her students] assume their humanity' (*Home* 21–2). She compares her pupils' epiphanies to 'Keats in Cheapside', when he first reads Chapman's translation of Homer and thereby discovers whole new worlds (22).[52] She knows that her teaching of certain texts to her students has helped them to realise that they are 'human beings, keepers of lore, makers of it' (22).

Crucially, Robinson's chosen word here, 'lore', functions as a pun on 'law'. In the transformative vision within *Home* there is a faith in human beings as makers (and changers) of law, and an endorsement of the symbiosis that the nineteenth-century reformers took for granted: a faith in power that the Humanities can have in the struggle for racial justice. The same connection is there in Glory's meditation at the end of the novel, when she imagines young Robert Boughton (Della and Jack's mixed-race son) returning to the Boughton family home at some time in the future. Her vision symbolises the transformed America that Robinson's work as a whole proposes, while also embodying this character's personal hopes and dreams. Young Robert's return would fulfil her wish (and Robinson's) that 'new love would transform the old and make its relics wonderful' (337). The word 'relic', as used here and elsewhere in the Robinsonian oeuvre, encapsulates the novelist's sense of the potential restorative nature of both 'pagan' antiquity and the Christian past. In *Gilead*, Ames mentions that his father can no longer identify with the town Gilead, because 'from any distance' it seemed to be 'a relic, an archaism', a place in which 'history' involved 'old, unhappy far-off things and battles long ago' (268).[53] While Ames senior, the abolitionist, is keen to distance Gilead's honourable nineteenth century into an ancient, quasi-classical epic past, the impulse of Robinson's work is just the opposite. Her novels strive to re-engage the power and energy that she perceives in the past, and they suggest just how transformative its 'relics' can be.

Notes

1. Another essay key to this discussion is Robinson's 'Humanism', which opens *The Givenness of Things* (2015). She also references both Pindar and Caesar within that collection (274, 260).
2. Robinson's fifth novel, *Jack* (2020), was published too late for consideration in this book.
3. For useful biographical sketches see Robinson, 'Art of Fiction', and Stevens, 'Introduction'.
4. On etymology and translation see for example Robinson, *Givenness* 142 or 157, and *When* 25 or 66.
5. Note Robinson's interest in epic films that explore Roman/Christian interactions: *The Robe* (1953), *Demetrius and the Gladiators* (1954) and *Ben-Hur* (1925) (see *Givenness* 129, 135–6, 138).
6. See for example 'McGuffey and the Abolitionists' in *The Death of Adam*, especially 127.

7. On the learning of both Calvin and Marguerite de Navarre see *The Death of Adam*; therein Robinson celebrates all the classical texts that Calvin refused to ban (and so permitted to circulate): 'Apuleius, Martial, Plautus, Terence, Horace, Catullus, Tibullus, Propertius, . . . Ovid' (201).
8. For Robinson's account of Calvin's radicalism see *Death* 205–6. On the political dimensions of her work see Mariotti and Lane; Roynon, 'Everything'. See 'Reformation' in *Givenness*, especially pp. 25–6, for further discussion of 'the Promethean work of the reformers'; see 'Decline' on the role of the humanities in democracy (*Givenness* 119).
9. For her opposition to fundamentalism see for example 'President Obama and Marilynne Robinson' I and II; on her opposition to nostalgia see *When* xiv.
10. See 'Decline': *Givenness* 119ff.
11. See *Aeneid* I.462 – translated by Fairclough as 'tears for misfortune'.
12. For Robinson's account of America and Americans as 'transforming' or 'self-transforming' see *Givenness* 157; *When* xii.
13. See *Givenness* 59.
14. See *When* 29. On Robinson's classicism and civil rights see Roynon, 'Everything'.
15. See for example *Death* 26–7.
16. This passage compares interestingly with Hannah Arendt's conception of the pearl diver in her 1968 *New Yorker* essay, 'Reflections: Walter Benjamin'; and with Adrienne Rich's poem, 'Diving into the Wreck', and 1972 essay, 'When We Dead Awaken' (see Rich, *Poetry and Prose*).
17. Other collections/special issues include Daly, and Sykes et al.
18. See especially Hungerford 743.
19. Buell 427; Showalter 471–4.
20. See also Stevens, 'Interview' 266.
21. See Mauro 152–3; also 160 on *anagnorisis* ('recognition') as both classical and Christian, particularly with regard to the prodigal son narrative in *Home*.
22. See also *Death* 8.
23. See 'Reformation' in *Givenness*: 'His work was read so widely that he is credited with creating French . . . as an international language' (18).
24. As classical scholar R. T. Ridley argues, there is no classical source for the fact of the sowing of Carthage with salt and it appears to be a nineteenth-century invention. Interestingly, it is 'documented' in George Ripley and Charles Dana's *New Cyclopædia of America*, published in 1858 (see vol. IV, p. 495ff, specifically 497), while Ridley cites one key source of the misinformation as the *Cambridge Ancient History*. From 'records' such as these, the myth presumably became

common 'knowledge'. My thanks to Stephen Harrison for directing me to Ridley.

25. See 'dragon's teeth' in glossary.
26. For Aeneas and Anchises in the underworld see *Aeneid* VI.679–898, especially 679–703.
27. This passage in *Housekeeping* about messages among leaves (discussed again later here) recalls Aeneas's advice to the Sibyl (*Aeneid* VI.74–5): 'Only trust not your verses to leaves, lest they fly in disorder . . .'.
28. See *Met.* I.262ff.
29. For Pygmalion and Galatea see Ovid, *Met.* X.243–98.
30. The girls in *Housekeeping* gather 'huckleberries' (14); compare also Robinson, *Lila* (103).
31. See *When* 89; see for example *Housekeeping* 38, 158.
32. Compare also *Housekeeping* 199: 'The fruit trees were all bare, and their leaves on the ground were as limp and noisome as wet leather.'
33. See Oswald, *Memorial* 73: from 'Like leaves who could write a history of leaves' to 'Which matters no more than the leaves'.
34. Compare the Bible, King James Version, I Corinthians 15: 51–4.
35. See pp. 198–201 for quotations from, and discussions of, Robinson's non-fictional reflections on this subject.
36. See Roynon, 'Everything' for further discussion of classicism, abolition and civil rights.
37. For symbolic references to leaves in *Gilead* see there 186 and 218.
38. See *Aeneid* VI.700–3; also discussed in relation to *Housekeeping* at pp. 206–7.
39. On 'moriturus' in the *Aeneid* see Petrini 38.
40. Compare Freud's *Civilization and its Discontents* 6–9, also referenced in my introduction here (with thanks to Daniel Orrells). For the most part, Robinson in her non-fiction expresses scepticism about rather than admiration for Freudian thought.
41. Compare p. 91 above on Faulkner's deployment of the same passage from Ovid.
42. See Roynon, 'Everything' for further discussion, including of Robinson's invocation of the anti-pastoral sunflowers in Morrison's *The Bluest Eye*.
43. See Mauro 152.
44. Compare Robinson on how Darwin is not Prometheus: *Death* 31.
45. See Hesiod, *Theogony* 521–616; Ovid, *Met.* I.82 (where Prometheus is called 'son of Iapetus'). See Chapters 3, 4 and 6 for the importance of Prometheus to Faulkner, Ellison and Roth respectively.
46. On Prometheus in American racial and class contexts see for example Hall, 'The Problem with Prometheus'; B. Foley; Hickman. See also Dougherty, *Prometheus*.
47. See *Home* 49–50. On Prometheus in Du Bois see Hawkins.

48. On Prometheus as/and Christ in Augustine and Tertullian see McLelland 32. Note that Jack also implicitly and half-jokingly compares himself to Christ (*Home* 269). On Prometheus see also Dougherty, *Prometheus*.
49. For Robinson on Theodore Dwight Weld, and on the great learning of many of the radical abolitionists, see her essay 'Who Was Oberlin?': *When* 165–81, in particular 177. See also her earlier essay 'McGuffey and the Abolitionists': *Death* 126–49.
50. See pp. 126–7 and 164; see also Roynon, 'Everything'.
51. See also *When* 29 and *Givenness* 97.
52. See John Keats, 'On First Looking into Chapman's Homer': 'Then felt I like some watcher of the skies / When a new planet swims into his ken; / Or like stout Cortez, when with eagle eyes / He stared at the Pacific' (602).
53. Compare *Housekeeping* on Sylvie and Ruth's motive for attempting to burn down their home: they 'could not leave that house, which was stashed like a brain, a reliquary, like a brain, its relics to be pawed and sorted and parcelled out among the needy and the parsimonious of Fingerbone' (209).

Further Reading

Mauro, Aaron. 'Ordinary Happiness: Marilynne Robinson's Tragic Economies of Debt and Forgiveness'. *symploke* 22.1–2 (2014): 149–66.

Robinson, Marilynne. 'Freedom of Thought', 'When I Was a Child' and 'Who Was Oberlin?' in *When I Was a Child I Read Books*. London: Virago, 2012.

Robinson, Marilynne. 'Humanism' and 'Reformation' in *The Givenness of Things: Essays*. London: Virago, 2015.

Roynon, Tessa. '"Everything Can Change": Civil Rights, Civil War and Radical Transformation in *Home* and *Gilead*'. *Marilynne Robinson: Essays*. Ed. Rachel Sykes, Jennifer Daly and Anna Maguire Elliott. Manchester: Manchester University Press, 2020. Pages not yet known.

Williams, Gary. 'Resurrecting Carthage: *Housekeeping* and Cultural History'. *English Language Notes* 29 (1991): 70–8.

Conclusion: The Diversity of Modern American Fiction's Classicism

Marilynne Robinson's fourth novel, *Lila* (2014), sheds significant light both on her classicism and on the relationship between the modern American novel and antiquity as a whole. 'There is something about being human that makes us love and crave grand narratives,' Robinson tells us in her essay 'Wondrous Love'. 'Greek and Roman boys memorized Homer,' she notes, and as 'memorizing the *Koran* is now for many boys in Islamic cultures, . . . this is one means by which important traditions are preserved and made in effect the major dialects of their civilizations' (*When* 126). It is arguable that with *Lila* Robinson herself creates a 'grand narrative', one that constitutes a 'major dialect' of American civilisation. Despite the obvious fact that Lila herself is not at all grand in the conventional sense, and despite there also being, in this novel, not one single explicit invocation of classical antiquity, *Lila* is a vernacular epic that inherits much from Homer, Virgil and Ovid. Thanks in no small measure to its elements of pastoral, elegy and tragedy, this novel indubitably achieves the 'high sentiment' that the author attributes to Sophocles (*When* 89). Like its ancient textual ancestors, *Lila* is at once 'grievous' and 'beautiful' (*Death* 27).

The absence of direct classical allusions is presumably explained by Robinson's fidelity to Lila's as-yet-little-educated consciousness. Given that the novel depicts the eponymous character's developing literacy and gradual acquaintance with the Bible, it is inevitable that the free indirect discourse through which Robinson depicts Lila's processing of experience is without even the limited mythological referents that Ruth, in *Housekeeping*, has acquired from school. There are implicit allusions that merit further analysis: the description of Doll's birthmark as a 'wound' or 'scar' resonates with the same combination of Christian and mythological resonances as these words do in the three prior novels, for example (*Lila* 24). The detail that when Lila washes her clothes in the river they resemble 'her own flayed skin' might be heard as a distorted echo of Ovid's account (in *Metamorphoses* Book VI) of the flaying of Marsyas and the river of tears named after him (*Lila* 78). And even the fact that Robinson records Lila seeing and liking the 1945 film of *The Picture of Dorian Gray* (dir. Albert Lewin) could indicate a dialogue with Wilde's Ovid-infused novel that is of such importance to Faulkner, Fitzgerald and Ellison.

Yet the primary 'classic' intertext in *Lila* is surely *Huckleberry Finn*. Both are deeply indebted to the *Odyssey* in their themes of wandering and journeying, the search for home, strangerhood, hospitality and belonging/unbelonging. With *Lila*, Robinson builds on *Housekeeping* to develop Twain's archetype of the parentless, transient young person existing on the margins of American society in significant ways. Not only does Lila herself remember a violent and abusive man who may be her father (bringing Huck's 'Pap' immediately to mind), but the father of the Huck-like boy who inherits her hut is similar. Lest we are in doubt about the relationship between the two novels, Robinson calls this vagrant boy 'George Peterson', clearly indicating he is a literary successor of Huck, who adopts the pseudonym 'George Peters' when he goes to visit Mrs Judith Loftus (Robinson, *Lila* 162; Twain 116). Moreover, both *Lila* and *Huckleberry Finn* are written in forms of 'Western' vernacular (Midwestern and Southwestern respectively). Though these of course do not sound identical, the texts have in common an extraordinary oral quality, a striking richness and beauty.

There is, nonetheless, an important difference in tone between Twain's and Robinson's novels. While Huck Finn's first-person narrative constantly shifts between the heroic and the comic, the elegiac and the satirical or anti-heroic, the third-person narrative of *Lila* is not without humour, but it is never satirical, ironic or comic at its protagonist's expense. It is noteworthy that other American novels that have affinities with both the *Odyssey* and *Huckleberry Finn* – such as Ellison's *Invisible Man* and Morrison's *Song of Solomon* – follow James Joyce in depicting the trials and *Bildung* of the 'ordinary hero' through extensive use of parody and the mock-heroic. Neither Milkman nor the Invisible Man gets to be dignified for more than the briefest of moments. *Lila* therefore stands out as an unironised epic, replete with epic similes that consolidate rather than mock the protagonist's dignity. With regard to the trajectory of novelists discussed in this book as a whole, it is interesting to conclude that almost exactly one century after the publication of Cather's *My Ántonia*, Robinson achieves the profundity, the universality, the scale of epic in a novel that is not just entirely without overt classical allusion, but also without any parody or irony directed at its protagonist.

Lila's unlikeness, in this regard, to nearly every other novel discussed in detail in this book testifies to the obvious but nonetheless noteworthy diversity of modern American fiction's classicism. To survey the chapters of this book is of course to note the recurrence of certain key figures and tropes – ones that appeal to different novelists (for different or for similar reasons) over time. These range from predictable favourites such as Odysseus, Oedipus, Julius Caesar or Aeneas to more surprising (or at least less talked about) figures such as Prometheus and Pygmalion. Prometheus, present in myriad context-specific conflicting politics of class and race, for example, constitutes an unexpected connection between the novels of Ellison, Roth and Robinson, while the ambiguously powerful artist Pygmalion links the fiction of Cather, Ellison and Morrison with Robinson once again. The recurring presence of Prometheus and Pygmalion (along with Icarus, Narcissus, Philomela, Proserpina et al.) itself testifies, in turn, to the extensive and long-overlooked fascination that Ovid's *Metamorphoses* holds for modern American novelists. Ovid is if anything more useful to them in their confrontations with America's dramatic and fraught history – that 'shifty hall of mirrors', as Ellison's Hickman calls it (*Three Days* 579) – than are Homer, Virgil and the Greek tragedians. Yet, despite these commonalities and continuities, the multivalence in both method and effect of the American novel's classical allusiveness complicates the very notion of tradition or genealogy that my book delineates.

As I intimated in my preface, *The Classical Tradition in Modern American Fiction* is to a great extent a discussion of how fiction writers transform their educations and reading practices through their own creative voices. In charting the principal ways by which my chosen authors have accessed classical antiquity and its legacies, I have emphasised not just their reading of translated (and sometimes untranslated) classical texts, but also their significant encounters with the ancient world via their reading in more modern literature, whether this be by Dante, Milton, Pope, Keats, Melville,

Swinburne, France, Jewett, Wilde, Housman or Malraux, to name but a few. James Joyce and T. S. Eliot stand uncontested as primary influences, in terms of both the manner and the meanings of their allusiveness, on the specific modernist aesthetics of Fitzgerald, Faulkner and Ellison (and probably of Morrison and Roth too). It is equally important to note, however, the extent to which Cather (in *My Ántonia*, for example) anticipates those canonical high modernists as much as she inherits and revises them. And Robinson, in turn, for the most part deploys antiquity to articulate not alienation, dislocation and the mock-heroic, but rather their antitheses: belonging, connectedness and the heroic.

To recall Cather's and Morrison's respective interest in the neoclassical architecture that characterised the landscapes and townscapes of the slaveholding South (and Roth's attention to similar styles in the WASP and academic environments of the north); Fitzgerald's use of a film set of the Roman Forum in *Tender Is the Night*; Faulkner's invocations of Confederate memorial statuary in *Light in August*; Ellison's reference to Saint-Gaudens's neoclassical memorial to the Unionist Colonel Robert Shaw and the African American regiment (in his 1981 introduction to *Invisible Man*); or Robinson's meditation on a diver's recovery of 'a piece of statuary under the Mediterranean' (*When* 87) is to recognise the significant role of visual cultures and the built environment within the classicisms that these authors engage. Panning across these various ekphrastic moments also reinforces the contrasting and conflicting ideologies that the classical tradition has underpinned, often simultaneously, throughout America's history. The seven authors discussed here have reflected and refracted American cultural deployments of antiquity as an articulation of independent, republican pride; of democratic ideals; of imperial ambition; of both pro-slavery and abolitionist perspectives; of both racist and anti-racist beliefs; of various pastoral idylls; of capitalist luxury and decadent pleasure; of decline and ruin; of military heroism in both triumphant victory and elegiac defeat; of patriarchy and of resistance to patriarchy; of both highbrow intellectual elitism and middlebrow 'common knowledge'; and as both a threat and a complement to Christianity.

The classical tradition's apparently infinite adaptability explains its extraordinarily diverse presences in a whole spectrum of modern American fiction that extends far beyond the seven authors who are the primary focus of this book. It is in this sense that my discussions here are a starting point only. They are an invitation to future scholars and students not only to continue the analysis of these palimpsestic texts and authors, but also to develop critical discussion on numerous other classically allusive works. This further analysis might include, for example, the entire oeuvre of Eudora Welty, whose fiction would have received a chapter in its own right within this book had space allowed. Also meriting discussion are thematic trajectories or fictional groupings such as those novels concerned with American masculinity (ranging from Norman Mailer's *An American Dream* (1965) to John Williams's *Stoner* (1965)); novels about the modern and postmodern condition such as E. L. Doctorow's *Ragtime* (1975) or Don DeLillo's *White Noise* (1985); those novels that epitomise postmodernism in their form, such as the short-story collections *Lost in the Funhouse* (1968) by John Barth and *Brief Interviews with Hideous Men* (1999) by David Foster Wallace; and novels that constitute a deep psychological engagement with particular characters and relationships from antiquity, such as Madeline Miller in her *Song of Achilles* (2011) and more recent *Circe* (2019). Contemporary fiction that engages antiquity in its depictions of the American Civil War – ranging from Charles Frazier's *Cold Mountain* (1997) to Irish author Sebastian Barry's *Days Without End* (2016) – invariably attracts both critical acclaim and strong sales. And there are, of course, numerous *sui generis* texts that (except for in their classical allusiveness) do not fit readily within any grouping or trajectory. These range from Kurt Vonnegut's *Cat's Cradle* (1963), Donna Tartt's *The Secret History* (1992) and Jeffrey Eugenides's *Middlesex* (2002) to Junot Díaz's *The Brief Wondrous Life of Oscar Wao* (2007), Jhumpa Lahiri's *Unaccustomed Earth* (2008) and Dinaw Mengestu's *How to Read the Air* (2010).

The diverse identities of the authors of these last three texts – Dominican American, South Asian American and Ethiopian American, respectively – illustrate one of the implicit points of my book as a whole: that in the twentieth and twenty-first centuries, classical antiquity is less than ever the preserve of a WASP male elite. Ellison's observation in that 1955 letter from Rome that 'the Renaissance' (as he calls it) 'belongs to anyone who can dig it' of course sounds trite when taken out of context, but it is an insight both important and true (*Trading* 98–9). While my discussions of Ellison and Morrison attest to their respective significant positions within black classicist cultural practice, my analyses of the representations of racial politics in texts by Cather, Faulkner and Robinson have shown how black classical radicalism can also operate powerfully within white-authored texts. At the same time, there is a wealth of classically allusive modern and contemporary fiction by other black American writers that merits far more sustained attention than I can give it here. This ranges from the subversive, experimental African-classicist novels of the Black Arts era and its aftermath such as Ishmael Reed's *Mumbo Jumbo* (1972) and Toni Cade Bambara's *The Salt Eaters* (1980) to Percival Everett's deeply irreverent *Erasure* (2001) and beyond. In this last, Everett's novelist-protagonist wins literary acclaim with a spoof protest novel when his serious fictional reworkings of Aeschylus and Euripides fail to succeed.

Also notable here is Paul Beatty's equally politically incorrect, comically ironic *The Sellout* (2015), a quotation from which begins this book, together with Fran Ross's undervalued but hilarious feminist satire of black and Jewish stereotypes, *Oreo*, which was first published in 1974 but republished, to great fanfare, by New Directions in 2015. While Ross engages the *Odyssey* and Theseus's slaying of the minotaur, Jesmyn Ward, in her completely differently toned *Salvage the Bones* of 2011, makes direct and repeated references to Edith Hamilton's *Mythology* in her interweaving of the lives of a contemporary black family. The fifteen-year-old female narrator, Esch, who lives on the Mississippi Gulf Coast and whose traumatic experiences include encountering the full force of Hurricane Katrina, has been reading the Hamilton book at school. Different again from either Ross's or Ward's texts, both in the nature of its classical allusiveness and in its form and tone, is Marcia Southgate's 2002 novel, *The Fall of Rome*. A realist narrative, it uses a fraught relationship between an African American scholarship student and his more privileged black Latin teacher at an elite Connecticut prep school to examine the complexities of racial and class identity in the post-Civil Rights/ pre-Obama era. While these texts are currently less frequently read and studied than those by DeLillo or Tartt or Eugenides, if one outcome of my book is that it precipitates much-needed further analysis of the classicism in these African American works, then it will have fulfilled one of its most longstanding aims.

In closing, it is important to note that there is, of course, nothing exceptionally American about modernity's fascination for antiquity. While United States novelists invariably enlist classical allusions in their explorations of history, power relations and identity within their own nation, contemporary Caribbean, Canadian and Latin American authors likewise make use of the same classical resources in numerous different contexts and to numerous different ends. Within the last two or three years alone, meanwhile, British and Irish writers too have published a range of stunning texts that engage with the Greek and Roman past: witness Colm Tóibín's *House of Names* (2017), Kamila Shamsie's *Home Fire* (2017), Pat Barker's *The Silence of the Girls* (2018) and Natalie Haynes's *A Thousand Ships* (2019). It is presumably no coincidence that while classical reception studies initially paid greater attention to verse and drama than to prose fiction, this could not remain and has not remained the case. Recent works of scholarship such as the essay collection *Ancient Greek Myth in World Fiction since 1989* (edited by Justine McConnell and Edith Hall, and published in 2016) attest to the fact that classical antiquity appeals to contemporary prose fiction writers across the globe. They have shored up the status of the modern novel as an important site of reception.

The Classical Tradition in Modern American Fiction, then, implicitly argues that the significant classical presences in American novels contribute to their 'global' nature as much as to their 'Americanness'. While my close readings of the seven major writers studied here testify to the always-shifting meanings and effects that allusions to antiquity can involve, as a whole my book demonstrates the importance and the rewards of paying sustained and bold attention to the classicisms of these and of every text. The photograph on the front cover here depicts the view from a window in the fretted corona of the Smithsonian's most recent museum: the National Museum of African American History and Culture. This view constitutes one major new perspective, in the built environment of Washington DC, on already-familiar icons of American classicism. This book itself, I believe, has enabled not dissimilar recalibrations of iconic American fiction. I hope it has also opened up further vistas, or new windows, through which we can glimpse the vast and varied work that still needs to be done.

Appendix 1 – Glossary of Classical Terms Used in this Book

This glossary includes names of deities and of mythical, legendary and historical people; place names; authors of classical texts; titles of classical texts (italicised); and concepts/phrases in Greek or Latin (italicised).

Note: nearly all the information in this glossary is taken either from the *Oxford Classical Dictionary* (<https://oxfordre.com/classics>) or from *Who's Who in the Ancient World* by Betty Radice (1973).

Achates	loyal comrade of Aeneas in Virgil's *Aeneid*
Achilles	Greek hero, key player in the Trojan War and the *Iliad*
Acropolis, the	central steep hill/fortress in ancient Athens, site of the Parthenon etc.
Actaeon	huntsman who (e.g. in Ovid's *Metamorphoses*) encounters Diana naked
Aeneas	central protagonist/hero of Virgil's *Aeneid*
***Aeneid*, the**	epic poem in Latin by Virgil, composed between and 30 and 19 BCE
Aeolus	deity that rules the winds
Aeschylus	Greek (Athenian) tragic playwright, ?525/4–456/5 BCE
Aesop	legendary author of *Fables* (in Greek), probably from sixth century BCE
Aesop's Fables	see **Aesop**
Agamemnon	king who led Greek forces in the Trojan War, husband of Clytemnestra
Agamemnon	first play in tragic trilogy, the *Oresteia*, by Aeschylus; the eponymous king is killed
Aglauros	envious sister in Ovid's *Metamorphoses*
Ajax	Greek hero in the *Iliad*, protagonist in Sophocles's tragedy *Ajax*
Alexander the Great	King of Macedonia and empire builder, 356–323 BCE
Amazonians	mythical female warriors

anagnorisis	Greek concept in Aristotle's *Poetics*: a moment of insight or recognition
Anchises	father of Aeneas, in Virgil's *Aeneid*
Antigone	daughter of Oedipus, protagonist in Sophocles's tragedy *Antigone*
Aphrodite	Greek goddess of love and beauty (Roman: Venus)
Apollo	Greek god associated with light, music and archery (Roman epithet: Phoebus)
Apollonius	of Rhodes, Greek epic poet of third century BCE, author of *Argonautica*
Appian	Greek historian, born in Alexandria at end of first century CE
Apuleius	Roman writer, born 125 CE, author of *The Golden Ass* (*Metamorphoses*)
Argos	ancient city in Argive region
Aristophanes	Greek comic dramatist, c. 450–c. 385 BCE
Aristotle	Greek scientist and philosopher, 384–322 BCE; author of *Poetics*
Atalanta	heroine who loses race (by picking up golden apples) in Ovid's *Metamorphoses*
Athena, Athene	see **Pallas Athena, Athene**
Atreus (house of)	descendants of Mycenean King Atreus (e.g. Agamemnon and Menelaus)
Attic	adjective describing things/people from, or relating to, Attica and/or Athens
Attica	territory in which ancient Athens was situated
Augustine	Father of the Christian church, writer and saint, 354–450 CE
Augustus	first Roman emperor, from 27 BCE to 14 CE
Aurora	Roman goddess of the dawn (Greek: Eos)
Bacchus	Roman god of wine (Greek: Dionysus)
Ben-Hur	eponymous fictional hero of Lew Wallace's novel of 1880, and later film
Briseis	Achilles's slave-concubine in the *Iliad*
Brutus	Roman statesman who led the conspiracy to murder Julius Caesar; killed himself in 42 BCE
Cadmus (house of)	descendants of Cadmus, who founded Thebes (see **dragon's teeth**)
Caesar, Julius	c. 100–44 BCE; Roman patrician, statesman and dictator; author of *Gallic Wars*
Calchas	seer (prophet/fortune-teller) and priest of Apollo in the *Iliad* and the *Agamemnon*
Caligula	Roman emperor 37–41 CE

Carthage	Phoenician colony, then Roman city in present-day Tunisia; home of Dido in the *Aeneid*
Cassandra	daughter of King Priam of Troy; has prophetic powers
Cato	Pro-republic Roman statesman; committed suicide (in 46 BCE) when Caesar defeated Pompey
Catullus	Roman poet c. 84–54 BCE
Cerberus	Many-headed dog that guards the entrance to the underworld, e.g. in the *Aeneid*
Ceres	Roman goddess of corn/the harvest (Greek name: Demeter); mother of Proserpina
Charite	bride-to-be in Apuleius's *The Golden Ass* who is told the 'Cupid and Psyche' story
Chryseis	young Trojan woman (a.k.a. Cressida); Agamemnon's slave-concubine before the *Iliad* opens
Cicero	Roman statesman, orator and writer, 106–43 BCE
Cinyras	legendary king of Cyprus; father of Myrrha in Ovid's *Metamorphoses*
Circe	divine sorceress who bewitches Odysseus's men and seduces him in the *Odyssey*
Claudia	wife of Roman emperor Nero
Claudius	Roman emperor from 41 to 54 CE
Clytemnestra	wife of Agamemnon; mother of Orestes, Electra, Iphigenia; features in the *Oresteia*
Croesus	exceptionally wealthy king of Lydia, sixth century BCE
Cumae	see also **Sibyl (Sybil) of Cumae**; coastal colony north-west of Naples
Cupid	Roman god of love (Greek: Eros)
'Cupid and Psyche'	tale told within Apuleius's *The Golden Ass*
Cyclops	race of one-eyed giants; one is Polyphemus
Daedalus	legendary inventor/engineer/artist; makes wings for son, Icarus, in Ovid's *Metamorphoses*
Danaë	raped by Zeus in the form of a shower of gold in Ovid's *Metamorphoses*
Daphne	nymph who transforms into laurel tree when pursued by Apollo in Ovid's *Metamorphoses*
Dawn	see **Aurora**
De rerum natura	philosophical poem in six books by Lucretius; title means 'On the Nature of Things'
Delphi	holy site on lower slopes of Mount Parnassus (Greece); site of priests/oracle of Apollo
Demeter	Greek goddess of the corn/harvest (Roman: Ceres)
Demosthenes	384–322 BCE; brilliant Athenian orator

Deucalion	survives flood and (with Pyrrha) repopulates earth from stones in Ovid's *Metamorphoses*
deus ex machina	Latin for 'the god from the machine' – literally refers to figure of deity suspended from crane in classical drama; figuratively can mean any miraculous or apparently divine solution
Diana	Italian (pre-Roman) goddess of woods, women and moon (Greek: Artemis)
Dido	founding queen of Carthage; kills herself when her lover, Aeneas, leaves her in the *Aeneid*
Diocletian	Roman emperor 284–305 CE
Diomedes	Greek warrior in the *Iliad*
Dionysus	Greek god of wine (Roman: Bacchus)
dragon's teeth	sown in the ground by Cadmus and by Jason (two separate myths); they sprout as men
Echo	nymph who can only repeat others' words; rejected by Narcissus in Ovid's *Metamorphoses*
Eclogue	individual poem within Virgil's *Eclogues* (see below)
Eclogues	ten short pastoral poems (in Latin) by Virgil, published 39–38 BCE
***ekphrasis* (n), *ekphrastic* (adj.)**	a detailed verbal or literary description of a visual work of art
Elagabalus	Roman emperor 270–275 CE
Electra	daughter of Agamemnon; sister of Orestes, whom she assists in killing their mother, Clytemnestra
Encolpius	narrator in the *Satyricon* by Petronius
Etruscans	a people indigenous to pre-Roman Italy
Euripides	Greek (Athenian) tragic dramatist, c. 480–406 BCE
Europa	princess from Tyre raped by Zeus in the form of a bull in Ovid's *Metamorphoses*
Eurydice	nymph, wife of Orpheus; he fails in his attempt to bring her back from the underworld
***fama*/Fama**	Latin for 'rumour'; personified as a monster in the *Aeneid* and Ovid's *Metamorphoses*
Fates, the	see ***Moirai***
faun	mythical half-human goat-legged creature
Faunus	Italian (pre-Roman) god associated with woods and herdsmen
Faustina	reputedly promiscuous and decadent wife of Roman emperor Marcus Aurelius
Forum, the	main public square in ancient Rome – site of temples, the senate, etc.

Furies, Fury	Greek spirits of revenge, known as *Eumenides* ('kindly ones') in Aeschylus's *Oresteia*
Galatea	name of the woman transformed from Pygmalion's sculpture in Ovid's *Metamorphoses*
Gallic Wars	Latin prose account by Julius Caesar of Rome's military conquest of Gaul (58–51 BCE)
Ganymede	Trojan prince raped and abducted by Zeus to be his cup-bearer
Georgic	individual poem within the collection *Georgics* (see below)
Georgics	Latin poem in four books by Virgil, about agriculture; published c. 29 BCE
Glaucus	warrior in the Trojan army who exchanges armour with Diomedes in the *Iliad*
Golden Age, the	mythical, idyllic, long-vanished age of peace and prosperity; described in the *Georgics* and Ovid's *Metamorphoses*
Golden Ass, The	novel by Apuleius; a.k.a. *Metamorphoses*; contains the 'Cupid and Psyche' story
Hades	Greek name for god of the underworld (also Dis; Pluto); can also refer to the underworld itself
Hector	Trojan prince, eldest son of King Priam; killed by Achilles near the end of the *Iliad*
Helen, Helen of Troy	Greek wife of Menelaus, abducted to Troy by Paris, hence the Trojan War
Heraclitus	Greek philosopher (from Asia Minor) of around 500 BCE, famous for theory of flux
Hercules	Roman name for Greek hero Heracles, who completed the twelve labours/tasks
Herodotus	c. 484–420 BCE; Greek historian (from Asia Minor), known as 'father of history'
Hesiod	Greek poet from around 700 BCE; author of *Works and Days*
Hestia	Greek goddess of hearth and home (Roman: Vesta)
Histories	history of Rome written by Livy
Homer	legendary Greek poet from around 700 BCE, conventionally understood (though contested and unprovable) as author of the *Iliad* and *Odyssey*
Homeric Hymn to Demeter	long poem by unknown author, c. 700–600 BCE, relating Hades's abduction of Persephone
Horace	65–8 BCE; Roman poet
Horatius	legendary hero who saved Rome by preventing Etruscans crossing a bridge into the city, late sixth century BCE

Huns	Mongolian nomadic people; invaded and advanced through central Europe in early 400s CE
Icarus	son of Daedalus; fell fatally when the sun melted his wax wings in Ovid's *Metamorphoses*
***Iliad*, the**	Greek epic poem dated c. 750 BCE, attributed to Homer; relates the Trojan War and its heroes
Iphigenia	daughter of Clytemnestra and Agamemnon; he sacrificed her to enable the sailing to Troy
ira	Latin word for anger
Iris	Greek goddess of the rainbow and a messenger of the gods
Itys	son of Procne and Tereus; in Ovid's *Metamorphoses* the rapist Tereus unknowingly feasts on him
Josephus	born c. 37 CE; Jewish historian (writing in Greek) of Jewish resistance to Roman rule
Julius Caesar	see **Caesar, Julius**
Jupiter	Roman father of the gods (Greek: Zeus)
Juvenal	c. 60–130 CE; Roman poet; wrote satires
katabasis	Greek word that conventionally describes a descent to the underworld and back
koine hestia	Greek for the 'common hearth': civic site of communal hearth or flame in Greek cities
lacrimae rerum	Latin phrase in Virgil's *Aeneid*: 'the sadness of things' or 'the tears in things'
Lavinium	city in Latium, south of Rome (and its forerunner), founded by Aeneas
Leda	princess and mother of Clytemnestra; raped by Zeus-as-a-swan in Ovid's *Metamorphoses*
lena	Latin word for procuress
Leonidas	King of Sparta famed for military leadership against the Persians at Thermopylae
Lethe	one of six rivers in the underworld; its waters have care-forgetting properties when drunk
Libation Bearers	second play in Aeschylus's *Oresteia* trilogy; Orestes kills his mother, Clytemnestra
Lina	see **Messalina**
Livy	59 BCE–17 CE; Roman historian; wrote a history of Rome in 142 books: *Histories*
Lucan	Roman epic poet, 39–65 CE
Lucretius	Roman philosopher and poet, 95–c. 55 BCE; author of *De rerum natura*
Lutetia	Roman city in France, on site of what is now Paris
Maecenas	wealthy Roman diplomat who was patron of writers such as Virgil, 70–8 BCE

Marathon	town in Attica; site of historic Greek victory over Persians in 490 BCE
Marcellus	a young Roman noble selected by Augustus (his uncle) as his son-in-law and potential successor, whose premature death in 23 BCE is referenced by Virgil in the *Aeneid*
Marcus Aurelius	Roman emperor 161–180 CE; husband of Faustina
Mars	Roman god of war (Greek: Ares)
Marsyas	flute-player who is flayed for losing a contest with Apollo; in Ovid's *Metamorphoses*
Martial	Roman poet who wrote epigrams, c. 40–104 CE
Medea	daughter of the King of Colchis, reputed to be a priestess and witch
Medea	Greek tragedy by Euripides centred on Medea's vengeful killing of the unfaithful Jason
Medusa	type of female monster (a.k.a. 'gorgon') that turns to stone anyone who looks at her
Meliboeus	name of shepherd (friend of Tityrus) in Virgil's first Eclogue
Messalina	wife of the Roman emperor Claudius; notorious for promiscuity and profligacy
***Metamorphoses*, the**	i) epic poem on the theme of transformation, completed by Ovid c. 8 CE ii) alternative name for *The Golden Ass* by Apuleius
miasma	Greek concept of pollution/contamination
Midas	legendary king whose every touch turns things into gold; in Ovid's *Metamorphoses*
Minoan (culture)	Bronze Age civilisation of Crete, c. 3500–1100 BCE
Moirai	trio of Greek goddesses of fate (the 'Fates'), named by Hesiod as Lachesis, Clotho, Atropos
moriturus	Latin word meaning 'he who is about to die'
mutatis mutandis	Latin phrase meaning 'after the necessary changes have been made'
Mycenean (culture)	late Bronze Age civilisation on Greek mainland
Myron	Greek sculptor, active 470–440 BCE
Myrrha	daughter of Cinyras; indulges an incestuous passion for him in Ovid's *Metamorphoses*
Nag Hammadi library	sacred Gnostic texts of the third and fourth centuries CE, written in Coptic
naiad	a type of water nymph
Narcissus	in Ovid's *Metamorphoses*; falls in love with his own reflection; rejects Echo
nefas	Latin word for unspeakable wrong
Nemesis	divine personification of retribution or avenging fate

Neptune	Roman god of the sea (Greek: Poseidon)
Nero	Roman emperor 54–68 CE
Niobe	woman who turns into a dripping rock from weeping prompted by the deaths of her twelve children; in Ovid's *Metamorphoses*
nostos	Greek word for homecoming or return
Odysseus	Greek hero; protagonist in the *Odyssey* (Roman: Ulysses)
Odyssey, the	Greek epic poem attributed to Homer, dated c. 725 BCE; relates Odysseus's adventures on voyage home from the Trojan War
Oedipus	King of Thebes who inadvertently marries his own mother, Jocasta
Oedipus Rex	tragedy by Sophocles relating Oedipus's killing his father, marrying his mother and unhappy end
oikonomia	Greek word for domestic (household) economy
oikos	Greek word for house/household
Olympian	refers to any one of the twelve main Greek gods, who live on Mount Olympus
Olympus	highest mountain in Greece; in mythology, home of the twelve main Greek gods
Oresteia	trilogy of tragedies written by Aeschylus: *Agamemnon*, *Libation Bearers*, *Eumenides*
Orpheus	mythological musician (song and lyre) and poet; married to Eurydice
otium	Latin word for leisure
Ovid	43 BCE–17/18 CE; Roman poet; works include *Metamorphoses*
Pallas Athena, Athene	Greek goddess of war and wisdom (Roman: Minerva)
Pan	goat-eared and goat-legged god of shepherds and herdsmen, associated with fertility and lust
Parnassus	mountain north-east of Delphi sacred to Apollo and the Muses
Parthenon, the	temple to Athene on Athenian acropolis; includes famous friezes (e.g. Elgin Marbles)
patria	Latin word for fatherland, homeland or birthplace
Penelope	wife of Odysseus; stays faithfully at home in Ithaca during his wanderings in the *Odyssey*
Peri Hippikes	instruction manual for cavalry soldiers by Xenophon; title (Greek): 'On Horsemanship'
Persephone	daughter of Demeter; abducted to the underworld by Hades (Roman: Proserpina)
Petronius	Roman satirist; author of the *Satyricon*; probably lived during latter half of first century CE

Phaethon	young man who in Ovid's *Metamorphoses* drives and crashes the chariot of the sun (which belongs to his father, Phoebus, a.k.a. Helios)
Phidias	Athenian sculptor, active 465–425 BCE
Philoctetes	Greek leader in Trojan War; famous for wound incurred through snake bite
Philoctetes	Greek tragic drama by Sophocles about the wounded Philoctetes
Philomel, Philomela	in Ovid's *Metamorphoses*, abducted, raped, mutilated by brother-in-law Tereus
Phocian	belonging to Phocis, a region in central ancient Greece
Phoebe	name means 'bright'; minor deity often associated with Diana/the moon
Phoebus	alternative name for Apollo, especially as sun-god (Greek: Helios/Hyperion)
Phoenician(s)	ancient people occupying eastern Mediterranean coast (present-day Syria/Lebanon)
Pindar	Greek lyric poet, 518–438 BCE
Plato	Greek philosopher, 429–347 BCE; works include the *Republic*
Plautus	Roman comic dramatist, 254–184 BCE
Plutarch	Greek essayist and biographer (including of Greek and Roman statesmen), c. 46–126 CE
Poetics	work of literary criticism/theory by Aristotle; includes definitions of tragedy and tragic hero
Polyphemus	cyclops who captures Odysseus and crew in the *Odyssey*
Pomona	Roman goddess of fruit; raped by Vertumnus in Ovid's *Metamorphoses*
Procne	sister of Philomel, wife of Tereus; in Ovid's *Metamorphoses*
Prometheus	early Greek titan; in Hesiod created men from clay, and stole fire from gods for man
Prometheus Bound	Greek tragedy by Aeschylus; Prometheus is chained to a rock for theft of fire
Propertius	Roman elegiac poet, c. 50 BCE–16 CE
Proserpina	daughter of Ceres, abducted to the underworld by Pluto (Greek: Persephone)
Proteus	shapeshifting minor sea god; described in the *Odyssey* and Ovid's *Metamorphoses*
prytaneion	central sacred/civic site in city, housing eternal flame (see ***koine hestia***)

Prytaneum	see **prytaneion**
Psyche	female personification of the soul, beloved of Cupid in Apuleius's *The Golden Ass*
Pygmalion	sculptor in Ovid's *Metamorphoses*; marries his statue of a woman (Galatea), once it's brought to life by Venus
Pyramus	doomed lover of Thisbe in Ovid's *Metamorphoses*
Pyrrha	wife of Deucalion in Ovid's *Metamorphoses*
Pythagoras	Greek philosopher and mathematician of sixth century BCE
Republic	work of political theory/discussion by Plato, written approximately mid-career
Romulus	mythical founder of Rome (with his brother Remus, whom later he possibly killed)
Roscius	a famed Roman actor of the first century BCE
Sabine, Sabinii	a people of ancient (pre-Roman) Italy, colonised by and assimilated into Rome
Sallust	Roman historian, c. 86–35 BCE
Sapphic(s)	pertaining to Sappho or her verse
Sappho	ancient Greek lyric poet (female); born on Lesbos in the second half of the seventh century BCE
satyr	male creature (often horse-human or goat-human) inhabiting the wild; connotes lust
***Satyricon*, the**	Latin novel by Petronius; includes 'Trimalchio's Feast' (scholarly title: *Satyrica*)
Seneca	Roman playwright/philosopher; best known today for his tragedies, c. 4 BCE–65 CE
Seven Against Thebes	Greek tragedy by Aeschylus
sibyl/sybil	prophetic woman/oracle figure in Greek religion
Sibyl (Sybil) of Cumae	prophetic woman who directs Aeneas to the golden bough in the *Aeneid*
siren(s)	mythical female beings who, in the *Odyssey*, lure sailors to their doom through their singing
Socrates	Athenian philosopher whose ideas were written down by Plato; 469–399 BCE
Solon	Athenian statesman and law-maker, c. 640–560 BCE
Sophocles	Greek (Athenian) tragic dramatist, 496–406 BCE
sparagmos	Greek word for ritual dismemberment of animal or human, usually in Dionysiac rite (see **Dionysus**)
Sparta	a Greek city-state in the Peloponnese region
Spartacus	gladiator from Thrace who led slave revolt against Roman rule in 73 BCE
Spartan	from or of Sparta

Statius	Roman poet, 45–96 CE
strophe and antistrophe	two alternating parts of Greek choric ode
Styx	river in the underworld over which the ferryman, Charon, transports dead souls
Suetonius	Roman historian and biographer, c. 69–140 CE
sui generis	Latin phrase meaning ‘of its own kind’, ‘one of a kind’
Sybarite(s)	people of Greek colony in southern Italy; known for luxurious living
Tanagra figures	terracotta figurines found among remains of Tanagra (city in central ancient Greece)
Tarquin	legendary last king of Rome (534–510 BCE)
Tatius	King of the Sabines, who ruled early Rome jointly with Romulus
Terence	Roman comic playwright; originally from North Africa, c. 185–160 BCE
Tertullian	Christian theologian from Carthage, c. 160–240 CE
Theatre of Dionysus	main theatre in ancient Athens, built into southern slopes of Acropolis in fifth/fourth century BCE
Themis	primordial Greek goddess associated with justice and law; associated with Apollo
Theocritus	Greek pastoral poet, 300–260 BCE
Thermopylae	site of significant battle between Greeks (led by Leonidas) and Persians, c. 480 BCE
Theseus	legendary King of Athens from the period of heroic myth
Thisbe	doomed lover of Pyramus in Ovid’s *Metamorphoses*
Thucydides	Greek historian of the Peloponnesian War (460–400 BCE)
Tiberius	Roman emperor 14–37 CE
Tibullus	Roman elegiac poet, 55/48–19 BCE
Tiresias	legendary blind seer from Thebes; (in Ovid) he gains physical attributes of both sexes
titan	pre-Olympian gods/demi-gods (such as Prometheus)
Tityrus	name of shepherd (friend of Meliboeus) in Virgil’s first Eclogue
Trimalchio	protagonist in best-known surviving section of Petronius’s *Satyricon*
triumvirate	board of three officers in Roman public life
Trojan War, the	legendary ten-year war between Trojans and Greeks, around thirteenth century BCE; related in the *Iliad*
Trojans	citizens (and/or army) of Troy

Troy	ancient city/culture in present-day Turkey; site of Trojan War
Ulysses	Latin name for Greek hero; protagonist of the *Odyssey* (Greek: Odysseus)
Valerian	Roman emperor 253–260 CE
Venus	Roman goddess of love and beauty (Greek: Aphrodite)
Vergil	alternative spelling of 'Virgil'
Vertumnus	Pre-Roman (Etruscan?) god of changing seasons, and money-changing; rapes Pomona
Vesta	Roman goddess of hearth and home (Greek: Hestia)
Vestal Virgins	six priestesses of Vesta, at her temple in the Roman Forum
Virgil	Roman poet; author of *Aeneid*, *Eclogues*, *Georgics*; 70–19 BCE
voluptas	Latin word for pleasure (associated by Lucretius, for example, with Aphrodite)
Voluptas	name of Cupid and Psyche's daughter in Apuleius's *The Golden Ass*
Works and Days	Greek poem by Hesiod; gives advice about life and work
Xenophon	Greek historian, c. 428–354 BCE
Zeus	Greek father of the gods (Roman: Jupiter)

Appendix 2 – Resources on Classical Antiquity

Versions of Classical Texts

There are numerous English translations of the *Iliad*, the *Odyssey*, the *Aeneid*, the *Metamorphoses*, etc. The most recent translations in the Norton Critical Edition series, the Oxford World Classics or the Penguin Classics are all excellent starting points.

The best 'one-stop' edition of translated Greek tragedies, for purposes related to American fiction, is the University of Chicago's multi-volume *Complete Greek Tragedies*, edited by David Grene et al. (numerous publication dates).

For all the epics above (and several other texts), the English translations referred to and quoted within my book are the Loeb Classical Library editions published by Harvard University Press (each is listed separately in my Works Cited, under its classical author's name). These editions publish the original Greek or Latin text on one page and the translation on the page facing it. Many university libraries now subscribe to the online edition of the 'new Loeb', a fantastic resource which provides searchable versions of all these texts. Tufts University hosts an open access website called Perseus (<www.perseus.tufts.edu>), which in its 'Greek and Roman Materials' section (under 'Collections/Texts') includes English translations of many classical texts, but the resources are quite uneven and not especially easy to use at first.

Myths

There are numerous retellings, in English, of the Greek and Roman myths in print. The 'old-fashioned' and traditional collections include Edith Hamilton's *Mythology*, first published in 1942 (and still used in many American high schools), and Robert Graves's two-volume *The Greek Myths* (originally published in 1955). At the other end of the spectrum are the more user-friendly handbook-type works. Among these, highly recommended is *The Greek and Roman Myths: A Guide to the Classical Stories* by Philip Matyszak (2010), which combines continuous text with charts, key information boxes and beautiful images.

Reference Works

The standard reference work used by classicists is the *Oxford Classical Dictionary*, available online (by subscription) at <https://oxfordre.com/classics>. Many university libraries subscribe to this resource. Although the entries in the former hard copy of the *OCD* were very detailed and assumed some prior knowledge, the recent online entries are increasingly user-friendly and suited to the non-specialist.

Other accessible reference works include *Who's Who in the Ancient World* by Betty Radice (1973; now out of print, but second-hand copies are available) and the *Penguin Dictionary of Classical Mythology* (edited by Pierre Grimal; concise paperback published in 1991).

Works Cited

Abdur-Rahman, Aliyyah. '"What Moves at the Margin": William Faulkner and Race'. Matthews 444–58.

Adams, Richard. *Faulkner: Myth and Motion*. Princeton: Princeton University Press, 1968.

Aeschylus. *Agamemnon*. Trans. Richmond Lattimore. *Greek Tragedies*. Ed. David Grene and Richmond Lattimore. Vol. 1. 2nd edn. Chicago: University of Chicago Press, 1991. 1–60.

—. *The Libation Bearers*. Trans. Richmond Lattimore. *Greek Tragedies*. Ed. David Grene and Richmond Lattimore. Vol. 2. Chicago: University of Chicago Press, 1960. 1–44.

—. *The Oresteia: Agamemnon, The Libation Bearers, The Eumenides*. Trans. Robert Fagles. Harmondsworth: Penguin, 1979.

Anderson, John. 'Horses'. Hornblower and Spawforth 728.

Andreach, Robert. *Drawing Upon the Past: Classical Theatre in the Contemporary American Theatre*. Oxford: Oxford University Press, 2003.

Apuleius. *The Golden Ass*. Trans. P. G. Walsh. Oxford: Oxford University Press, 1994.

Arendt, Hannah. 'Reflections: Walter Benjamin'. *The New Yorker*. 19 October 1968. 65–6.

Arnold, Marilyn. 'The Allusive Cather'. *Cather Studies* 3 (1996): 137–48.

Auerbach, Erich. *Mimesis: The Representation of Reality in Western Literature*. Princeton: Princeton University Press, 2003.

Awkward, Michael. '"Unruly and Let Loose": Myth, Ideology and Gender in *Song of Solomon*'. *Callaloo* 13.3 (1990): 492–8.

Azérad, Hugues. 'A New Region of the World: Faulkner, Glissant, and the Caribbean'. Matthews 164–84.

Baker, Anne. '"Terrible Women": Gender, Platonism, and Christianity in Willa Cather's *The Professor's House*'. *Western American Literature* 45.3 (2010): 252–72.

Baker, Houston. *Blues, Ideology, and Afro-American Literature: A Vernacular Theory*. Chicago: University of Chicago Press, 1984.

Bakewell, Geoffrey. 'Philip Roth's Oedipal *Stain*'. *Classical and Modern Literature* 24.2 (2004): 29–46.

Barnard, John Levi. *Empire of Ruin: Black Classicism and American Imperial Culture*. Oxford: Oxford University Press, 2017.

Baugh, Albert. *A Literary History of England*. London: Routledge & Kegan Paul, 1948.

Beam, Alex. *A Great Idea at the Time: The Rise, Fall and Curious Afterlife of the Great Books*. New York: Public Affairs, 2008.

Beatty, Paul. *The Sellout*. London: Oneworld Books, 2016.

Bender, Bert. '"His Mind Aglow": The Biological Undercurrent in Fitzgerald's *Gatsby* and Other Works'. *Journal of American Studies* 32.3 (1998): 399–420.

Bennett, Mildred. 'The Childhood Worlds of Willa Cather'. *Great Plains Quarterly* 2.4 (1982): 204–9.

—. *The World of Willa Cather*. London and Lincoln: University of Nebraska Press, 1989.

Benston, Kimberly. 'Re-weaving the "Ulysses Scene": Enchantment, Post-Oedipal Identity and the Buried Text of Blackness in *Song of Solomon*'. *Comparative American Identities: Race, Sex and Nationality in the Modern Text*. Ed. Hortense Spillers. New York: Routledge, 1991. 87–109.

Berman, Ronald. 'Fitzgerald's Intellectual Context'. *A Historical Guide to F. Scott Fitzgerald*. Ed. Kirk Curnutt. Oxford: Oxford University Press, 2004. 69–84.

Bernal, Martin. *Black Athena: The Afroasiatic Roots of Classical Civilization. Vol. 1: The Fabrication of Ancient Greece*. New Brunswick, NJ: Rutgers University Press, 1987.

Björk, Lennart. 'Ancient Myths and the Moral Framework of *Absalom, Absalom!*'. *American Literature* 35.2 (May 1963): 196–204.

Blazek, William and Laura Rattray, eds. *Twenty-First-Century Readings of 'Tender Is the Night'*. Liverpool: Liverpool University Press, 2007.

Bleikasten, André. '*Light in August*: The Closed Society and its Subjects'. Millgate 81–102.

Blight, David. *Race and Reunion: The Civil War in American Memory*. Cambridge, MA: Belknap-Harvard University Press, 2001.

Blotner, Joseph. *Faulkner: A Biography*. 2 vols. London: Chatto & Windus, 1974.

—. *William Faulkner's Library: A Catalogue*. Charlottesville: University of Virginia Press, 1964.

—, ed. *Selected Letters of William Faulkner*. London: The Scholar Press, 1977.

Bluefarb, Sam. '*The Human Stain*: A Satiric Tragedy of the Politically Incorrect'. *Playful and Serious: Philip Roth as a Comic Writer*. Ed. Jay Halio and Ben Siegel. Newark: University of Delaware Press, 2010. 222–8.

Boddy, Kasia. 'Philip Roth's Great Books: A Reading of *The Human Stain*'. *Cambridge Quarterly* 39.1 (2010): 39–60.

Bohlke, L. Brent. *Willa Cather in Person: Interviews, Speeches, and Letters.* Lincoln: University of Nebraska Press, 1986.

Bosher, Kathryn, Fiona Macintosh, Justine McConnell and Patrice Rankine, eds. *The Oxford Handbook of Greek Tragedy in the Americas.* Oxford: Oxford University Press, 2015.

Brauner, David. *Philip Roth.* Manchester: Manchester University Press, 2007.

Briggs, Ward. 'Petronius and Virgil in *The Great Gatsby*'. *International Journal of the Classical Tradition* 6.2 (1999): 226–35.

—. 'The Ur-Gatsby'. *International Journal of the Classical Tradition* 6.4 (2000): 577–84.

Brooks, Cleanth. 'The Community and the Pariah'. *Virginia Quarterly Review* 39.2 (Spring 1963): 236–53.

—. 'History and the Sense of the Tragic'. *William Faulkner's 'Absalom, Absalom!': A Casebook.* Ed. Fred Hobson. Oxford: Oxford University Press, 2003. 17–46.

Brown, David. *Paradise Lost: A Life of F. Scott Fitzgerald.* Cambridge, MA: Belknap-Harvard University Press, 2017.

Brown, E. K. *Willa Cather: A Critical Biography.* New York: Knopf, 1953.

Bruccoli, Matthew. Afterword and Notes. Fitzgerald, *Trimalchio: A Facsimile Edition* 1–13.

—. *F. Scott Fitzgerald: A Life in Letters.* New York: Scribners, 2014.

—. *Some Sort of Epic Grandeur: The Life of F. Scott Fitzgerald.* London: Hodder & Stoughton, 1981.

Bruccoli, Matthew and Judith Baughman. *Conversations with F. Scott Fitzgerald.* Jackson: University Press of Mississippi, 2004.

Bryer, Jackson, Ruth Prigozy and Milton Stern. *F. Scott Fitzgerald in the Twenty-First Century.* Tuscaloosa: University of Alabama Press, 2003.

Brylowski, Walter. *Faulkner's Olympian Laugh: Myth in the Novels.* Detroit: Wayne State University Press, 1968.

Buell, Lawrence. *The Dream of the Great American Novel.* Cambridge, MA: Harvard University Press, 2014.

Bulfinch, Thomas. *Bulfinch's Mythology.* Ed. Richard Martin. New York: HarperCollins, 1991.

Butler, Robert. 'Dante's *Inferno* and Ellison's *Invisible Man*: A Study in Literary Continuity'. *The Critical Response to Ralph Ellison's 'Invisible Man'.* Ed. Robert Butler. Westport, CT: Greenwood Press, 2000. 95–105.

Callahan, John. Introduction to *Flying Home.* Ellison, *Flying Home* ix–xxxiii.

Callahan, John and Marc Conner, eds. *The Selected Letters of Ralph Ellison.* New York: Random House, 2019.

Canales, Gustavo Sáncho. 'The Classical World and Modern Academia in Philip Roth's *The Human Stain*'. *Philip Roth Studies* 5.1 (2009): 111–28.

—. '"There Is a Bomb Blast in the Most Elegant Greek Revival House": Classical Motifs in Philip Roth's *American Pastoral*'. *Reading Philip Roth's 'American Pastoral'*. Ed. Velichka Ivanova. Toulouse: Presses Universitaires du Mirail, 2011. 205–19.

Carlyle, Thomas. *Heroes, Hero-Worship and the Heroic in History*. London: Chapman & Hall, 1840.

Cassuto, Leonard, ed. *The Cambridge History of the American Novel*. Cambridge: Cambridge University Press, 2011.

Cather, Willa. *April Twilights and Other Poems*. New York: Knopf, 2013.

—. 'Cather 10'. Manuscript of *Sapphira and the Slave Girl*. Willa Cather Collection, Drew University Library.

—. *A Lost Lady*. Scholarly edition. Lincoln: University of Nebraska Press, 1997.

—. *My Ántonia*. Scholarly edition. Lincoln: University of Nebraska Press, 1994.

—. *My Ántonia*. London: Vintage, 1994.

—. 'The Namesake' [poem]. Cather, *April Twilights* 83–4.

—. 'The Namesake' [story]. Cather, *Stories, Poems and Other Writings* 52–63.

—. *Not Under Forty*. Cather, *Stories, Poems and Other Writings* 881–4.

—. *On Writing: Critical Studies on Writing as an Art*. New York: Knopf, 1949.

—. *One of Ours*. London: Virago, 1987.

—. *The Professor's House*. Scholarly edition. Lincoln: University of Nebraska Press, 2002.

—. *Sapphira and the Slave Girl*. Scholarly edition. Lincoln: University of Nebraska Press, 2009.

—. *The Song of the Lark*. London: Virago, 1993.

—. *Stories, Poems and Other Writings*. New York: Library of America, 1992.

Clark, Keith. 'Man on the Margin: Lucas Beauchamp and the Limitations of Space'. *Faulkner Journal* 6.1 (Fall 1990): 67–79.

Collar, William and Moses Daniell. *Collar and Daniell's First Year Latin*. London: Forgotten Books, 2015.

Collins, Carvel. 'The Pairing of *The Sound and the Fury* and *As I Lay Dying*'. *Princeton University Library Chronicle* 18.1 (1957): 114–23.

Conner, Marc. 'Father Abraham: Ellison's Agon with the Fathers in *Three Days Before the Shooting . . .*'. Conner and Morel 167–93.

—. 'Introduction: Aesthetics and the African-American Novel'. *The Aesthetics of Toni Morrison: Speaking the Unspeakable*. Ed. Conner. Jackson: University Press of Mississippi, 2000. ix–xxviii.

—. 'Modernity and the Homeless: Toni Morrison and the Fictions of Modernism'. Seward and Tally 19–32.

—. 'Wild Women and Graceful Girls: Toni Morrison's Winter's Tale'. *Nature, Woman, and the Art of Politics*. Ed. Eduardo Velásquez. New York and Oxford: Rowman & Littlefield, 2000. 341–67.

Conner, Marc and Lucas Morel. Introduction to *The New Territory*. Conner and Morel 3–36.

—, eds. *The New Territory: Ralph Ellison and the Twenty-First Century*. Jackson: University Press of Mississippi, 2016.

Connolly, Joy. 'Classical Culture and the Early American Democratic Style'. Stephens and Vasunia 78–99.

Cook, William and James Tatum. *African American Writers and Classical Tradition*. Chicago: University of Chicago Press, 2010.

Cornell, Tim. 'Sabini'. Hornblower and Spawforth 1342.

Cowart, David. '"Babylon Revisited": The Tragedy of Charlie Wales'. *Journal of the Short Story in English* 3 (1984): 21–7.

—. 'Faulkner and Joyce in Toni Morrison's *Song of Solomon*'. *American Literature* 62.1 (1990): 87–100.

Cowley, Malcolm. Introduction to *The Portable Faulkner*. Ed. Cowley. New York: Viking Press, 1946. 1–24.

Crable, Bryan. 'Ellison's Appropriation of Jane Ellen Harrison's *Themis*: From Sacrifice to Sacrament'. Roynon and Conner, pages not yet known.

—. 'Who Invents Rituals? Ralph Ellison Reads Lord Raglan'. *Literature of the Americas* 5 (2018): 27–42.

Crèvecœur, J. Hector St. John. *Letters from an American Farmer*. New York and London: Penguin, 1986.

Crowell, Ellen. 'The Picture of Charles Bon: Oscar Wilde's Trip through Faulkner's Yoknapatawpha'. *Modern Fiction Studies* 50.3 (Fall 2004): 595–633.

Curran, Leo. 'Rape and Rape Victims in the *Metamorphoses*'. *Women and the Ancient World: The Arethusa Papers*. Ed. John Peradotto and John Sullivan. Albany: SUNY Press, 1984. 263–86.

Curtin, William, ed. *The World and the Parish: Willa Cather's Articles and Reviews, 1893–1902*. 2 vols. Lincoln: University of Nebraska Press, 1970.

Dahl, Curtis. 'An American Georgic: Willa Cather's *My Ántonia*'. *Comparative Literature* 7.1 (1955): 43–51.

Daly, Jennifer. Issue 6 Editorial: Special Issue on Marilynne Robinson. *Irish Journal of American Studies*. 2017. <http://ijas.iaas.ie/issue-6-editorial/> (last accessed 9 June 2020).

Daniel, Anne Margaret. '"Blue as the Sky, Gentlemen": Fitzgerald's Princeton through *The Prince*'. Bryer et al. 10–37.

Dante. *Divine Comedy*. <https://digitaldante.columbia.edu/dante/divine-comedy/> (last accessed 29 April 2020).

Daugherty, Christa and James West III. 'Josephine Baker, Petronius, and the Text of "Babylon Revisited"'. *F. Scott Fitzgerald Review* 1.1 (2002): 3–15.

Davis, Angela. *Angela Davis: An Autobiography*. New York: Random House, 1974.

De La Piedra, Benji. 'Ellison's White Liberal Rhinehart: The Negro American Core of Book I of *Three Days Before the Shooting . . .*'. *Literature of the Americas* 5 (2018): 132–50.

Demetrakapoulos, Stephanie and Karla Holloway. *New Dimensions of Spirituality: A Biracial and Bicultural Reading of the Novels of Toni Morrison*. New York: Greenwood Press, 1987.

Denard, Carolyn. *Toni Morrison: Conversations*. Jackson: University Press of Mississippi, 2008.

Deneen, Patrick. 'Was Huck Greek? The "Odyssey" of Mark Twain'. *Modern Language Studies* 32.2 (2002): 35–44.

Dennis, Helen. Introduction. Dennis, *Willa Cather* iii–xi.

—. '"Tonight Mrs Forrester Began with 'Once upon a Time'": Origins and Traces in the Work of Willa Cather'. Dennis, *Willa Cather* 33–52.

—, ed. *Willa Cather and European Cultural Influences*. Lewiston, NY: Edward Mellen Press, 1996.

Devlin, Paul. 'A Literary Archaeology of Reverend Hickman's Juneteenth Sermon in Ralph Ellison's Second Novel'. *Literature of the Americas* 5 (2018): 116–31.

Dimino, Andrea. 'Toni Morrison and William Faulkner: Remapping Culture'. Kolmerten et al. 31–47.

Dodds, E. R. *The Greeks and the Irrational*. Berkeley: University of California Press, 1951.

Domestico, Anthony. '"Imagine a Carthage Sown with Salt": Creeds, Memory, and Vision in Marilynne Robinson's *Housekeeping*'. *Literature & Theology* 28.1 (2014): 92–109.

Donaldson, Susan. 'Faulkner's Versions of Pastoral, Gothic and the Sublime'. *A Companion to Faulkner*. Ed. Richard Moreland. Hoboken: Wiley Blackwell, 2007. 351–72.

Donnell, Alison. 'Signifying the Subaltern: Europe's Others in Selected Texts of Willa Cather'. Dennis 53–66.

Donovan, Josephine. *After the Fall: The Demeter-Persephone Myth in Wharton, Cather, and Glasgow*. University Park: Pennsylvania State University Press, 1989.

Dougherty, Carol. 'Homecomings and Housekeepings: Homer's *Odyssey* and Marilynne Robinson's *Housekeeping*'. *Odyssean Identities in Modern Cultures: The Journey Home*. Ed. Hunter Gardner and Sheila Murnaghan. Columbus: Ohio State University Press, 2014. 281–302.

—. *Prometheus*. New York: Routledge, 2006.

Draper, R. D. *Tragedy: Developments in Criticism*. Basingstoke: Macmillan, 1980.

Drennan, William. '"I Know Old Niceros and He's No Liar": Nick Carraway's Name in *The Great Gatsby*'. *ANQ* 2.4 (1989): 145–6.

duBois, Page. *Sowing the Body: Pyschoanalysis and Ancient Representations of Women*. Chicago: University of Chicago Press, 1988.

Duvall, John. 'Doe Hunting and Masculinity: *Song of Solomon* and *Go Down, Moses*'. *Toni Morrison's 'Song of Solomon': A Casebook*. Ed. Jan Furman. Oxford: Oxford University Press, 2003. 113–36.

—. 'Morrison and the Anxiety of Faulknerian Influence'. Kolmerten et al. 3–16.

—. 'Silencing Women in "The Fire and the Hearth" and "Tomorrow"'. *College Literature* 16.1 (1989): 75–82.

Eaton, Alice Knox, Maxine Montgomery and Shirley Stave. *New Critical Essays on Toni Morrison's 'God Help the Child': Race, Culture, and History*. Jackson: University Press of Mississippi, 2020.

Edwards, Catharine, ed. *Roman Presences: Receptions of Rome in European Culture, 1789–1945*. Cambridge: Cambridge University Press, 1999.

Eliot, T. S. '*Ulysses*, Order, and Myth'. Rainey 165–7.

—. *The Waste Land*. Rainey 123–42.

Ellison, Ralph. *Collected Essays*. New York: Modern Library, 2003.

—. *Flying Home and Other Stories*. London: Penguin, 1996.

—. *Invisible Man*. New York: Vintage, 1992.

—. *Three Days Before the Shooting* . . . New York: Modern Library, 2011.

—. *Trading Twelves: The Selected Letters of Ralph Ellison and Albert Murray*. New York: Vintage, 2001.

Endres, Nikolai. 'Petronius in West Egg: *The Satyricon* and *The Great Gatsby*'. Futre Pinheiro and Harrison 111–24.

Enterline, Lynn. *The Rhetoric of the Body from Ovid to Shakespeare*. Cambridge: Cambridge University Press, 2000.

Falkner, Murry. *The Falkners of Mississippi: A Memoir*. Baton Rouge: Louisiana State University Press, 1967.

Farmer, David. *Oxford Dictionary of Saints*. 5th edn. Oxford: Oxford University Press, 2004.

Faulkner, William. *Absalom, Absalom!* New York: Vintage, 1990.

—. 'Compson 1699–1945' ('The Compson Appendix'). Faulkner, *The Sound and the Fury* 203–15.

—. *Go Down, Moses*. New York: Vintage, 1990.

—. *Light in August*. New York: Vintage, 1990.

—. *The Sound and the Fury*. New York: Norton, 1994.

Ferrero, Guglielmo. *Ancient Rome and Modern America: A Comparative Study of Morals and Manners*. New York: G. Putnam, 1914.

Fertik, Harriet and Mattias Hanses, eds. *Above the Veil: Re-visiting the Classicism of W. E. B. Du Bois*. Special issue. *International Journal of the Classical Tradition* 26.1 (2019).

Fitzgerald, F. Scott. *The Beautiful and Damned*. Cambridge: Cambridge University Press, 2014.

—. *The Crack-Up*. New York: New Directions, 1993.

—. *Flappers and Philosophers: The Collected Short Stories*. London: Penguin, 2010.

—. *F. Scott Fitzgerald's Ledger*. Washington, DC: NCR Microcard Editions, 1972.

—. *The Great Gatsby*. Cambridge: Cambridge University Press, 1991.

—. *Last Kiss*. Cambridge: Cambridge University Press, 2017.

—. *Spires and Gargoyles: Early Writings, 1909–1919*. Cambridge: Cambridge University Press, 2010.

—. *Tender Is the Night*. Cambridge: Cambridge University Press, 2012.

—. *This Side of Paradise*. Cambridge: Cambridge University Press, 2012.

—. *Trimalchio: An Early Version of 'The Great Gatsby'*. Ed. James West. Cambridge: Cambridge University Press, 2002.

—. *Trimalchio: A Facsimile Edition of the Original Galley Proofs for 'The Great Gatsby'*. Ed. Matthew Bruccoli. Columbia: University of South Carolina Press, 2000.

Foley, Barbara. *Wrestling with the Left: The Making of Ralph Ellison's 'Invisible Man'*. Durham, NC: Duke University Press, 2010.

Foley, Helene. *Re-imagining Greek Tragedy on the American Stage*. Berkeley: University of California Press, 2012.

Forrest, Susanna. *The Age of the Horse: An Equine Journey through Human History*. London: Atlantic, 2016.

Foster, Richard. 'Time's Exile: Dick Diver and the Heroic Idea'. *Mosaic* 8.3 (1975): 89–108.

Freiert, William. 'Classical Themes in Toni Morrison's *Song of Solomon*'. *Helios* 10 (1988): 161–70.

Freud, Sigmund. *Civilization and its Discontents*. London: Penguin, 2002.

Futre Pinheiro, Marília and Stephen Harrison, eds. *Fictional Traces: Receptions of the Ancient Novel*. Vol. 2. Groningen: Barkhuis Publishing, 2011.

Gardner, Helen, ed. *New Oxford Book of English Verse, 1250–1950*. Oxford: Oxford University Press, 1972.

Gates, Henry Louis. *The Signifying Monkey: A Theory of African-American Literary Criticism*. New York and Oxford: Oxford University Press, 1988.

Gillin, Edward. 'Princeton, Pragmatism and Fitzgerald's Sentimental Journey'. Bryer et al. 38–53.

Gilroy, Paul. *The Black Atlantic: Modernity and Double Consciousness*. London and New York: Verso, 1993.

—. 'Living Memory: An Interview with Toni Morrison'. *Small Acts: Thoughts on the Politics of Black Cultures*. London: Serpent's Tail, 1993. 175–82.

Giltrow, Janet and David Stouck. 'Pastoral Mode and Language in *The Great Gatsby*'. Bryer et al. 139–52.

Girard, Philippe. *Toussaint Louverture: A Revolutionary Life*. London: Basic, 2016.

Glaser, Jennifer. 'The Jew in the Canon: Reading Race and Literary History in Philip Roth's *The Human Stain*'. *PMLA* 123.5 (2008): 1465–78.

Godden, Richard. '*Absalom, Absalom!*, Haiti and Labor History: Reading Unreadable Revolutions'. *ELH* 61.3 (1994): 685–720.

—. 'Agricultural Adjustment, Revenants, Remnants and Counter-Revolution in Faulkner's "The Fire and the Hearth"'. *Faulkner Journal* 12.2 (1997): 41–55.

Goff, Barbara and Michael Simpson. *Crossroads in the Black Aegean: Oedipus, Antigone and Dramas of the African Diaspora*. Oxford: Oxford University Press, 2007.

Goings, Kenneth and Eugene O'Connor. '"My Name is Nobody": African-American and Classical Modes of the Trickster in Ralph Ellison's *Invisible Man*'. *Lit* 1.3 (1990): 217–27.

Good, Dorothy Ballweg. '"A Romance and a Reading List": The Literary References in *This Side of Paradise*'. *Fitzgerald/Hemingway Annual* (1976): 35–64.

Goodrich, Samuel Griswold. *Peter Parley's Universal History, on the Basis of Geography*. London: William Tegg, 1881.

Gordon, Andrew. 'When in Rome: Philip Roth's *Portnoy's Complaint* and Bernard Malamud's *Picture of Fidelman*'. *Philip Roth Studies* 4.1 (2008): 39–46.

Graham, Maryemma and Amritjit Singh, eds. *Conversations with Ralph Ellison*. Jackson: University Press of Mississippi, 1995.

Gray, Richard. *The Life of William Faulkner: A Critical Biography*. Oxford: Blackwell, 1994.

Greenwood, Emily. 'Re-rooting the Classical Tradition: New Directions in Black Classicism'. *Classical Receptions Journal* 1.1 (2009): 87–103.

Guillory, John. *Cultural Capital: The Problem of Literary Canon Formation*. Chicago: University of Chicago Press, 1993.

Gupta, Nikhil. 'Fashioning Bernice and Belinda: F. Scott Fitzgerald's Revision of Alexander Pope's Mock Epic'. *Texas Studies in Literature and Language* 57.1 (2015): 31–52.

Gwin, Minrose. 'Her Shape, His Hand: The Spaces of African-American Women in *Go Down, Moses*'. Wagner-Martin 73–100.

Gwynn, Frederick and Joseph Blotner, eds. *Faulkner in the University: Class Conferences at the University of Virginia, 1957–58*. Charlottesville: University of Virginia Press, 1959.

Haley, Shelley. 'Self-Definition, Community and Resistance: Euripides' *Medea* and Toni Morrison's *Beloved*'. *Thamyris* 2.2 (1995): 177–206.

Hall, Edith. Introduction. Hall et al. 1–40.

—. 'The Migrant Muse: Greek Drama as Feminist Window on American Identity, 1900–1925'. Bosher et al. 149–65.

—. 'The Problem with Prometheus: Myth, Abolition, and Radicalism'. Hall et al. 209–46.

Hall, Edith, Richard Alston and Justine McConnell, eds. *Ancient Slavery and Abolition: From Hobbes to Hollywood*. Oxford: Oxford University Press, 2011.

Hamblin, Robert. 'Mythic and Archetypal Criticism'. *Companion to Faulkner Studies*. Ed. Charles Peek and Robert Hamblin. Westport, CT: Greenwood Press, 2004. 1–26.

Hamilton, Edith. *Mythology: Timeless Tales of Gods and Heroes*. New York: Mass Market, 2011.

Hardie, Philip. *Rumour and Renown: Representations of 'Fama' in Western Literature*. Cambridge: Cambridge University Press, 2012.

Hardwick, Lorna. 'Fuzzy Connections: Classical Texts and Modern Poetry'. *Tradition, Translation, Trauma: The Classic and the Modern*. Ed. Jan Parker and Timothy Mathews. Oxford: Oxford University Press, 2011. 39–60.

—. *Reception Studies*. Oxford: Oxford University Press, 2003.

Hardwick, Lorna and Stephen Harrison, eds. *Classics in the Modern World: A Democratic Turn?* Oxford: Oxford University Press, 2013.

Harris, Leslie. 'Myth as Structure in Toni Morrison's *Song of Solomon*'. *MELUS* 7.3 (1980): 69–76.

Harrison, Stephen. 'Petronius Arbiter'. Hornblower and Spawforth 1149–50.

Hart, Jeffrey. *The Living Moment: Modernism in a Broken World*. Evanston, IL: Northwestern University Press, 2012.

Hawkins, Tom. 'The Veil, the Cave and the Fire-Bringer'. *International Journal of the Classical Tradition* 26.1 (2019): 38–53.

Hayes, Patrick. 'Not Quite *Letting Go*: Rethinking the "Tragic Sense of Life" in Roth's First Novel'. *Philip Roth Studies* 9.2 (2013): 7–22.

—. '"To Rake Suburban Life over the Barbecue Coals": Cultural Criticism in Philip Roth's Early Fiction and Journalism'. Pozorski 97–118.

Hays, Peter L. '*As I Lay Dying* and the *Odyssey*'. *Classical and Modern Literature* 18.3 (1998): 241–5.

Hedrick, Tace and Marilynne Robinson. 'On Influence and Appropriation'. *Iowa Review* 22.1 (1992): 1–7.

Heseltine, Michael. Introduction. Petronius ix–xlvi.

Hesiod. *Theogony* and *Works and Days*. Trans. M. L. West. Oxford: Oxford University Press, 2008.

Hickman, Jared. *Black Prometheus: Race and Radicalism in the Age of Atlantic Slavery*. Oxford: Oxford University Press, 2016.

Hinds, Stephen. *Allusion and Intertext: Dynamics of Appropriation in Roman Poetry*. Cambridge: Cambridge University Press, 1998.

Hirsch, Marianne. *The Mother/Daughter Plot: Narrative, Psychoanalysis, Feminism*. Bloomington: Indiana University Press, 1989.

Høgsbjerg, Christian, ed. *Toussaint Louverture by C. L. R. James*. Durham, NC: Duke University Press, 2012.

Hokom, Matthew. 'Pompeii and the House of the Tragic Poet in *A Lost Lady*'. *Cather Studies* 10 (2015): 349–73.

Holland-Toll, Linda J. 'Absence Absolute: The Recurring Patten of Faulknerian Tragedy'. *Mississippi Quarterly* 51.3 (1998): 435–52.

Homer. *The Iliad*. 2 vols. Trans. A. Murray. Rev. William Wyatt. Cambridge, MA: Harvard University Press, 1999.

—. *The Odyssey*. 2 vols. Trans. A. Murray. Rev. George Dimock. Cambridge, MA: Harvard University Press, 1998.

Hornblower, Simon and Antony Spawforth, eds. *Oxford Classical Dictionary*. 3rd edn rev. Oxford: Oxford University Press, 2003.

'Howard University Bulletin'. College of Liberal Arts 1951–2, 1952–3. Vol. 51.8. 1 February 1953.

Hughes, Lisa. 'Gender, Sexuality and Writing in Plato and Cather'. *Classical and Modern Literature* 22.1 (2002): 49–60.

Hungerford, Amy. 'Religion and the Twentieth-Century American Novel'. Cassuto 732–5.

Hutton, Clare. *Serial Encounters: 'Ulysses' and 'The Little Review'*. Oxford: Oxford University Press, 2019.

Iannone, Carol. 'An American Tragedy'. *Commentary* 104.2 (1997): 55–7.

Jacks, L. V. 'The Classics and Willa Cather'. *Prairie Schooner* 35.4 (1961–2): 289–96.

Jackson, Lawrence. *Ralph Ellison: Emergence of Genius*. New York: Wiley, 2002.

James, Pearl. 'History and Masculinity in F. Scott Fitzgerald's *This Side of Paradise*'. *Modern Fiction Studies* 51.2 (2005): 1–33.

Jennings, La Vinia Delois. *Toni Morrison and the Idea of Africa*. Cambridge: Cambridge University Press, 2008.

Jewell, Andrew and Janis Stout, eds. *The Selected Letters of Willa Cather*. New York: Knopf, 2013.

Jones, Bessie. 'Greek Tragic Motifs in *Song of Solomon*'. *The World of Toni Morrison: Explorations in Literary Criticism*. Ed. Bessie Jones and Audrey Vinson. Dubuque: Kendall Hunt, 1985. 103–14.

Joyce, James. *Portrait of the Artist as a Young Man. The Essential James Joyce*. London: Triad Gratfton, 1989. 175–366.

—. *Ulysses*. London: Penguin, 1992.

Kalisch, Michael. 'A Late Adventure of the Feelings: Eulogizing Male Intimacy in *I Married a Communist* and *The Human Stain*'. *Philip Roth Studies* 12.2 (2016): 83–96.

Kartiganer, Donald M. *The Fragile Thread: The Meaning of Form in Faulkner's Novels*. Amherst: University of Massachusetts Press, 1979.

—. 'The Role of Myth in *Absalom, Absalom!*'. *Modern Fiction Studies* 9 (1964): 357–69.

Keats, John. 'On First Looking into Chapman's Homer'. Gardner 602.

Kelly, Adam. 'Imagining Tragedy: Philip Roth's *The Human Stain*'. *Philip Roth Studies* 6.2 (2010): 189–205.

Kennedy, Gerald J. 'Fitzgerald's Expatriate Years and the European Stories'. Prigozy 118–42.

King James Bible. Cambridge: Cambridge University Press (undated).

Kolmerten, Carol, Judith Bryant Wittenberg and Stephen M. Ross, eds. *Unflinching Gaze: Morrison and Faulkner Re-envisioned*. Jackson: University Press of Mississippi, 1997.

Kreiswirth, Martin. 'Plots and Counterplots: The Structure of *Light in August*'. Millgate 55–79.

Kuehl, John. 'Scott Fitzgerald's Reading'. *Princeton University Library Chronicle* 22.2 (1961): 58–90.

Kuhnle, John H. '*The Great Gatsby* as Pastoral Elegy'. *Fitzgerald/Hemingway Annual* (1978): 141–54.

Lake, Sean and Theresa Levy. 'Preserving and Commodifying the Past: Allusions to the Classical World in *The Professor's House*'. *Willa Cather Review* 51.1 (2007): 15–20.

Lateiner, Donald. 'Mythic and Non-Mythic Artists in Ovid's *Metamorphoses*'. *Ramus* 13.1 (1984): 1–30.

Lee, Hermione. *Willa Cather: A Life Saved Up*. London: Virago, 1989.

Levine, Lawrence. *Black Culture and Black Consciousness: Afro-American Thought from Slavery to Freedom*. Oxford: Oxford University Press, 1977.

Levins, Lynn Gartrell. *Faulkner's Heroic Design: The Yoknapatawpha Novels*. Athens: University of Georgia Press, 1976.

Lewis, Edith. *Willa Cather Living: A Personal Record*. New York: Knopf, 1953.

Lewis, R. W. B. *The American Adam: Innocence, Tragedy and Tradition in the Nineteenth Century*. Chicago: University of Chicago Press, 1955.

Lind, Ilse Dusoir. 'The Design and Meaning of *Absalom, Absalom!*'. *PMLA* 70.5 (1955): 887–912.

Lindemann, Marilee, ed. *The Cambridge Companion to Willa Cather*. Cambridge: Cambridge University Press, 2005.

Lindenberg, Nicole. '"What if Movie is Bliss's Own Life?": The Symbolic Violence of the Movie in Ralph Ellison's Unfinished Second Novel, *Three Days Before the Shooting . . .*'. *Literature of the Americas* 5 (2018): 116–31.

List, Robert. *Dedalus in Harlem: The Joyce-Ellison Connection*. Washington, DC: University Press of America, 1982.

Little, Alan. *Myth and Society in Attic Drama*. New York: Columbia University Press, 1942.

Lively, Genevieve. 'Reading Resistance in Ovid's *Metamorphoses*'. *Ovidian Transformations: Essays on Ovid's 'Metamorphoses' and its Reception*. Ed. Stephen Hinds, Alessandro Barchiesi and Philip Hardie. Cambridge: Cambridge Philological Society, 1999. 197–213.

Locke, Alain. 'The New Negro'. *The New Negro: Voices of the Harlem Renaissance*. Ed. Locke. New York: Simon & Schuster, 1992. 3–18.

Longley, John Lewis, Jr. *The Tragic Mask: A Study of Faulkner's Heroes*. Chapel Hill: University of North Carolina Press, 1963.

Losemann, Volker. 'The Nazi Concept of Rome'. Edwards 221–35.

Ludot-Vlasak, Ronan. *Essais sur Melville et l'Antiquité classique: 'Etranger en son lieu'*. Paris: Honoré Champion, 2018.

Lutz, Tom. 'Cather and the Regional Imagination'. Cassuto 437–51.

Lyons, Bonnie. 'Philip Roth's American Tragedies'. *Turning Up the Flame: Philip Roth's Later Novels*. Ed. Jay Halio and Ben Siegel. Newark: University of Delaware Press, 2005. 125–30.

McCluskey, Alan. 'Cosmopolitanism and Tragic Silence in Philip Roth's *The Human Stain*'. *Philip Roth Studies* 10.2 (2014): 7–19.

McConnell, Justine. *Black Odysseys: The Homeric Odyssey in the African Diaspora since 1939*. Oxford: Oxford University Press, 2013.

—. 'Invisible Odysseus: A Homeric Hero in Ralph Ellison's *Invisible Man*?'. *Zero to Hero, Hero to Zero: In Search of the Classical Hero*. Ed. Lydia Langerwerf and Cressida Ryan. Newcastle: Cambridge Scholars Publishing, 2010. 161–82.

—. 'Postcolonial *Sparagmos*: Toni Morrison's *Sula* and Wole Soyinka's *The Bacchae of Euripides: A Communion Rite*'. *Classical Receptions Journal* 8.2 (2016): 133–54.

McConnell, Justine and Edith Hall, eds. *Ancient Greek Myth in World Fiction since 1989*. London: Bloomsbury, 2016.

McGowan, Grace. '"I Know I Can't Change the Future, but I Can Change the Past": Toni Morrison, Robin Coste Lewis, and the Classical Tradition'. *Contemporary Women's Writing* 13.3 (2019): 339–56.

McGowan, Philip. 'Reading Fitzgerald Reading Keats'. Blazek and Rattray 204–20.

MacKendrick, Paul. '*The Great Gatsby* and Trimalchio'. *Classical Journal* 45.7 (1950): 307–14.

MacKethan, Lucinda. 'The Grandfather Clause: Reading the Legacy from "The Bear" to *Song of Solomon*'. Kolmerten et al. 99–114.

McLelland, Joseph. *Prometheus Rebound: The Irony of Atheism*. Waterloo: Wilfred Laurier University Press, 1988.

McQuade, Molly. *An Unsentimental Education: Writers and Chicago*. Chicago: University of Chicago Press, 1995.

Maddox, Lucy. *Locating American Studies: The Evolution of a Discipline*. Baltimore: Johns Hopkins University Press, 1999.

Malamud, Margaret. *African Americans and the Classics: Antiquity, Abolition and Activism*. London: I. B. Tauris, 2016.

—. *Ancient Rome and Modern America*. Malden, MA: Wiley-Blackwell, 2009.

Malik, Shushma. 'The Criminal Emperors of Ancient Rome and Oscar Wilde's "True Historical Sense"'. Riley et al. 305–21.

Marcus, Greil and Werner Sollors, eds. *New Literary History of America*. Cambridge, MA: Harvard University Press, 2009.

Mariotti, Shannon and Joseph Lane, eds. *A Political Companion to Marilynne Robinson*. Lexington: University Press of Kentucky, 2016.

Markowitz, Norman. 'William Faulkner's "Tragic Legend": Southern History and *Absalom, Absalom!*'. *Minnesota Review* 17 (1981): 104–17.

Marlowe, Christopher. 'The Passionate Shepherd to his Love'. Gardner 109–10.

Marx, Leo. *The Machine in the Garden: Technology and the Pastoral Ideal in America*. Oxford: Oxford University Press, 1964.

Matthews, John. 'Touching Race in *Go Down, Moses*'. Wagner-Martin 21–48.

—, ed. *The New Cambridge Companion to William Faulkner*. Cambridge: Cambridge University Press, 2015.

Mauro, Aaron. 'Ordinary Happiness: Marilynne Robinson's Tragic Economies of Debt and Forgiveness'. *symploke* 22.1–2 (2014): 149–66.

May, Regine and Stephen Harrison, eds. *Cupid and Psyche: The Reception of Apuleius' Love Story since 1600*. Cambridge and Berlin: De Gruyter, 2020.

Melton, Barbara Lawatsch. 'Appropriations of Cicero and Cato in the Making of American Civic Identity'. Hardwick and Harrison 79–88.

Melville, Herman. *Moby-Dick*. London: Penguin, 1994.

Merrill, Robert. '*Tender Is the Night* as a Tragic Action'. *Texas Studies in Literature and Language* 25.4 (1983): 597–615.

Michaels, Walter Benn. *Our America: Nativism, Modernism, and Pluralism*. Durham, NC: Duke University Press, 1995.

Mikalson, Jon. 'Hestia'. Hornblower and Spawforth 701.

Miller, Stephen. *The Prytaneion: Its Function and Architectural Form*. Berkeley: University of California Press, 1978.

Millgate, Michael, ed. *New Essays on 'Light in August'*. Cambridge: Cambridge University Press, 1987.

Milton, John. *Paradise Lost*. London: Penguin, 1989.

Miner, Madonne. 'Lady No Longer Sings the Blues: Rape, Madness, and Silence in *The Bluest Eye*'. *Modern Critical Views: Toni Morrison*. Ed. Harold Bloom. New York: Chelsea House, 1990. 85–99.

Monoson, Sara. 'Recollecting Aristotle: Pro-Slavery Thought in Antebellum America and the Argument of *Politics* Book I'. Hall et al. 247–78.

Montgomery, Maxine. '"You Not the Woman I Want": Toni Morrison's *God Help the Child* and the Legend of Galatea'. Eaton et al. 106–22.

Morley, Catherine. *Modern American Literature*. Edinburgh: Edinburgh University Press, 2012.

—. *The Quest for Epic in Contemporary American Fiction: John Updike, Philip Roth and Don DeLillo*. New York: Routledge, 2008.

—. 'Willa Cather and Dutch Golden Age Painting'. *Modernist Cultures* 11.1 (2016): 118–36.

Morrison, Toni. *Beloved*. New York: Vintage, 2005.

—. *The Bluest Eye*. New York: Vintage, 1999.

—. 'City Limits, Village Values: Concepts of the Neighbourhood in Black Fiction'. *Literature and the American Urban Experience: Essays on the City and Literature*. Ed. Michael Jayne and Ann Chalmers Watts. Manchester: Manchester University Press, 1981. 35–44.

—. *God Help the Child*. London: Chatto & Windus, 2015.

—. *Home*. London: Chatto & Windus, 2012.

—. *Jazz*. New York: Vintage, 2005.

—. *The Origin of Others*. Cambridge, MA: Harvard University Press, 2017.

—. *Paradise*. New York: Vintage, 1999.

—. *Playing in the Dark: Whiteness and the Literary Imagination*. Cambridge, MA: Harvard University Press, 1992.

—. *Song of Solomon*. New York: Vintage, 2005.

—. *Sula*. New York: Vintage, 2005.

—. 'Unspeakable Things Unspoken: The Afro-American Presence in American Literature'. *Within the Circle: An Anthology of African American Literary Criticism from the Harlem Renaissance to the Present*. Ed. Angelyn Mitchell. Durham, NC: Duke University Press, 1994. 368–98.

— (Chloe Ardelia Wofford). 'Virginia Woolf's and William Faulkner's Treatment of the Alienated'. MA thesis. Cornell University, 1955.

—. *What Moves at the Margin: Selected Nonfiction*. Ed. Carolyn Denard. Jackson: University Press of Mississippi, 2008.

Mortimer, Gail. 'Faulkner's Playful Bestiary: Seeing Gender through Ovidian Eyes'. *Faulkner at 100: Retrospect and Prospect*. Ed. Donald M. Kartiganer and Ann J. Abadie. Jackson: University Press of Mississippi, 2000. 53–9.

Murphy, John. 'Euripides' *Hippolytus* and Cather's *A Lost Lady*'. *American Literature* 53.1 (1981): 72–86.

Murray, Gilbert. *The Classical Tradition in Poetry*. Oxford: Oxford University Press, 1927.

Muse, Clifford, Jr. 'The Howard University Players'. *Howard University Archives Net*. February 2001. <http://www.huarchivesnet.howard.edu/howarcorSketch1.htm> (last accessed 7 May 2020).

Nadel, Alan. *Invisible Criticism: Ralph Ellison and the American Canon*. Iowa City: University of Iowa Press, 1988.

Nussbaum, Martha. 'Invisibility and Recognition: Sophocles's *Philoctetes* and Ellison's *Invisible Man*'. *Philosophy and Literature* 23 (1999): 257–83.

O'Brien, Sharon. *Willa Cather: The Emerging Voice*. New York and Oxford: Oxford University Press, 1987.

O'Connor, Margaret Anne. *Willa Cather: The Contemporary Reviews*. Cambridge: Cambridge University Press, 2001.

Orrells, Daniel, Gurminder Bhambra and Tessa Roynon, eds. *African Athena: New Agendas*. Oxford: Oxford University Press, 2011.

Oswald, Alice. *Memorial*. London: Faber, 2011.

Otten, Terry. 'Transfiguring the Narrative: *Beloved* from Melodrama to Tragedy'. *Critical Essays on Toni Morrison's 'Beloved'*. Ed. Barbara Solomon. Boston: G. K. Hall, 1998. 284–99.

Ovid. *Metamorphoses*. 2 vols. Trans. Frank Justus Miller. Rev. G. P. Goold. Cambridge, MA: Harvard University Press, 2004.

Pantel, Pauline Schmitt and Louise Bruit Zidman. *Religion in the Ancient Greek City*. Trans. Paul Cartledge. Cambridge: Cambridge University Press, 1989.

Parini, Jay. *One Matchless Time: A Life of William Faulkner*. New York: HarperCollins, 2004.

Park, Jungoh. 'Faulkner's Mythical Method: The Use of the Demeter/Persephone Myth'. *Feminist Studies in English Literature* 11.1 (2003): 121–41.

Parker, Robert. *Athenian Religion: A History*. Oxford: Clarendon Press, 1996.

—. *Miasma: Pollution and Purification in Early Greece*. Oxford: Clarendon Press, 1983.

Parrish, Timothy. *The Cambridge Companion to Philip Roth*. Cambridge: Cambridge University Press, 2007.

—. Introduction. Parrish, *Cambridge Companion* 1–8.

—. 'Ralph Ellison's *Three Days*: The Aesthetics of Political Change'. Conner and Morel 194–217.

Petrini, Mark. *The Child and the Hero: Coming of Age in Catullus and Vergil*. Ann Arbor: University of Michigan Press, 1997.

Petronius. *Satyricon*. Trans. Michael Heseltine. Rev. E. H. Warmington. *Petronius; Seneca, Apocolocyntosis*. Cambridge, MA: Harvard University Press, 1987. 1–384.

Phelan, James. 'Sethe's Choice: *Beloved* and the Ethics of Reading'. *Style* 32.2 (1998): 318–33.

Pierpont, Claudia Roth. *Roth Unbound: A Writer and his Books*. New York: Farrar, Straus and Giroux, 2014.

Pladott, Dinnah. 'William Faulkner: The Tragic Enigma'. *Journal of Narrative Theory* 15.2 (1985): 97–118.

Posnock, Ross, ed. *The Cambridge Companion to Ralph Ellison*. Cambridge: Cambridge University Press, 2005.

—. 'Introduction: Ellison's Joking'. Posnock, *Cambridge Companion* 1–10.

—. 'Mourning and Melancholy: Explaining the Ellison Animus'. Conner and Morel 285–93.

Pound, Ezra and Ernest Fenellosa. 'The Chinese Written Character as a Medium for Poetry'. Rainey 99–112.

Powell, David McKay. 'Henry Adams's Gothic Disposition in Fitzgerald's *This Side of Paradise*'. *F. Scott Fitzgerald Review* 10 (2012): 93–107.

Pozorski, Aimee, ed. *Critical Insights: Philip Roth*. Ipswich, MA: Grey House, 2013.

'President Obama and Marilynne Robinson: A Conversation in Iowa'. Part I. *New York Review of Books*. 5 November 2015. <https://www.nybooks.com/articles/2015/11/05/president-obama-marilynne-robinson-conversation/> (last accessed 29 April 2020).

'President Obama and Marilynne Robinson: A Conversation in Iowa'. Part II. *New York Review of Books*. 19 November 2015. <https://www.nybooks.com/articles/2015/11/19/president-obama-marilynne-robinson-conversation-2/> (last accessed 29 April 2020).

Prettejohn, Elizabeth. '"The Monstrous Diversion of a Show of Gladiators": Simeon Solomon's *Habet!*'. Edwards 157–72.

Prigozy, Ruth, ed. *The Cambridge Companion to F. Scott Fitzgerald*. Cambridge: Cambridge University Press, 2002.

Provencal, Vernon. 'Faulkner's Reception(s) of Apuleius' *Cupid and Psyche* in *The Reivers*'. May and Harrison 339–56.

Quinn, K. *Virgil's 'Aeneid': A Critical Description*. Exeter: Bristol Phoenix, 2005.

Rainey, Lawrence, ed. *Modernism: An Anthology*. Malden, MA, and Oxford: Blackwell, 2005. 165–7.

Rampersad, Arnold. *Ralph Ellison: A Biography*. New York: Vintage, 2008.

Rankine, Patrice. '*Black is, black ain't*: Classical Reception and Nothingness in Ralph Ellison, Derek Walcott and Wole Soyinka'. *Revue de littérature comparée* 344 (2012): 457–74.

—. 'Passing as Tragedy: Philip Roth's *The Human Stain*, the Oedipus Myth, and the Self-Made Man'. *Critique* 47.1 (2005): 101–12.

—. *Ulysses in Black: Ralph Ellison, Classicism, and African American Literature*. Madison: University of Wisconsin Press, 2006.

Ransom, John Crow. 'Reconstructed but Unregenerate'. *I'll Take My Stand: The South and the Agrarian Tradition*. Ed. Donald Davidson et al. New York: Peter Smith, 1951.1–27.

Raubichek, Walter. 'The Catholic Romanticism of *This Side of Paradise*'. Bryer et al. 55–64.

Raulff, Ulrich. *Farewell to the Horse: The Final Century of our Relationship*. Trans. Ruth Ahmedzai Kemp. London: Penguin, 2018.

Reinhold, Meyer. *Classica Americana: The Greek and Roman Heritage in the United States*. Detroit: Wayne State University Press, 1984.

Reynolds, Guy. *Willa Cather in Context: Progress, Race, Empire*. Basingstoke: Macmillan, 1996.

Ricciardi, Caterina. 'F. Scott Fitzgerald and Rome'. *RSA Journal* 10 (1999): 29–46.

Rich, Adrienne. *Adrienne Rich's Poetry and Prose*. New York: Norton, 1992.

Richard, Carl. *The Founders and the Classics: Greece, Rome and the American Enlightenment*. Cambridge, MA: Harvard University Press, 1994.

Richlin, Amy. 'Reading Ovid's Rapes'. *Pornography and Representation in Greece and Rome*. Ed. Richlin. Oxford: Oxford University Press, 1992. 158–79.

Ridley, R. T. 'To Be Taken with a Pinch of Salt: The Destruction of Carthage'. *Classical Philology* 81.2 (1986): 140–6.

Riley, Kathleen, Alastair Blanchard and Iarla Manny, eds. *Oscar Wilde and Classical Antiquity*. Oxford: Oxford University Press, 2018.

Ripley, George and Charles Dana, eds. *The New Cyclopædia of America*. Vol. IV. New York: Appleton, 1858.

Robinson, James, ed. *The Nag Hammadi Library in English*. 4th edn rev. New York: E. J. Brill, 1996.

Robinson, Marilynne. 'The Art of Fiction No. 198'. *Paris Review* 186 (2008): 37–65.

—. *The Death of Adam: Essays on Modern Thought*. New York: Picador, 2005.

—. *Gilead*. London: Virago, 2005.

—. *The Givenness of Things: Essays*. London: Virago, 2015.

—. *Home*. London: Virago, 2008.
—. *Housekeeping*. London: Faber, 2005.
—. *Lila*. London: Virago, 2014.
—. *When I Was a Child I Read Books*. London: Virago, 2012.
Robinson, Phyllis. *Willa: The Life of Willa Cather*. Garden City, NY: Doubleday, 1983.
Rogers, Gayle. 'American Modernisms in the World'. *The Cambridge Companion to the American Modernist Novel*. Ed. Joshua Miller. Cambridge: Cambridge University Press, 2015. 227–44.
Ronnick, Michele. 'Black Classicism: "Tell Them We Are Rising!"'. *Classical Journal* 106 (2011): 259–70.
—. 'Classicism, black'. *Encyclopedia Africana*. 2nd edn. 5 vols. Vol. 2. Ed. Henry Louis Gates and Kwame Anthony Appiah. Oxford: Oxford University Press, 2005. 120–3.
Roth, Philip. *American Pastoral*. New York: Vintage, 1998.
—. *The Facts: A Novelist's Autobiography*. London: Jonathan Cape, 1998.
—. *The Ghost Writer*. Roth, *Zuckerman Bound* 1–116.
—. *The Human Stain*. New York: Vintage, 2005.
—. 'I Have Fallen in Love with American Names'. *The New Yorker*. 5 and 12 June 2017. 46–7.
—. *I Married a Communist*. New York: Vintage, 1999.
—. *Letting Go. Novels and Stories 1959–62*. New York: Library of America, 2005. 227–896.
—. *Portnoy's Complaint. Novels 1967–72*. New York: Library of America, 2005. 277–486.
—. *Zuckerman Bound: A Trilogy and Epilogue: 1979–85*. New York: Library of America, 2007.
—. *Zuckerman Unbound*. Roth, *Zuckerman Bound* 117–262.
Roulston, Richard. 'Dick Diver's Plunge into the Roman Void: The Setting of *Tender Is the Night*'. *South Atlantic Quarterly* 77.1 (1978): 85–97.
—. 'Something Borrowed, Something New: A Discussion of Literary Influences on *The Great Gatsby*'. *Critical Essays on F. Scott Fitzgerald's 'The Great Gatsby'*. Ed. Scott Donaldson. Boston: G. K. Hall, 1984. 34–65.
Roynon, Tessa. 'The Africanness of Classicism'. Orrells et al. 381–97.
—. *The Cambridge Introduction to Toni Morrison*. Cambridge: Cambridge University Press, 2012.
—. 'Ellison and the *Metamorphoses* of Ovid: Transformative Allusions'. Roynon and Conner, pages not yet known.
—. '"Everything Can Change": Civil Rights, Civil War and Radical Transformation in *Home* and *Gilead*'. Sykes et al., pages not yet known.
—. 'Ovid, Race and Identity in E. L. Doctorow's *Ragtime* (1975) and Jeffrey Eugenides's *Middlesex* (2002)'. *Ovid and Identity in the Twenty-First*

Century. Special issue. *International Journal of the Classical Tradition* 26.4 (2019): 377–96.
—. *Toni Morrison and the Classical Tradition: Transforming American Culture*. Oxford: Oxford University Press, 2013.
—. '"We Are Individuals": Ralph Ellison and Selfhood in the 1940s'. *Ralph Ellison: Biographical Approaches*. Ed. Marc Conner. Forthcoming.
Roynon, Tessa and Marc Conner, eds. *Global Ralph Ellison: Transnational Aesthetics and Politics*. Oxford: Peter Lang, 2021.
Ryder, Mary Ruth. *Willa Cather and Classical Myth: The Search for a New Parnassus*. Lewiston, NY: Edward Mellen Press, 1990.
Safer, Elaine. 'Tragedy and Farce in Roth's *The Human Stain*'. *Critique: Studies in Contemporary Fiction* 43.3 (2002): 211–27.
Sanders, Archie. 'Odysseus in Black: An Analysis of the Structure of *Invisible Man*'. *CLA Journal* 13.3 (1970): 217–28.
Sanderson, Rena. 'Women in Fitzgerald's Fiction'. Prigozy 143–63.
Schallück, Paul. 'Schwarzer Odysseus'. *Hamburger Anzeiger*. 8 May 1954. 10.
Schleiner, Winifred. 'In the Lumber Room of Faulkner's Memory: *As I Lay Dying* and Hellenic Myths'. *Literatur in Wissenschaft und Unterricht* 20.1 (1987): 131–40.
Schwartz, Richard A. 'Modernist American Classical Tragedy: *Absalom, Absalom!*'. *Journal of Evolutionary Psychology* 15.3–4 (1994): 212–21.
Scruggs, Charles. 'Ralph Ellison's Use of *The Aeneid* in *Invisible Man*'. *CLA Journal* 17.3 (1974): 368–78.
Searles, George. *Conversations with Philip Roth*. Jackson: University Press of Mississippi, 1992.
Segall, Jeffrey. *Joyce in America: Cultural Politics and the Trials of 'Ulysses'*. Berkeley: University of California Press, 1993.
Sensibar, Judith L. 'Who Wears the Mask? Memory, Desire and Race in *Go Down, Moses*'. Wagner-Martin 101–28.
Serafin, Joan. *Faulkner's Uses of the Classics*. Ann Arbor and Epping: UMI Research Press, 1983.
Settle, Glenn. 'Fitzgerald's Daisy: The Siren Voice'. *American Literature* 57.1 (1985): 115–24.
Seward, Adrienne Lanier and Justine Tally, eds. *Toni Morrison: Memory and Meaning*. Jackson: University Press of Mississippi, 2014.
Shaw, George Bernard. Preface to *Pygmalion*. *Androcles and the Lion; Overruled; Pygmalion*. London: Constable, 1949. 195–9.
Shields, John. *The American Aeneas: Classical Origins of the American Self*. Knoxville: University of Tennessee Press, 2001.
Shostak, Deborah. 'Roth and Gender'. Parrish, *Cambridge Companion* 111–27.
Showalter, Elaine. *A Jury of her Peers: American Women Writers from Anne Bradstreet to Annie Proulx*. London: Hachette, 2009.

Shreve, Grant. 'Ralph Ellison's *Three Days Before the Shooting* . . . and the Implicit Morality of Form'. Conner and Morel 218–44.

Sklar, Robert. *F. Scott Fitzgerald: The Last Lacoön*. Oxford: Oxford University Press, 1967.

Sklenar, Robert. 'Anti-Petronian Elements in *The Great Gatsby*'. *F. Scott Fitzgerald Review* 6 (2007–8): 121–8.

Slater, Niall W. '"His Career as Trimalchio": Petronian Character and Narrative in Fitzgerald's Great American Novel'. Futre Pinheiro and Harrison 125–53.

Slote, Bernice, ed. *The Kingdom of Art: Willa Cather's First Principles and Critical Statements, 1893–1896*. Lincoln: University of Nebraska Press, 1966.

Smith, Amanda. 'Toni Morrison'. *Publisher's Weekly*. 21 August 1987. 50–1.

Snell, Susan. *Phil Stone of Oxford: A Vicarious Life*. Athens: University of Georgia Press, 1991.

Snowden, Frank M., Jr. 'Bernal's "Blacks" and the Afrocentrists'. *'Black Athena' Revisited*. Ed. Mary Lefkowitz and Guy Maclean Rogers. Chapel Hill: University of North Carolina Press, 1996. 112–28.

Solomon, Jack. '*Huckleberry Finn* and the Tradition of the *Odyssey*'. *South Atlantic Bulletin* 33.2 (1968): 11–13.

Soyinka, Wole. *Myth, Literature and the African World*. Cambridge: Cambridge University Press, 1976.

St. Jean, Shawn. *Pagan Dreiser: Songs from American Mythology*. Madison: Fairleigh Dickinson University Press, 2001.

Stanford, W. B. *The Ulysses Theme: A Study in the Adaptability of a Traditional Hero*. 2nd edn. Oxford: Blackwell, 1964.

Stangherlin, Nicholas. '*Nemesis* and the Persistence of Tragic Framing: Bucky Cantor as Job, Hebrew Prometheus, and Reverse Oedipus'. *Philip Roth Studies* 12.1 (2016): 73–87.

Stark, John. '*Invisible Man*: Ellison's Black Odyssey'. *Negro American Literature Forum* 7.2 (1973): 60–3.

Stavrou, C. N. 'Ambiguity in Faulkner's Affirmation'. *The Personalist* 40 (1959): 169–77.

Stephens, Susan and Phiroze Vasunia. *Classics and National Cultures*. Oxford: Oxford University Press, 2010.

Stern, Milton R. '*Tender Is the Night* and American History'. Prigozy 95–117.

Stevens, Jason. 'Marilynne Robinson: A Chronology'. Stevens, *This Life, This World* xi–xvii.

—. 'Interview with Marilynne Robinson'. Stevens, *This Life, This World* 254–70.

—. Introduction. Stevens, *This Life, This World* 1–23.

—, ed. *This Life, This World: New Essays on Marilynne Robinson's 'Housekeeping', 'Gilead', and 'Home'*. Leiden: Brill, 2016.

Stoddard, Lothrop. *The Rising Tide of Color Against White World-Supremacy*. Brighton: Historical Review Press, 1980.

Stout, Janis. 'Daughter of a War Lost, Won, and Evaded: Cather and the Ambiguities of the Civil War'. *Cather Studies* 10 (2015): 133–49.

—. *Willa Cather: The Writer and her World*. Charlottesville and London: University Press of Virginia, 2000.

Sundquist, Eric. *Faulkner: The House Divided*. Baltimore: Johns Hopkins University Press, 1983.

—. 'Ralph Ellison in his Labyrinth'. Conner and Morel 117–41.

Sutherland, Donald. 'Willa Cather: The Classic Voice'. *The Art of Willa Cather*. Ed Bernice Slote and Virginia Faulkner. Lincoln: University of Nebraska Press, 1974. 156–79.

Swift, John. 'Willa Cather's *My Ántonia* and the Politics of Modernist Classicism'. *Narratives of Nostalgia, Gender and Nationalism*. Ed. Suzanne Kehde and Jean Pickering. London: Palgrave Macmillan, Springer, 1997. 107–20.

Sykes, Rachel, Jennifer Daly and Anna Maguire Elliott, eds. *Marilynne Robinson: Essays*. Manchester: Manchester University Press, 2020.

Tally, Justine. *Toni Morrison's 'Beloved': Origins*. New York: Routledge, 2008.

Tanner, Tony. Introduction to F. Scott Fitzgerald, *The Great Gatsby*. Harmondsworth: Penguin, 1990. vii–lvi.

Taylor, Carole Anne. '*Light in August*: The Epistemology of Tragic Paradox'. *Texas Studies in Literature and Language* 22 (1980): 48–68.

Taylor-Guthrie, Danille, ed. *Conversations with Toni Morrison*. Jackson: University Press of Mississippi, 1994.

Thurin, Erik Ingvar. *The Humanization of Willa Cather: Classicism in an American Classic*. Lund: Lund University Press, 1990.

Tischler, Nancy. 'Negro Literature and Classical Form'. *Contemporary Literature* 103 (1969): 352–65.

Toohey, Peter. *Reading Epic: An Introduction to the Ancient Narratives*. New York: Routledge, 1992.

Towner, Theresa. *The Cambridge Introduction to William Faulkner*. Cambridge: Cambridge University Press, 2008.

Traylor, Eleanor. 'The Fabulous World of Toni Morrison: *Tar Baby*'. *Critical Essays on Toni Morrison*. Ed. Nellie McKay. Boston: G. K. Hall, 1988. 135–49.

Turnbull, Andrew. *Scott Fitzgerald*. London: Bodley Head, 1962.

—, ed. *The Letters of F. Scott Fitzgerald*. London: Bodley Head, 1964.

Twain, Mark. *The Adventures of Huckleberry Finn*. London: Penguin, 1985.

Van Arsdale, Nancy. 'Princeton as Modernist's Hermeneutics: Rereading *This Side of Paradise*'. *F. Scott Fitzgerald: New Perspectives*. Ed. Jackson Bryer, Alan Margolies and Ruth Prigozy. Athens: University of Georgia Press, 2000. 39–50.

Vance, Norman. 'Decadence and the Subversion of Empire'. Edwards 110–24.

Vandiver, Elizabeth. *Stand in the Trench, Achilles: Classical Receptions in British Poetry of the Great War*. Oxford: Oxford University Press, 2010.

Virgil. *Aeneid*. Books I–VI. Virgil, *Eclogues, Georgics, Aeneid 1–6* 261–597.

—. *Aeneid*. Books VII–XII. *Aeneid Books 7–12; Appendix Vergiliana*. Trans. H. R. Fairclough. Rev. G. P. Goold. Cambridge, MA: Harvard University Press, 2000. 2–369.

—. *The Eclogues. The Georgics*. Trans C. Day Lewis. Oxford: Oxford University Press, 1983.

—. *Eclogues, Georgics, Aeneid 1–6*. Trans. H. R. Fairclough. Rev. G. P. Goold. Cambridge, MA: Harvard University Press, 2000.

Wadlington, Warwick. *Reading Faulknerian Tragedy*. Ithaca: Cornell University Press, 1987.

Wagner-Martin, Linda, ed. *New Essays on 'Go Down, Moses'*. Cambridge: Cambridge University Press, 1996.

Wallace, Michele. *Black Macho and the Myth of the Superwoman*. New York: Verso, 1990.

Walters, Tracey. *African American Literature and the Classicist Tradition: Black Women Writers from Wheatley to Morrison*. New York: Palgrave Macmillan, 2007.

Wasson, Ben. *Count No 'Count: Flashbacks to Faulkner*. Jackson: University Press of Mississippi, 1983.

Watts, Jerry Gafio. *Heroism and the Black Intellectual: Ralph Ellison, Politics and Afro-American Intellectual Life*. Chapel Hill: University of North Carolina Press, 1994.

Weisenburger, Steven. *Modern Medea: A Family Story of Slavery and Child-Murder in the Old South*. New York: Hill & Wang, 1998.

Welsh, Alexander. 'On the Difference between Prevailing and Enduring'. Millgate 123–47.

Wilde, Oscar. *The Picture of Dorian Gray*. 2nd edn. New York and London: Norton, 2007.

Williams, Dana. 'To Make a Humanist Black: Toni Wofford's Howard Years'. Seward and Tally 42–52.

Williams, Gary. 'Resurrecting Carthage: *Housekeeping* and Cultural History'. *English Language Notes* 29 (1991): 70–8.

Willis, Susan. *Specifying: Black Women Writing the American Experience*. Madison: University of Wisconsin Press, 1987.

Winterer, Caroline. *The Culture of Classicism: Ancient Greece and Rome in American Intellectual Life, 1780–1910*. Baltimore: Johns Hopkins University Press, 2002.

—. *The Mirror of Antiquity: American Women and the Classical Tradition, 1750–1900*. Ithaca: Cornell University Press, 2007.

Wolff, Cynthia Griffin. 'Time and Memory in *Sapphira and the Slave Girl*: Sex, Abuse, and Art'. *Cather Studies* 3 (1996): 213–31.

Woodress, James. *Willa Cather: A Literary Life*. Lincoln: University of Nebraska Press, 1987.

Wyatt, Jean. *Love and Narrative Form in Toni Morrison's Later Novels*. Athens: University of Georgia Press, 2017.

Wyke, Maria. *Caesar in the USA*. Berkeley: University of California Press, 2012.

Young, Stark. *The Colonnade*. London: Ernest Benn, 1924.

Zender, Karl. 'Lucas Beauchamp's Choices'. *Faulkner in the Twenty-First Century: Faulkner and Yoknapatawpha 2000*. Ed. Robert Hamblin and Ann Abadie. Jackson: University Press of Mississippi, 2003. 119–75.

Index

Series Editors: Martin Halliwell, Professor of American Studies at the University of Leicester; and Emily West, Professor of American History at the University of Reading.

The British Association for American Studies (BAAS)

The British Association for American Studies was founded in 1955 to promote the study of the United States of America. It welcomes applications for membership from anyone interested in the history, society, government and politics, economics, geography, literature, creative arts, culture and thought of the USA.

The Association publishes a newsletter twice yearly, holds an annual national conference, supports regional branches and provides other membership services, including preferential subscription rates to the *Journal of American Studies*.

Membership enquiries may be addressed to the BAAS Secretary. For contact details visit our website: www.baas.ac.uk